# Authors & Artists for Young Adults

ISSN 1040-5682

# *Authors & Artists for Young Adults*

## VOLUME 83

GALE
CENGAGE Learning

Detroit • New York • San Francisco • New Haven, Conn • Waterville, Maine • London

GALE
CENGAGE Learning

**Authors and Artists for Young Adults, Volume 83**

Project Editor: Dana Ferguson, Mary Ruby

Permissions: Jacqueline Flowers, Savannah Gignac, Jhanay Williams

Imaging and Multimedia: John Watkins

Composition and Electronic Capture: Amy Darga

Manufacturing: Rita Wimberley

Product Manager: Meggin Condino

For product information and technology assistance, contact us at
**Gale Customer Support, 1-800-877-4253.**
For permission to use material from this text or product,
submit all requests online at **www.cengage.com/permissions.**
Further permissions questions can be emailed to
**permissionrequest@cengage.com**

Since this page cannot legibly accommodate all copyright notices, the acknowledgments constitute an extension of the copyright notice.

While every effort has been made to ensure the reliability of the information presented in this publication, Gale, a part of Cengage Learning, does not guarantee the accuracy of the data contained herein. Gale accepts no payment for listing; and inclusion in the publication of any organization, agency, institution, publication, service, or individual does not imply endorsement of the editors or publisher. Errors brought to the attention of the publisher and verified to the satisfaction of the publisher will be corrected in future editions.

EDITORIAL DATA PRIVACY POLICY. Does this product contain information about you as an individual? If so, for more information about our editorial data privacy policies, please see our Privacy Statement at www.gale.cengage.com.

*Gale*
27500 Drake Rd.
Farmington Hills, MI, 48331-3535

LIBRARY OF CONGRESS CATALOG CARD NUMBER 89-641100

ISBN-13: 978-0-7876-9476-0
ISBN-10: 0-7876-9476-2

ISSN 1040-5682

Printed in the United States of America
1 2 3 4 5 6 7 14 13 12 11 10

# Contents

# Introduction

*Authors and Artists for Young Adults* is a reference series designed to serve the needs of middle school, junior high, and high school students interested in creative artists. Originally inspired by the need to bridge the gap between Gale's *Something about the Author,* created for children, and *Contemporary Authors,* intended for older students and adults, *Authors and Artists for Young Adults* has been expanded to cover not only an international scope of authors, but also a wide variety of other artists.

Although the emphasis of the series remains on the writer for young adults, we recognize that these readers have diverse interests covering a wide range of reading levels. The series therefore contains not only those creative artists who are of high interest to young adults, including cartoonists, graphic novelists, photographers, music composers, bestselling authors of adult novels, media directors, producers, and performers, but also literary and artistic figures studied in academic curricula, such as influential novelists, playwrights, poets, and painters. The goal of *Authors and Artists for Young Adults* is to present this great diversity of creative artists in a format that is entertaining, informative, and understandable to the young adult reader.

## Entry Format

Each volume of *Authors and Artists for Young Adults* will furnish in-depth coverage of approximately twenty-five authors and artists. The typical entry consists of:

—A detailed biographical section that includes date of birth, marriage, children, education, and addresses.

—A comprehensive bibliography or filmography including publishers, producers, and years.

—Adaptations into other media forms.

—Works in progress.

—A distinctive essay featuring comments on an artist's life, career, artistic intentions, world views, and controversies.

—References for further reading.

—Extensive illustrations, photographs, movie stills, cartoons, book covers, and other relevant visual material.

A cumulative index to featured authors and artists appears in each volume.

## Compilation Methods

The editors of *Authors and Artists for Young Adults* make every effort to secure information directly from the authors and artists through personal correspondence and interviews. Sketches on living authors and artists are sent to the biographee for review prior to publication. Any sketches not personally reviewed by biographees or their representatives are marked with an asterisk (*).

## Highlights of Forthcoming Volumes

Among the authors and artists planned for future volumes are:

Laurie Halse Anderson
David Benioff
Sandro Botticelli
Ray Bradbury
James Lee Burke
Julia Margaret Cameron
Matt de la Peña
Cory Doctorow
Siobhan Dowd
Frances O'Roark Dowell
Zaha Hadid
Henry James
Ursula K. Le Guin
Ian McEwan
Marcia Muller
Amos Oz
Shonda Rhimes
Andrew Stanton
François Truffaut
Jacqueline Woodson

## Contact the Editor

We encourage our readers to examine the entire *AAYA* series. Please write and tell us if we can make *AAYA* even more helpful to you. Give your comments and suggestions to the editor:

BY MAIL: The Editor, *Authors and Artists for Young Adults*, 27500 Drake Rd., Farmington Hills, MI 48331-3535.

BY TELEPHONE: (800) 347-GALE

# *Authors and Artists for Young Adults* Product Advisory Board

The editors of *Authors and Artists for Young Adults* are dedicated to maintaining a high standard of excellence by publishing comprehensive, accurate, and highly readable entries on writers, artists, and filmmakers of interest to middle and high school students. In addition to the quality of the entries, the editors take pride in the graphic design of the series, which is intended to be orderly yet appealing, allowing readers to utilize the pages of *AAYA* easily, enjoyably, and with efficiency. Despite the success of the *AAYA* print series, we are mindful that the vitality of a literary reference product is dependent on its ability to serve its readers over time. As critical attitudes about literature, art, and media constantly evolve, so do the reference needs of students and teachers. To be certain that we continue to keep pace with the expectations of our readers, the editors of *AAYA* listen carefully to their comments regarding the value, utility, and quality of the series. Librarians, who have firsthand knowledge of the needs of library users, are a valuable resource for us. The *Authors and Artists for Young Adults* Product Advisory Board, made up of school, public, and academic librarians, is a forum to promote focused feedback about *AAYA* on a regular basis, as well as to help steer our coverage of new authors and artists. The advisory board includes the following individuals, whom the editors wish to thank for sharing their expertise:

- **Eva M. Davis,** Youth Department Manager, Ann Arbor District Library, Ann Arbor, Michigan

- **Joan B. Eisenberg,** Lower School Librarian, Milton Academy, Milton, Massachusetts

- **Susan Dove Lempke,** Children's Services Supervisor, Niles Public Library District, Niles, Illinois

- **Robyn Lupa,** Head of Children's Services, Jefferson County Public Library, Lakewood, Colorado

- **Caryn Sipos,** Community Librarian, Three Creeks Community Library, Vancouver, Washington

- **Stephen Weiner,** Director, Maynard Public Library, Maynard, Massachusetts

# Diane Arbus

(Reproduced by permission of Stephen Frank.)

## ■ Personal

Born March 14, 1923, in New York, NY; committed suicide, July 26, 1971, in New York, NY; daughter of David Irwin (a store owner and furrier) and Gertrude Nemerov; married Allen Arbus, 1941 (divorced, 1969); children: Doon, Amy. *Education:* Attended the Ethical Culture School, Fieldston School, and Cummington School of the Arts; studied photography with photographer Alexey Brodovitch, 1954; studied under Lisette Model at New School for Social Research, New York, 1955-57.

## ■ Career

Photographer. Taught at Parsons School of Design, 1955-56, Rhode Island School of Design, and Cooper Union. *Exhibitions:* Work contained in the permanent collections of the Museum of Modern Art, New York, NY, and the George Eastman House, Rochester, NY. Work exhibited in art shows, including Museum of Modern Art Group Show, New York, NY, 1965; Guggenheim Group Show, Philadelphia, PA, 1966; Museum of Modern Art New Documents, New York, NY, 1967; American Photography Show, 1970; Eastman Kodak Show, 1970; and Osaka

World's Fair, 1970; "Diane Arbus Revelations," Metropolitan Museum of Art, New York, NY, 2005. Work also exhibited in the International Museum of Photography; Library of Congress, Washington, DC; Minneapolis Institute of Art, Minneapolis, MN; New Orleans Museum of Art, New Orleans, LA; Museum of Fine Arts, Houston, TX; Center for Creative Photography, University of Arizona, Tucson; National Gallery of Canada, Ottawa, Ontario, Canada; Museum of Fine Arts, Boston, MA; and Bibliothèque Nationale, Paris, France.

## ■ Awards, Honors

Guggenheim fellowships, 1963 and 1966.

## ■ Writings

*New Photography U.S.A.,* Museum of Modern Art (New York, NY), 1971.

*Diane Arbus: An Aperture Monograph,* edited by Doon Arbus and Marvin Israel, Aperture (New York, NY), 1972, 25th anniversary edition, 1997.

*USA; XXXVI International Biennial Exhibition of Art/ Venice, June 11-October 1, 1972: Diane Arbus, Ron Davis, Richard Estes, Sam Gilliam, James Nutt, Keith Sonnier,* 1972.

*The Woman's Eye* (selections from the work of Arbus and others), edited by Anne Tucker, Knopf (New York, NY), 1973.

*The Presence of Walker Evans: Diane Arbus, William Christenberry, Robert Frank, Lee Friedlander, Helen Levitt, Alston Purvis, John Szarkowski, Jerry Thompson, June 27-September 3, 1978, The Institute of Contemporary Art, Boston,* The Institute (Boston, MA), 1978.

*Diane Arbus: Magazine Work,* edited by Doon Arbus and Marvin Israel, essay by Thomas W. Southall, Aperture (Millerton, NY), 1984.

*Untitled: Diane Arbus,* edited by Doon Arbus and Yolanda Cuomo, Aperture (New York, NY), 1995.

*Diane Arbus: Revelations,* text by Anthony W. Lee and John Pultz, Random House (New York, NY), 2003.

*Diane Arbus: Family Albums,* text by Sandra S. Phillips and others, Yale University, (New Haven, CT), 2003.

Contributor to magazines, including *Harper's Bazaar, Esquire, Show, Glamour, Vogue, Infinity,* and the *New York Times Magazine.*

■ **Sidelights**

Diane Arbus, one of the foremost figures of twentieth-century documentary photography, captured segments of modern life in the lens of her camera, revealing what Hilton Als, writing in the *New Yorker,* called a "visual narrative of disenfranchisement." She portrayed everything from ordinary suburban couples and people sitting placidly on park benches to the "freaks" of the world, as she termed them in the introduction to *Untitled: Diane Arbus.* "Most people go through life dreading they'll have a traumatic experience," wrote Arbus, who committed suicide in 1971. "Freaks were born with their trauma. They've already passed their test in life. They're aristocrats." Among such "aristocrats," Arbus focused her lens on dwarfs, hermaphrodites, transvestites, prostitutes, and circus performers.

With the controversial photos collected in 1995's *Untitled,* Arbus's work at various residences housing the mentally retarded was given full view. And though such photos are far outnumbered by more sedate photo-journalistic studies, Arbus has long been connected with what was, at the time, the shocking image, the attention grabber. There is the startling image of a cross-dresser, "Seated Man in Bra and Stockings" from 1967, or the equally famous "A Jewish Giant at Home with His Parents in the Bronx," in which a huge young man stoops in a living room so that his head will not brush the ceiling, dwarfing his parents who stand next to him. Such images are indelibly linked with Arbus. According to Patricia Bosworth in *Diane Arbus: A Biography,* the photographer "drastically altered our sense of what is permissible in photography; she extended the range of what can be called acceptable subject matter. And she deliberately explored the visual ambiguity of people on the fringe and at the center of society."

Janet Malcolm commented about such photographic subject matter in the *New York Review of Books:* "Arbus celebrates her own encounter with the marginal and taboo, relishing the success with which she—a straight woman from a rich Jewish family . . .—has penetrated a sordid closed world and, through her journalist's too-niceness, become privy to its exciting and pathetic secrets." Arbus herself noted in the introduction to her 1972 collection, *Diane Arbus: An Aperture Monograph,* "I do feel I have some slight corner on something about the quality of things. I mean it's very subtle and a little embarrassing to me, but I really believe there are things which nobody would see unless I photographed them."

Arbus was born in 1923, the daughter of wealthy furrier David Nemerov, who owned a fashionable Fifth Avenue clothing store called Russek's. Arbus, brought up in a world of privilege, once said that she and her siblings were so overly protected as children that they did not even realize they were Jewish. Her brother, Howard, later became a noted poet; artistic and cultural excellence were admired qualities in the Nemerov home. Arbus attended private schools in New York City, including the progressive Ethical Culture School and later the Fieldston School in the Bronx.

Graduating in 1941, Arbus married Allan Arbus, an advertising clerk employed by her father, who taught his wife the camera skills he had learned in the photography division of the U.S. Army Signal Corps. With the aid of her father, Arbus and her husband set up a studio specializing in fashion photography. However, as Arbus became increasingly interested in photography herself, and studied technique with Alexey Brodovitch, she began to leave fashion photography—and her husband—behind. By 1956, Arbus and her husband were no longer working together; by the 1960s they had separated.

**From Fashion to Freaks**

Arbus began attending workshops held by Lisette Model in 1957, and this proved to be a turning point in her career. Model specialized in photographs of grotesques and societal outsiders, and Arbus began to concentrate on such subjects as well, spending time at a well-known freak show in New York's Time Square and also at a club where female impersonators met. As a biographer of Arbus in *American Cultural Leaders* noted, the photographer "seemed more interested in prowling the night streets and visiting circuses and sideshows with her Rollieflex camera, photographing 'the losers of the world'." Her earlier fashion work, appearing in the pages of *Glamour* and *Harper's Bazaar,* was replaced with her new edgy, urban portraits which found a home in publications from the *Sunday Times Magazine* to *Esquire.*

Arbus developed a face-on, hyper-realistic style with which she photographed ordinary people in everyday situations and brought out the uniqueness in the quotidian. Such documentary portraits revealed hidden texts such as alienation and pretension. Both admired and derided for her controversial subject matter, Arbus gained a name nationally, exhibiting widely and teaching at such prestigious schools as the Parsons School of Design, the Rhode Island School of Design, and the Cooper Union. She won Guggenheim Awards in 1963 and 1966, and was included in a 1967 exhibition at the Museum of Modern Art in New York.

Arbus suffered from depression, however, and despite her success, ended her life in 1971 by taking sleeping pills and cutting her wrists. She was found in her bathtub. Her final journal entry read, "The last supper." After her death Arbus's work was featured in museums in the United States, Europe, Japan, New Zealand, and Australia. Collections of her work were also published posthumously. A contributor for *USA Today Magazine* noted of her early passing: "At the time of her death, Arbus already was a significant influence—even something of a legend—among serious photographers, although only a relatively small number of her most important pictures were widely known at the time."

## The Arbus Legend

Arbus's fame has spread since the time of her death, in part because of the efforts of her daughter Doon, who has helped prepare several volumes of the photographer's work for publication, and also because of the continued discovery of some of Arbus's work and subsequent exhibitions. In 2006, there was even a feature film about the photographer's life: *Fur: An Imaginary Portrait of Diane Arbus,* which starred Nicole Kidman,. *New Republic* contributor Doris Grumback reviewed the first of the posthumous collections, 1972's *Diane Arbus,* edited

by Doon and Marvin Israel, and called it an "affecting and profound collection." A *New Yorker* reviewer commented that Arbus "sought out pain, ugliness, and disorder, and looked at it harder than probably any other photographer has done." Writing in *Time* magazine, Robert Hughes noted, "Arbus did what hardly seemed possible for a still photographer. She altered our experience of the face." Hughes further remarked, "Arbus became perhaps the least sentimental photographer who ever caught a face in the viewfinder." The art and film critic Richard Schickel noted in *Commentary* that Arbus accomplished "a radical purification of the photographic image." There was something resembling the snapshot in Arbus's work, but critics largely agree that she elevated that form to art. Hal Hinson, writing in *Atlantic,* noted the "astringent purity" and "pointedness" to Arbus's work, and commented that it was the "quality of a personal mission . . . [that] makes her work so enthralling." Hinson further commented, "In her hands photography became a medium of whispers and shadowy dreams, a kind of dark medieval science."

The later collection *Diane Arbus: Magazine Work* shows "a softer, less corrosive side," noted Hinson. The book contains black-and-white portraits of celebrities, artists, and other figures in addition to Arbus's "geeks and sexual adventurers." A *Publishers Weekly* reviewer said the photos and the selections from Arbus's journal "provide a new and warm understanding of her sometimes off-putting images." Milton Meltzer wrote in *Library Journal* that Thomas W. Southall's essay "enriches the book's contribution to the understanding of a major figure."

*Untitled* is a collection of photographs taken by Arbus at homes for the mentally retarded between 1969 and 1971. Patrick Skene Catling wrote in a *Spectator* review of *Untitled* that Arbus "was always shy but good at overcoming her shyness. . . . Carrying a camera gave her the nerve to prowl about in Central Park and the back streets of New York, and the insidious strength to penetrate into the mean rooms of misfits who lived as if light-years away from her family. Intruding, with the subjects' consent, to photograph intimate physical squalor made her feel she was at last encountering reality and empathizing with previously unimaginable psychic agony." Catling noted that "some of these photographs are even out of focus, intensifying an impression of awful rawness." Publication of these photographs, however, also caused a stir: some critics wondered about the ethics of using such subjects, questioning if it were art or voyeurism. Andy Grundberg, writing in the *New York Times Book Review,* noted that the inmates' "participation in Arbus's theater of the human grotesque is simulta-

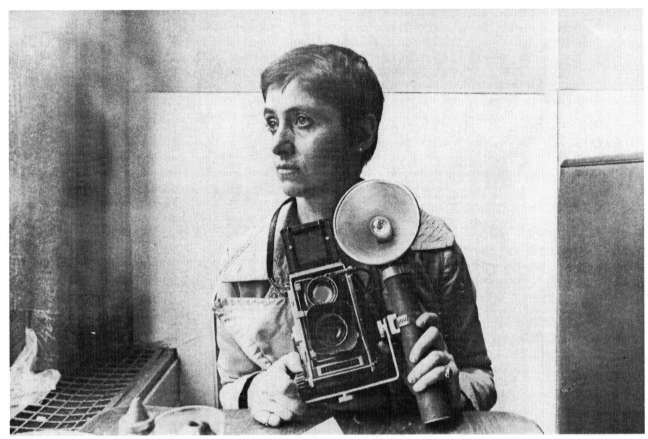

**Arbus was noted for her spare, evocative photographs of unusual subjects, including dwarfs, circus performers, and the mentally challenged.** (Photograph courtesy of Roz Kelly/Michael Ochs Archives/Getty Images.)

neously emotionally touching and ethically disturbing." Others, such as A.D. Coleman in the London *Observer*, felt that such photos even violated the "rights of the mentally challenged," and that "no responsible administrator of such a facility would or could permit" such pictures to be taken today. In a climate of political correctness, Arbus's work with so-called freaks takes on different connotations in some quarters, smacking of exploitation and simple bad manners.

Others defended the artist. Als, writing in the *New Yorker*, commented that the photographs of the mentally retarded "can't be confined by critical categorization, because they are purely ecstatic; they are the pictures Arbus had been waiting all her life to take. . . . People whose power stemmed from the fact that they were unaware of their vulnerability." Als concluded that the photographs "don't feel exploitative in the least, because they are filled with love and discipline. . . . In fact, this is the warmest collection of Arbus's work to date, in part because of the intimacy that exists among the subjects themselves. . . . But several of these

photographs also express great love for and trust in their photographer." Raul Nino noted in *Booklist* that Arbus's "jarring yet magical" images "give a lyrical poke at our collective subconscious, to wake us up—and remind us to look." Reviewing both *Diane Arbus: Family Albums* and *Diane Arbus: Revelations, New Yorker* contributor Judith Thurman observed, "Even before her death, in 1971, Arbus was exalted as a genius and reviled as a predator who conned her subjects out of their dignity. The judicious books that accompany two new shows give perspective to her intentions and, in the process, to her character."

### The Arbus Legacy

Two further collections appeared in 2003: *Diane Arbus: Family Albums*, the catalogue of a retrospective exhibition of the same name, and *Diane Arbus: Revelations*. In the former, editors grouped previously unseen photographs recording Arbus's concept of the family that she had been working on in her final months. Arbus's photographs are set against similarly themed photos by artists such as Walker Evans and August Sander. There are also numerous photographs Arbus took of the family of producer Konrad Matthaei. Conversely, *Diane Arbus: Revelations,* both the exhibition and the companion volume, is a major retrospective of the artist's work and life. Francine Prose noted of *Revelations* in *Harper's,* "Arbus's work can seem like the bible of a faith to which one can almost imagine subscribing—the temple of the individual and irreducible human soul, the church of obsessive fascination and compassion for those fellow mortals whom, on the basis of mere surface impressions, we thoughtlessly misidentify as the wretched of the earth." Similarly, *Time* magazine art critic Richard Lacayo felt this collection is "powerful and weirdly but irresistibly moving." Lacayo further noted: "Arbus worked at the point where the voyeuristic and the sacramental converge. She lies in wait for your first misstep in her direction. Then she dares you to stare at something—a little boy with a toy hand grenade, a dominatrix embracing her client—until you admit your own complicity with whatever it is in there that frightens you. At that point, all the picture's traps unfold, and it confers its rough grace. Like it or not." And Richard B. Woodward, writing about both the exhibition and the book for *ARTnews,* concluded: "No photojournalist on the front lines of Vietnam or the civil rights struggle recorded her times with more urgency. Arbus's images are proof that a camera is a deadly weapon."

---

If you enjoy the works of Diane Arbus, you may also want to check out the following:

The works of Brazilian photojournalist Sebastião Salgado (1944-), Mexican photographer Manuel Alvarez Bravo (1902-2002), and American documentary photographers Jacob Riis (1849-1914), Lee Friedlander (1934-), and Emmet Gowin (1941-).

---

Arbus's achievement in her chosen art helped to shape twentieth-century photography. Arbus "produced a body of photographs that reformulated a whole generation's attitudes toward portraiture and the documentary image," commented Jim Jordan in *Artweek.* Jordan noted further that Arbus has, since

her death, "become a figure of myth," an artist like Van Gogh whose life story has become intertwined with the art. Working as she did, in the 1950s and 1960s, Arbus had to contend not only with the difficulties of being a woman in a man's profession, but also against the prevailing society "so immersed in illusion that verisimilitude . . . was considered a form of fantasy," according to Jordan. For Jordan, the Halloween photographs later collected in *Untitled* represent the "penultimate point" in Arbus's "search for photographic integrity." Describing the photographer's legacy, a *USA Today Magazine* contributor noted: "Arbus' gift for rendering strange those things we consider most familiar continues to challenge our assumptions about the nature of everyday life and compels us to look at the world in a new way." The same writer also felt that Arbus created "a body of work that often is shocking in its purity, with a commitment to the celebration of things as they are." A further assessment of Arbus's accomplishment was offered by *New Statesman* contributor Sue Hubbard, who stated: "Perhaps, in the end, this is the true power of [Arbus's] images— that they not only throw light on those who seem odd and dispossessed, but that they illuminate our own responses when faced with the different and the damaged. In that sense Arbus is a revealer of souls."

■ **Biographical and Critical Sources**

*BOOKS*

Arbus, Diane, *Diane Arbus: An Aperture Monograph,* Aperture (New York, NY), 1972, 25th anniversary edition, 1997.

Arbus, Diane, *Untitled: Diane Arbus,* Aperture (New York, NY), 1995.

Bosworth, Patricia, *Diane Arbus: A Biography,* Knopf (New York, NY), 1984, published with a new afterword by the author, Norton (New York, NY), 2005.

*Contemporary Women Artists,* St. James Press (Detroit, MI), 1999.

Harmon, Justin, and others, *American Cultural Leaders,* ABC-Clio (Santa Barbara, CA), 1993.

*PERIODICALS*

*Afterimage,* March, 1985, review of *Diane Arbus: Magazine Work,* p. 9; November-December, 2003, Frederick Gross, review of *Diane Arbus: Revelations* and *Diane Arbus: Family Albums,* p. 16.

*American Photographer*, February, 1985, review of *Diane Arbus: Magazine Work*, p. 24.

*Art in America*, January, 1985, review of *Diane Arbus: Magazine Work*, p. 11.

*ARTnews*, October, 1984, review of *Diane Arbus: Magazine Work*, p. 29; April, 1995, review of *Untitled: Diane Arbus*, p. 145; October, 2003, Richard B. Woodward, "Shooting from the Hip."

*Artweek*, January 31, 1987, Jim Jordan, "The Masked and the Naked," p. 11.

*Atlantic*, November, 1984, Hal Hinson, review of *Diane Arbus: Magazine Work*, p. 129.

*Booklist*, October 15, 1984, John Brosnahan, review of *Diane Arbus: Magazine Work*, p. 274; October 15, 1995, Raul Nino, review of *Untitled: Diane Arbus*, p. 376.

*California*, April, 1985, review of *Diane Arbus: Magazine Work*, p. 48.

*Chatelaine*, September, 1984, review of *Diane Arbus: Magazine Work*, p. 4.

*Commentary*, March, 1973, Richard Schickel, "The Art of Diane Arbus," p. 73.

*Cosmopolitan*, July, 1984, review of *Diane Arbus: Magazine Work*, p. 30.

*Entertainment Weekly*, November 17, 2006, Owen Gleiberman, review of *Fur: An Imaginary Portrait of Diane Arbus*, p. 100.

*Film Journal International*, December, 2006, Bruce Feld, review of *Fur*, p. 63.

*Guardian Weekly*, March 3, 1985, review of *Diane Arbus: Magazine Work*, p. 22.

*Harper's*, November, 2003, Francine Prose, review of *Diane Arbus: Revelations*, p. 84.

*Harper's Bazaar*, December, 1984, review of *Diane Arbus: Magazine Work*, p. 103.

*Kirkus Reviews*, November 1, 1972, review of *Diane Arbus: An Aperture Monograph*, p. 1297.

*Library Journal*, October 15, 1984, Milton Meltzer, review of *Diane Arbus: Magazine Work*, p. 1939; October 1, 1995, Eric Bryant, review of *Untitled*, p. 80, January, 2004, Douglas Smith, review of *Diane Arbus: Revelations* and *Diane Arbus: Family Albums*, p. 98.

*Life*, August, 1984, review of *Diane Arbus: Magazine Work*, p. 7.

*Los Angeles Times Book Review*, November 11, 1984, review of *Diane Arbus: Magazine Work*, p. 6; November 5, 1995, review of *Untitled*, p. 10.

*Mademoiselle*, August, 1984, review of *Diane Arbus: Magazine Work*, p. 108.

*Modern Photography*, July, 1985, review of *Diane Arbus: Magazine Work*, p. 80.

*Nation*, December 4, 2006, Stewart Klawans, review of *Fur*, p. 32.

*New Leader*, June 25, 1984, review of *Diane Arbus: Magazine Work*, p. 15.

*New Republic*, December 1, 1973, Doris Grumback, review of *Diane Arbus*, p. 32.

*New Statesman*, June 8, 2009, Sue Hubbard, "A Revealer of Souls," p. 50.

*Newsweek*, December 11, 1972, review of *Diane Arbus: An Aperture Monograph*, p. 111; October 22, 1984, review of *Diane Arbus: Magazine Work*, p. 88; November 20, 2006, David Ansen, review of *Fur*, p. 19.

*New Yorker*, December 23, 1972, review of *Diane Arbus: An Aperture Monograph*, p. 80; November 27, 1995, Hilton Als, "Unmasked," p. 92; October 13, 2003, Judith Thurman, "Exposure Time," p. 103; March 21, 2005, Peter Schjeldahl, "Looking Back," p. 78; November 13, 2006, David Denby, review of *Fur*, p. 102.

*New York Review of Books*, February 1, 1996, Janet Malcolm, "Aristocrats," p. 7.

*New York Times*, September 14, 2003, Arthur Lubow, "Arbus Reconsidered."

*New York Times Book Review*, December 3, 1972, review of *Diane Arbus: An Aperture Monograph*, p. 5; December 2, 1984, review of *Diane Arbus: Magazine Work*, p. 16; October 22, 1995, review of *Untitled*, p. 36; December 3, 1995, Andy Grundberg, review of *Untitled*, p. 58.

*Observer* (London, England), September 17, 1995, A.D. Coleman, review of *Untitled*, p. 16.

*Photo District News*, March 1, 2004, Roberta Bernstein, "Diane Arbus."

*Popular Photography*, December, 1984, review of *Diane Arbus: Magazine Work*, pp. 72, 85.

*Publishers Weekly*, August 31, 1984, review of *Diane Arbus: Magazine Work*, p. 430; September 9, 2003, review of *Diane Arbus: Family Albums*, p. 72.

*Quill & Quire*, February, 1985, review of *Diane Arbus: Magazine Work*, p. 45.

*Spectator*, October 14, 1995, Patrick Skene Catling, review of *Untitled*, p. 48.

*Time*, November 13, 1972, Robert Hughes, "To Hades with Lens," p. 83; June 4, 1984, review of *Diane Arbus: Magazine Work*, p. 70; November 3, 2003, Richard Lacayo, "Visionary Voyeurism," p. 69.

*Tribune Books* (Chicago, IL), December 17, 1995, review of *Untitled*, p. 5.

*USA Today*, December 5, 1984, review of *Diane Arbus: Magazine Work*, p. 6D.

*USA Today Magazine*, January, 2004, "Diane Arbus' Revelations of Life."

*Village Voice*, September 24, 1985, review of *Diane Arbus: Magazine Work*, p. 54.

*Washington Monthly*, October, 1984, review of *Diane Arbus: Magazine Work*, p. 12.


ONLINE


*Artcyclopedia*, http://www.artcyclopedia.com/ (January 11, 2010), "Diane Arbus."

*Artnet,* http://www.artnet.com/ (January 11, 2010), "Diane Arbus."

*Masters of Photography,* http://www.masters-of-photography.com/ (January 11, 2010), "Diane Arbus."

OTHER

*Fur: An Imaginary Portrait of Diane Arbus* (feature film based on the biography by Patricia Bosworth), Picturehouse, 2006.*

(Photography courtesy of Chuck Berman/Chicago Tribune/Newscom.)

# Brian Azzarello

## ■ Personal

Born in Cleveland, OH; married Jill Thompson (a cartoonist and illustrator). *Education:* Received B.F.A. in painting.

## ■ Addresses

*Home*—Chicago, IL.

## ■ Career

Writer and comic-book creator. Formerly worked as a painter and a furniture restorer.

## ■ Awards, Honors

Eisner Award nominations for best new series, 2000, for "100 Bullets," and for best serialized story, 2000, for "100 Bullets," issues 1-3; Eisner Award for best serialized story, 2001, for "Hang up on the Hang Low"; Harvey Award for best writer and for best continuing or limited story, both 2002, both for "100 Bullets"; Eisner Award for best continuing story, 2002, for "100 Bullets," and Eisner Award nominations for best single issue, 2002, for "Idol Chatter," for best serialized story, 2002, for "Highwater," and for best writer, 2002, for "100 Bullets," and "Hellblazer"; Harvey Award nominations for best writer and for best continuing or limited series, both 2003, both for "100 Bullets," Harvey Award nomination for best graphic album of original work, 2004, for *Sgt. Rock: Between Hell and a Hard Place;* Eisner Award for best continuing story, 2004, for "100 Bullets," and Eisner Award nomination for best writer, 2004, for "100 Bullets," *Sgt. Rock: Between Hell and a Hard Place,* and *Batman;* Crimespree Award for favorite comics writer, 2007.

## ■ Writings

*"100 BULLETS" SERIES; COLLECTIONS*

*First Shot, Last Call,* illustrated by Eduardo Risso, Vertigo (New York, NY), 2000.
*Split Second Chance,* illustrated by Eduardo Risso, Vertigo (New York, NY), 2001.
*Hang up on the Hang Low,* illustrated by Eduardo Risso, Vertigo (New York, NY), 2001.
*A Foregone Tomorrow,* illustrated by Eduardo Risso, Vertigo (New York, NY), 2002.

*The Counterfifth Detective*, illustrated by Eduardo Risso, Vertigo (New York, NY), 2003.

*Six Feet under the Gun*, illustrated by Eduardo Risso, Vertigo (New York, NY), 2003.

*Samurai*, illustrated by Eduardo Risso, Vertigo (New York, NY), 2004.

*The Hard Way*, illustrated by Eduardo Risso, Vertigo (New York, NY), 2005.

*Strychnine Lives*, illustrated by Eduardo Risso, Vertigo (New York, NY), 2006.

*Decayed*, illustrated by Eduardo Risso, Vertigo (New York, NY), 2006.

*Once upon a Crime*, illustrated by Eduardo Risso, Vertigo (New York, NY), 2007.

*Dirty*, illustrated by Eduardo Risso, Vertigo (New York, NY), 2008.

*Wilt*, illustrated by Eduardo Risso, Vertigo (New York, NY), 2009.

*"HELLBLAZER" SERIES; COLLECTIONS*

*Hellblazer: Hard Time*, illustrated by Richard Corben, Vertigo (New York, NY), 2000.

*Hellblazer: Good Intentions*, illustrated by Marcelo Frusin, Vertigo (New York, NY), 2002.

*Hellblazer: Freezes Over*, illustrated by Marcelo Frusin, Guy Davis, and Steve Dillon, Vertigo (New York, NY), 2003.

*Hellblazer: Highwater*, illustrated by Marcelo Frusin, Giuseppe Camuncoli, and Cameron Stewart, Vertigo (New York, NY), 2004.

*"LOVELESS" SERIES; COLLECTIONS*

*A Kin of Homecoming*, illustrated by Marcelo Frusin, Vertigo (New York, NY), 2006.

*Thicker Than Blackwater*, illustrated by Danijel Zezelj, Marcelo Frusin, and Werther Dell'Edera, Vertigo (New York, NY), 2007.

*Blackwater Falls*, illustrated by Danijel Zezelj and Werther Dell'Edera, Vertigo (New York, NY), 2008.

*GRAPHIC NOVELS AND COMIC COLLECTIONS*

(With others) *Gangland*, DC Comics (New York, NY), 2000.

*Startling Stories: Banner*, illustrated by Richard Corben, Marvel (New York, NY), 2001.

*Jonny Double*, illustrated by Eduardo Risso, DC Comics (New York, NY), 2002.

*Cage*, illustrated by Richard Corben, Marvel (New York, NY), 2002.

*Sgt. Rock: Between Hell and a Hard Place*, illustrated by Joe Kubert, Vertigo (New York, NY), 2003.

*Batman/Deathblow: After the Fire*, illustrated by Lee Bermejo, DC Comics (New York, NY), 2003.

*Batman: Broken City*, illustrated by Eduardo Risso, DC Comics (New York, NY), 2004.

*Superman: For Tomorrow*, illustrated by Jim Lee, DC Comics (New York, NY), 2005, deluxe edition published as *Absolute Superman: For Tomorrow*, 2009.

*Lex Luthor: Man of Steel*, illustrated by Lee Bermejo, DC Comics (New York, NY), 2005.

(With others) *Batman: Black and White*, Volume 3, DC Comics (New York, NY), 2007.

*Dr. Thirteen: Architecture and Mortality*, illustrated by Cliff Chiang, Titan Books (London, England), 2007.

*El Diablo*, illustrated by Danijel Zezelj, Vertigo (New York, NY), 2008.

*Joker*, illustrated by Lee Bermejo, Vertigo (New York, NY), 2008.

*Deathblow: And Then You Live*, illustrated by Carlos D'Anda, Wildstorm (New York, NY), 2008.

*Filthy Rich*, illustrated by Victor Santos, Vertigo (New York, NY), 2009.

*OTHER*

Contributor to comic books and comic-book series, including *Weird War Tales, Hearthrobs, Flinch, JSA All-Stars, Strange Adventures, Batman, Spider-Man's Tangled Web, Solo, Winter's Edge, First Wave, Wednesday Comics,* and *Noir.* Author of segment for *Batman: Gotham Knight* (animated direct-to-DVD anthology film), Warner Bros. Animation, 2008.

■ **Sidelights**

"There are few writers in comics who write as subtly and as powerfully as Brian Azzarello," asserted Daniel Robert Epstein in a *UGO.com* profile of the Eisner and Harvey Award winner. Best known for his acclaimed noir series "100 Bullets," Azzarello has also earned plaudits for his work on the "Hellblazer" series of supernatural thrillers as well as "Loveless," a dark western. Additionally, Azzarello has applied his gritty personal vision to such iconic characters as Batman, Superman, and the Incredible Hulk, "infuriating some traditionalist fans and picking up some more of his own at the same time," remarked *Acid Logic* interviewer Tom Waters. "He is to comics what Lon Chaney was to method actors. He dives into his dialogue head first and soaks it up on subways, street corners and dive bars. He knows the street and the words his characters bluster and swear and shout with is genuine."

A native of Cleveland, Ohio, Azzarello began reading comics at a young age and found himself drawn to horror tales and war stories. Though he wasn't fond of superhero comics, Azzarello told *Sequential Tart* interviewer Lauren Vega-Rasner that the 200th issue of *Thor* had a profound effect on him. "It was the story of Ragnorok, and all the Norse gods died, the mighty Thor included," he recalled. "That was something, y'know? I mean at the time, it never occurred to my young mind that comic characters—or gods for that matter—could die."

After graduating from high school and earning a bachelor's degree in fine art in college, Azzarello worked as a painter and a furniture restorer. He entered the world of comicdom in 1992, serving as an editor for *Slash,* and his debut story, "The Assassin's Song," appeared in *Primer* in 1996. He first teamed with artist Eduardo Risso, who would become a frequent and trusted collaborator, on *Jonny Double,* a four-issue series about an aging private investigator that ran in 1998. The pair joined forces again for Azzarello's ground-breaking "100 Bullets," "an ink-dark crime series about consequence-free revenge," according to *New York Times* contributor Alexandra Marshall.

## A Stunning Series

Spanning 100 issues and taking ten years to complete, the "100 Bullets" series contains stories of revenge centering on a shadowy operative known as Agent Graves. To each person he approaches, Graves offers three items: a dossier proving that the individual has been grievously wronged by another person, a gun, and one hundred untraceable bullets. "There was this old TV show called *The Millionaire* where this mysterious man would give a million dollars to a different character each week, and the episode would focus on how the money changed that person's life," Azzarello commented to Vega-Rasner. "Same thing with *100 Bullets.* Only real darker. Agent Graves ain't handing out cash, he's handing out the ways, means, and carte blanche immunity to get revenge on someone who's done you serious harm in the past. So what do you do with it? That's our character's dilemma."

In *First Shot, Last Call,* which collects several early stories in the "100 Bullets" saga, Latina gangbanger Dizzy Cordova is given the opportunity to avenge the murders of her husband and child, who were killed in a drive-by shooting, while a bartender is likewise able to seek atonement for his ruined life. "It's not that premise that makes *100 Bullets . . .* the best crime fiction going, in any medium. It's the characters—a series of losers, low-lifes and dead-enders whose voices resonate with the rhythm of the street, whose dialogue is accented with the cold reality of despair," stated Andrew A. Smith in the Toronto *Globe and Mail.*

As the series progresses, readers learn that Graves heads an elite cadre of agents, the Minutemen, who act as enforcers for a secret organization of crime families known as "The Trust" but who now seek to retaliate against the group's corrupt leaders. "Characters with questionable morals are sexy," Azzarello remarked to Marshall. "They get away with things we would be afraid to try." In the second story arc, published in book form as *Split Second Chance,* details of the manipulative Graves's past begin to surface. A third collection, *Hang up on the Hang Low,* contains an Eisner Award-winning tale. Here Graves initiates a young man named Loop Hughes into his web of conspiracy, and Loop, who finds his long-lost mob-boss father, is drawn into mob enforcement. In *The Counterfifth Detective,* the individual who receives the gun and bullets is private investigator Milo Garret, whose face must be swathed in bandages following an automobile accident. Gordon Flagg commented in *Booklist* that Eduardo Risso's art "perfectly suits Azzarello's sparse, hardboiled scripts; this is one of the most effective writer-artist teams in comics."

As the story arcs in "100 Bullets" continue, new characters are introduced and new details of Graves's past are revealed. The concept of the Trust becomes central to the overall history of the series, explained Chris Arrant in *Newsarama.com.* "Forged in the first days of the 'New World' in the 1600s, the Trust has, for all intents and purposes, carte blanche on the world around them," Arrant wrote. "Responsible for some of the world's most deadly and [ambiguous] crimes and murders in the past three centuries, the Trust is the dark hand playing with the world's future." At one point, when Graves refused to follow the Trust's orders, he was targeted for assassination and left for dead. Since that time, he has been gathering his own group of enforcers as part of an elaborate revenge scheme. "Azzarello's involved plotlines are among the most complex in comics," Flagg stated.

## 100 Issues Later

Azzarello completed his "100 Bullets" saga in 2009. The series garnered critical praise for its large and finely drawn cast of characters, sprawling and suspenseful narrative, terse dialog, and atmospheric art. Reviewing the collection *Six Feet under the Gun*, a *Publishers Weekly* critic observed that "the comic brilliantly sustains a sense of nervous doubt," and *New York Times* contributor John Hodgman noted that "while the backbone plot [of "100 Bullets"] is occasionally preposterous, the self-contained, beautiful and uncompromising little crime stories that are its vertebrae are often astonishing." Over the series' ten-year run, Flagg commented in a review of *Wilt*, the final collection, "neither Azzarello's knotty plotlines and stark characterizations nor Risso's stylish visuals let up for an instant." Reflecting on "100 Bullets" in an interview with *Publishers Weekly* contributor Laura Hudson, Azzarello stated, "Some people have said that it didn't end the way they thought it would, but it couldn't have ended any other way. We've known the ending since we began. That's the way you're supposed to write. And that's the reason we were able to seed different things and reference back it over a hundred issues, because we knew where we were going."

In addition to his work on "100 Bullets," Azzarello has written for a number of other well-known titles. In 2000 he became the first American to pen stories for the popular "Hellblazer" series featuring magician and confidence man John Constantine. "My take on the guy is he's at his best when he's playing all sides against the middle; he may not be in control of the game, but everyone else playing thinks he is," the writer told Vega-Rasner. "That's part of the illusion he creates." Set in post-Civil War America, Azzarello's "Loveless" series follows the exploits of Wes Cutter, a Confederate soldier who returns to his Union-occupied hometown of Blackwater, Missouri. At its root, the series deals with "the way people behave and what motivates them, and they're two different things," Azzarello said in an interview with Carlos Ruiz on *Playback:stl.* "On the surface there is a lot of hatred. Politically based hatred, but underneath it's personal hatred." "Narratively, Azzarello uses flashbacks distinctively, weaving images of the past into present-set scenes," Flagg stated in a review of *A Kin of Homecoming*, a work in the "Loveless" saga.

## Pens Tales for Comic Icons

The author also contributed to the history of two of the most respected characters in American comic fiction: Batman and Superman. In the dark thriller *Batman: Broken City*, the Caped Crusader pursues the murderer of a young girl. According to a *Publishers Weekly* contributor, Azzarello portrays Batman as an anti-hero, "moving among crooks like an old, incestuous acquaintance." Batman tries to solve a

decades-old mystery in *Batman/Deathblow: After the Fire*. When Bruce Wayne's friend is killed in a flash fire, suspicion falls on a pyromaniac villain named Firebug, who escaped from a special agent named Deathblow years earlier. *Booklist* reviewer Ray Olson wrote that although Batman is "brutal and nihilistic," he "remains heroic." Azzarello looks at the Batman's most notorious adversary in *Joker*, "a memorably cringe-worthy story," wrote a *Publishers Weekly* reviewer. The work revolves around the efforts of the Clown Prince of Crime to retake control of Gotham City following his release from Arkham Asylum. "Azzarello has learned how to create a menacing, morally ambivalent atmosphere," the *Publishers Weekly* critic stated.

In *Superman: For Tomorrow,* the superhero attempts to solve the mystery behind the Vanishing, an astonishing event in which one million people, including Lois Lane, disappeared from the face of the Earth. Azzarello "provides an unusually dark take on the Man of Steel, making him a grim and haunted figure," Steve Raiteri noted in *Library Journal.* Azzarello presents his take on Superman's greatest foe in *Lex Luthor: Man of Steel.* According to *School Library Journal* reviewer John Leighton, Azzarello's "treatment of an old relationship is squarely in the tradition of sophisticated alternate treatments of classic heroes."

Azzarello revived one of his favorite childhood characters in the graphic novel *Sgt. Rock: Between Hell and a Hard Place,* drawn by veteran penciller Joe Kubert. Set during World War II, the work centers on three captive German soldiers who are murdered while in the custody of Rock's Easy Company. "The powerful story is amplified by the strength and grit of Kubert's highly accomplished artwork and coloring," Raiteri observed in *Library Journal.* The author returned to the western genre with *El Diablo,* which focuses on a sheriff's desperate search for an vicious outlaw. "Azzarello spills out the incredibly violent, tersely rendered story . . . in tantalizing bits and pieces," *Booklist* critic Ian Chipman noted.

---

If you enjoy the works of Brian Azzarello, you may also want to check out the following graphic novels:

Kevin Baker, *Luna Park*, 2009.
Ed Brubaker, *Incognito*, 2009.
Ian Ranking, *Dark Entries*, 2009.

With the success of "100 Bullets" and other titles, Azzarello has established himself as one of the most significant writers in the comic world. As Arrant stated, "In an industry of numerous creators of all varieties, Azzarello's work is one of the few that is bound to provoke a strong reaction every issue, every time." Azzarello's hard-boiled heroes and earthy subject matter are the keys to his success, Bill Baker noted on the *Comic Book Resources* Web site: "He concerns himself mainly with the ugly, terrible and often stupid things that every man, woman and child does just make it through the day. He works in the shadows cast by the horrible secrets that people keep hidden from each other, from their closest friends and loved ones, and often even from themselves. However, this doesn't mean his characters and their stories aren't engrossing, or without worth." Baker concluded, "They're interesting, and worthy our of attention because of the simple fact that they're profoundly human, and real."

### ■ Biographical and Critical Sources

*PERIODICALS*

*Booklist*, May 1, 2003, Gordon Flagg, review of *The Counterfifth Detective*, p. 1531; May 15, 2003, Ray Olson, review of *Batman/Deathblow: After the Fire*, p. 1626; December 1, 2003, Gordon Flagg, review of *Six Feet under the Gun*, p. 656; September 1, 2004, Ray Olson, review of *Broken City*, p. 76; October 1, 2004, Gordon Flagg, reviews of *Hellblazer: Highwater* and *Samurai*, p. 319; September 1, 2005, Gordon Flagg, review of *The Hard Way*, p. 76; October 15, 2005, Gordon Flagg, review of *Superman: For Tomorrow*, p. 38; August 1, 2006, Gordon Flagg, reviews of *Strychnine Lives* and *A Kin of Homecoming*, p. 59; February 15, 2007, Gordon Flagg, review of *Decayed*, p. 47; March 15, 2007, Gordon Flagg, review of *Thicker than Blackwater*, p. 36; July 1, 2007, Gordon Flagg, review of *Batman: Black and White*, p. 45; September 15, 2007, Gordon Flagg, review of *Once upon a Crime*, p. 55; November 15, 2007, Gordon Flagg, review of *Dr. Thirteen: Architecture and Mortality*, p. 26; March 15, 2008, Ian Chipman, review of *El Diablo*, p. 40; November 15, 2008, Carl Hays, review of *Blackwater Falls*, p. 24, and Gordon Flagg, review of *Dirty*, p. 24; December 1, 2008, Gordon Flagg, review of *Joker*, p. 39; July 1, 2009, Gordon Flagg, review of *Wilt*, p. 48.

*CrimeSpree*, July-August, 2009, Sean Chercover, interview with Azzarello.

*Entertainment Weekly*, January 26, 2001, Ken Tucker, review of *100 Bullets*, p. 96; November 21, 2003, Tom Sinclair, "Veteran's Day," review of *Sgt. Rock: Between Hell and a Hard Place*, p. 42; November 7, 2008, Ken Tucker, review of *Joker*, p. 97.

*Globe and Mail* (Toronto, Ontario, Canada), January 5, 2001, Andrew A. Smith, "Comic Antiheroes with Tragic Agendas: In *100 Bullets*, Writer Brian Azzarello Lets His Cast of Low-Lifes Get Their Revenge."

*Kirkus Reviews*, September 1, 2005, "Graphic Novel & Comics Spotlight," review of *First Shot, Last Call*.

*Library Journal*, March 1, 2004, Steve Raiteri, review of *Sgt. Rock: Between Hell and a Hard Place*, p. 61; September 15, 2005, Steve Raiteri, review of *Superman: For Tomorrow*, p. 52.

*New York Times*, July 18, 2004, John Hodgman, "Chronicle Comics: No More Wascally Wabbits," review of *Samurai*; March 13, 2005, Alexandra Marshall, "The Talk: Cape Fear."

*Publishers Weekly*, May 7, 2001, review of *Split Second Chance*, p. 226; November 24, 2003, review of *Cage*, p. 43; February 9, 2004, review of *Six Feet under the Gun*, p. 60; May 24, 2004, review of *Batman: Broken City*, p. 46; July 18, 2005, review of *The Hard Way*, p. 191; February 26, 2007, review of *Thicker than Blackwater*, p. 68; November 17, 2008, review of *Joker*, p. 48; April 28, 2009, Laura Hudson, "Brian Azzarello's 100th Bullet"; July 20, 2009, review of *Wilt*, p. 129; February 16, 2010, Kiel Phegley, "Azzarello Reinvents Pulp Icons & Superheroes in *First Wave*."

*School Library Journal*, January, 2006, Jennifer Feigelman, review of *The Hard Way*, p. 168; May, 2006, Steev Baker, review of *Superman*, p. 162; July, 2006, John Leighton, review of *Lex Luthor: Man of Steel*, p. 129; November, 2006, Jennifer Feigelman, review of *Loveless: A Kin of Homecoming*, p. 168; November, 2007, Benjamin Russell, review of *Thicker than Blackwater*, p. 158; March, 2008, Douglas P. Davey, review of *Doctor Thirteen: Architecture and Mortality*, p. 228; January, 2010, Matthew L. Moffett, review of *Filthy Rich*, p. 131.

*USA Today*, March 3, 2010, Brian Truitt, "'First Wave' Reintroduces Pulp Heroes to New Readers."

*ONLINE*

*Acid Logic*, http://www.acidlogic.com/ (December 1, 2006), Tom Waters, "Rapid Fire with Brian Azzarello."

*Broken Frontier*, http://www.brokenfrontier.com/ (September 2, 2008), Sam Moyerman, "Bad Azz Mojo—Part 1," and "Azzarello & Chiang Talk Doctor Thirteen—Part 7."

*Comic Book Database*, http://www.comicbookdb.com/ (April 1, 2010), "Brian Azzarello."

*Comic Book Resources*, http://www.comicbookresources.com/ (June 1, 2000), Bill Baker, "100 Sound Bytes: Brian Azzarello Interview"; (August

18, 2005), Dave Richards, "Reconstructing the Western: Azzarello talks *Loveless*"; (August 11, 2009), Jeffrey Renaud, "Azzarello Reimagines Doc Savage."

*Comics Bulletin Webzine,* http://www.comicsbulletin. com/ (November 1, 2002), Ray Tate, review of *Batman/Deathblow;* (October 2, 2007), Matthew McLean, "Brian Azzarello: Crafting Stories from Mistakes."

*GraphicNovelReporter.com,* http://www.graphicnovel reporter.com/ (April 1, 2010), William Jones, review of *100 Bullets.*

*Newsarama.com,* http://newsarama.com/ (June 29, 2006), Chris Arrant, "The Big Picture: Brian Azzarello"; (September 2, 2008), Steve Ekstrom, "Exploring the Joker—Brian Azzarello Talks."

*Playback:stl,* http://www.playbackstl.com/ (March 27, 2008), Carlos Ruiz, "First Call, First Shot"; (April 3, 2008), Carlos Ruiz, "Last Call, Second Shot."

*Sequential Tart Webzine,* http://www.sequentialtart. com/ (August, 1999), Lauren Vega-Rasner, "Blood Letters and Badmen"; (March 3, 2008), Henrik Andreasen, "Here Comes the Future!! An Interview with Brian Azzarello & Tim Bradstreet."

*UGO.com,* http://www.ugo.com/ (September 2, 2008), Daniel Robert Epstein, "Brian Azzarello Interview."

*Wired,* http://www.wired.com/ (April 14, 2009), Scott Thill, "Brian Azzarello's 100 Bullets Runs Out of Ammo."*

# Alan Ball

(Photograph courtesy of Frank Trapper/Corbis.)

## ■ Personal

Born May 13, 1957, in Atlanta, GA; son of an aircraft inspector and a homemaker. *Education:* Florida State University, bachelor's degree in theater, c. 1981.

## ■ Addresses

*Agent*—c/o United Talent Agency, 9560 Wilshire Blvd., Suite 500, Beverly Hills, CA 90212-2401.

## ■ Career

Screenwriter, producer, and director. Wrote for public access television in Sarasota, FL; moved to New York, NY, and worked as a graphic designer for *Adweek* while writing plays for Alarm Dog Repertory, 1986-93; staff writer for television shows *Grace under Fire,* 1993-95, and *Cybill,* 1995-98; creator, producer, and writer of television series *Oh Grow Up,* 1999, *Six Feet Under,* 2001-05, and *True Blood,* 2008—. Director of television episodes and films, including *Towelhead,* 2008.

## ■ Member

Writers Guild of America West, Directors Guild of America.

## ■ Awards, Honors

Academy Award for best original screenplay, Academy for Motion Picture Arts and Sciences, Golden Globe for best screenplay, Hollywood Foreign Press Association, WGA Award for best screenplay written directly for the screen, Writers Guild of America, Critics Choice Award for best original screenplay, Broadcast Film Critics, ShoWest Award for Screenwriter of the Year, and London Critics' Circle Film Award for screenwriter of the year, all 2000, all for *American Beauty;* Directors Guild of America Award for Outstanding Directorial Achievement in Dramatic Series, and Emmy Award for Outstanding Directing for a Drama Series, both 2002, both for pilot of *Six Feet Under;* Stephen Kolzak Award, Gay and Lesbian Alliance Against Defamation (GLAAD), 2002, and GLAAD Awards for Outstanding Drama Series, 2002, 2003, and 2005, all for *Six Feet Under;* PGA Award for producer of the year in episodic television, Producers Guild of America, 2004, for *Six Feet Under;* ShoWest Award for Groundbreaking Filmmaker of the Year, 2008, for *Towelhead.*

## ■ Writings

*PLAYS*

*Power Lunch* (first produced in New York, NY, 1989), published in *Five One-Act Plays*, Dramatists Play Service (New York, NY), 1994.

*Your Mother's Butt* (first produced in New York, NY, 1990), published in *Five One-Act Plays*, Dramatists Play Service (New York, NY), 1994.

*Bachelor Holiday* (first produced in New York, NY, 1991), published in *Five One-Act Plays*, Dramatists Play Service (New York, NY), 1994.

*The M Word* (first produced in Jamestown, NY, 1991), published in *Five One-Act Plays*, Dramatists Play Service (New York, NY), 1994.

*Five Women Wearing the Same Dress*, Dramatists Play Service (New York, NY), 1993.

*Five One-Act Plays* (contains *Made for a Woman, Bachelor Holiday, Power Lunch, The M Word,* and *Your Mother's Butt*), Dramatists Play Service (New York, NY), 1994.

*The Amazing Adventures of Tense Guy*, produced in New York, NY, at Paradise Theatre, 1994.

*All That I Will Ever Be*, produced in New York, NY, 2007.

*FILMS*

*American Beauty*, Dreamworks SKG, 1999, published as *American Beauty: The Shooting Script*, introduction by Sam Mendes, Newmarket Press (New York, NY), 1999.

(And director and producer) *Towelhead* (based on the novel by Alicia Erian; also screened under title *Nothing Is Private*), Warner Independent Pictures, 2008.

Also author of short film, *The M Word*, 2004.

*TELEVISION*

(And show creator and producer) *Oh Grow Up*, American Broadcasting Company (ABC-TV), 1999.

(And show creator and producer) *Six Feet Under*, Home Box Office (HBO), 2001–05.

(And show creator and producer) *True Blood*, Home Box Office (HBO), 2008–2010.

Also writer of episodes of *Grace under Fire*, 1993-95, and *Cybill*, 1995-98.

*OTHER*

(Editor, with Alan Poul) *Six Feet Under: Better Living through Death*, Pocket Books (New York, NY), 2003.

## ■ Sidelights

Screenwriter, producer, and director Alan Ball has become one of the most well-known and respected artists in Hollywood. After stunning Hollywood with his first film script, the Academy Award-winning *American Beauty*, Ball has gone on to success in television as the creator of the cult shows *True Blood* and *Six Feet Under*. He has also earned accolades as a director, earning Emmy and Directors Guild of America Awards for *Six Feet Under*. and helming his first feature film, *Towelhead*, in 2008.

Ball was born in Atlanta, Georgia, in 1957, and was raised in the Atlanta suburb of Marietta. He was the youngest of four children of a homemaker and an aircraft inspector. His family was disrupted by tragedy during his youth: when he was thirteen, he was in a car accident while riding with his older sister, Mary Ann. Ball was unhurt, but Mary Ann was killed. He told Dan Snierson in *Entertainment Weekly*, "That really made it impossible for me to ever go home again, because the person I was closest to was gone. My whole family sort of exploded apart." Although his family would later try to reconnect, they would have lasting psychological and spiritual wounds from this experience.

### From NYC to Hollywood

Ball graduated from Florida State University with a degree in theater, and then moved to Sarasota, Florida, where he worked with the Florida Studio Theatre. When he had trouble getting acting jobs, "I started writing to give myself things to do because nobody was casting me," he told a IFP/West screenwriting conference in a talk reproduced on the *Inside Film* Web site. With cowriter and college friend Nancy Oliver, Ball wrote comedies and one-act plays for public access television, but their work received little recognition. In 1986, looking for greater opportunities, Ball moved to New York City, where he created the Alarm Dog Repertory Theatre. With the group Ball staged several plays, including the one-acts *The M Word* (which premiered at the Lucille Ball Festival of New American Comedy in 1991), *Made for a Woman, Bachelor Holiday,* and *Your*

*Mother's Butt*, as well as *The Amazing Adventures of Tense Guy*. Like many writers, actors, and artists, he also found a day job, working as a graphic artist for the magazine *Adweek*. He told Kay Kioling in *Sarasota Magazine*, "I was good at the graphics job, and it would have been a career, but to me it was just a day job."

At the time, Ball told Scott Robson in *Variety*, "I never imagined I'd be standing on a stage someday accepting an Oscar or an Emmy. I was pursuing a career as a playwright. It never occurred to me I'd actually be working in Hollywood." Although his *Adweek* job did not involve writing, Ball found it almost restful not to have to immerse himself in the work, telling Robson, "there's something Zenlike about putting together those graphs." His situation changed after his play *Five Women Wearing the Same Dress* was produced at the Manhattan Class Company, starring future TV stars Thomas Gibson, Ally Walker, and Allison Janney. Ball described the play to Kioling as the story of "a big, old-money society wedding" where "five women are the bridesmaids,

all wearing the same horrible dress." The play received good reviews and was optioned by Columbia Pictures. The production also brought Ball an offer to write for the television situation comedy *Grace under Fire*, which starred comedian Brett Butler.

Bored and ready to try something new, Ball moved to Hollywood, where he suffered culture shock. In the New York theater world, writers are respected, but in television, he remarked to Kioling, they are "just grist for the mill." He added that while *Grace under Fire* was a hit, Butler "screamed at me, called me [an] amateur in front of people—she was a train wreck. . . . I spent a year there just morally disgusted." Ball moved on to another sitcom, *Cybill*, where he was a writer and eventually became the show's co-executive producer. Although the emotional tone behind the scenes was much calmer, Ball told Kioling, "[I turned] off my emotions about my writing, to become just a craftsman, a factory worker." He commented to Marc Peyser in *Newsweek* that in both sitcoms, "the stars basically looked

**Ball explores the dark side of suburban life in *American Beauty*, an Academy Award-winning 1999 film featuring Kevin Spacey and Annette Bening.** (Photograph courtesy of Dreamworks LLC/The Kobal Collection/Sebastian, Lorey/The Picture Desk, Inc.)

at those shows as PR for their own lives. We'd get notes like, 'I would never do that. That makes me look stupid.'"

## A Stunning Film Debut

While TV work taught Ball a lot about storytelling, he continually yearned to write "something that meant something, at least to me," as he recalled to Kioling. By the third season on *Cybill*, "I really wanted to leave, but they backed the money truck up to my house and I stayed," he told Chris Ayres in the London *Times Online*. "But I felt like such a whore, and at nights I dumped all of my frustration into the script of *American Beauty*. It's a very angry script. It's what you get when you've been working with a crazy person who walks into the room and says: 'I got a bad haircut, let's write a show about that.'" Ball also wove into the script his own experiences as a gay man, his awareness of his father's deep unhappiness, and his meditations on death. Additionally, he drew on his experiences working for *Adweek* to imbue the script with a biting disgust for corporate structure.

*American Beauty* opens with adman Lester Burnham (played by Oscar-winning actor Kevin Spacey) telling viewers they are about to witness the last months of his life. During that time Burnham quits his job, confronts his controlling wife, becomes infatuated with his teenaged daughter's friend, and searches for ways to make his life meaningful. *Newsweek*'s David Ansen noted that the film's theme was "the painful gulf between [our] fantasies and the reality we can't seem to grasp," and called it "a very funny film that packs an unexpected emotional wallop." While *New York Times* critic Janet Maslin found the satire on suburbia "none too fresh," she also observed that Ball's "crisp" writing uses "little things that turn the stereotype into something memorable." "Alan Ball's script evinces a keen ear for both unconscious cruelties . . . and unconscious self-indictment," Richard Alleva noted in *Commonweal*. *Time* critic Richard Schickel noted that while the film's subject of suburban discontent is a familiar one, "the writing . . . consistently surprises—not so much in what it says, but in how it says it." Although the film debuted with little fanfare, it eventually grossed more than $130 million and earned five Academy Awards, including best picture and best original screenplay for Ball.

The success was disorienting for Ball. While the film took off, he was busy working on his first television series and scarcely had time for premieres or reviews. At the Academy Awards ceremony, Ball felt more than a bit overwhelmed. He told *Newsweek*'s Peyser, "I usually watch the Oscars at home with friends, drinking martinis and throwing socks at the TV. And all of a sudden, I was there. It was really weird." He keeps the statue representing the award on a shelf in his home—dressed in a pink Barbie jacket. "He [the statue] looks so pretentious. The jacket cuts him down to size a little bit."

## A Deadly Serious Show

Ball returned to television in 1999 as executive producer of the ABC series *Oh Grow Up*. The sitcom about three former college friends sharing a Brooklyn house received poor ratings, however, and was soon canceled. Two years later Ball returned with another series, *Six Feet Under*, which was set in a funeral home, featured a family of undertakers, and emphasized the dark underside of suburban life. The show was commissioned by HBO, and that cable network's freedom, relative to the restrictions placed on broadcast networks, gave Ball the room he wanted to explore his characters' sexuality as well as address themes such as love, family dynamics, and mortality. He told *Entertainment Weekly*'s Snierson, "I think our culture tends to deny the reality of death. We're a little bit in the closet about it. This show is trying to demystify the whole process." He added, "It's about people attempting to live an authentic life in a world that's increasingly inauthentic."

The series begins with the death of family patriarch Nathaniel Fisher and the repercussions it has on his widow and three children. The eldest son, free-wheeling Nate, left home and wanted nothing to do with the family business, yet he has been left a share of the funeral home; the second son, uptight David, is resentful because he helped run the business; and the youngest, sensitive Claire, copes with the vagaries of teenage life. Peyser, who described the show as "funny, warm, [and] offbeat," noted that a typical episode "opens with a ghoulishly hilarious death. The Fisher family then tends to the survivors, once it gets over its own crises." These crises are often sparked by unexpected revelations, such as the widow Ruth's affairs and David's closeted homosexuality.

The public reacted favorably to *Six Feet Under*, and so did the critics. *Variety* reviewer Steven Oxman called the show "a smart, brooding, fanciful character-driven ensemble piece" that "ambitiously takes on death as its primary subject, providing a mix of the blackest of black comedy with deep psychological drama." *Entertainment Weekly*'s Snier-

**Peter Krause (left) and Michael C. Hall starred as the dysfunctional owners of a family-run funeral home in Ball's acclaimed television series *Six Feet Under*.** (Photograph courtesy of HBO/The Kobal Collection/The Picture Desk, Inc.)

son commented, "HBO is once again offering up a blast of fresh air. *Six Feet Under* is a frank, trippy, spiritual, witty drama." "It is often funny but never exactly fun; it's icier, more rarified and easier to admire than to love," James Poniewozik observed in *Time.* "It's also audacious, psychologically acute and beautifully shot." *American Prospect* contributor Joshua Gamson called the show a "blend of a family melodrama and a comedy of sex, death, and theology. The mix is sometimes very affecting and sometimes just confused and slippery, but it certainly makes *Six Feet Under* interesting."

In addition to receiving critical acclaim, Ball received an Emmy Award and the Directors Guild of America's Award for the pilot of *Six Feet Under.* In recognition of the realistic portrayal of gay characters on the show, he also received the Gay and Lesbian Alliance Against Defamation Stephen Kolzak Award. The character of David is based on his younger self, Ball told James Greenberg in *Los Angeles Magazine.* Ball didn't come out as a homosexual until his thirties, telling Greenberg that he

"bought into the whole propaganda that you can't be happy if you're gay, that you have to be this sad, tortured person, which is such a lie." While the writer was pleased viewers were sympathetic to David's character, he didn't want it to be the focus of the show: "Certainly it informs my work in that there is a whole gay story line, but I don't focus on my sexuality as the defining aspect of who I am. I like living in the world."

Ball told *Entertainment Weekly*'s Snierson that in writing for *Six Feet Under,* "I feel very fortunate. For the first time ever in television, I feel like the people who hired me to do this job actually trust me and don't question every little instinct I have." The show ran for five seasons, during which its cast and crew garnered a host of Emmy Awards. The finale, broadcast in 2005, is regarded as one of the finest in television history. "Most series end in ambiguity, leaving viewers alone to imagine what may have happened to their favorite characters," wrote *Miami Herald* contributor Michael Hamersly. "Not so here. Claire's tearful drive away begins a masterful montage that chronologically wraps everything up." Hamersly observed that "the gripping sequence . . . shows us the future we're desperate to see. Since *Six Feet Under* centered on death, it was essential to tell us the end of the story—a wholly unexpected, yet in retrospect, absolutely necessary choice."

Although he was pleased with his experiences on *Six Feet Under,* Ball was eager to move on and discover new characters. The protagonist of his 2007 play *All That I Will Ever Be* is a gay hustler who is struggling with his identity and is unsure about how to deal with real love. Although the play received mixed reviews, *Hollywood Reporter* contributor Larry Worth remarked that it "proves that even a flawed work from Ball leaves viewers with plenty to think about and debate, long after the curtain has fallen."

Ball returned to films the following year to direct his first feature-length project. When his agent sent him Alicia Erian's novel *Towelhead,* Ball was struck by the protagonist's voice and the book's subject: a thirteen-year-old Arab-American girl struggling with her developing sexuality. Ball's film centers on Jasira, who is sent to live with her divorced father in the suburbs after she attracts the attention of her mother's boyfriend. She then becomes involved with both an African-American classmate and an older neighbor. The film is a companion piece to *American Beauty* in "its unwavering examination of the dirty little secrets and raging hypocrisies lurking just beyond all those manicured suburban lawns," Michael Rechtshaffen noted in the *Hollywood Reporter,* adding that "Ball orchestrates all the goings-on with a seasoned agility that belies his feature directorial debut." Critical reception was mixed—*USA Today*'s Claudia Puig noted that the "movie feels both tedious and prurient, an odd combination that takes away from the story's potential to affect and rattle us"—but it earned Ball a Groundbreaking Filmmaker of the Year citation from the ShoWest convention.

### The Vampire Chronicles

After five years exploring life and death with *Six Feet Under,* Ball recalled to Ayres, "I thought to

**Ball, seen here on the set of *Six Feet Under,* served as the creator, writer, and producer of the series.** (Photograph courtesy of Seth Joel/Corbis.)

**In *True Blood*, a wildly popular vampire series, Ball mixes elements of horror, political allegory, and social satire.**
(Photograph courtesy of HBO/The Kobal Collection/The Picture Desk, Inc.)

myself: 'OK, I'm done looking into the abyss now. I'm ready for a theme park ride.'" He was considering his options when he began reading Charlaine Harris's first "Sookie Stackhouse" novel. "I promised myself I'd read a chapter before I went to bed," he told Ayres, "and before I switched out the light I'd read seven." He bought the rights and began filming the series for HBO as *True Blood*. The pilot introduces Louisiana waitress and telepath Sookie Stackhouse, who can hear the thoughts of everyone around her. When a vampire walks into her bar, she

is intrigued—not just because vampires have only recently "come out of the coffin" and revealed themselves to humanity, but because the vampire Bill's thoughts are hidden to her. The two become emotionally involved as they try to discover who—vampire or human—is committing a series of murders.

*True Blood* became a word-of-mouth hit for HBO, gaining viewers with each new episode of its first season. "While the show is a trifle hokey," Brian

Lowry noted in *Variety*, "its soapy elements, gothic atmosphere and cliffhanger endings—coupled with Anna Paquin's knockout performance [as Sookie]—do reel viewers in, laying the groundwork for what might be the cultish, undemanding romp HBO needs to inject much-needed life into its lineup." Alessandra Stanley commented in the *New York Times* that "Ball has taken what is basically a quirky romance novel and turned it into an R-rated melodrama puffed up with erotic tension and campy gore. It's creepy, steamy and funny at times, and it's also a muddle, a comic murder mystery that is a little too enthralled with its own exoticism." Other reviewers saw deeper meaning in the show. "Ball is again tweaking stereotypes," Andy Olin remarked in the *Houston Chronicle*, adding that "though vampires easily can be seen as a metaphor for homosexuals, they can also represent anyone who is discriminated against." Reviewing the second season, Robert Bianco observed in *USA Today* that "what we're seeing this season is a show that has grown confident and comfortable enough to expand its universe while maintaining its tonal control. Almost every comic scene includes the threat of horror, and almost every horrific scene has some small touch of comic relief. All in all, *True Blood* is one of TV's true joys."

For Ball, part of the fun of *True Blood* lies in writing about complex characters who possess both positive and negative traits. "I'm not interested in stereotypical heroes and villains," he told Karen Idelson in *Daily Variety*. "It's much more compelling if you have a hero who can also be narcissistic and dark and a villain who can be good and kind." The challenge of creating multi-faceted characters keeps his work fresh, Ball notes. "I'm drawn to characters and stories that surprise me and force me to face my own limitations in how I see the world," Ball told Cynthia Lucia in *Cineaste*. While *American Beauty* "was a huge step forward in discovering my voice," he added, "we adapt, we change over time, and one's voice changes, hopefully. I don't want to do the same thing over and over again."

If you enjoy the works of Alan Ball, you may also want to check out the following films:

*Harold and Maude*, starring Ruth Gordon and Bud Cort, 1971.
*The Ice Storm*, directed by Ang Lee, 1997.
*Little Miss Sunshine*, starring Steve Carell, 2006.

Ball also enjoys the collaborative nature of the dramatic arts. "I feel like as a writer you have a very specific vision when you're writing a piece, but the main purpose of that vision is to get the piece on paper," he remarked in his IFP/West speech. "And once it's there, it's going to become a collaborative thing, and other people are going to bring stuff to it that improves it." Although he enjoys his occasional forays into feature films, Ball told Lucia that he finds television especially rewarding: "You can really get to know the characters and be with them and grow with them in a way that you can't really do in film because in film you've got two hours—you've got to get there, to the resolution; there's this one issue the characters are dealing with, they deal with it, you get on the other side. A TV series can sprawl in ways that, for a writer, is very rich and nourishing and satisfying—well, for me at least."

## ■ Biographical and Critical Sources

*PERIODICALS*

*Advocate*, January 18, 2000, Gregg Kilday, "Worth a Closer Look," review of *American Beauty*, p. 91; July 3, 2001, Paul Clinton, "Diggin' Six Feet Under," p. 50; June 21, 2005, Jeremy Podeswa, "Six Feet Over," p. 154.
*American Prospect*, July 2, 2001, Joshua Gamson, "Death Becomes Them," p. 36.
*Back Stage*, June 24, 1994, David Sheward, review of *The Amazing Adventures of Tense Guy*, p. 36.
*Cineaste*, fall, 2008, Cynthia Lucia, "Sexual Politics and Awakenings in *Towelhead*: An Interview with Alan Ball," p. 14.
*Commonweal*, November 5, 1999, Richard Alleva, "No 'Leave It to Beaver,'" p. 19.
*Daily Variety*, April 9, 2002, Kevin Maynard, "Groundbreaking Creator Pushes Inclusive Images," p. A4; August 30, 2002, Alan Sepinwall, "Alan Ball: Oscar Winner Gives Death a Good Name While Becoming a Sunday Night Staple," p. 18; June 18, 2009, Karen Idelson, "*True Blood*: HBO," p. A5.
*Entertainment Weekly*, June 8, 2001, Dan Snierson, "Embalms Away!," p. 36.
*Harper's Bazaar*, July, 2001, "Exit, Laughing: With His New Comedy Series Set in a Mortuary, *American Beauty* Scribe Alan Ball Revisits the Nuclear Family's Dark Side," p. 76.
*Hollywood Reporter*, February 21, 2007, Larry Worth, review of *All That I Will Ever Be*, p. 27; September 13, 2007, Michael Rechtshaffen, "Nothing Is Private," p. 9.

*Houston Chronicle,* September 5, 2008, Andy Olin, "Writer Gives Vampire Series Some Teeth," p. 8.

*Los Angeles Magazine,* June, 2001, James Greenberg, "Family Plot," p. 52.

*Miami Herald,* August 22, 2005, Michael Hamersly, "*Six Feet Under* Finale Raises the Bar with Perfect Ending."

*Newsweek,* September 27, 1999, David Ansen, "What 'American' Dream?," p. 68; May 28, 2001, Marc Peyser, "A Family Drama to Die For," p. 62.

*New York Times,* September 15, 1999, Janet Maslin, "Dad's Dead, and He's Still a Funny Guy"; September 5, 2008, Alessandra Stanley, "Handsome Stranger? Be Careful. He Bites," p. E1.

*Sarasota Magazine,* February, 2000, Kay Kioling, "Coming up Roses," p. 46.

*Time,* September 20, 1999, Richard Schickel, "Dark Side of the Dream," p. 79; June 4, 2001, James Poniewozik, "Where the Hearse Is," p. 76.

*USA Today,* September 12, 2008, Claudia Puig, "*Towelhead:* Solid, but Draped in Discomfort," p. 5D; July 10, 2009, Robert Bianco, "*True Blood* Gets Truly Great Now," p. 9D.

*Variety,* May 28, 2001, Steven Oxman, review of *Six Feet Under,* p. 29; December 8, 2003, Scott Robson, "Alan Ball: From *Adweek* to Oscar," p. S24; September 8, 2008, Brian Lowry, "A Soap with Teeth," p. 22.

ONLINE

*HBO Web site,* http://www.hbo.com/ (December 20, 2009), "Alan Ball."

*Inside Film Web site,* http://www.insidefilm.com/ (March 18-19, 2000), "American Beauty Screenwriter Alan Ball Conducts Case Study at the IFP/West Screenwriters Conference" (lecture transcript).

*Times Online* (London, England), http://entertainment.timesonline.co.uk/ (September 30, 2009), Chris Ayres, "Alan Ball Finds True Blood Six Feet Under."*

# Alison Bechdel

(Photograph by Greg Martin. Photograph courtesy of Alison Bechdel.)

## ■ Personal

Born September 10, 1960, in Lock Haven, PA; daughter of Bruce Allen (a high school English teacher, antiques dealer, and funeral director) and Helen (a high school English teacher and actress) Bechdel. *Education:* Simon's Rock Early College (now Simon's Rock of Bard College), A.A., 1979; Oberlin College, B.A., 1981. *Politics:* "Correct." *Religion:* "Unaffiliated."

## ■ Addresses

*Home*—VT. *Office*—P.O. Box 215, Jonesville, VT 05466. *Agent*—(literary) Sydelle Kramer, Susan Rabiner Literary Agency, sydellekrabiner.net; (speaking) The Agency Group, 1880 Century Park E., Suite 711, Los Angeles, CA 90067. *E-mail*— dyke@dykestowatchoutfor.com.

## ■ Career

Writer and comic artist. Creator of syndicated comic *Dykes to Watch Out For*, 1983-2008; creator of comic *Servant to the Cause*, published in the *Advocate*, 1988-90. Word processor in New York, NY, 1981-85; worker at a food bank warehouse in Hadley, MA, 1985-86; *Equal Time* (gay/lesbian newspaper), Minneapolis, MN, production manager, 1986-90.

## ■ Awards, Honors

Lambda Book Award for gay and lesbian humor, 1990, for *New, Improved! Dykes to Watch Out For*, 1992, for *Dykes to Watch Out For: The Sequel*, 1993, for *Spawn of Dykes to Watch Out For*, 1993, for lesbian biography/autobiography, and 1998, for *The Indelible Alison Bechdel: Confessions, Comix, and Miscellaneous Dykes to Watch Out For*; National Book Critics Circle Award nomination for memoir/autobiography, Lambda Literary Award for lesbian memoir/biography, Gay and Lesbian Alliance Against Defamation (GLAAD) Media Award for outstanding comic book, Will Eisner Comic Industry Award for best reality-based work, Judy Grahn Award for lesbian nonfiction, The Publishing Triangle, and Stonewall Book Award for nonfiction, American Library Association, all 2007, all for *Fun Home: A Family Tragicomic*; two Vice Versa Awards for excellence from the Gay and Lesbian Press.

## ■ Writings

*COMIC COLLECTIONS*

*Dykes to Watch Out For*, Firebrand Books (Ithaca, NY), 1986.

*More Dykes to Watch Out For*, Firebrand Books (Ithaca, NY), 1988.

*New, Improved! Dykes to Watch Out For*, Firebrand Books (Ithaca, NY), 1990.

*Dykes to Watch Out For: The Sequel*, Firebrand Books (Ithaca, NY), 1992.

*Spawn of Dykes to Watch Out For*, Firebrand Books (Ithaca, NY), 1993.

*Unnatural Dykes to Watch Out For*, Firebrand Books (Ithaca, NY), 1995.

*Hot, Throbbing Dykes to Watch Out For*, Firebrand Books (Ithaca, NY), 1997.

*Split-level Dykes to Watch Out For*, Firebrand Books (Ithaca, NY), 1998.

*Post-Dykes to Watch Out For*, Firebrand Books (Ithaca, NY), 2000.

*Dykes and Sundry Other Carbon-based Life Forms to Watch Out For*, Alyson Books (Los Angeles, CA), 2003.

*Invasion of Dykes to Watch Out For*, Alyson Books (Los Angeles, CA), 2005.

*The Essential Dykes to Watch out For*, Houghton Mifflin Harcourt (Boston, MA), 2008.

*OTHER*

*The Indelible Alison Bechdel: Confessions, Comix, and Miscellaneous Dykes to Watch Out For* (autobiography), Firebrand Books (Ithaca, NY), 1998.

(Illustrator) Louise Rafkin, *What Do Dogs Dream?*, Andrews & McMeel (Kansas City, MO), 1998.

(Illustrator) Louise Rafkin, *What Do Cats Dream?*, Andrews & McMeel (Kansas City, MO), 1998.

*Fun Home: A Family Tragicomic* (graphic novel), Houghton Mifflin (Boston, MA), 2006.

Work represented in anthologies, including *American Splendor*, edited by Harvey Pekar. Contributor to periodicals, including *Gay Comix, Wimmen's Comix, Village Voice, Strip AIDS USA, Womanews*, and *Choices*.

■ **Sidelights**

Since the mid-1980s, Alison Bechdel has been a well-known name in the gay community for her long-running comic strip, *Dykes to Watch Out For*. The successful feature was a comics-page staple of several dozen alternative newspapers for twenty-five years and was regularly collected into book form. "With each image that Bechdel has created, she invites the lesbian community, both in the United States and internationally, to gaze into a mir-

ror that reflects its passions, politics, and idiosyncrasies," noted a contributor in *Gay & Lesbian Biography*. In 2006, Bechdel earned more mainstream media attention for her acclaimed memoir, a graphic novel she titled *Fun Home: A Family Tragicomic*. In it, she recounts her youth in a small Pennsylvania town, where her father served as the local mortician—and lived as a closeted gay man, which she learned not long after revealing her own sexual orientation to her parents when she was in college.

Born in 1960, Bechdel grew up in the central Pennsylvania town of Beech Creek, population 800, where both of her parents taught at the local high school. Her father Bruce also had a side job as the director of the town's funeral home, which Bechdel and her two younger brothers rather morbidly dubbed the "Fun Home." Her father Bruce's true calling, however, came in his restoration of their actual home, a 4,000-square-foot Gothic Revival mansion he restored to its original 1880s condition, complete with period furnishings and custom reproduction wallpaper. "One thing I remember vividly from my childhood is sitting in a car outside an antique store, for what would seem like forever," Bechdel recalled in an interview with Ginia Bellafante of the *New York Times*. "I'd die of boredom." Her father, she noted years later in her memoir, had a strong-willed personality, and she and the rest of her family occasionally locked horns with him over innocuous household-related issues. "I think I was drawn to cartooning because of the absence of color," she theorized in the same *New York Times* interview. "It was such a rejection of the environment I grew up in, and my father had no aesthetic criteria for judging it."

**Strange Beginnings**

Bechdel's artistic gifts became apparent at an early age and were actively encouraged by her parents. Many of the artists she encountered as a child would have a lasting influence on her work. The cartoonists of *Mad* magazine were among them, as well as "Norman Rockwell and certain children's book illustrators," as she told Anne Rubenstein in the *Comics Journal*. "We had some books of children's poetry that Edward Gorey illustrated. . . . I also loved Hillary Knight's work, the guy who did the Eloise books. And Dr. Seuss. And Richard Scarry's picture books." While her early childhood felt ordinary, as the artist grew into her teens she began to suspect her family was different from those around her, aside from the fact that the Bechdels lived in what amounted to a carefully arranged decorative-arts museum. As she wrote years later in her memoir *Fun Home*, "My father began to seem

**Bechdel's** alternative comic strip *Dykes to Watch Out For,* which chronicles the lives and loves of a group of lesbian friends, ran for twenty-five years. (Houghton Mifflin Harcourt, 2008. Illustration copyright © 2008 by Alison Bechdel. Reproduced by permission of Harcourt.)

morally suspect to me long before I knew that he actually had a dark secret." The male students he befriended, who babysat for Bechdel and her brothers and even went on vacation with the family, were one sign that something might have been amiss. On another occasion, her father was arrested for buying beer for a teen.

Like her parents, Bechdel was an avid reader, and during her high school years seemed to find common ground with her father in their discussions of literature. She left home to attend Simon's Rock of Bard College in Great Barrington, Massachusetts, but transferred to Oberlin College in Ohio after her sophomore year. It was during her first year at Oberlin that Bechdel wrote a letter to her parents informing them that she was gay. She had worried they would be upset but was unprepared for what followed. "My father called after receiving it," she recounted in her memoir. "He seemed oddly pleased to think I was having some kind of orgy. Mom wouldn't come to the phone." Bechdel soon learned the truth: that her father had had homosexual encounters himself. Bechdel's mother soon began divorce proceedings, but four months after the letter was sent, Bruce Bechdel was struck and killed by a truck while crossing the road near another old home he was in the process of restoring. The family considered it an accident, but Bechdel wondered privately if her father had made a deliberate decision to step into the road that day.

### Makes Mark with Alternative Comic

After graduating from Oberlin in 1981, Bechdel moved to New York City and did secretarial work for a few years before moving on to Hadley, Massachusetts, and then Minneapolis, Minnesota. The first cartoons she ever drew appeared in the margins of letters she wrote to friends, and one of her correspondents suggested that she try her hand at drawing a comic strip. Fascinated by contemporary lesbian subculture, she came up with the idea for *Dykes to Watch Out For*, which first appeared in 1983 on the pages of a feminist publication called *Womanews*. She was excited by the reaction she saw after distributing the paper at a lesbian march. "I was so elated that my work was getting passed around, and getting read," Bechdel told Rubenstein. "It was really thrilling to actually see people react to my cartoons, to laugh. I was so happy. I knew that was something I wanted." The strip was picked up for syndication two years later and began appearing in alternative newspapers around the United States. It became a cult read in lesbian communities across the United States for its wry, witty take on gay women and their relationships. It was

also successful enough to generate a line of T-shirts, mugs, and other products, and by 1990 the extra income allowed Bechdel to quit her day job as a newspaper production manager to work on the strip full-time.

*Dykes to Watch Out For* focused on a group of characters anchored by Mo—Bechdel's bespectacled, close-cropped alter ego—who works in a women's bookstore, and whose friends and partners comprise the full range of lesbian stereotypes in their hometown of Erewhon, a fictional city that shares many similarities with Minneapolis. The series was regularly assembled into book form at roughly two-year intervals, bearing titles such as *Spawn of Dykes to Watch out For* and *Split-level Dykes to Watch out For*. Writing for the London *Independent on Sunday*, Louise Gray called the strip "one of the most subtle comedies of modern manners to come along in the last two decades. That they happen to be gay mores is neither here nor there." This was the artist's goal, Bechdel revealed to Gray, asserting that her "characters are as human as anyone else, and I really am insistent about letting them be universal." Bechdel added, "The strip is about all kinds of things, not just gay and lesbian issues, although the world is seen through that lens. These events—births, deaths and everything in-between—happen to everyone."

Bechdel succeeded in that goal well enough that in 1994 Universal Press Syndicate approached her about creating a mainstream comic strip. "I thought about it for a couple of weeks," she told Rubenstein, "but eventually I came to my senses. . . . I have less than no interest in speaking to the mainstream. I mean, if my work ever got banal enough to make it into a mainstream newspaper, I hope someone would just put me out of my misery." Besides, Bechdel had a new project in mind. In the late 1990s she reduced the frequency of *Dykes* and ended her licensing agreements to explore the possibility of writing her family's story in a graphic novel format. The idea had intrigued her since her father's death, and she finally decided that the time had come. She began *Fun Home* in 1998, and it took her several years to write. A large part of the work involved staging each of the cartoon frames with the help of a digital camera; she positioned herself in each one as the different family members, including herself looking at her father in his casket, to produce the photographs from which she drew the story.

### A Haunting Autobiography

*Fun Home* was published by Houghton Mifflin in 2006 as the first graphic novel the company had ever issued. Critics greeted the work with unstint-

In *Dykes to Watch Out For,* Bechdel addresses a range of issues, including relationships and politics, with intelligence and humor. (Houghton Mifflin Harcourt, 2008. Illustration copyright © 2008 by Alison Bechdel. Reproduced by permission of Harcourt.)

ing praise, with most writing appreciatively of Bechdel's candor in dealing with such sensitive topics as suicide and families with closeted parents. *Entertainment Weekly*'s Jennifer Reese commended the "openness that distinguishes Bechdel's generous and intelligent work. Unlike so many memoirs, this one never tries to set the record straight, and while *Fun Home* takes only a couple of hours to read, it has a depth and sweetness few can match at five times the length." Writing in the *Lambda Book Report*, Nisa Donnelly found that Bechdel's chronicle of her family "takes readers into a dark and daring place, much like a confessional. It is an intimate look at the underpinnings of a family, and especially of a lesbian daughter's relationship to her complicated father."

Donnelly also characterized Bechdel's memoir as "extraordinarily literary," a sentiment echoed by Sean Wilsey in his *New York Times Book Review* critique. Wilsey described *Fun Home* as "a comic book for lovers of words" in which "Bechdel's rich language and precise images combine to create a lush piece of work—a memoir where concision and detail are melded for maximum, obsessive density. She has obviously spent years getting this memoir right, and it shows." The book also earned recommendations from *People, Booklist,* and *Time* magazine, which deemed it one of the ten best books of 2006. It also earned a National Book Critics Circle Award nomination for memoir/autobiography, and an Eisner Award for best reality-based work from her comic book artist peers.

Some of the reticence that Bechdel harbored for years about revealing her family's story was fueled by external issues. By the time she was midway through, she told Rachel Deahl in a *Publishers Weekly* article, "the culture had really changed. It didn't feel like it was such a terrible thing to reveal my father was gay, as it had 20 years earlier." Despite that progress, *Fun Home* was the target of censorship crusades in a few conservative communities, whose residents objected to its presence on library shelves. There were a few others uncomfortable with the book for more personal reasons: though Bechdel's mother and brothers knew of her project during its genesis, and she thanked them in the book's acknowledgements page for "not trying to stop me," she admitted in an interview with the London *Guardian* that they were uneasy with the final result. "I've discovered that there's something inherently hostile about having someone else write about your life," she remarked to Oliver Burkeman, "no matter how well-intentioned that other person might be."

Some of the family's unease was tied to the nature of Bruce Bechdel's death—was it an accident, or suicide? Even a quarter-century later, the question remained an unanswered one. "I think it's part of my father's brilliance, the fact that his death was so ambiguous," she told Burkeman in the *Guardian* interview. "The idea that he could pull that off. That it was his last great wheeze. I want to believe that he went out triumphantly." There was another factor that also weighed heavily on her in the decade following his death: In her job at the Minneapolis weekly *Equal Time* in the late 1980s, she arranged pages of obituary notices and tributes for men who had died of acquired immune-deficiency syndrome (AIDS), the disease that spread with deadly force in the gay community beginning in the early 1980s. "When I try to project what Dad's life might have been like if he hadn't died in 1980, I don't get very far," Bechdel mused in her memoir. She also wrote of the prejudices of the era as "a narrative of injustice, of sexual shame and fear of life considered expendable. It's tempting to say that, in fact, this is my father's story. There's a certain emotional expedience to claiming him as a tragic victim of homophobia. But that's a problematic line of thought. For one thing, it makes it harder for me to blame him."

## Drawing to a Close

From her home in Vermont, Bechdel continued drawing her cult-favorite comic strip throughout the late 2000s. The storylines threading through *Dykes to Watch Out For* over the years have reflected many changes in the gay, lesbian, and transgender community—a journey that can be traced in *The Essential Dykes to Watch out For*, a 2008 collection of most of her strips. *New York Times* contributor Dwight Garner noted that the collected panels "offer the chance to watch a group of very appealing women grow and change (and struggle to have better sex) over the course of more than two decades." He continued: "The most important thing to know about *The Essential Dykes to Watch out For,* however, is how deeply amusing it is. It crackles with one-liners." "What cannot be overemphasized is the sheer scope of the collection, which follows these women from idealistic young adulthood to contentedly disillusioned middle age and, for some, parenthood," a *Publishers Weekly* critic commented. "Bechdel's characters are alive. You know them, you recognize them, you've seen them before. They are the dykes next door, or the dykes you didn't know lived next door," Trina Robbins stated in the *Women's Review of Books*. The critic added that one can view the progress of Bechdel's art throughout the strips and in a cleverly inked introduction, and "in short, she is a damn good artist." As *Booklist*'s Ray Olson concluded, while *Fun Home* brought the author a wider audience than *Dykes*, "make no mistake—the strip is her masterpiece."

In her memoir *Fun Home: A Family Tragicomic,* Bechdel recounts her often difficult relationship with her father, a **closeted homosexual.** (A Mariner Book, 2007. Illustration copyright © 2006 by Alison Bechdel. Reproduced by permission of Houghton Mifflin Company.)

Although in 2003 Bechdel told Gray in the *Independent on Sunday* that "I have a hazy fantasy about lying on my deathbed when I'm 117 and completing the last panel" of *Dykes to Watch Out For,* in 2008 she retired from the strip. "The longer I wrote about these people, the fewer possibilities were open to everyone based on the choices they made. Everyone's lives started to narrow," Bechdel told Kera Bolonik in *New York* magazine. In addition, while once she had seen her role "really as a kind of cultural anthropologist," as she told Lisa London in the *Women's Review of Books,* she felt the world had caught up to the gay subculture. "When I was young, there was this very cohesive little gay world, an alternative world to the mainstream," she told Emma Brockes in the London *Guardian.* "That's not the case anymore. Things have gotten so assimilated. I feel in some ways I was longing for those days, in a way that I eventually had to let go of. The whole purpose of a liberation movement is to render itself obsolete. You can't go on clinging to it."

---

If you enjoy the works of Alison Bechdel, you may also want to check out the following graphic novels:

Craig Thompson, *Blankets,* 2003.
Linda Barry, *One! Hundred! Demons!,* 2005.
David Small, *Stitches,* 2009.

---

By leaving *Dykes* behind, Bechdel instead planned on returning to the graphic memoir genre and taking advantage of having "the luxury of just completely immersing myself in one project," as she told Bolonik. In her new project she planned to explore her coming of age and relationships as a lesbian, "but using it as a laboratory to look at bigger and more abstract issues about the self and other," she revealed to Brockes. "I don't know if I can pull it off." In a *Nerve* interview with Peter Smith she acknowledged the pressure of matching the success of *Fun Home:* "[It was] a pretty good story, and I can't top it. So I decided I wouldn't even try. I guess I've sort of gotten used to this problem, just from doing creative work for so many years. Every time I do an episode of my comic strip I feel like I have to top what I did last time, so it's a kind of pressure I've learned to manage." She concluded to Smith, "I guess I sort of almost assume the second book is just going to disappoint people, and there's nothing I can do about that, so I just get on with it."

## ■ Biographical and Critical Sources

*BOOKS*

Bechdel, Alison, *The Indelible Alison Bechdel: Confessions, Comix, and Miscellaneous Dykes to Watch Out For,* Firebrand Books (Ithaca, NY), 1998.
Bechdel, Alison, *Fun Home: A Family Tragicomic,* Houghton Mifflin (Boston, MA), 2006.
*Gay & Lesbian Biography,* St. James Press (Detroit, MI), 1997.

*PERIODICALS*

*Advocate,* July 18, 2000, Etelka Lehoczky, "Still a Dyke to Watch," p. 46; November 8, 2005, review of *An Invasion of Dykes to Watch Out For,* p. 66; June 20, 2006, Regina Marler, "Drawn to the Truth," p. 120.
*Booklist,* June 15, 1992, Ray Olson, review of *Dykes to Watch Out For: The Sequel,* p. 1814; July, 1997, Ray Olson, review of *Hot, Throbbing Dykes to Watch Out For,* p. 1788; November 15, 1998, Ray Olson, review of *Split-level Dykes to Watch Out For,* p. 557; September 15, 2003, Ray Olson, review of *Dykes and Sundry Other Carbon-based Life Forms to Watch Out For,* p. 219; March 15, 2006, Ray Olson, review of *Fun Home: A Family Tragicomic,* p. 37; November 1, 2008, Ray Olson, review of *The Essential Dykes to Watch Out For,* p. 32.
*Comics Journal,* August, 1995, Anne Rubenstein, "Alison Bechdel Interview," pp. 112-121.
*Editor & Publisher,* December 8, 2003, Dave Astor, "Readers Watch Out for 'Dykes' Feature: The Self-Syndicated Comic Turns 20 and Appears in Its 10th Book," p. 21.
*Entertainment Weekly,* June 2, 2006, Jennifer Reese, "Drawing Blood," review of *Fun Home,* p. 86.
*Feminist Collections,* winter, 2004, Briana Smith, "Watch Out! Alison Bechdel's Comics as Cultural Commentary," p. 1.
*Gay & Lesbian Review Worldwide,* May-June, 2006, Diane Ellen Hamer, "My Father, My Self," review of *Fun Home,* p. 37.
*Guardian* (London, England), October 16, 2006, Oliver Burkeman, "A Life Stripped Bare," p. 14; December 1, 2008, Emma Brockes, "'I Don't Know Why I Reveal These Things.'"
*Independent on Sunday* (London, England), October 19, 2003, Louise Gray, "Just an Everyday Story of Lesbian Folk at Home," p. 8.
*Kirkus Reviews,* March 1, 2006, review of *Fun Home,* p. 216.
*Lambda Book Report,* January-February, 1994, Nedhera Landers, review of *Spawn of Dykes to Watch Out For,* p. 42; September, 1997, Jeannine DeLom-

bard, review of *Hot, Throbbing Dykes to Watch Out For,* p. 26; July, 1998, Sarah Van Arsdale, "Drawing on Life: Alison Bechdel Shows and Tells," p. 1; February, 1999, Julia Willis, review of *Split-level Dykes to Watch Out For,* p. 32; October-November, 2003, Marissa Pareles, "Role Models: *Dykes and Sundry Other Carbon-based Life Forms to Watch Out For,*" p. 37; spring, 2006, Nisa Donnelly, review of *Fun Home,* p. 14.

*New York,* December 1, 2008, Kera Bolonik, "Alison Bechdel Retires Her Infamous 'Dykes,'" p. 81.

*New York Times,* August 3, 2006, Ginia Bellafante, "Twenty Years Later, the Walls Still Talk"; December 3, 2008, Dwight Garner, "The Days Of Their Lives: Lesbians Star In Funny Pages," p. C1.

*New York Times Book Review,* June 18, 2006, Sean Wilsey, "The Things They Buried," p. 9.

*People Weekly,* June 12, 2006, Bob Meadows, review of *Fun Home,* p. 51.

*Publishers Weekly,* March 16, 1992, review of *Dykes to Look Out For: The Sequel,* p. 75; November 1, 1993, review of *Spawn of Dykes to Watch Out For,* p. 73; November 9, 1998, review of *Split-level Dykes to Watch Out For,* p. 59; July 10, 2000, review of *Post-Dykes to Watch Out For,* p. 44; November 17, 2003, review of *Dykes and Sundry Other Carbon-based Life Forms to Watch Out For,* p. 46; February 27, 2006, review of *Fun Home,* p. 40; June 5, 2006, Rachel Deahl, "Family History in Pictures and Prose," p. 25; November 17, 2008, review of *The Essential Dykes to Watch Out For,* p. 48.

*Women's Review of Books,* November, 1997, Harriet Malinowitz, review of *Hot, Throbbing Dykes to Watch Out For,* p. 6; December, 2003, Lisa London, review of *Dykes and Sundry Other Carbon-based Life Forms to Watch Out For,* p. 10; May-June, 2009, Trina Robbins, "Desperate Housemates," p. 10.

*ONLINE*

*AfterEllen.com,* http://www.afterellen.com/ (October 4, 2006), Shauna Swartz, portrait of Alison Bechdel and discussion of *Fun Home.*

*Dykes to Watch Out For,* http://www.dykestowatchoutfor.com (March 30, 2010).

*Goblin Magazine Archives,* http://www.sonic.net/~goblin/ (October 16, 2006), "Sing Lesbian Cat, Fly Lesbian Seagull: Interview with Alison Bechdel."

*Nerve,* http://www.nerve.com/ (February 7, 2007), Peter Smith, "House of Pain: Alison Bechdel on the success of *Fun Home.*"*

# *Barbara Taylor Bradford*

(Photograph courtesy of Larry Marano/Getty Images.)

## ■ Personal

Born May 10, 1933, in Upper Armley, Leeds, Yorkshire, England; immigrated to United States, 1963; dual U.S. and British citizenship; daughter of Winston (an industrial engineer) and Freda (a children's nurse and nanny) Taylor; married Robert Bradford (a movie producer), December 24, 1963. *Education:* Studied at private schools in England.

## ■ Addresses

*Home*—New York, NY. *Office*—Bradford Enterprises, 450 Park Ave., New York, NY 10022-2605. *Agent*—Morton Janklow, Janklow & Nesbit Associates, 445 Park Ave., New York, NY 10022. *E-mail*—btbweb@barbarataylorbradford.com.

## ■ Career

Writer and journalist. *Yorkshire Evening Post,* Yorkshire, England, reporter, 1949-51, women's page editor, 1951-53; *Woman's Own,* London, England, fashion editor, 1953-54; *London Evening News,* London, columnist, 1955-57; *London American,* London, executive editor, 1959-62; *Today* magazine, columnist, 1962-63; National Design Center, New York, NY, editor-in-chief of decorating and design magazines, 1965-69; *Newsday,* Long Island, NY, syndicated columnist, 1966-70; *Chicago Tribune/New York News* syndicate, New York, columnist, 1970-75; *Los Angeles Times* syndicate, columnist, 1975-81. March of Dimes, ambassador, 1999; also associated with other charities, among them City-Meals-on-Wheels and the Susan G. Koman Breast Cancer Foundation. Member of board, Police Athletic League (PAL; charity for underprivileged children) and Girls Inc. (national charity for underprivileged girls). Also associated with various charities in the United Kingdom, several of them in Yorkshire.

## ■ Member

Authors Guild of America (member of council, 1989—), National Society of Interior Designers, American Society of Interior Designers.

## ■ Awards, Honors

Distinguished Editorial Award, 1969; National Society of Interior Designers award; Dorothy Dawe Award, American Furniture Mart, 1970 and 1971;

National Press Award, 1971; Matrix Award, New York chapter of Women in Communications, 1985; Editorial Award for Writing, American Society of Interior Designers, 1985; honorary doctorate of Letters, Leeds University, 1990; special jury prize for body of literature, Festival of American Film, Deauville, France, 1994; Spirit of Life Award and establishment of the Barbara Taylor Bradford Research Fellowship in Pediatric Leukemia, City of Hope, 1995; She Knows Where She's Going Award, Girls Inc., 1995; "Gala 12" Woman of Distinction Award, Birmingham-Southern College, 1995; honorary doctorate of Letters, University of Bradford, 1995; Woman of the Year Award, Police Athletic League, 1995; honorary doctorate of Humane Letters, Teikyo Post University, 1996; Spirit of Achievement Award, Albert Einstein College of Medicine, 1996; award of achievement for outstanding accomplishments in the field of literature, Five Towns Music and Art Foundation, 1997; British Excellence Award (given aboard the QE2), 1998; inducted into Matrix Hall of Fame, 1998; inducted into the Writers Hall of Fame of America, 2003; named Order of the British Empire for her services to literature, 2007. Bradford's image was used on postal stamps in St. Vincent and the Grenadines and Grenada, 2000, and on the British Isle of Man, 2003; Bradford was also celebrated in the postage stamp series *Great Writers of the 20th Century*.

# ■ Writings

*NOVELS*

*Voice of the Heart*, Doubleday (Garden City, NY), 1983.

*Act of Will*, Doubleday (Garden City, NY), 1986.

*The Women in His Life*, Random House (New York, NY), 1990.

*Remember*, Random House (New York, NY), 1991.

*Barbara Taylor Bradford: Three Complete Novels* (contains *Hold the Dream, To Be the Best,* and *Act of Will*), Wings (New York, NY), 1992.

*Angel*, Random House (New York, NY), 1993.

*Everything to Gain*, HarperCollins (New York, NY), 1994.

*Dangerous to Know*, HarperCollins (New York, NY), 1995.

*Love in Another Town*, HarperCollins (New York, NY), 1995.

*Her Own Rules*, HarperCollins (New York, NY), 1996.

*A Secret Affair*, HarperCollins (New York, NY), 1996.

*Power of a Woman*, HarperCollins (New York, NY), 1997.

*A Sudden Change of Heart*, Doubleday (New York, NY), 1999.

*Where You Belong*, Doubleday (New York, NY), 2000.

*Barbara Taylor Bradford—Three Complete Novels: Love in Another Town, Everything to Gain, A Secret Affair*, Wings (New York, NY), 2000.

*The Triumph of Katie Byrne*, Doubleday (New York, NY), 2001.

*Three Weeks in Paris*, Doubleday (New York, NY), 2002.

*"HARTE FAMILY SAGA" SERIES*

*A Woman of Substance*, Doubleday (Garden City, NY), 1979.

*Hold the Dream*, Doubleday (Garden City, NY), 1985.

*To Be the Best*, Doubleday (New York, NY), 1988.

*Emma's Secret*, St. Martin's Press (New York, NY), 2004.

*Unexpected Blessings*, St. Martin's Press (New York, NY), 2005.

*Just Rewards*, St. Martin's Press (New York, NY), 2006.

*Breaking the Rules*, St. Martin's Press (New York, NY), 2009.

*"RAVENSCAR" TRILOGY*

*The Ravenscar Dynasty*, St. Martin's Press (New York, NY), 2006.

*The Heirs of Ravenscar*, Collins (London, England), 2007, published as *The Heir*, St. Martin's Press (New York, NY), 2007.

*Being Elizabeth*, St. Martin's Press (New York, NY), 2008.

*JUVENILE; EDITOR, EXCEPT AS NOTED*

(Author) *Children's Stories of the Bible from the Old Testament*, illustrated by Laszlo Matulay, Lion Press (New York, NY), 1966.

*Children's Stories of Jesus from the New Testament*, Lion Press (New York, NY), 1966.

Samuel Nisenson, *The Dictionary of One Thousand and One Famous People: Outstanding Personages in the World of Science, the Arts, Music, and Literature*, Lion Press (New York, NY), 1966.

(Author) *A Garland of Children's Verse*, Lion Press (New York, NY), 1968.

*Children's Stories of the Bible from the Old and New Testament*, Crown (New York, NY), 1988.

*NONFICTION*

*The Complete Encyclopedia of Homemaking Ideas,* Meredith (New York, NY), 1968.

*How to Be the Perfect Wife: Etiquette to Please Him,* Essandess (New York, NY), 1969.

*How to Be the Perfect Wife: Entertaining to Please Him,* Essandess (New York, NY), 1969.

*How to Be the Perfect Wife: Fashions That Please Him,* Essandess (New York, NY), 1970.

*Easy Steps to Successful Decorating,* Simon & Schuster (New York, NY), 1971.

*How to Solve Your Decorating Problems,* Simon & Schuster (New York, NY), 1976.

*Decorating Ideas for Casual Living,* Simon & Schuster (New York, NY), 1977.

*Making Space Grow,* Simon & Schuster (New York, NY), 1979.

*Luxury Designs for Apartment Living,* Doubleday (New York, NY), 1981.

*Barbara Taylor Bradford's Living Romantically Every Day,* Andrews McMeel Publishers (Kansas City, MO), 2002.

Editor-in-chief, *Guide to Home Decorating Ideas;* creator/author of the award-winning syndicated column "Designing Woman."

*OTHER*

*Hold the Dream* (screenplay; television miniseries adaptation of her novel), Taft Entertainment Television/Bradford Portman Productions, 1986.

Contributor to periodicals, including *Writer.* Author's works have been translated into more than forty languages; author archive held in the Brotherton Collection of the Brotherton Library at the University of Leeds.

## ■ Adaptations

Many of Bradford's novels have been adapted as television miniseries or movies of the week, earning award nominations and airing in various countries; eight of the miniseries were produced by Robert Bradford; the adapted novels include: *A Woman of Substance,* Portman/Artemis Productions, *Voice of the Heart,* Bradford Portman Productions, *Act of Will,* Bradford Portman Productions, *To Be the Best,* Robert Bradford Production/Bradford Entertainment, *Remember,* H.R. Productions, List/Estrin Productions, *Everything to Gain,* Adelson Entertainment/Bradford Entertainment for the CBS Network, *Love in Another*

*Town,* Adelson Entertainment/Bradford Entertainment for the CBS Network, *Her Own Rules,* Adelson Entertainment/ Bradford Entertainment for the CBS Network, and *A Secret Affair,* Adelson Entertainment/Bradford Entertainment for the CBS Network. *The Women in His Life* was adapted and aired as a radio play by BBC Radio Drama. All of Bradford's novels are on CD.

## ■ Sidelights

Best-selling romance author Barbara Taylor Bradford has earned a wide readership with her mainstream fiction featuring strong women who succeed against all odds. As *Bookseller* contributor Alice O'Keeffe noted in a profile of the prolific and popular author, Bradford has made herself into "a worldwide super-brand" with her two dozen novels published since 1979, including her series about the powerful Harte family. "It is in capturing the complexities within women that Barbara Taylor Bradford succeeds," a *Contemporary Popular Writers* essayist stated. "Truly a commercial storyteller, Bradford adds class to a genre that receives little respect." An essayist in *Twentieth-Century Romance & Historical Writers* also praised the author's works, stating, "Bradford's novels allow her audience to glimpse the glamorous lives and enjoy the exotic playgrounds of the rich and famous while developing characters who engage the reader's interest and emotions."

Prior to her best-selling debut as a novelist, Bradford completed several books for juveniles and a number of nonfiction works, among them *The Complete Encyclopedia of Homemaking Ideas, How to Be the Perfect Wife: Etiquette to Please Him,* and *Easy Steps to Successful Decorating.* A former journalist covering everything from crime to show business, Bradford expressed great satisfaction over the turn her writing career has taken. "If anyone asks me whether I like being a popular writer," she told *New York Times* interviewer Rachel Billington, "I ask them whether they think I'd rather be an unpopular writer." As of 2010, Bradford's works had sold more than eighty million copies, had been translated into more than forty languages, and were published in more than ninety countries. Ten of her novels were adapted as television miniseries or movies of the week.

Bradford grew up in the north of England, an imaginative youngster who had read all the works of Charles Dickens and the Brontë sisters by the time she was twelve. When she was ten years old she sold her first short story to a British children's

A NOVEL

BY THE

#1 *NEW YORK TIMES*

BESTSELLING

AUTHOR

barbara taylor bradford

a woman of substance

WITH A NEW INTRODUCTION BY THE AUTHOR

**Bradford's debut novel, *A Woman of Substance*, has sold more than nineteen million copies worldwide.** (St. Martin's Griffin, 2009. Reproduced with permission of Palgrave Macmillan.)

magazine for seven shillings and sixpence. Determined to become a writer, Bradford left school at sixteen to work as a typist at the *Yorkshire Evening Post*. Six months later she was a cub reporter, then a reporter, and within two years she was promoted to women's page editor; at eighteen years of age she was the youngest newspaper editor in the whole of England. When she was twenty, Bradford went to London as fashion editor of a weekly magazine, *Woman's Own*. But she missed newspapers, and after a year joined the *London Evening News* as a feature writer and columnist. Later she was a columnist for *Today* magazine and served as the executive editor of the *London American*, a weekly newspaper.

In 1963 Barbara married Robert Bradford, an American movie producer, and moved to the United States, where she continued her career as a journalist. After she wrote a best-selling book on interior design, the *Newsday* syndicate offered her a column. "Designing Woman" covered lifestyle and interior design topics; Bradford also wrote a number of books on interior design, including *How to Solve Your Decorating Problems* and *Luxury Designs for Apartment Living*.

## From Journalism to Novels

Between 1969 and 1976 Bradford started but did not finish four novels. Having never lost sight of her childhood dream to be a novelist, she was determined to complete a work of fiction. She did so when she delivered *A Woman of Substance* to Doubleday. Begun in 1976, the novel was completed two years later and released in 1979. The debut work sold 25,000 copies in hardcover, but it was the paperback edition that broke records. *A Woman of Substance* stayed on the paperback best-seller lists for more than a year, including fourteen months on the *New York Times* best-seller list. More than three-and-a-half million copies of the book were sold in that time in the United States.

Since then, *A Woman of Substance* has become a classic, selling over nineteen million copies worldwide. The book begins the saga of Emma Harte, a Yorkshire woman who rises from obscurity to found a great retail empire and family dynasty and to enact revenge on the family of a young man who seduced and abandoned her when she was a girl. In her *New York Times* interview with Billington, Bradford characterized Emma as "a powerful woman who started with nothing but acquired dignity and polish." Bradford added that she strove to make Emma—and her other female characters—"tough but not hard." She wrote two sequels to *A Woman of Substance: Hold the Dream* and *To Be the Best*.

Some of Bradford's subsequent novels, such as *The Women in His Life*, feature male protagonists, but she remains best known for her strong heroines. In *Everything to Gain*, she presents the story of a woman with a seemingly idyllic life who in an instant loses everything that matters to her. Bradford portrays the character's charmed early years, then her subsequent journey from the brink of suicide to a renewed love of life. A writer for *Kirkus Reviews* commented: "The sunshine half of this novel is a fun glide through Beautiful Living, and the dark stuff has a weepier potential for the susceptible." The reviewer rated *Everything to Gain* as "stronger" than some of Bradford's more intricately plotted books. *Booklist* writer Denise Perry Donavin noted: "Bradford's fans won't be disappointed."

## On the Bestseller Lists

While a strong female lead is almost a given in Bradford's novels, many critics contend that her books are far from formulaic. Her writings often illuminate interesting or little-known aspects of history. For example, *Her Own Rules* explores the British practice of exiling children in orphanages to the far corners of the empire—a practice that continued even after World War II. Other books simply offer enjoyable entertainment. For example, *Love in Another Town* details a complicated May-September romance, and *A Secret Affair* is the story of an illicit relationship that plunges into mystery.

*A Sudden Change of Heart* explores how two close friends, Laura and Claire, enjoy privileged childhoods that do not prepare them for the troubles they will face as adults. Reunited in Paris, Laura and Claire face the fallout from their failed marriages and Claire's struggle with cancer. Laura investigates the possibility that some of the artwork she wants to purchase may have been illegally pilfered by the Nazis, and Claire gradually comes to terms with a childhood that might not have been as perfect as it seemed. Although Bettie Alston Shea in *Library Journal* felt that Bradford had covered this territory in other novels, the critic nonetheless stated: "It's fun to read about wealthy, famous, and otherwise successful people." A *Publishers Weekly* contributor found Laura to be yet another "indefatigable, headstrong heroine," particularly in the scenes where Laura's marriage unravels. In *Booklist*, Hughes suggested that *A Sudden Change of Heart* "will certainly please fans of [Bradford's] particular brand of contemporary women's fiction."

THE *NEW YORK TIMES* BESTSELLER BY THE AUTHOR OF *THE TRIUMPH OF KATIE BYRNE*

BARBARA TAYLOR BRADFORD

*Three Weeks in Paris*

Once, Paris shaped four women for a lifetime.
Now it will change them forever....

*Three Weeks in Paris* **centers on the stormy reunion of four young women who studied together at an exclusive Paris art school.** (Dell, 2002. Cover photo illustration copyright © 2002 by Debra Lill. Used by permission of Doubleday, a division of Random House, Inc.)

## Writers Write

Bradford's success can be traced in part to her incredible work ethic. Her writing days begin at six in the morning and can last ten to twelve hours. She reportedly adapted her novel *Hold the Dream* for television in just five weeks. Although she often emphasizes how much she loves her work, she also pointed out to *Atlanta Journal-Constitution* writer Don O'Briant that "there's nothing glamorous about it." She went on to describe writing novels as "the hardest work I've ever done." Yet she told *Writer's Digest* contributor Candy Schulman that she derives tremendous satisfaction from her labors. "I *need* it," she reflected. "If I didn't write fiction, they'd take me away in a straitjacket, because I have all this . . . *stuff* going on in my head. I have to get it out."

Bradford put her skills to the test when creating her 2000 novel, *Where You Belong*. After completing 250 pages and nearing her publishing deadline, she suddenly decided to switch narrative perspectives. She related in a *Writer* article that the voice of Val, her protagonist, "was coming through . . . so strongly—consistently and insistently" that she finally attended to the voice, revising her third-person draft into the novel's existing first-person format. Although she had written two earlier novels—*Everything to Gain* and *Dangerous to Know*—in the first person, she remained slightly uneasy about the style. "Writing a novel in the first person is terribly difficult, probably the hardest way to write fiction," she stated in her *Writer* essay, adding that the novelist "cannot move away from the actual in order to get into the heads, hearts, minds, and souls of the other characters." However, Bradford stated that she was glad she changed perspectives and was pleased with the final angle of storytelling.

In *Where You Belong,* readers follow Valentine, an American photojournalist who leaves her Paris home and enters Kosovo to document the ethnic conflict there, accompanied by Tony, her colleague and lover. The pair, along with Jake, an American photojournalist, are caught in an ambush and wounded, and Val's lover eventually dies. After the two survivors return to Paris, Val discovers that her lover was married. The news devastates her, and she and Jake take refuge together in southern France. Jake professes his love for Val and helps her redefine her family ties and her career. Bradford described Val's personal struggles in *Writer:* "Val takes [readers] with her when she goes to make peace with an estranged sibling, when she uncovers the mystery of her unhappy childhood, and confronts her mother and her painful past. [Readers] are by her side when she finally accepts where she belongs in life and with whom. Her journey is fascinating."

In a *Library Journal* review of *Where You Belong,* Bettie Alston Shea commented that Bradford's readers "will cheer on Val in her spiritual journey." A *Publishers Weekly* critic liked the "timeliness" of the plot and added that the story "will probably satisfy Bradford's more loyal fans." *Booklist* correspondent Kristin Kloberdanz cited Val as yet another of Bradford's "admirable, tough" heroines, "who, in her quest for self-fulfillment, does not always get it right."

Bradford's *The Triumph of Katie Byrne* and *Three Weeks in Paris* also helped her to usher in the twenty-first century high on the best-seller lists. In *The Triumph of Katie Byrne,* a talented young actress must overcome her horrific memories of the murder of two friends—and her suspicion that the murderer wants to kill her, too—in order to pursue a career on the stage. "Romantic suspense readers look first for colorful characters and plenty of romance," maintained Kathleen Hughes in *Booklist.* "[Bradford] delivers both in abundance here." Four young women whose friendship has been compromised are drawn together in *Three Weeks in Paris.* In the work, an aging schoolmistress wishes to celebrate her eighty-fifth birthday and calls the former friends to a party. There the four women confront both the surprising difficulties of material success and the circumstance that forced them apart. According to a *Publishers Weekly* contributor, "Bradford's knack for depicting elegant surroundings and happy-ever-after romance" serves her well in this title. According to Kristine Huntley in *Booklist:* "Watching each woman sort out her love life and find happiness is certainly entertaining."

## Returns to Familiar Territory

In 2004 Bradford returned to her "Emma Harte" series, publishing a fourth novel linked to *A Woman of Substance. Emma's Secret,* published on the twenty-fifth anniversary of the release of *A Woman of Substance,* explores the lives of Emma's granddaughters and great-granddaughters as they seek to run the vast Harte empire. American Evan Hughes follows her dying grandmother's advice and travels to London to meet Emma, only to discover that Emma has been dead for twenty years. Nevertheless, subsequent generations of Emma's family hire Evan to work with them on a retrospective of Emma's couture. Evan's entrée into the extended clan sparks suspicions and even some romance; indeed, her resemblance to certain family members is curious. Secrets await as Emma's granddaughter discovers a lost diary that might hold clues to Evan's parentage.

A *Publishers Weekly* reviewer commented that *Emma's Secret* would be "best appreciated by those with an irresistible desire to follow the further adventures of the Harte clan." In a similar vein, *Booklist* contributor Kristine Huntley observed that readers "familiar with Emma Harte and her large family will feel right at home." In her *Library Journal* review, Samantha J. Gust noted that readers might benefit from having read the prior "Emma Harte" titles, but the critic also wrote that *Emma's Secret* "has plenty of drama, romance, and intrigue."

Just prior to the publication of *Emma's Secret,* Bradford found herself in the difficult position of having to sue a company in India—Sahara TV—over a made-for-television miniseries they were about to air that had taken themes, characters, situations, and even complete scenes from her "Emma Harte" series. Bradford made the trip to India herself and took the company to court, where she won an injunction that prevented them from airing *Karishima: Miracle of Destiny,* the work in question. Despite the court order, Sahara TV did go ahead and air the first episode; however, this action caused them to be in contempt of court and further episodes were pulled. Bradford explained her actions to Steven Zeitchik in an interview for *Publishers Weekly:* "I realized they were doing 260 episodes. They had put up 800 billboards. This was a big deal. And I thought, 'The arrogance. They just plagiarized my work.'" The writer of the screenplay behind the miniseries sued Bradford in turn for defamation of character, insisting that the script was entirely original work. Ultimately, the court ruled in favor of the production company, allowing the miniseries to air, and rather than face a long, drawn-out case in the traditional Indian courts, Bradford decided not to further her suit.

*Unexpected Blessings* takes up where *Emma's Secret* leaves off. Taking her place in the Harte conglomerate, Evan Hughes has learned her true relationship to the extended Harte family. As she becomes involved with their troubles, Evan faces a number of challenges, from the abduction of a child to intrigues aimed at the vast Harte fortune. A *Publishers Weekly* contributor wrote that the extended adventures of Bradford's fictitious Harte clan "make for lusty escapist fiction." In *Just Rewards*, Bradford continues the Harte family saga begun with *A Woman of Substance*. In this tale, Emma's great-granddaughter, Linnet O'Neill, is newly married and battling her nefarious uncle Jonathan Ainsley for control of the family business. Gust, writing in *Library Journal*, complimented the novel's "juicy storylines," and Huntley observed in *Booklist:* "Readers who have followed the trilogy . . . will be pleased with this romantic conclusion to the long-running saga."

## A Fresh Start with Another Clan

After extending the story of Emma Harte's family, Bradford began chronicling the lives of another powerful clan. *The Ravenscar Dynasty,* the first book in a trilogy by the author, focuses on the Deravenel family of London. Set at the turn of the twentieth century, the novel revolves around the wealthy entrepreneurial family's loves and battles. When patriarch Richard Deravenel dies in an arson fire with several other members of his family, seventeen-year-old Edward Deravenel is quickly brought in to learn the family business. Edward has more on his mind than business, however, as he and his cousin Neville Watkins set out to avenge the death of their family members. A *Publishers Weekly* contributor directed readers to anticipate "a plot rich with period detail."

Bradford's next offering in the "Ravenscar" trilogy is *The Heir,* which was originally published in England as *The Heirs of Ravenscar.* The year is 1918, and Edward Deravenel has been the head of the family's company since 1904, when he took the reins at a youthful age. He has since become a powerful businessman who has built the trading company into a major global force against which few can hope to compete. The business is a varied one, with interests in everything from oil in Persia to fine wine in France. Happily married, he also has two sons, ensuring the succession of the family dynasty, as well as a daughter. In the years since Edward has taken over, he has also restored a sense of peace to the family, or so he thinks. In reality there is a certain amount of treachery taking place in the ranks, specifically relating to his younger brother George, who gambles recklessly and resents his elder brother's position as Deravenel patriarch, an attitude that results in his being sent off to France to keep him out of the public eye. But not all family crises can be dispatched with such ease, and when Edward suffers a heart attack and his two sons suddenly go missing, the company is in serious danger. The book received uneven reviews from critics. One contributor to *Kirkus Reviews* remarked that "Bradford's plodding exposition—she's no exponent of late-in, early-out scene-crafting—makes for novelistic terrain almost as rock-strewn as Ravenscar." However, Carol Haggas, writing for *Booklist,* observed that the book "packs as much intrigue as any Shakespearean royal drama."

Bradford continues the saga with the 2008 title *Being Elizabeth.* In this installment, young Elizabeth Deravenel Turner takes over the family business. Elizabeth comes to this position as the result of the sudden death of her half sister, Mary, but others in the family feel they too have a claim on the position of power. Elizabeth, however, is undaunted by these challenges and forges ahead to rebuild the Deravenel business, with a good deal of success. Soon, though, professional cares are mitigated by the arrival of an unexpected love interest in Elizabeth's life. Robert Dunley is an old childhood friends of hers, and sparks fly when the two reunite. Elizabeth and Robert begin a relationship, and scandal erupts because, though long separated, Dunley is still married. "Each time life seems to be settling into a comfortable routine, scandal rears its head again," noted *Bookreporter.com* reviewer Amie Taylor of this novel. "And every time, Elizabeth scales each mountain with aplomb. Will she emerge victorious, or will the events and dramas of her life and business finally get the better of her?" Taylor had praise for this work, further noting, "Bradford transports us to a world of opulence, power and riches that few of us will ever experience." Reviewing the same work in *Booklist,* Haggas observed, "Bradford saturates her novel with the kind of intricate internecine plotting best suited to a Shakespearean drama."

Published on the thirtieth anniversary of *A Woman of Substance,* Bradford's twenty-fifth novel, *Breaking the Rules,* features a great-granddaughter of Emma Harte. Bradford's protagonist is known only as "M." At the age of twenty-three, M leaves England in hopes of starting a modeling career in New York. M is motivated by more than mere ambition, however, for she was violently attacked and now must leave her native country behind. At first things work out well for her: she is soon a supermodel and finds love with an English actor. However, her fame and

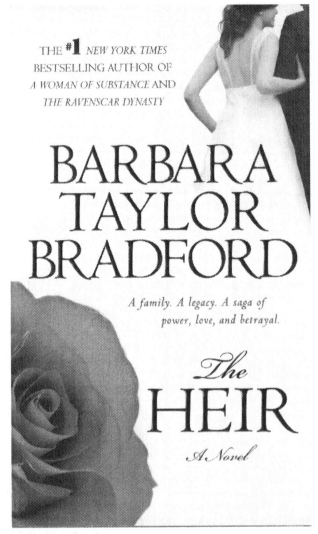

THE #1 *NEW YORK TIMES* BESTSELLING AUTHOR OF *A WOMAN OF SUBSTANCE* AND *THE RAVENSCAR DYNASTY*

# BARBARA TAYLOR BRADFORD

*A family. A legacy. A saga of power, love, and betrayal.*

## *The* HEIR

*A Novel*

**Bradford explores the power struggles within the Deravenel clan in *The Heir*, the second work in her "Ravenscar" trilogy.** (St. Martin's Press, 2008. Reproduced with permission of Palgrave Macmillan.)

notoriety put her in the sights of family enemies once again. A *Publishers Weekly* reviewer commented that Bradford's "plot, while contrived, satisfies on the fashion-and-passion front." The same reviewer further noted Bradford's usual "determined heroine" is at the heart of the narrative. Huntley, writing for *Booklist*, termed *Breaking the Rules* a "sprawling novel." Huntley further thought that readers will be "happy to dwell in the glamorous world of Bradford's sophisticated characters."

Asked by O'Keeffe in her *Bookseller* interview if she has any plans to retire from writing, Bradford responded most definitely in the negative: "I don't know what I'd do! I've got no children, I've got no grandchildren, I've got two dogs but you can't boss

If you enjoy the works of Barbara Taylor Bradford, you may also want to check out the following romance novels:

Nora Roberts, *Hidden Riches*, 1994.
Danielle Steele, *Answered Prayers*, 2002.
Jude Deveraux, *Lavender Morning*, 2009.

them around. Bob [her husband] is at the office. Just tell me, what would I do? I like being busy. I love writing books. I love telling stories, I love telling all those lies!"

## ■ Biographical and Critical Sources

*BOOKS*

*Contemporary Popular Writers*, St. James Press (Detroit, MI), 1997.

Dudgeon, Piers, *A Woman of Substance: The Life and Works of Barbara Taylor Bradford*, HarperCollins (London, England), 2005, published as *The Woman of Substance: The Secret Life That Inspired the Renowned Storyteller Barbara Taylor Bradford*, St. Martin's Press (New York, NY), 2005.

*Twentieth-Century Romance & Historical Writers*, 3rd edition, St. James Press (Detroit, MI), 1994.

*PERIODICALS*

*Atlanta Journal-Constitution*, July 13, 1995, Don O'Briant, "Bradford's Novels Full of Feisty Heroines," p. C1.

*Booklist*, July, 1994, Denise Perry Donavin, review of *Everything to Gain*, p. 1893; January 1, 1999, Kathleen Hughes, review of *A Sudden Change of Heart*, p. 791; February 1, 2000, Kristin Kloberdanz, review of *Where You Belong*, p. 995; August, 2000, Nancy Spillman, review of *Where You Belong*, p. 2163; February 15, 2001, Kathleen Hughes, review of *The Triumph of Katie Byrne*, p. 1084; February 1, 2002, Kristine Huntley, review of *Three Weeks in Paris*, p. 907; October 15, 2003, Kristine Huntley, review of *Emma's Secret*, p. 356; November 1, 2004, Kristine Huntley, review of *Unexpected Blessings*, p. 444; November 1, 2005, Kristine Huntley, review of *Just Rewards*, p. 4; November 15, 2006, Kristine Huntley, review of *The Ravenscar Dynasty*, p. 4; September 15, 2007, Carol Haggas, review of

*The Heir,* p. 5; August 1, 2008, Carol Haggas, review of *Being Elizabeth,* p. 4; September 1, 2009, Kristine Huntley, review of *Breaking the Rules,* p. 5.

*Bookseller,* March 3, 2006, review of *Just Rewards,* p. 12; October 2, 2009, Alice O'Keeffe, "A Woman of Substance: Barbara Taylor Bradford Is a Publishing Phenomenon," p. 22.

*Entertainment Weekly,* June 28, 1996, Rhonda Johnson, review of *Her Own Rules,* p. 101.

*Guardian* (London, England), July 22, 1995, Megan Tresidder, "A Woman Worried by Good Reviews," p. 29.

*Independent* (London, England), July 29, 1995, John Walsh, "She's a Friend of Norman Mailer and Is the Richest Englishwoman after the Queen. Her Name Is Barbara Taylor Bradford," p. S3.

*Kirkus Reviews,* July 1, 1994, review of *Everything to Gain,* p. 861; October 15, 2003, review of *Emma's Secret,* p. 1238; January 1, 2005, review of *Unexpected Blessings,* p. 5; November 15, 2005, review of *Just Rewards,* p. 1201; November 15, 2006, review of *The Ravenscar Dynasty,* p. 1141; October 1, 2007, review of *The Heir;* October 1, 2009, review of *Breaking the Rules.*

*Library Journal,* April 15, 1998, Catherine Swenson, review of *Power of a Woman,* p. 134; February 1, 1999, Bettie Alston Shea, review of *A Sudden Change of Heart,* p. 118; March 15, 2000, Bettie Alston Shea, review of *Where You Belong,* p. 124; December, 2003, Samantha J. Gust, review of *Emma's Secret,* p. 163; December 1, 2005, Samantha Gust, review of *Just Rewards,* p. 110; February 15, 2009, Denise A. Garofalo, review of *Being Elizabeth,* p. 78.

*Maclean's,* March 8, 1999, "The Bradford Take on Writing," p. 55.

*McCall's,* September, 1998, Sophia Dembling, "The Last Words on Romance," p. 53.

*New York Times,* October 26, 1986, Rachel Billington, "Novelist Becomes Script Writer in One Hectic Lesson."

*New York Times Book Review,* April 24, 1983, Mel Watkins, review of *Voice of the Heart,* p. 16; June 9, 1985, Kiki Olson, review of *Hold the Dream,* p. 22; July 20, 1986, Andrew Postman, review of *Act of Will,* p. 18; July 31, 1988, Joyce Cohen, review of *To Be the Best,* p. 18.

*People,* October 14, 1996, "Barbara Taylor Bradford's *Everything to Gain,*" p. 20; February 22, 1999, Francine Prose, review of *A Sudden Change of Heart,* p. 44; April 17, 2000, Lan N. Nguyen, review of *Where You Belong,* p. 47.

*Publishers Weekly,* January 4, 1999, review of *A Sudden Change of Heart,* p. 75; February 28, 2000, review of *Where You Belong,* p. 58; February 26, 2001, review of *The Triumph of Katie Byrne,* p. 57; February 11, 2002, review of *Three Weeks in Paris,* p. 164; April 8, 2002, John F. Baker, "Bradford's Big Move," p. 16; May 26, 2003, Steven Zeitchik, "Bradford Creates Legal Stir in India," p. 17; August 11, 2003, Karen Holt, "Bradford Drops Costly Challenge to Indian Series," p. 116; November 10, 2003, review of *Emma's Secret,* p. 41; December 6, 2004, review of *Unexpected Blessings,* p. 43; November 28, 2005, review of *Just Rewards,* p. 24; November 20, 2006, review of *The Ravenscar Dynasty,* p. 35; August 31, 2009, review of *Breaking the Rules,* p. 30.

*School Library Journal,* February, 1997, Katherine Fitch, review of *Her Own Rules,* p. 134.

*Spectator,* November 16, 1996, David Sexton, review of *A Secret Affair,* p. 48.

*Times* (London, England), January 3, 1995, Julia Llewellyn Smith, "Model for a Woman of Substance," p. 11.

*Wall Street Journal,* September 10, 1986, Joanne Kaufman, "Heft and Heavy Breathing," p. 30; February 11, 2000, "Barbara Taylor Bradford," p. W2.

*Writer,* March, 1986, Barbara Taylor Bradford, "So You Want to Write a Bestseller?," p. 7; September, 1991, Billie Figg, "Novel Ideas," p. 9; May, 1996, Barbara Taylor Bradford, "The Making of a Novelist," p. 7; October, 2000, Barbara Taylor Bradford, "In Whose Voice?," p. 7.

*Writer's Digest,* June, 1987, Candy Schulman, "Barbara Taylor Bradford's Acts of Will," p. 3.

*ONLINE*

*Barbara Taylor Bradford Home Page,* http://www.barbarataylorbradford.com (April 1, 2010).

*Bookreporter.com,* http://www.bookreporter.com/ (January 13, 2010), Amie Taylor, review of *Being Elizabeth;* Hillary Wagy, review of *Breaking the Rules.**

# Harlan Coben

(Photograph courtesy of Ulf Andersen/Getty Images.)

## ■ Personal

Born January 4, 1962, in Newark, NJ; son of Carl Gerald (an attorney) and Barbara Coben; married Anne Armstrong (a pediatrician), November 5, 1988; children: four, including Charlotte and Benjamin. *Education:* Amherst College, B.A., 1984.

## ■ Addresses

*Home*—Ridgewood, NJ. *Agent*—Aaron Priest Literary Agency, 708 3rd Ave., New York, NY 10017. *E-mail*—me@harlancoben.com.

## ■ Career

Writer. Previously worked in travel industry.

## ■ Member

Mystery Writers of America, Sisters in Crime.

## ■ Awards, Honors

Anthony Award for best paperback original novel, World Mystery Conference, and Edgar Award nomination, Mystery Writers of America, both 1996, and Nero Wolfe award nomination, all for *Deal Breaker*; Edgar Award for best paperback original mystery novel, Mystery Writers of America, Shamus Award for best paperback original novel, Private Eye Writers of America, and On-line Mystery Award (OLMA) for best paperback original, American Online/Microsoft/Internet Newsgroups, all 1997, all for *Fade Away*; Fresh Talent Award, United Kingdom, for *One False Move*; Edgar Allan Poe Award nomination in best novel category, Mystery Writers of America, 2002, and Le Grand Prix des Lectrices de Elle for fiction, France, both for *Tell No One*; "Thumping Good Read" Award, W.H. Smith, for *Gone for Good*; Bestseller Dagger Award, Crime Writers' Association, 2009.

## ■ Writings

NOVELS

*Play Dead*, British American Publishing (Latham, NY), 1990.

*Miracle Cure*, British American Publishing (Latham, NY), 1991.

*Tell No One*, Delacorte (New York, NY), 2001.

*Gone for Good*, Delacorte (New York, NY), 2002.
*No Second Chance*, Dutton (New York, NY), 2003.
*Just One Look*, Dutton (New York, NY), 2004.
*The Innocent*, Dutton (New York, NY), 2005.
*The Woods*, Dutton (New York, NY), 2007.
*Hold Tight*, Dutton (New York, NY), 2008.
*Caught*, Dutton (New York, NY), 2010.

*"MYRON BOLITAR" SERIES; MYSTERY NOVELS*

*Deal Breaker*, Dell (New York, NY), 1995.
*Drop Shot*, Dell (New York, NY), 1996.
*Fade Away*, Dell (New York, NY), 1996.
*Back Spin*, Dell (New York, NY), 1997.
*One False Move*, Dell (New York, NY), 1997.
*The Final Detail*, Dell (New York, NY), 2000.
*Darkest Fear*, Dell (New York, NY), 2000.
*Three Great Novels: Deal Breaker/Drop Shot/Fade Away*
    (omnibus), Orion (London, England), 2001.
*Promise Me*, Dutton (New York, NY), 2006.
*Long Lost*, Dutton (New York, NY), 2009.

*OTHER*

(Editor, and contributor) *Mystery Writers of America Presents Death Do Us Part: New Stories about Love, Lust, and Murder*, Little, Brown (New York, NY), 2006.

Contributor to periodicals, including the *New York Times*. Books have been published in twenty-two languages.

■ **Adaptations**

*Tell No One* was adapted as the French film *Ne le dis à personne*, 2006; *The Innocent* was optioned for a feature film by Plum Pictures. Several novels have been adapted as audiobooks, including *No Second Chance*, Books on Tape, 2003, *Just One Look*, Penguin Audio, 2004, and *Promise Me*, Brilliance Audio, 2006.

■ **Sidelights**

Harlan Coben is the first mystery writer to win the Edgar Award, the Shamus Award, and the Anthony Award. With forty-seven million books in print around the world, Coben has made his pesky sports agent and unwilling sleuth Myron Bolitar an international sensation. According to Leslie Garisto Pfaff in the *Writer*, "the author has established himself as a master of breakneck pacing, and his sinuous plots and sleight-of-hand twists have earned him critical accolades and a devoted readership." He has also garnered a worldwide audience for his stand-alone fiction; the French film adaptation of *Tell No One*, for example, became a box office hit and earned numerous film awards in France. Explaining, in part, the immense popularity of Coben's non-series fiction, Pfaff noted, "His protagonists are everyday people caught up in extraordinary circumstances, inhabiting that gray area where good can suddenly look a lot like evil and evil isn't always what it seems."

Coben was born in Newark, New Jersey. His father was a lawyer, and he raised the family in Livingston, New Jersey, which Coben often uses as a location in his novels. "We weren't that well off; we were the poor Jews in Livingston," Coben explained to Konigsberg. Coben was not an avid reader as a child, and a career in writing was not something he planned. By his senior year in college, however, Coben was already working on a humorous novel. Rather than going to law school following graduation, he continued writing, living in his parents' basement and working in his grandfather's travel bureau by day. Finally, Coben and his college sweetheart married and moved into a condominium. Not long after, his first novel sold.

**Early Works Garner Attention**

Coben made his mark in the 1990s with crime novels that examine the world of professional sports. His first work, *Play Dead*, concerns professional basketball star David Baskin, a member of the Boston Celtics, who fakes his own death while on his honeymoon in Australia. Baskin's wife, supermodel Laura Ayars, investigates the strange circumstances surrounding her husband's apparent demise, only to find that the people she wishes to interview about the case have a habit of turning up dead. David, meanwhile, has resurfaced—in disguise and with a new identity—and begins playing once again for the Celtics. *Library Journal* contributor Marylaine Block noted that *Play Dead* is "an engrossing suspense novel," and a *Publishers Weekly* contributor commented that the work is "manipulative but otherwise engaging." In *School Library Journal*, Katherine Fitch wrote that the author "weaves a delicate web of intrigue." Fitch went on to describe the novel as "a fast-moving thriller with a rapidly twisting plot."

Fitch found Coben's second novel, *Miracle Cure*, a "fast moving mystery." In the work, a pair of brilliant researchers develop an antidote for AIDS, yet

"You race to turn the pages...both suspenseful and often surprisingly funny." —*People*

# HARLAN COBEN

NEW YORK TIMES BESTSELLING AUTHOR OF *PROMISE ME*

# DEAL BREAKER

The First Myron Bolitar Novel

"What sets Harlan Coben above the crowd are wit...and an entertaining plot." —*LA Times*

**Coben introduced his entertaining sports-agent-turned-sleuth Myron Bolitar in the mystery *Deal Breaker*.** (Dell, 2005. Used by permission of Dell Publishing, a division of Random House, Inc.)

their success is short-lived when one of them is murdered, as are several patients at their clinic, including the son of a U.S. senator. When sports star Michael Silverman, a friend of the researchers, is diagnosed as HIV-positive, his wife, television journalist Sara Lowell, begins investigating the clinic murders with the help of New York City homicide detective Max Bernstein, a closeted homosexual. Suspicion falls on a host of characters, including a government official, a research rival of the researchers, and a televangelist. *Library Journal* contributor A.J. Wright, despite calling the novel's characters "an uneasy stew of American types," declared that "Coben keeps the reader's interest by fleshing out the stereotypes a little bit and moving the plot fast enough to overcome the more incredible aspects."

## Enter Myron Bolitar

Coben then began a series of mystery novels centered on Bolitar, an offbeat investigative hero featured in works such as *Deal Breaker, One False Move,* and *Final Detail.* A former professional basketball player turned sports agent, Bolitar delves into a host of unusual cases with the help of Windsor ("Win") Horne Lockwood III, a lethally powerful young man with a head for business, and Esperanza Diaz, a former wrestler who serves as Bolitar's secretary. In *Deal Breaker,* which introduces the series, Bolitar looks into the bizarre circumstances surrounding the death of the fiancée of rookie quarterback Christian Steele, Bolitar's prized client. *Deal Breaker* received the Anthony Award for best paperback original novel.

Bolitar looks into the murder of a tennis player in *Drop Shot.* Valerie Simpson, a former teen phenomenon trying to revive her career, is shot dead while at the U.S. Open, and Bolitar's latest client, an up-and-coming player, may know the assassin's identity. *Publishers Weekly* contributor Maria Simson commented that the novel's "rapid-fire dialogue" reminded her of the "Fletch" novels by Gregory Mcdonald. "Dry humor and a self-deprecating attitude make Myron an appealing hero, and minor characters are delineated with attitude and verve," Simson wrote. Margo Kaufman, critiquing *Drop Shot* in the *Los Angeles Times Book Review,* wrote that the plot twists were not surprising but that Coben's "depiction of the sports marketing scene is hilarious." *Armchair Detective* contributor Ronald C. Miller called the novel "a solid mystery with an interesting sports background, a fast-paced plot, witty dialogue, and a you'll-never-guess-whodunit denouement." He added: "Harlan Coben brings a new and exciting voice to the mystery novel."

Other Bolitar novels followed. In *Fade Away,* the sleuth gets the chance to enter the basketball arena once again after a coach hires him to find a player who disappears; the player in question was once Bolitar's rival on the court. "Coben writes a fast-moving narrative in a style witty enough to keep pace without straining too hard," wrote a *Publishers Weekly* reviewer of this book. A star golfer loses her son to kidnappers in *Back Spin,* a work in which the "characters are deftly etched and the details keenly observed," according to a *Publishers Weekly* contributor. In *One False Move,* Bolitar takes on a new client, Brenda Slaughter, a young woman who could be a star basketball player. Brenda is also the daughter of Bolitar's former coach, and now he and the young woman join forces to locate her missing father. *Booklist* contributor Wes Lukowsky said of this series installment, "Bolitar is a solid protagonist who is plenty tough but also smart enough to accept his shortcomings." A *Publishers Weekly* contributor called the same book is "a stylish and successful package."

In *Final Detail,* Bolitar tries to prove his now-partner, Esperanza, innocent of murdering one of her clients. For *Booklist* contributor Jenny McLarin, this is a "winner on all counts." Similarly, a *Publishers Weekly* reviewer felt it is the "strongest entry yet in a series that deftly balances realism with excitement, while refusing to fall back on genre cliches." In *Darkest Fear* Bolitar learns that he is the father of an adolescent boy who is dying. The child needs a bone marrow transplant to save his life and Bolitar is the only match, but before he can do anything the youngster is kidnapped. Lukowsky, writing for

**In *Fade Away,* Bolitar, a former pro basketball player, returns to the court to solve a perplexing mystery.** (Dell, 1998. Used by permission of Dell Publishing, a division of Random House, Inc.)

*Booklist,* felt this series addition was filled with "thought-provoking issues and mind-numbing terror made more real by their human context." A reviewer for *Publishers Weekly* had praise for not only this seventh installment, but also for the entire "wonderfully rich series."

### A Breakthrough with Stand-Alone Thrillers

Coben attracted a wide audience for his books featuring Bolitar and won numerous awards for those titles, but in 2001 he left his series behind to write stand-alone thrillers. "Though Coben's protagonists are male," *Atlantic* contributor Eric Konigsberg noted of these works, "they're husbands and fathers, and the crimes they're unwittingly called upon to solve involve not so much intrigue as middle-class desperation." *Tell No One* "moves from heartbreaking to heartstopping without missing a beat," according to Connie Fletcher in *Booklist.* The novel centers on Dr. David Beck, whose wife, supposedly brutally murdered eight years earlier, returns from the dead, appearing on a Web camera. This vision sends Beck on a desperate search for the truth. For *Library Journal* reviewer Jeff Ayers, *Tell No One* is "the book everyone should take to the beach this summer." Coben's novel became a bestseller on both sides of the Atlantic, and set the writer on a course away from his humorous mysteries featuring Bolitar, and instead toward domestic thrillers.

In Coben's novel *No Second Chance,* Dr. Marc Seidman wakes up in a hospital after being in a coma for twelve days following an attack. Also present at the attack was his wife, who was killed, and his baby daughter, who has been kidnapped. When Seidman pays a ransom to the kidnappers, they take off with the money but do not return his daughter. Months later, the criminals contact the doctor asking for more money, and Seidman sets out to get his daughter back. Writing in the *South Florida Sun-Sentinel,* Oline H. Cogdill commented that the "action-laden plot spins on false endings, surprise revelations and a pathos that accentuates the story." Cogdill added: "Coben sharply shapes the characters as realistic, flawed human beings capable of extreme courage and cowardice."

*Just One Look* opens as Grace Lawson, looking through a group of family photos, finds a picture that doesn't seem to belong with the others. Nevertheless, one of the individuals in that picture looks like her husband, Jack, when he was a college student, and one of the women accompanying him in the photo has her faced crossed out. After revealing the picture to her husband, he suddenly disappears, and Grace sets out to look for him. In the process, secrets from her husband's past come to light. Fletcher, writing in *Booklist,* noted the author's ability "to get readers to identify so passionately with the beleaguered principal character that they disappear into the story." A *Publishers Weekly* contributor commented that *Just One Look* "highlights the author's customary strengths (swift pacing, strong lead characters)," and Joe Heim, writing in *People*, noted: "The tension doesn't build slowly; it snaps and crackles right from the get-go."

*The Innocent* tells the story of Matt Hunter, a paralegal who has built a happy life with Olivia, his newly pregnant wife. When Olivia goes on business trip, Hunter receives a photo sent to his cell phone that apparently shows his wife having an affair with another man. Hunter, who spent four years in prison for killing another student in college during a brawl, is soon caught up in a mystery that includes a nun's murder. A *Kirkus Reviews* contributor commented that "there's a record number of jaw-dropping plot twists," and a reviewer writing in *Publishers Weekly* called *The Innocent* Coben's "best book to date." *Booklist* contributor Connie Fletcher noted the novel's "intriguing start . . . [that] hurtles into a fast-paced hunter-and-hunted drama."

### Bolitar Rides Again

Coben returns to his protagonist Myron Bolitar in the 2006 novel *Promise Me*. In the work, the sleuthing sports agent convinces a pair of neighbors to phone him rather than accept a ride from their intoxicated pals. A few nights later Bolitar receives a call from one of the girls and drives her to a friend's house. When the girl disappears without ever making it to her own home, however, Bolitar decides it is his duty to find her. A *Kirkus Reviews* contributor stated that the author "piles on the plot twists, false leads, violent set pieces and climactic surprises." Writing in *Booklist*, Fletcher praised the novel's "melding of high suspense and high technology with a somewhat battered, very canny, questing hero," and *Entertainment Weekly* critic Adam B. Vary pointed out the author's "skillful pacing and truly surprising turns of plot."

Bolitar is featured once again in *Long Lost*. Here the investigator goes to Paris to be with a former lover, Terese Collins, a television journalist. She lets Bolitar know that her ex-husband, an investigative reporter, recently got in touch with her to discuss a huge story he was covering. When this man's corpse turns up, Collins becomes a prime suspect, and soon Bolitar is caught up in a whirlwind of activities involving international terrorists. *Booklist* contributor Joanne Wilkinson termed this novel an "action-

A doctor receives an eerie vision of his wife, who was presumed dead eight years earlier, in the thriller *Tell No One.* (Dell, 2009. Used by permission of Dell Publishing, a division of Random House, Inc.)

packed thriller with a horrific yet credible premise." A *Publishers Weekly* reviewer noted, "Bolitar fans will cheer their hero every step of the way."

The past comes back to haunt a New Jersey country prosecutor named Paul Copeland in *The Woods*. Twenty years earlier, Copeland's sister, Camille, went missing and was declared dead at a summer camp where he worked as a counselor. More recently, Copeland has lost his loving wife to cancer, and his father has now disappeared while searching for Camille. Left to raise his only daughter by himself, Copeland is working on a rape case in which two fraternity boys are charged with the crime. Then the remains of one of Camille's friends is discovered, providing ammunition for the parents of the college students, who are searching for ways to attack Copeland's integrity. "The exploration of ordinary people with life-shattering secrets is a common thread in Coben's novels," pointed out *Library Journal* contributor Ayers. Some critics, however, felt that the author missed his mark with this mystery. "Less than compelling characters fail to compensate for a host of implausibilities," remarked one *Publishers Weekly* writer. Fletcher offered a more positive assessment of the work, asserting in *Booklist* that "Coben has an uncanny knack for getting readers to care deeply about his main characters" in this "gripper." "I prefer to work in the grays," Coben was quoted as saying in a *Kirkus Reviews* article about his 2007 thriller. "No character comes out of *The Woods* unscathed or innocent."

Coben followed *The Woods* with a technothriller called *Hold Tight*, which explores a number of issues concerning parents' supervision of children's electronic devices. Coben's "genius is to make the seemingly mundane terrifying," observed Fletcher in another *Booklist* review. Coben alternates two seemingly unrelated plots: one featuring a serial killer out to murder women and the other about a couple who install a program on their son's computer that records his every keystroke. Through this juxtaposition, the author is able to highlight themes that include the right to privacy. A *Publishers Weekly* contributor noted that Coben also addresses issues such as the need to balance work and family responsibilities and the importance of honesty within a marriage. "Coben plucks each of these strings like a virtuoso," concluded the critic.

Speaking with Pfaff in the *Writer,* Coben noted that, despite the great success of his thrillers, he doesn't consider himself simply a mystery novelist. "I've never looked at the crime novel as a genre; I look at it as a form," he stated. "It's like saying 'haiku' or 'sonata' to me. And within that form, I can do whatever I want—and I have done so. I've done friendship, loss, family, relationships, sexism, racism. But what I love about the form, and why I

*Tell No One* **was adapted as the award-winning French film** *Ne le dis à personne* **in 2006.** (Photograph courtesy of Les Productions du Trésor/Europa Corp/The Kobal Collection/The Picture Desk, Inc.)

If you enjoy the works of Harlan Coben, you may also want to check out the following books:

Elmore Leonard, *Out of Sight*, 1996.
Robert Crais, *The Forgotten Man*, 2005.
Rick Riordan, *Rebel Island*, 2007.

think it's so vital right now, is that it forces you to tell a story; you're compelled to make it suspenseful; you're not just meandering along."

## ■ Biographical and Critical Sources

*PERIODICALS*

*Armchair Detective*, spring, 1996, Ronald C. Miller, review of *Drop Shot*, p. 242.

*Atlantic*, July-August, 2007, Eric Konigsberg, "Paperback Writer," p. 98.

*Booklist*, May 15, 1998, Wes Lukowsky, review of *One False Move*, p. 1598; April 15, 1999, Jenny McLarin, review of *The Final Detail*, p. 1470; May 1, 2000, Wes Lukowsky, review of *Darkest Fear*, p. 1614; May 1, 2001, Connie Fletcher, review of *Tell No One*, p. 1624; March 1, 2004, Connie Fletcher, review of *Just One Look*, p. 1100; March 1, 2005, Connie Fletcher, review of *The Innocent*, p. 1101; April 1, 2006, Connie Fletcher, review of *Promise Me*, p. 4; July 1, 2006, David Pitt, review of *Mystery Writers of America Presents Death Do Us Part: New Stories about Love, Lust, and Murder*, p. 37; February 15, 2007, Connie Fletcher, review of *The Woods*, p. 4; March 1, 2008, Connie Fletcher, review of *Hold Tight*, p. 29; January 1, 2009, Joanne Wilkinson, review of *Long Lost*, p. 22.

*Detroit Free Press*, May 4, 2005, Ron Bernas, review of *The Innocent*.

*Entertainment Weekly*, April 30, 2004, Adam B. Vary, review of *Just One Look*, p. 168; April 29, 2005, Jennifer Reese, review of *The Innocent*, p. 155; April 28, 2006, Adam B. Vary, review of *Promise Me*, p. 139; April 20, 2007, Paul Katz, review of *The Woods*, p. 67.

*Kirkus Reviews*, September 1, 1991, review of *Miracle Cure*, p. 1106; March 15, 2004, review of *Just One Look*, p. 239; March 1, 2005, review of *The Innocent*, p. 244; March 15, 2006, review of *Promise Me*, p. 263; June 15, 2006, review of *Mystery Writers of America Presents Death Do Us Part*, p. 602; February 1, 2007, review of *The Woods*, p. 7; February 15, 2007, review of *The Woods*; February 1, 2009, review of *Long Lost*.

*Library Journal*, April 1, 1990, Marylaine Block, review of *Play Dead*, p. 136; November 1, 1991, A.J. Wright, review of *Miracle Cure*, p. 130; May 1, 1998, Rex E. Klett, review of *One False Move*, p. 143; May 1, 2000, Rex Klett, review of *Darkest Fear*, p. 156; April 15, 2001, Jeff Ayers, review of *Tell No One*, p. 130; May 1, 2004, Jeff Ayers, review of *Just One Look*, p. 139; April 1, 2005, Jeff Ayers, review of *The Innocent*, p. 84; May 1, 2006, Jeff Ayers, review of *Promise Me*, p. 77; March 15, 2007, Jeff Ayers, review of *The Woods*, p. 56; March 1, 2009, Rebecca Vnuk, review of *Long Lost*, p. 63.

*Los Angeles Times Book Review*, March 10, 1996, Margo Kaufman, review of *Drop Shot*, p. 11.

*New York Times*, September 9, 1990, Shirley Horner, "Harlan Coben: Getting Published on the First Attempt"; April 5, 2009, Robin Finn, "Local Writer, Worldwide Following."

*Orlando Sentinel*, May 26, 2004, Nancy Pate, review of *Just One Look*.

*People*, May 3, 2004, Joe Heim, review of *Just One Look*, p. 47.

*Publishers Weekly*, April 6, 1990, review of *Play Dead*, p. 101; February 5, 1996, Maria Simson, review of *Drop Shot*, p. 82; October 28, 1996, review of *Fade Away*, p. 76; June 23, 1997, review of *Back Spin*, p. 87; March 30, 1998, review of *One False Move*, p. 72; April 19, 1999, review of *The Final Detail*, p. 64; April 24, 2000, review of *Darkest Fear*, p. 64; May 7, 2001, review of *Tell No One*, p. 220; March 29, 2004, review of *Just One Look*, p. 36; May 10, 2004, Daisy Maryles, "It's Coben Time," p. 16; March 7, 2005, review of *The Innocent*, p. 50; March 6, 2006, review of *Promise Me*, p. 48; June 5, 2006, review of *Mystery Writers of America Presents Death Do Us Part*, p. 40; February 12, 2007, review of *The Woods*, p. 62; February 18, 2008, Robert C. Hahn, "*PW* talks with Harlan Coben," p. 134, and review of *Hold Tight*, p. 136.

*San Jose Mercury News*, April 21, 2004, John Orr, review of *Just One Look*.

*School Library Journal*, October, 1990, Katherine Fitch, review of *Play Dead*, p. 150; May, 1992, Katherine Fitch, review of *Miracle Cure*, p. 151; November, 2000, Katherine Fitch, review of *Darkest Fear*, p. 182.

*South Florida Sun-Sentinel* (Fort Lauderdale, FL), May 5, 2003, Oline H. Cogdill, review of *No Second Chance*; April 28, 2004, Oline H. Cogdill, review of *Just One Look*; April 27, 2005, Oline H. Cogdill, review of *The Innocent*; April 26, 2006, Oline H. Cogdill, review of *Promise Me*; August 9, 2006, Oline H. Cogdill, review of *Deal Breaker*.

*Writer*, September, 2006, Leslie Garisto Pfaff, "In the Gray Zone with Harlan Coben," p. 20.

ONLINE

*BookPage.com*, http://www.bookpage.com/ (December 26, 2006), Stephanie Swilley, "Harlan Coben Tells All."

*Bookreporter.com*, http://www.bookreporter.com/ (May, 2003), interview with Coben; (December 26, 2006), Joe Hartlaub, reviews of *Promise Me, The Innocent, Just One Look,* and *Gone for Good;* Bob Rhubart, review of *No Second Chance.*

*Harlan Coben Home Page*, http://www.harlancoben. com (January 14, 2010).*

# Junot Díaz

(Photograph courtesy of Ulf Andersen/Getty Images.)

Has also worked at a copy shop, and as a dishwasher, steelworker, pool-table delivery person, clerk, and editorial assistant.

## ■ Personal

Born December 31, 1968, in Santo Domingo, Dominican Republic; immigrated to the United States, 1975; naturalized citizen. *Education:* Attended Kean College; Rutgers University, B.A., 1992; Cornell University, M.F.A., 1995.

## ■ Addresses

*Home*—Cambridge, MA. *Office*—Massachusetts Institute of Technology, 77 Massachusetts Ave., Cambridge, MA 02139. *E-mail*—junot@mit.edu.

## ■ Career

Writer and educator. Freelance writer, 1996—; Syracuse University, Syracuse, NY, member of creative writing faculty, 1997-2002; Massachusetts Institute of Technology (MIT), Cambridge, MA, 2003—, began as associate professor of writing, currently Rudge and Nancy Allen Professor of Writing.

## ■ Awards, Honors

Named one of the "New Faces of 1996," *Newsweek* magazine; Guggenheim Fellowship; Eugene McDermott Award in the Arts, Massachusetts Institute of Technology; Lila Wallace-Reader's Digest Writers' Award; Radcliffe Institute for Advanced Study fellowship, Harvard University; PEN/Malamud Award, 2002; U.S.-Japan Creative Artist Fellowship, National Endowment for the Arts, 2003; *Los Angeles Times* Book Prize nomination, 2007, John Sargent, Sr., First Novel Prize, Mercantile Library Center for Fiction, 2007, National Book Critics Circle Award for fiction, 2007, Pulitzer Prize for fiction, 2008, Anisfield-Wolf Book Award, Cleveland Foundation, 2008, and Dayton Literary Peace Prize, 2008, all for *The Brief Wondrous Life of Oscar Wao.*

## ■ Writings

*Drown* (stories), Riverhead Books (New York, NY), 1996.

(Editor) *The Beacon Best of 2001: Great Writing by Women and Men of All Colors and Cultures,* Beacon Books (Boston, MA), 2001.

*The Brief Wondrous Life of Oscar Wao* (novel), River-head Books (New York, NY), 2007.

Stories from *Drown* were translated into Spanish and published as *Negocios,* Vintage Books (New York, NY), 1997. Contributor to the anthology *Best American Short Stories 1996;* contributor of fiction to periodicals, including the *New Yorker, Story, Paris Review,* and *African Verse.* Has also written book reviews for *Entertainment Weekly.*

## ■ Adaptations

The film rights to *The Brief Wondrous Life of Oscar Wao* were purchased by Miramax and producer Scott Rudin.

## ■ Sidelights

Like the characters in many of his stories, Junot Díaz was born in the Dominican Republic and spent his early childhood in that nation before his father was able to bring the family to the United States. But there the similarity ends. Several of Díaz's characters are adolescent drug dealers, while he himself obtained a literature and history degree from Rutgers University in New Jersey and studied creative writing at Cornell University in New York City. *New York Times* contributor Barbara Stewart called Díaz "an unflinching observer, an insider, of tough teen-age Latino immigrants in New Jersey. Of hand-to-mouth lives and of mind-numbing jobs. Of young men who get money making penny-ante drug sales and give some to their mothers to spend at the mall, or who steal from the boss's cash register to buy lingerie for a girlfriend. He writes of what he knows without compromise, but he invests his stories with love." Díaz's first novel, *The Brief Wondrous Life of Oscar Wao,* claimed both the National Book Critics Circle Award and the Pulitzer Prize, and "decisively" established Díaz "as one of contemporary fiction's most distinctive and irresistible new voices," according to *New York Times* critic Michiko Kakutani.

Díaz spent his early years in the Dominican Republic, living in poverty while his father tried to earn enough to bring his family to America. The family joined his father in New Jersey when Díaz was just six, in a neighborhood bordered by a landfill and a highway. Díaz remembers being fascinated by the number of electric lights in his neighborhood. "That was one of thousands of things that reminded me I was in a new world," he told *Milwaukee Journal Sentinel* columnist Geeta Sharma-Jensen. "You have a number of reactions. You protect yourself against it because it's overwhelming. Or you begin to explore." Because he had an easier time learning to read English than to speak it, books—particularly science fiction and comics—became Díaz's way of exploring his environment. "I was trying to answer the question, first of all, what is the United States, and how do I get along in this culture, this strange place, better? And also, who am I and how did I get here? And the way I was doing it was through books," he told Steve Inskeep of National Public Radio's "Morning Edition." He added, "When they'd showed me the library when I was a kid, a light went off at me in every cell of my body. Books became the map with which I navigated this new world."

Díaz eventually found ways to fit in with his neighbors and classmates, and the family was getting by until his father was laid off and his parents split up. Díaz's mother ended up supporting her five children by working multiple jobs, often performing menial labor. To complicate matters, the author's older brother was diagnosed with leukemia (he later recovered). As a result, the young teen "felt like my life was entering this huge, vast silence," Díaz told a contributor in *People Weekly,* and he began writing as a way to deal with his frustrations. His love of reading and writing pegged him as a nerd, "but to be a nerd in my neighborhood meant you could beat up just about any kid from outside your neighborhood," he joked with Fritz Lanham of the *Houston Chronicle.* It didn't necessarily mean academic success, either; Díaz's grades were poor, and when he wasn't reading he spent most of his free time drinking or smoking. Living next to a garbage landfill, "I felt that we were as far from the world as you could possibly get," he told Sam Anderson in *New York.* "I was so desperate to escape."

### Literary Beginnings

Díaz hadn't thought to escape through a career as a writer, but his life changed after his mother convinced him to apply to Kean College, a small local school. He planned to attend for a year, just to humor her, but he discovered he loved his studies and eventually transferred to Rutgers University. He earned his bachelor's degree in 1992 and was accepted into the creative writing program at Cornell University, an Ivy League school. Although he called his early work "junk," he graduated in 1995 and was soon placing stories in prestigious publications like the *New Yorker.* He acquired an agent and hoped for a steady income through writing. Díaz was writing at night and supporting himself with a clerical job when his agent struck gold, earning Díaz a six-figure deal for his first collection of short stories and an unfinished novel. Soon *Newsweek* was listing him among its "New Faces of 1996" and he published his first fiction collection, *Drown.*

The stories in *Drown* feature young Dominican characters struggling with life's obstacles, both in the Caribbean and in their immigrant neighborhoods in New Jersey. The title story concerns an adolescent narrator—a drug dealer—reacting to the knowledge that his best friend is gay. "Ysrael," set in the Dominican Republic, tells the tale of a boy whose face has been chewed off by a pig, and the taunting he suffers from his peers. The same

NATIONAL BESTSELLER

DROWN

Junot Díaz

Author of the Pulitzer Prize-winning *The Brief Wondrous Life of Oscar Wao*

*Drown,* **a short-story collection by Díaz, features a number of characters from the Dominican Republic, where the author was born.** (Riverhead Books, 1997. Front cover photograph © 1996 by Ken Schles.)

character shows up in another story in *Drown;* by now he has come to America and is set to have reconstructive surgery. "Aguantando" centers on Yunior, a child in the Dominican Republic who watches his mother try to support the family while they wait for his father, who has settled in the United States, to send for them. "Fiesta, 1980" takes place after Yunior has been reunited with his father, and readers are shown his father's unsympathetic nature through his reaction to his son's chronic carsickness. One of the more controversial stories in *Drown* is "How to Date a Browngirl, Blackgirl, Whitegirl, or Halfie." "Although each [story] stands on its own," Vanessa V. Friedman remarked in *Entertainment Weekly,* "when read together Díaz's remarkable stories enhance and illuminate each other to create a work greater than its parts."

*Drown* earned Díaz some head-turning reviews. A critic in *Publishers Weekly* called it an "intense debut collection," and went on to observe that the tales in it possess "a lasting resonance." *New York Times Book Review* contributor David Gates placed Díaz's alienated characters firmly within the American literary tradition and added that the author "transfigures disorder and disorientation with a rigorous sense of form." His frequent protagonist, Yunior, has a voice that "is tough, realistic, penetrating," James Hannah noted in the *Houston Chronicle.* "But at the same time, like all youths, he wants to believe in hope; he would like his frail faith to be strengthened by circumstances." As Roberto Santiago concluded in *American Visions:* "To read the short fiction in *Drown* is to be exposed to one of the most original, vibrant and engrossing voices to come along in many years."

In the wake of *Drown*'s success, Díaz was catapulted into the literary limelight, something which brought its own set of troubles. "I don't want people to think I'm not grateful for what's happened," he told Lanham of the *Houston Chronicle.* "I don't mind eating regularly. I get to send money to my mother, and to me that's important. At the same time . . . it's got another edge to it." The weight of lofty expectations and Díaz's meticulous writing style all contributed to a severe case of writer's block. "You want to talk about a perfect storm," he told *New York* contributor Boris Kachka. "This was a perfect storm of insecurity and madness and pressure and you name it." It would take Díaz more than a decade to produce his first novel, *The Brief Wondrous Life of Oscar Wao.* Contributing to the delay was Díaz's belief that the novel's complex and intricate plot required time to fully develop. In a *Bomb* interview with Edwidge Danticat, Díaz explained: "Ultimately the novel wouldn't have it any other way. This book wanted x number of years out of my life. Perhaps I could have written a book in a shorter time but it wouldn't have been this book and this was the book I wanted to write."

### A Wondrous Success

The 2007 novel *The Brief Wondrous Life of Oscar Wao* examines the often violent history of the Dominican Republic through three generations of the Cabral family. The novel focuses on Oscar de León, a lovesick, overweight Dominican-American youngster who dreams of becoming the next great fantasy writer (like J.R.R. Tolkien), and Oscar's relationship with his domineering mother, Beli, who fled her native country after the death of its brutal dictator, Rafael Trujillo. According to Armando Celayo and David Shook, writing in *World Literature Today,* the novel is more than a coming-of-age story; "it's an honest and poignant narrative that looks at the overbearing weight of history as it influences generations upon generations of Americans, who often don't realize the impact it has on them." The story is narrated both by Oscar's knockout sister, Lola, and Díaz's recurring narrator, Yunior, in a mixture of Spanglish (phrases combining Spanish and English), pop culture references, and historical footnotes.

*The Brief Wondrous Life of Oscar Wao* garnered strong reviews, particularly for Díaz's vibrant, energetic prose. "Like his shattering 1996 debut collection, *Drown,* Díaz's first novel is dense and thick, teeming with observations stacked tight like staples," Allison Glock commented in *Esquire. New York Times* critic Kakutani stated that the book "is funny, street-smart and keenly observed, and it unfolds from a comic portrait of a second-generation Dominican geek into a harrowing meditation on public and private history and the burdens of familial history." The novel "shows a novelist engaged with the culture, high and low, and its polyglot language," *Newsweek* contributor David Gates observed, adding that other writers "will find that the bar just got set higher." As Alice O'Keeffe concluded in *New Statesman:* Díaz "is a rare treat: a new author who has both something original to say and a fresh and idiosyncratic way of saying it."

Along with the critical accolades, *The Brief Wondrous Life of Oscar Wao* garnered numerous honors, including the National Book Critics Circle Award and the Pulitzer Prize. The arduous journey to complete the novel, Díaz noted, was worth more than any literary award. As he told *Newsweek Online* interviewer Jesse Ellison, "I think it was an incredibly difficult

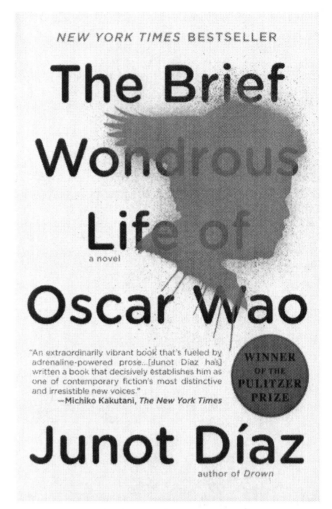

Díaz garnered the National Book Critics Circle Award and the Pulitzer Prize for fiction for *The Brief Wondrous Life of Oscar Wao,* his first novel. (Riverhead Books, 2008. Used by permission of Penguin Group (USA) Inc.)

struggle. I tell a lot of young people I work with that nothing should be more inspirational than my dumb ass. It took me 11 years to struggle through one dumb book, and every day you just want to give up. But you don't find out you're an artist because you do something really well. You find out you're an artist because when you fail you have something within you—strength or belief or just craziness—that picks you back up again."

After hitting the bestseller lists with *Oscar Wao,* Díaz returned to short fiction with other stories featuring Yunior as the narrator. In the 2010 story "The Pura Principle," Yunior's older brother deals with leukemia, and this detail, along with biographical similarities in other works, have inspired many to wonder whether the character is based on the author himself. "I consider Yunior my alter-ego,"

Díaz told Matt Okie of *Identity Theory*. "But for me an alter-ego is less about pursuing my autobiographical details than it is just having a conversation about how in this age, we're very hungry for autobiographical details in an area, fiction, where we should not be looking for them. . . . I think the reason why I make Yunior my alter-ego is because he is good at representing how many sides we have to us. I've always liked that."

## Establishing an Identity

Díaz is often referred to as a "Latino" or "Dominican" writer, and he says that such labels do not bother him. As he told Wajahat Ali in an interview for the *CounterPunch* Web site, "I think as a writer of color, as an artist of color, especially one who identifies himself or herself as such, and thinks there is nothing limiting or ghetto-izing of calling oneself a writer of color, simply stating that doesn't absolve me from universality, in fact I think it brings me closer to it. The universal is found in the specific." In using Spanglish throughout his work, he told Stewart, "I write for the people I grew up with. I took extreme pains for my book to not be a native informant. Not: 'This is Dominican food. This is a Spanish word.' I trust my readers, even non-Spanish ones."

---

If you enjoy the works of Junot Díaz, you may also want to check out the following books:

Elías Miguel Muñoz, *Crazy Love*, 1989.
Julia Alvarez, *How the García Girls Lost Their Accents*, 1991.
Reinaldo Arenas, *Before Night Falls: A Memoir*, 1993.

---

Díaz believes he would be a slow, methodical writer even if he were writing full-time, but since 2003 he has also taught writing at the Massachusetts Institute of Technology (MIT). He hopes to inspire other writers through his example. "I was always encouraged and motivated by other artists' breaking down trails for us," he told Connie Ogle in the *Miami Herald*. "The best thing about these awards is that you encourage someone you don't even know and may never meet. I keep thinking all this will go away, and no one will remember any of it, but maybe some young immigrant girl somewhere will pick up a book someday and say, 'I can do this.'" To affect a reader is Díaz's ultimate goal. "As a writer, if I help two people in my lifetime on their journey to, like, a better sense of the human within themselves, that's well worth it. That's more than anybody who runs a company can say," he told Okie of *Identity Theory*. "I'm trying to reach into, like, one person at the most—that's what you pray for. And the impact that an artist has on a person and what that impact has on a collective cannot be measured. It's a mystery."

## ■ Biographical and Critical Sources

*PERIODICALS*

*American Visions*, October-November, 1996, Roberto Santiago, review of *Drown*, p. 28.
*Bomb*, fall, 2007, Edwidge Danticat, "Junot Díaz."
*Boston Globe*, September 10, 2007, Johnny Díaz, "Eleven Years Later . . .: Call It a Curse or Writer's Block, but after the Acclaim of His First Novel, Junot Díaz Struggled to Write the Follow-Up."
*Entertainment Weekly*, October 4, 1996, Vanessa V. Friedman, review of *Drown*, p. 56; August 31, 2007, review of *The Brief Wondrous Life of Oscar Wao*, p. 70.
*Esquire*, September, 2007, Allison Glock, "We Are All Fuku'd," p. 86.
*Hispanic*, November, 2000, Ana Radelat, "Junot Díaz," p. 32; October, 2001, review of *The Beacon Best of 2001: Great Writing by Women and Men of All Colors and Cultures*, p. 18.
*Houston Chronicle*, September 15, 1996, James Hannah, "*Drown* Reveals Strong New Voice," p. 23; October 6, 1996, Fritz Lanham, "Adrift in Success," p. 20.
*London Review of Books*, March 20, 2008, Philip Connors, review of *The Brief Wondrous Life of Oscar Wao*, p. 30.
*Miami Herald*, April 8, 2008, Connie Ogle, "Prize 'Astonishes' Brilliant Writer."
*Milwaukee Journal Sentinel*, October 5, 2008, Geeta Sharma-Jensen, "A Wondrous Guest."
*Nation*, November 26, 2007, William Deresiewicz, review of *The Brief Wondrous Life of Oscar Wao*, p. 36.
*New Statesman*, February 25, 2008, Alice O'Keeffe, "Spanglish Surrealism," p. 58.
*Newsweek*, September 10, 2007, David Gates, "From a Sunny Mordor to the Garden State," p. 51.

*New York*, September 16, 1996, review of *Drown*, p. 41; August 24, 2007, Boris Kachka, "Junot Díaz Karate-Chops His Writer's Block," p. 102; October 6, 2008, Sam Anderson, "Two New York Novelists on the Death of Times Square, the Afterbirth of the Lower East Side, and the Importance of Ghosts," p. 130.

*New Yorker*, June 14, 2004, Junot Díaz, "Homecoming, with Turtle," p. 90.

*New York Times*, September 15, 1996, Somini Sengupta, "More Orchard Beach than Elaine's" (author interview); December 8, 1996, Barbara Stewart, "Outsider with a Voice"; September 4, 2007, Michiko Kakutani, "Travails of an Outcast."

*New York Times Book Review*, September 29, 1996, David Gates, "English Lessons," review of *Drown*; September 30, 2007, A.O. Scott, review of *The Brief Wondrous Life of Oscar Wao*, p. 9.

*People Weekly*, January 13, 1997, "Giving His People a Voice," p. 77; September 17, 2007, Jonathan Durbin, review of *The Brief Wondrous Life of Oscar Wao*, p. 59.

*Publishers Weekly*, July 8, 1996, review of *Drown*, p. 71; August 13, 2001, review of *The Beacon Best of 2001*, p. 297.

*San Francisco Chronicle*, April 22, 2006, Edward Guthmann, "It's a Scary Time for Latin American Immigrants, and Writer Junot Díaz Feels the Pressure to Help."

*Time*, September 3, 2007, Lev Grossman, review of *The Brief Wondrous Life of Oscar Wao*, p. 62.

*Times Literary Supplement*, February 1, 2008, Bill Broun, review of *The Brief Wondrous Life of Oscar Wao*, p. 21.

*USA Today*, September 11, 2007, Carol Memmott, "*Oscar Wao* Packs Punch of Erotic Latino Persuasion," p. 4D.

*Washington Post Book World*, September 30, 2007, Jabari Asim, review of *The Brief Wondrous Life of Oscar Wao*, p. 3.

*World Literature Today*, March-April, 2008, Armando Celayo and David Shook, "In Darkness We Meet: A Conversation with Junot Díaz," p. 12, and Jim Hannan, review of *The Brief Wondrous Life of Oscar Wao*, p. 65.

*ONLINE*

*Bookslut*, http://www.bookslut.com/ (September 4, 2007), John Zuarino, "An Interview with Junot Díaz."

*CounterPunch*, http://www.counterpunch.org/ (April 11, 2008), Wajahat Ali, "Revenge of the Ghetto Nerd: An Interview with Pulitzer Prize-Winning Novelist Junot Díaz."

*Identity Theory*, http://www.identitytheory.com/ (September 2, 2008), Matt Okie, "Mil Máscaras: An Interview with Pulitzer-Winner Junot Díaz."

*Junot Díaz Home Page*, http://www.junotdiaz.com (March 16, 2010).

*LAist Web site*, http://laist.com/ (April 10, 2008), Carrie Meathrell and Osmany Rodriguez, author interview.

*National Public Radio Web site*, http://www.npr.org/ (November 24, 2008), Steve Inskeep, "Morning Edition: Junot Díaz on 'Becoming American'" (transcript).

*Newsweek Online*, http://www.newsweek.com (April 3, 2008), Jesse Ellison, "'I'm Nobody or I'm a Nation': Junot Díaz Talks about Authors and Ethnicity."

*New Yorker Online*, http://www.newyorker.com/ (March 15, 2010), Cressida Leyshon, "This Week in Fiction: Questions for Junot Díaz."

*Powells.com*, http://www.powells.com/ (August 19, 2007), Dave Weich, "Junot Díaz out of the Silence."

*Salon.com*, http://www.salon.com/ (May 19, 2002), review of *Drown*; (September 12, 2007), Roland Kelt, "*The Brief Wondrous Life of Oscar Wao*: Junot Díaz's Long-awaited Debut Novel Is a Portrait of the Artist as a Nerdy Young Latino—as Well as a Tribute to Tolkien, Magic Realism and Dominican History."

*Slate*, http://www.slate.com/ (November 8, 2007), Meghan O'Rourke, "*The Brief Wondrous Life of Oscar Wao*: Questions for Junot Díaz."

*Splice Today*, http://www.splicetoday.com/ (April 7, 2008), John Lingan, "Interview: Junot Díaz."*

# Margarita Engle

## ■ Personal

Born September 2, 1951, in Pasadena, CA; daughter of Martin (an artist) and Eloisa (a quilter) Mondrus; married Curtis E. Engle (a research biologist), 1978; children: Victor, Nicole. *Education:* California State Polytechnic University, B.S., 1974; Iowa State University, M.S., 1977; doctoral study at University of California, Riverside, 1983. *Politics:* "Human rights advocate." *Religion:* Christian. *Hobbies and other interests:* Horsemanship, western equitation, trail riding.

## ■ Addresses

*Agent*—Julie Castiglia, 1155 Camino Del Mar, Ste. 510, Del Mar, CA 92014.

## ■ Career

Poet, novelist, journalist, and botanist. California State Polytechnic University, Pomona, associate professor of agronomy, 1978-82.

## ■ Member

Pen USA West, Amnesty International, Freedom House of Human Rights, Freedom to Write Committee.

## ■ Awards, Honors

CINTAS fellow, Arts International, 1994-95; San Diego Book Award, 1996, for *Skywriting*; Willow Review Poetry Award, 2005; Best Books for Young Adults and Notable Children's Books selection, both American Library Association (ALA), Children's Book Award and Teachers' Choice award, both International Reading Association, Notable Children's Books in the Language Arts, National Council of Teachers of English, Best Children's Book of the Year, Bank Street College of Education, Books for the Teen Age selection, New York Public Library, Américas Award for Children's and Young Adult Literature, Consortium of Latin American Studies Programs, 2007, and Pura Belpré Award, ALA, 2008, all for *The Poet Slave of Cuba;* Claudia Lewis Award and Best Children's Book of the Year selection, both Bank Street College of Education, Lee Bennett Hopkins Poetry Award Honor Book, Notable Social Studies Trade Books for Young People, National Council for the Social Studies/Children's Book Council, Américas Award for Children's and Young Adult Literature, Consortium of Latin American Studies Programs, Amelia Bloomer Project/Feminist Task Force selection, ALA Best Books for Young Adults and Notable Children's Books selections, both ALA, Pura Belpré Award, ALA, 2009, and Newbery Honor Book, ALA, 2009, all for *The Surrender Tree;* Sydney Taylor Book Award, Association of Jewish Libraries, 2010, for *Tropical Secrets.*

## ■ Writings

*The Poet Slave of Cuba: A Biography of Juan Francisco Manzano,* illustrated by Sean Qualls, Henry Holt (New York, NY), 2006.
*The Surrender Tree: Poems of Cuba's Struggle for Freedom,* Henry Holt (New York, NY), 2008.

*Tropical Secrets: Holocaust Refugees in Cuba,* Henry Holt (New York, NY), 2009.

*The Firefly Letters: A Suffragette's Journey to Cuba,* Henry Holt (New York, NY), 2010.

*Summer Birds: The Butterflies of Maria Merian,* illustrated by Julie Paschkis, Henry Holt (New York, NY), 2010.

*FOR ADULTS*

*Singing to Cuba* (novel), Arte Público Press (Houston, TX), 1993.

*Skywriting: A Novel of Cuba,* Bantam (New York, NY), 1995.

Contributor to periodicals, including *Atlanta Review, Bilingual Review, California Quarterly, Caribbean Writer, Hawai'i Pacific Review,* and *Nimrod.*

## ■ Sidelights

The author of adult novels as well as books for young readers, Cuban-American writer Margarita Engle is the first Hispanic to earn a coveted Newbery Honor Book citation. She is known for her novels in verse for young readers, including *The Poet Slave of Cuba: A Biography of Juan Francisco Manzano, The Surrender Tree: Poems of Cuba's Struggle for Freedom, Tropical Secrets: Holocaust Refugees in Cuba,* and *The Firefly Letters: A Suffragette's Journey to Cuba,* all of which illuminate various aspects of her mother's native land. "I love the dreamlike quality of historical novels in verse," Engle told *Booklist* contributor Jeannine Atkins. "I know there are modern critics who dislike the combination of storytelling with poetry, but to me, it seems so natural and ancient, a form that has been rediscovered, not reinvented."

Born in 1951, Engle grew up in Los Angeles, California, but she spent her summers in Cuba. There she learned to appreciate her mother's extended family as well as the special feel of the island. With the rise to power of communist politician Fidel Castro, which resulted in travel restrictions from the United States to Cuba, however, she did not return to the island until 1991. "When we would visit Cuba we would visit my greatgrandmother," Engle remarked to *Publishers Weekly* interviewer Aida Bardales. "The last time I saw her was for my ninth birthday, in 1960. I do have very vivid memories, and I'm so glad I got to meet her. And of course I knew my grandmother, though there were many years when we were cut off; after the missile crisis it was impossible to visit."

### From Professor to Author

Engle developed an early interest in literature, she remarked on the *Macmillan* Web site. "I loved to read, especially travel books, adventure stories and poetry," she recalled. "I began writing poetry when I was very young. I remember going for walks, and making up poems about what I was seeing. I did not save any of those poems, but I can still remember the satisfied feeling I received from composing them." She also greatly enjoyed the outdoors even though she lived in a big city. While attending college she studied agronomy and botany as a way to connect with the wilderness she had been missing while growing up in Los Angeles. She became the first woman agronomy professor at Cal Poly Pomona and married Curtis E. Engle, an agricultural entomologist. "The study of natural history is compatible with an open mind and a sense of adventure," she remarked to Atkins. "I am especially fond of old-fashioned field botany, the kind of science that requires muddy boots. I am fascinated by aspects of biology that can never be fully quantified."

While raising her two children, she revisited her love of writing, submitting her haiku and having it published, as well as writing editorial columns for news organizations. After her trip to Cuba in 1991, thirty years after she had last visited as a child, Engle was inspired to write two adult novels about Cuba: *Singing to Cuba* and *Skywriting: A Novel of Cuba.* Thereafter, she left academia behind and turned to writing.

Reviewing *Singing to Cuba,* a *Publishers Weekly* contributor termed it a "pleasantly rambling first novel." The book tells the story of a Cuban-American poet who returns to Cuba, much like Engle did, after a long hiatus brought on by the Castro revolution. "Through the fictional, personal story of her nameless U.S.-born narrator," remarked *MELUS* contributor Gisele M. Requeña, "Engle tackles the controversial issues of 'Cubanness' and exile consciousness . . . and creates a story which embraces the general Cuban-American experience of disillusionment, loss, and oppression." In *Skywriting,* Engle focuses on the efforts of a young Cuban-American woman to free her half brother from one of Castro's prisons after he was caught trying to flee the island. A *Publishers Weekly* reviewer found this "a lush improvisation on Cuban politics and their effect on one family."

### Targets a Younger Audience with Verse Novels

While traveling in Cuba, Engle learned the story of Juan Francisco Manzano, a Cuban slave who became a well-known poet. She struggled for years to write a historical novel about Manzano, but the words never came. Eventually, she changed directions, writing a biography of Manzano through the use of lyrical poetry. A *Kirkus Reviews* contributor called *The Poet Slave of Cuba,* which won the Américas Award and the Pura Belpré Award, a "powerful and accessible biography." Engle "achieves an impressive synergy between poetry and biography," wrote a critic for *Publishers Weekly.* Commenting on Engle's depiction of Manzano telling himself stories while being beaten by his owners, Hazel Rochman wrote in *Booklist* that "today's readers will hear the stories . . . and never forget them," while in *School Library Journal* Carol Jones Collins concluded that *The Poet Slave of Cuba* "should be read by young and old, black and white, Anglo and Latino."

Like *The Poet Slave of Cuba, The Surrender Tree* is a story told in verse that focuses on the life of a Cuban slave. Rosa la Bayamesa was born into slavery, but after she was freed by her owner she became a rebel, fighting for Cuban independence from Spanish rule. She worked as a nurse, healing the wounded on both sides of the conflict. "*The Surrender Tree* is hauntingly beautiful, revealing pieces of Cuba's troubled past through the poetry of hidden moments," wrote Jill Heritage Maza in *School Library Journal,* commenting on the small details in Engle's poetry that illuminate the larger story. Jane Lopez-Santillana, writing in *Horn Book,* called Engle's poetry "haunting," and a *Kirkus Reviews* contributor concluded that "young readers will come away inspired by these portraits of courageous ordinary people."

Speaking with Alex Alvarez of *Guanabee,* Engle described *The Surrender Tree* as "a biographical novel in verse about the life of Rosa la Bayamesa, one of many Cuban women who became self-taught wilderness nurses." Engle added: "On another level, it is a universal story of ordinary people caught up in terrible circumstances, forced to make terrifying decisions. Rosa's decision was truly inspiring. Instead of seeking safety and comfort for herself, she chose to heal the wounds of colonial Spanish soldiers as well as Cuban rebels. Imagine deciding to heal your enemies! This is the image that I hope readers will remember. Imagine choosing kindness, even when history is cruel."

*The Surrender Tree* won numerous awards for Engle, including a Newbery Honor Book citation. In an interview with Debra Lau Whelan for *School Library Journal,* Engle commented on her reactions to receiving this prestigious prize: "I simply did not think of the Newbery Honor as within reach. When the committee called me, I was already in shock from learning that I had won the Pura Belpré Award two years

in a row. I am profoundly grateful, ridiculously excited, childishly thrilled, and also deeply humbled by thoughts of all the fantastic Latino authors who preceded me, before the time was ripe for recognition."

## Further Verse Dramas

With her 2009 title, *Tropical Secrets,* Engle alternates first-person narrative poems to tell the story of a holocaust refugee in World War II-era Cuba. Daniel is thirteen when he arrives in Cuba alone, for his parents were unable to secure passage aboard his ship. There he is helped by an elderly Jewish refugee and a young Cuban girl named Paloma. Engle remarked to Bardales that she was drawn to the subject "after reading about Cuban teenagers who volunteered to teach Spanish to the refugees. It seemed like such a simple way to help people who must have felt abandoned by the entire world. The German ships they were on had already been turned away from New York and Toronto. Havana Harbor was their last hope. Any refugees who were not accepted by Cuba would have been sent back to Germany."

Reviewing *Tropical Secrets* in *School Library Journal,* Geri Diorio remarked, "Engle's prose poems in this novel in verse are spare yet complete." A reviewer for *Tablet Magazine* also had praise for the work, calling *Tropical Secrets* "vibrant, exciting and moving." A *Kirkus Reviews* contributor was less impressed, though, observing that the "manipulation of characters and their fictional conflicts seem . . . formulaic." On the other hand, *Booklist* reviewer Rochman found the same work to be a "gripping story about refugees," while a *Publishers Weekly* contributor noted, "Engle gracefully packs a lot of information into a spare and elegant narrative."

In her 2010 book, *The Firefly Letters,* Engle looks at a different time period in Cuba, the mid-nineteenth century, through the eyes of three female narrators. One is Cecelia, a slave captured in Africa when she was eight, who is now a translator. Another is the historical Swedish suffragist Fredrika Bremer, who spent several months in Cuba in 1851, and who is helped by the services of Cecilia. A third perspective comes in the form of Elena, a privileged Cuban girl. "Using elegant free verse and alternating among each character's point of view, Engle offers powerful glimpses into Cuban life" during this era, Leah J. Sparks observed in *School Library Journal.* *Booklist* reviewer Rochman lauded the work as a "stirring, immediate story," told via a "moving combination of historical viewpoints." Further praise came from a *Kirkus Reviews* contributor who described Engle's writing in *The Firefly Letters* as a "gossamer thread of subtle beauty weaving together three memorable characters who together find hope and courage."

In 2010 Engle also released *Summer Birds: The Butterflies of Maria Merian,* a picture-book biography for young readers that recalls the author's love of nature. Unlike her previous titles, *Summer Birds* is set in seventeenth-century Germany and explores the life of Maria Sibylla Merian, a scientist and artist who, as a teenager, secretly studied the life cycle of the butterfly, a creature that was believed to possess supernatural powers. In the words of *Booklist* critic Gillian Engberg, the work "will spark children's own fascination with the natural world and its everyday dramas."

---

If you enjoy the works of Margarita Engle, you may also want to check out the following books:

Oscar Hijuelos, *The Mambo Kings Play Songs of Love,* 1989.
Ruth Behar, *Bridges to Cuba,* 1995.
Ron Koertge, *Margaux with an X,* 2004.

---

"Using free verse to tell a story feels like an ancient process, something that might have been done in the time of the *Iliad* and the *Odyssey,*" Engle remarked on the *Macmillan* Web site. "It feels ancestral in some universal, timeless way. When it works, it is a euphoric experience." The author further expounded on her choice of target audience and writing style in her *Publishers Weekly* interview with Bardales: "I want to write for young people, not just children but teenagers, because they are the future. I know how many distractions they have in their lives, and it's a privilege when they actually listen to a poem and ask amazingly intelligent questions, and they think about things and are aware of the world and surroundings. That spirit of wonder is so important in youth; anything we can do to slow down enough in our adulthoods to recapture that magical spirit of wonder is very valuable. For me poetry does that."

## ■ Biographical and Critical Sources

*PERIODICALS*

*Booklist,* February 15, 2006, Hazel Rochman, review of *The Poet Slave of Cuba: A Biography of Juan Francisco Manzano,* p. 95; March 15, 2008, Hazel Rochman, review of *The Surrender Tree: Poems of Cuba's Struggle for Freedom,* p. 53; January 1, 2009, Hazel Rochman, review of *Tropical Secrets: Holocaust Refugees in Cuba,* p. 74; December 15, 2009, Hazel Rochman, review of *The Firefly Letters: A Suffragette's Journey to Cuba,* p. 32; January 1, 2010, Jeannine Atkins, "Talking with Margarita Engle: The Newbery Honor-winning Author Talks about the Inspirations behind Her Novels in Verse," p. S38; March 15, 2010, Gillian Engberg, review of *Summer Birds: The Butterflies of Maria Meriana,* p. 43.

*Fresno Bee* (Fresno, CA), February 18, 2008, Felicia Cousart Matlosz, "Paying Homage to a Poet."

*Horn Book,* July-August, 2006, Lelac Almagor, review of *The Poet Slave of Cuba,* p. 459; July-August, 2008, Jane Lopez-Santillana, review of *The Surrender Tree,* p. 465; March-April, 2010, Sarah Ellis, review of *The Firefly Letters,* p. 54.

*Kirkus Reviews,* March 15, 2006, review of *The Poet Slave of Cuba,* p. 289; March 15, 2008, review of *The Surrender Tree;* February 1, 2009, review of *Tropical Secrets;* January 1, 2010, review of *The Firefly Letters.*

*MELUS,* spring, 1998, Gisele M. Requeña, "The Sounds of Silence: Remembering and Creating in Margarita Engle's *Singing to Cuba,*" p. 147.

*Publishers Weekly,* August 2, 1993, review of *Singing to Cuba,* p. 75; June 5, 1995, review of *Skywriting: A Novel of Cuba,* p. 52; April 17, 2006, review of *The Poet Slave of Cuba,* p. 190; April 6, 2009, review of *Tropical Secrets,* p. 48; March 15, 2010, review of *The Firefly Letters,* p. 55.

*School Library Journal,* April, 2006, Carol Jones Collins, review of *The Poet Slave of Cuba,* p. 154; June, 2008, Jill Heritage Maza, review of *The Surrender Tree,* p. 158; June, 2009, Geri Diorio, review of *Tropical Secrets,* p. 122; February, 2010, Leah J. Sparks, review of *The Firefly Letters,* p. 129.

*ONLINE*

*Guanabee,* http://guanabee.com/ (February 23, 2009), Alex Alvarez, "*Guanabee* Interviews Margarita Engle, Newbery Honor-Winning Author of *The Surrender Tree.*"

*Macmillan Web site,* http://us.macmillan.com/ (January 16, 2010), "Margarita Engle: Q & A."

*Publishers Weekly Online,* http://www.publishersweekly.com/ (April 16, 2009), Aida Bardales, "Q & A with Margarita Engle."

*School Library Journal Online,* http://www.schoollibraryjournal.com/ (March 4, 2009), Debra Lau Whelan, "Margarita Engle's Historic Newbery Honor."

*Tablet Magazine,* http://www.tabletmag.com/ (January 16, 2010), review of *Tropical Secrets.**

# Natasha Friend

## ■ Personal

Born April 28, 1972, in Norwich, NY; daughter of a college professor and a poet and actress; married, husband's name Erik; children: Jack, Ben, Emma. *Education:* Bates College, B.A., 1994; Clemson University, M.A., 1997.

## ■ Addresses

*Home*—Madison, CT.

## ■ Career

Writer and educator. Has taught at The Brearley School, New York, NY, and École Bilingue, Cambridge, MA. Brimmer and May Summer Camp, Chestnut Hill, MA, former director.

## ■ Awards, Honors

Milkweed Prize for Children's Literature, and Golden Sower Award, both for *Perfect;* Quick Pick for Reluctant Readers citation, American Library Association, for *Lush;* Best Books for the Teen Age list, New York Public Library, 2008, for *Bounce.*

## ■ Writings

*Perfect,* Milkweed Editions (Minneapolis, MN), 2004.
*Lush,* Milkweed Editions (Minneapolis, MN), 2006.
*Bounce,* Scholastic (New York, NY), 2007.
*For Keeps,* Viking Juvenile (New York, NY), 2010.

Contributor to periodicals, including *Family Fun,* and to anthologies, including *Chicken Soup for the Volunteer's Soul.*

## ■ Adaptations

*Perfect* was adapted as an audio book, Recorded Books, 2005.

## ■ Sidelights

Natasha Friend has written a series of young adult novels noted for their insight into teen emotions and their attention to dialogue, while at the same time examining difficult social and family issues, from bulimia to alcoholism to the death of a parent. "My fascination with human psychology . . . informs everything I write," the author told John Valeri in the *Hartford Books Examiner.* "I love how people think, and interact, and obsess, and grieve, and cope, and reinvent themselves, and grapple

Friend's debut novel, *Perfect*, received the Milkweed Prize for Children's Literature. (Milkweed Editions, 2004. Reproduced by permission.)

with problems in a whole variety of ways. All of my characters are flawed. Not every one of them is likable. But that's what makes them real."

Friend was born in 1972 in Norwich, New York, an upstate college town. Her father was an English professor and her mother a poet and actress. Growing up without a television in the house, Friend became a great reader and frequent visitor of the local library. "I wasn't just a reader; I was an inhaler of books," Friend remarked on her home page. One of her favorite authors as a young reader was Judy Blume, and after reading Blume's *Are You There, God? It's Me, Margaret,* she vowed to become a writer herself. For her tenth birthday her parents presented her with a manual typewriter, and Friend was on her way, writing numerous short stories. Then came junior high school. The author insists that the inspiration for her books comes from the

emotional turmoil she experienced during those years. "Nobody—and I mean nobody—comes out unscathed," Friend further remarked on her home page. "I don't care how beautiful you are, or how cool your clothes are, or how many friends you have; being 13 is a harrowing experience."

Friend eventually went on to college, earning a bachelor's degree from Bates College and a master's degree from Clemson University. She then began teaching at private schools in New York City and Boston, promising herself that at the end of five years—if she did not love her work—she would write a novel. After marrying her husband, Erik, Friend quit her teaching job and began work on her first book. Three months after the birth of her first son, Friend learned that *Perfect,* her debut novel, would be published by Milkweed Editions; the book was released in 2004.

## Problem Novels for Teen Readers

*Perfect* focuses on thirteen-year-old Isabelle Lee and the young woman's battle with bulimia. "As a former competitive gymnast I was introduced to the concept of dieting and weight control at an early age," Friend explained in a *Teenreads.com* interview, adding, "I went on my first diet at the age of eleven." Isabelle's bulimia is caused less by athletics than by grief: her father died several years earlier, and she is unable to cope except by bingeing on food and then throwing up. When Isabelle is sent to group therapy, she is surprised to meet Ashley Barnum, a gregarious and popular classmate who is also bulimic. The two girls begin spending time together, their friendship revolving around their eating disorders, until Isabelle realizes that Ashley isn't as "perfect" as she appears. "Friend knows middle school kids and delivers beautifully," wrote Mary R. Hofmann in a *School Library Journal* review of *Perfect.*

Other critics also offered praise for the novel. The "graphic binging and purging scenes" in *Perfect* "help explain the disease to readers without seeming didactic," wrote a *Publishers Weekly* reviewer. "Friend combines believable characters and real-life situations into a fine novel," Denise Moore concluded in *School Library Journal,* and a *Kirkus Reviews* contributor deemed the book "clearly and simply written with a nice balance of humor and drama." Noting the prevalence of eating disorders among teens, Claire Rosser wrote in *Kliatt* that *Perfect* "addresses the fact that eating disorders are plaguing ever-younger adolescent girls." Through her careful attention to Isabelle's voice, "Friend elevates what could have been just another problem novel to a truly worthwhile read," Debbie Carton concluded in *Booklist.*

## Coping with Difficult Circumstances

In Friend's second young adult novel, *Lush*, Samantha and her family are hiding her father's alcoholism from the world. The teen is tired of pretending, however, and she is angry and frustrated at her father's inability to change. She releases some of her burden in an anonymous letter she leaves in a library book, and she soon begins corresponding with an unknown library pen pal. While the content of the novel is heavy, "the author avoids a maudlin tone by infusing the plot with details of typical teen life," wrote Rebecca M. Jones in *School Library Journal*. "Sam comes across as a savvy as well as naive teen who tells her own story with humor, honesty and hope," a *Kirkus Reviews* writer noted, while Carton, again writing for *Booklist*, called *Lush* "a believable, sensitive, character-driven story, with realistic dialogue."

In *Bounce*, a lonely teen reluctantly welcomes six new stepsiblings into her life after her father remarries. (Scholastic, 2007. Reprinted by permission of Scholastic Inc.)

A sensitive teenager struggles to deal with her father's alcoholism in *Lush*. (Scholastic, 2007. Reprinted by permission of Scholastic Inc.)

*Bounce* centers on Evyn Linney, a lonely thirteen year old who lives with her widowed father and younger brother in Maine. When her father announces that he is marrying a woman with six children and moving the family to Boston, Evyn feels overwhelmed, and through a series of imaginary conversations, she begins seeking advice from her dead mother. As Evyn comes to know her stepsiblings and adjusts to her new private school, she grows accustomed to the changes in her life. "Friend offers no fairy-tale ending but presents, through hip conversations and humor, believable characters and a feel-good story," D. Maria LaRocco noted in her review for *School Library Journal*. Rosser noted in *Kliatt* that Friend gives readers "a chance to spend time with smart, caring, funny people" as she tells Evyn's story. "The realistic and genuinely humorous details of the newly formed Linney-Gartos family set this text apart," explained a *Kirkus Reviews* contributor. In *Publishers Weekly* a reviewer commended Friend for her "unmistakable gift for exploring family dynamics." Similarly, *Booklist* contributor Cindy Dobrez felt that Friend delivers a "satisfying blend of humor and empathy" in this tale, and that she endows the teen protagonist with "an authentic teen voice and emotions."

### Inspired by Life

In Friend's fourth young adult novel, *For Keeps*, the author tells the story of Josie, a junior in high school who has grown up with her single mom. Josie's mother, Kate, became pregnant at about Josie's age, and, soon thereafter, the father left the small Massachusetts town where Josie and Kate still live. For all these years, mom and daughter have been a close pair, but when Josie's biological father, Paul, comes back to town, her world is turned upside down. Her mother is emotionally distraught, reliving her teen sorrow. Meanwhile, Josie is having new experiences in her own life, entering a relationship with her first boyfriend, and fearing that her best friend, Liv, might be pregnant. Finally, Josie learns secrets about her father that make her re-evaluate all of the beliefs she has held about her parents. Reviewing this novel in *Booklist*, Hazel Rochman felt *For Keeps* was much more than merely a teen-issues novel. "There is a real plot," noted Rochman, "filled with fast, immediate dialogue and secrets."

---

If you enjoy the works of Natasha Friend, you may also want to check out the following books:

Jaye Murray, *Bottled Up*, 2003.
Sarah Dessen, *Just Listen*, 2006.
Kirsten Smith, *The Geography of Girlhood*, 2007.

---

Friend notes that the inspiration for her books come from a variety of sources. As she remarked on her home page, "Many ideas come straight from inner 13-year old girl. Some come from the lives of my friends, or from articles and books I've read. Often I begin with a seed—just the beginning of an idea, or a first sentence—and from there a plot begins to develop." Asked if she had any suggestions for aspiring young writers, Friend remarked to the contributor for *Teenreads.com*, "Read. It's bar none the best possible advice I could give."

## ■ Biographical and Critical Sources

*PERIODICALS*

*Booklist*, January 1, 2005, Debbie Carton, review of *Perfect*, p. 844; November 1, 2006, Debbie Carton, review of *Lush*, p. 41; November 1, 2007, Cindy Dobrez, review of *Bounce*, p. 36; January 1, 2010, Hazel Rochman, review of *For Keeps*, p. 60.

*Kirkus Reviews*, October 15, 2004, review of *Perfect*, p. 1006; October 15, 2006, review of *Lush*, p. 1071; August 1, 2007, review of *Bounce*.

*Kliatt*, November, 2004, Claire Rosser, review of *Perfect*, p. 8; September, 2007, Claire Rosser, review of *Bounce*, p. 12.

*Publishers Weekly*, November 8, 2004, review of *Perfect*, p. 57; July 30, 2007, review of *Lush*, p. 87; September 17, 2007, review of *Bounce*, p. 56.

*School Library Journal*, December, 2004, Denise Moore, review of *Perfect*, p. 146; November, 2005, Mary R. Hofmann, review of *Perfect*, p. 57; December, 2006, Rebecca M. Jones, review of *Lush*, p. 138; September, 2007, D. Maria LaRocco, review of *Bounce*, p. 196.

*ONLINE*

*Hartford Books Examiner*, http://www.examiner.com/ (April 6, 2010), John Valeri, "Madison Author Natasha Friend Plays For Keeps (A Q&A)."

*Natasha Friend Home Page*, http://www.natashafriend.com (January 23, 2010).

*Scholastic Web site*, http://www.scholastic.com/ (April 1, 2010), "Natasha Friend."

*Teenreads.com*, http://www.teenreads.com/ (March, 2005), "Author Talk: Natasha Friend."*

# Ricky Gervais

(Photograph courtesy of AP Images.)

## ■ Personal

Born June 25, 1961, in Reading, England; son of Jerry (a laborer) and Eva (a homemaker) Gervais; companion of Jane Fallon (a television producer and novelist). *Education:* University College London, B.A.

## ■ Addresses

*Home*—England. *Agent*—WME Entertainment, 1 William Morris Pl., Beverly Hills, CA 90212; United Agents, 12-26 Lexington St., London W1F 0LE, England; (commercials) Nicola Richardson, Qvoice, 193-197 High Holborn, 4th Floor, London WC1V 7BD, England.

## ■ Career

Actor, writer, broadcaster, and producer. Actor and program host in television, including *The 11 O'Clock Show*, 1998, *Meet Ricky Gervais*, 2000, *The Office* (original BBC version), 2001-03, *Legend of the Lost Tribe*, 2002, and *Extras*, 2005-07; actor in films, including *Dog Eat Dog*, 2001, *Valiant* (voice work), 2005, *For Your Consideration*, 2006, *Night at the Museum*, 2006, *Stardust*, 2007, *Ghost Town*, 2008, *Night at the Museum: Battle of the Smithsonian*, 2009, *The Invention of Lying*, 2009, and *Cemetery Junction*, 2010.

Director of television programs, including *Meet Ricky Gervais*, 2000, *The Office*, 2001-03, and *Extras*, 2005-07; director of films, including *The Invention of Lying*, 2009, and *Cemetery Junction*, 2010. Producer of television programs and specials, including *The Office* (U.S. version), 2005—, *Ricky Gervais Meets. . .*, 2006, *Extras*, 2006-07; producer of films, including *The Invention of Lying*, 2009, and *Cemetery Junction*, 2010. Has also worked variously as a pizza delivery boy, a band manager, and a disc jockey for XFM Radio, London, England.

## ■ Awards, Honors

British Comedy Award for best comedy actor, 2002, British Academy of Film and Television Arts (BAFTA) Television Award for best comedy performance and situation comedy award, 2002, 2003, and 2004, Broadcasting Press Guild Writer's Award, 2002 and 2003, Royal Television Society Award for best comedy performance, 2003, Silver Rose (sitcom), Festival Rose d'Or (Golden Rose Festival), Montreux, Switzerland, 2003, Television Critics Award for individual achievement in comedy, 2004, and Golden Globe Awards for best comedy series and best performance by an actor in a comedy, 2004, all for *The Office* (British version); corecipient, Rave award for podcast, *Wired* magazine, 2006; Emmy Award for outstanding comedy series, 2006, for *The Office* (U.S. version); Emmy Award for outstanding lead actor in a comedy series, 2007, BAFTA Award for best comedy performance, 2007, Golden Globe for best television series—musical or comedy, 2008, and British Comedy Award for best television comedy actor, 2008, all for *Extras*; Satellite Award for best actor in a motion picture comedy or musical, International Press Academy, 2008, for *Ghost Town*.

## ■ Writings

*FILMS*

(With Matthew Robinson, and codirector) *The Invention of Lying*, Warner Brothers/Universal, 2009.
(With Stephen Merchant, and codirector) *Cemetery Junction*, Sony Pictures, 2010.

*TELEVISION SERIES; WITH OTHERS*

*The 11 O'Clock Show*, TalkBack Productions, 1998.
*Bruiser*, British Broadcasting Corporation, 2000.
*Meet Ricky Gervais*, TalkBack Productions, 2000.
*The Sketch Show*, Avalon Television, 2001.
(With Stephen Merchant) *The Office*, British Broadcasting Corporation, 2001–2003.
*Stromberg*, Brainpool, 2004.
(With Stephen Merchant) *Extras*, Home Box Office, 2005–2007.
*Kelsey Grammer Presents: The Sketch Show*, Grammnet Productions, 2005.
*Ricky Gervais Meets . . .*, Objective Productions, 2006.
*The Ricky Gervais Show*, Home Box Office, 2010.

*TELEVISION SPECIALS AND EPISODES*

"Golden Years," *Comedy Lab*, Room 5, 1999.
*Ricky Gervais Live: Animals*, Channel 4 Television Corporation, 2003.
*Ricky Gervais Live 2: Politics*, Universal Studios, 2004.
"Homer Simpson: This Is Your Wife," *The Simpsons*, Twentieth Century Fox Television, 2006.
*Ricky Gervais Live 3: Fame*, Universal Video, 2007.
*Ricky Gervais: Out of England: The Stand-Up Special*, Moffitt-Lee Productions, 2008.

*CHILDREN'S BOOKS*

*Flanimals*, illustrated by Rob Steen, Faber & Faber (London, England), 2004, Putnam (New York, NY), 2005.
*More Flanimals*, illustrated by Rob Steen, Putnam (New York, NY), 2006.
*Flanimals Pop-up*, illustrated by Rob Steen, Candlewick Press (Somerville, MA), 2010.

## ■ Adaptations

Various adaptations of *The Office* have been made in countries worldwide, including Canada, Chile, France, Germany, and Israel. *Flanimals* has been optioned for film.

## ■ Sidelights

Writer and actor Ricky Gervais is a highly regarded British comedian who has achieved success on both sides of the Atlantic, and he did it after the age of forty. His "mockumentary" television series *The Office* became a cult hit in Britain before airing on the cable channel BBC America in the United States. There it became the first foreign-produced show to win a Golden Globe Award for best comedy series, and Gervais received a Golden Globe for best actor in a comedy series. The writer-actor also earned an Emmy Award for his performance on the television series *Extras*, and he has become a star of the big screen as well, appearing in such films as *The Invention of Lying*. As Alessandra Stanley remarked in the *New York Times*, Gervais is "a brilliant creator of comedy who keeps moving from theater to television and movies without overstaying his welcome in any one field."

Gervais grew up in Reading, England, some forty miles west of London. The son of a British mother and a French-Canadian father who served in England during World War Two, Gervais showed few signs early on that he was destined for great success, or even that he would become a performer. "The first thing I wanted to be was a marine biologist," Gervais told Scott Brown in *Entertainment Weekly*. "Then I wanted to be a vet." Still, as the youngest of four boys by several years, he had to learn to hold his own during family conversations. We "took the piss out of each other. You had to be able to answer back," he told Johnny Davis in the London *Independent*. He credits his mother with inspiring his sense of humor. "My mum used to say things like, 'You're about as much use as a one-legged man in an arse-kicking contest,'" Gervais told a *People Weekly* interviewer.

### Office Work

After graduating from University College London with a degree in philosophy, Gervais tried his hand at a number of jobs. These included work as a pizza delivery boy, an entertainment manager (coordinating both events and bands), and even a very short stint as a singer in a new wave pop duo. He eventually ended up working as a disc jockey for London radio station XFM. He hired comic and DJ Stephen Merchant as an assistant, and the two hosted a Saturday afternoon show in 1998 until station ownership changed hands and they were fired. Ger-

**Gervais holds a pair of British Comedy Awards for his work on the wildly popular sitcom *The Office*, which he co-created.** (Photograph courtesy of Rune Hellestad/Corbis.)

vais then tried stand-up comedy while trying to break into sketch shows. When both that and a talk show failed, he almost gave up on show business. Instead, however, he and Merchant decided to try their hands at writing a television script together, the result of which was the pilot for *The Office*.

While Gervais had toyed with sketch writing before this, he had never attempted anything as expansive as a television series script, but the effort paid off. The script was bought by the British Broadcasting Corporation (BBC) and developed into a television series in which Gervais also starred. Shot in a faux documentary style, the series revolved around a group of employees at a local paper merchant in Slough, England, with Gervais playing the role of the manager, David Brent. Brent suffers under the delusion that he is a wonderful fellow who is beloved at the company, and he sees himself as something of a philosopher who has a strong grasp on society's mores and behavior. In reality, Brent is a boor and an idiot who is in the midst of a mid-life crisis that he has failed to notice. The employees whom he manages must tolerate his numerous and often unbearable attempts to befriend them while also attempting to keep their jobs on track. "On a less carefully written show, the conceit would almost certainly pall after a few episodes," *New York Times* critic Stanley remarked. "*The Office* is instead addictive, less because viewers grow to love David and his batty employees than because the show refuses to let those characters grow too lovable."

The British version ran for two six-episode seasons with the addition of a couple of Christmas specials before Gervais and Merchant decided to conclude the show. Their intent was to go out while the series was successful and before they burned out creatively. "We're like a cottage industry, myself and my co-writer," Gervais told Robert Mackey in the *New York Times*. "We do everything from conceive it to worry about the font on the credits." In the meantime, the award-winning show began airing in the United States on cable channel BBC America. *The Office* became a cult hit, and Gervais was surprised when it received a Golden Globe Award nomination for best comedy series, along with a second nomination for Gervais for best actor. He publicly stated he expected to lose; instead, the show became the first non-American production to win the award, and Gervais the first winning actor from a non-American show.

*The Office* was not only a major hit in Great Britain, it inspired several versions rewritten to appeal to audiences in different countries. Gervais served as an executive producer for the American version, with comic actor Steve Carell playing Gervais's role

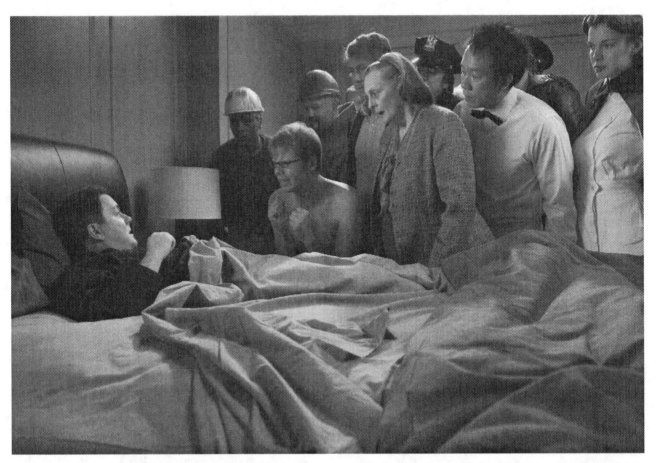

**Gervais portrays a dentist who can talk to spirits after a near-death experience in the 2008 comedy** *Ghost Town.*
(Photograph courtesy of Paramount/The Kobal Collection/The Picture Desk, Inc.)

as the manager of a paper company branch. While Gervais's original only ran for a dozen episodes over two seasons, the American version of the program was still going after six seasons and more than 100 episodes. Gervais believed the show's appeal lay in its universal themes: "What's nice about the comedy of embarrassment—and the fact that *The Office* is a fake documentary—is that we all make a fool of ourselves, but it's usually either in front of no one or one person," he told Mackey. As a producer of the American version, Gervais shared the Emmy Award for best comedy series the show won in 2006.

In the aftermath of *The Office*'s popularity, Gervais discovered that success was much easier to come by. He and Merchant were rehired by XFM for a Saturday morning show, and he had several successful stand-up comedy gigs—his first show in the U.S., a 2007 festival appearance at Madison Square Garden, sold out within hours. He began doing voice-over work and landed a number of smaller acting roles, including one in the popular film *Night at the Museum* and another in *For Your Consideration*,

an improvisational comedy by Christopher Guest, the same writer-director who helped create Gervais's favorite film, *This Is Spinal Tap*. Gervais also wrote a script and voiced a character for an episode of the long-running animated series *The Simpsons*. He turned down many more offers than he accepted, however. "The best way to keep a good batting average is not to bat very often," he told *Entertainment Weekly*'s Gilbert Cruz. "I could have been in 19 films playing the butler. . . . Now I'm getting offered excellent films, but what's the point? There's got to be a reason to do it. And it's never profile, never money, never fame."

### Lovable Losers

Gervais and Merchant's second television series, *Extras*, debuted in 2005 and gave viewers an insider's look at the film and television industry from the point of view of those performers who are hired to play nonspeaking parts. Gervais starred as Andy Millman, an aspiring actor who can't manage to find anything but work as an extra, partly because of his incompetent agent (played by Merchant). In the first season, Andy and his friend and fellow extra Maggie (played by Ashley Jensen) stand in the background of various film sets and observe the lead actors (played by a succession of real Hollywood stars) indulge in all sorts of bad behavior. Gervais told Devin Gordon of *Newsweek* that the show has all his favorite themes: "Ego, desperation, men behaving like boys. Same blood, different veins." Gervais added that Andy is a more self-aware character than David Brent, however: "He thinks the world is full of idiots, but he's burdened with a conscience. He really should fire his agent, but he can't bear to see the look on his stupid little face."

*Extras* aired on BBC2 in England and on Home Box Office (HBO) in the U.S., which ensured Gervais more creative freedom. Although Gervais announced the program on his Web site as "the show critics are already calling the disappointing follow-up to *The Office*," reaction to the show was generally positive. Gordon, in his review for *News-*

*week,* commented: "*The Office* is better than *Extras*—but only just." In the series' second season, Andy gains a measure of success: the BBC buys his idea for a TV series but won't produce it unless he dumbs it down to the lowest common denominator. Andy gains success and celebrity for a catchphrase he loathes saying, as it reminds him of his lost integrity. As a result, "*Extras*; is a compact, searingly original take on disappointment, fame and friendship," Tim Goodman observed in the *San Francisco Chronicle*. "It deserves to be sought out and sampled by American audiences who don't mind a fair dose of cringe-inducing humor and a fearless look at the darker sides of dreams come almost true." Gervais earned an Emmy Award for best actor in a comedy for the second season; as *USA Today* contributor Robert Bianco observed of his performance in the finale, "Gervais can spin a joke into something truly heartbreaking, and then just as quickly reel it back." After a second six-episode series and a final special, Gervais and Merchant ended the show. *Slant* contributor Brian Holcomb thought the characters deserved more

**Gervais made his big-screen directorial debut with the 2009 film** *The Invention of Lying.* (Photograph courtesy of Radar Pictures/The Kobal Collection/The Picture Desk, Inc.)

**In 2009 the talented British comedian premiered his live stand-up show** *Science* **at the Edinburgh Playhouse in Scotland.** (Photograph courtesy of David Cheskin/AP Images.)

episodes, concluding that "this is a true testament to the quality of the writing, which never sacrifices character for effect. So, for those who thought they were a one trick pony, *Extras* is proof positive that Gervais and Merchant have much more to contribute to our popular culture for some time to come."

### Tackling the Big Screen

After *Extras* Gervais returned to acting work, including his first film role as a leading man. In the 2008 comedy *Ghost Town*, the comic plays Bertram Pincus, a misanthropic dentist who nearly dies during routine surgery and comes back able to perceive ghosts. In helping one persistent spirit prevent his widow from dating a cad, Pincus achieves a measure of redemption. Although the plot is standard romantic comedy, "Gervais succeeds in elevating the material and also inducing his talented co-stars to up their comedy game," Michael Rechtshaffen wrote in the *Hollywood Reporter*. "The big screen is

all the richer for his presence." Although the film and especially Gervais generally got good notices— *USA Today*'s Claudia Puig noted "he proves himself an offbeat but undeniably charming leading man"— the film was a box office disappointment.

Throughout the late 2000s Gervais also had several stand-up comedy performances broadcast on HBO, many of them courting controversy by being politically incorrect. In the 2008 special *Ricky Gervais: Out of England*, for instance, most of his jokes "are scatological, smutty or politically incorrect, almost as if Mr. Gervais were testing squeamish American audiences to see just how far they will let him go," *New York Times* critic Stanley observed. "The jokes may seem cruel, but they're really ridiculing our fondness for cruelty and the sanctimonious pretense that we're above such things," Bianco of *USA Today* noted, concluding that "Ricky Gervais may be the funniest storyteller we have."

In 2009 Gervais returned to the big screen with *The Invention of Lying*, a film that he not only wrote but directed, along with Matthew Robinson. The film is set in a world where no one knows how to lie, until Mark Bellison (Gervais) accidentally makes up an untruth and discovers he can get away with it. It brings him success as a screenwriter (he invents fiction) and a prophet (he invents Heaven), and it may also bring him success with the woman he loves, if his conscience will allow it. The film received mixed reviews, mainly for turning a promising concept into a traditional romantic comedy. The *Hollywood Reporter*'s Rechtshaffen noted that the film's first half hour "is so sharply fresh, clever and laugh-out-loud hilarious that you can't help but wonder how they'll sustain it for another hour. To be honest, they can't. But even when it's merely mildly amusing, [the film] . . . is so wittily winsome you'll readily cut Gervais and Robinson some slack if they don't quite succeed in going the distance." "By adhering to the romantic-comedy formula, *The Invention of Lying* stops short of being truly inventive," Puig of *USA Today* likewise remarked. "But enough sequences are fresh and inspired to make this a comedy honestly worth catching."

### A Wealth of Projects

In 2010, Gervais and Merchant debuted a third television collaboration, *The Ricky Gervais Show*. The show was actually an animated version of the podcasts the duo had made with Karl Pilkington, a producer they met while working at XFM Radio. Pilkington's deadpan reactions and curious opinions made him the perfect foil for Gervais and Merchant to talk about various subjects. "Everything he says is honest and funny," Gervais told Dave Itzkoff in the *New York Times*. "I don't mean everything he says is true, but everything he says he thinks is true." When the show debuted on the Web in late 2005, the podcast officially set a Guinness World Record as most downloaded ever, with over one million downloads the first month. In the animated series, Gervais "serves as a bullying sidekick to Mr. Pilkington and steps out of the way, letting his strange and funny collaborator take the lead," *New York Times* critic Stanley observed. The critic added that much like early television programs that were merely recordings of radio shows, "the series is not a full-blown comedy show; it's a collection of Web-styled sketches and proof that big laughs can come in small doses."

Although he has numerous awards to his name, Gervais still finds it difficult to believe his accomplishments. "It's a shock to a Brit to be successful—that's where I'm coming from psychologically," he told Randee Dawn in the *Hollywood Reporter*. "Americans are told they can become the next president. British people are told, 'It won't happen to you.' So, I'm afraid my life is a constant

If you enjoy the works of Ricky Gervais, you may also want to check out the following:

*This Is Spinal Tap*, a film directed by Rob Reiner, 1984.
*The Larry Sanders Show*, a television series starring Garry Shandling, 1992-98.
*Best in Show*, a film directed by Christopher Guest, 2000.

shock." He has attributed his success to creating characters with whom people can identify. "Comedy is about misdirection and surprise, but mainly it's about empathy," he told Logan Hill in *New York*. "I have been blessed with being able to play the putz because we basically root for the underdog." Although his career is built on telling jokes, he continued, "I do take it seriously. Making people laugh is easy for me. I'm quite proud of that. But I'm prouder of silencing an audience for a minute because they're thinking about something. I use comedy as a Trojan horse, to deliver other things. And I try and make stories that take characters on an emotional journey. All of my favorite comedies have done that."

## ■ Biographical and Critical Sources

*PERIODICALS*

*Commonweal*, April 22, 2005, Celia Wren, "Not Bleak Enough: *The Office* Emigrates to U.S. TV," p. 22.
*Entertainment Weekly*, February 11, 2005, Scott Brown, "'Flanimal' Magnetism," p. 68; March 18, 2005, "Office Mates," p. 28; September 23, 2005, Dalton Ross, "Ready for His Not-So-Close-Up," p. 75; February 16, 2007, Gilbert Cruz, "Ricky Gervais," p. 23.
*Hollywood Reporter*, May 8, 2007, Randee Dawn, "Office Boy," p. 22; September 9, 2008, Michael Rechtshaffen, review of *Ghost Town*, p. 12; September 14, 2009, Michael Rechtshaffen, review of *The Invention of Lying*, p. 11.
*Independent* (London, England), August 24, 2001, Steve Jelbert, "More Than the Office Comedian," p. 9; October 23, 2005, Johnny Davis, "Ricky Gervais: My Life as a Superstar."
*Los Angeles Magazine*, July 1, 2008, "A Stand-Up Bloke: Comedian Ricky Gervais Comes to the Kodak," p. 145.

*Newsweek,* December 29, 2003, Susannah Meadows, "Q&A: Ricky Gervais," p. 32; January 24, 2005, Susannah Meadows, "Fast Chat: Elvis in London," p. 12; August 22, 2005, Devin Gordon, "Giving Us a Little 'Extra,'" p. 68; December 11, 2006, Devin Gordon and Nicki Gostin, "Newsmakers: Ricky Gervais, Pam, Kid, Paris, Lindsay and a Haiku," p. 109.

*New York,* December 10, 2007, Adam Sternbergh, "Having a Laff Yet?," p. 81; November 2, 2009, Logan Hill, "The Laugh Factory."

*New York Times,* October 8, 2003, Jesse McKinley, "Making Yanks Laugh? It's a Bit Dodgy, Mate," p. 1; October 10, 2003, Alessandra Stanley, "When the Boss Thinks He's Funny," p. E1; October 12, 2003, Robert Mackey, "Talking Comedy with the 'Office' Manager," p. AR26; December 14, 2007, Neil Genzlinger, "Extra Who Found Fame Has Now Found the Exit," p. 27; December 15, 2007, Edward Wyatt, "Going Out, Gervais Picks Bang over Whimper," p. 6; November 14, 2008, Alessandra Stanley, "He's out for Laughs, and No One Is Safe," p. C1; October 2, 2009, Manohla Dargis, "A World Where Truth Turns out Not to Be Beauty," p. C14; February 14, 2010, Dave Itzkoff, "Three Mates Laughing (Well, Two Are)," p. 18; February 19, 2010, Alessandra Stanley, "Taking the Podcast Back to a Simpler Time," p. C5.

*People Weekly,* May 3, 2004, *The Office*'s Ricky Gervais," p. 138; November 22, 2004, Ann Marie Cruz, "All-Purpose Awards," p. 146.

*Publishers Weekly,* January 31, 2005, review of *Flanimals,* p. 66, and Diane Roback, "Serving Up Some Flan," p. 67.

*San Francisco Chronicle,* January 12, 2007, Tim Goodman, "Pained Humiliation Returns on *Extras,*" p. E-4.

*School Library Journal,* October 1, 2006, Margaret Bush, review of *More Flanimals,* p. 110.

*Time,* April 12, 2004, "Q&A with Ricky Gervais," p. 83; October 25, 2004, James Poniewozik, *"The Office* Punches Out," p. 92; December 17, 2007, "10 Questions," p. 6.

*USA Today,* September 23, 2005, Robert Bianco, "The Good, the Not-bad and the Truly Ugly," p. 9E; December 14, 2007, Gary Levin, "Gervais Makes His Comic Mark on USA," p. 11; September 18, 2008, Donna Freydkin, "Gervais Believes in *Ghost,*" p. 8D; September 19, 2008, Claudia Puig, "Gervais Leads Spirited *Ghost,*" p. 1D; November 14, 2008, Robert Bianco, "Gervais' Jokes Are All in His Stage Persona," p. 15D; October 2, 2009, Claudia Puig, "Truth Is, *Lying* Has Big Laughs," p. 2D.

*ONLINE*

*A.V. Club,* http://www.avclub.com/ (April 21, 2004), Noel Murray, "Interview: Ricky Gervais"; (January 10, 2007), Scott Gordon, "Interview: Ricky Gervais."

*Ricky Gervais Home Page,* http://www.rickygervais. com (March 23, 2010).

*Slant Magazine,* http://www.slantmagazine.com/ (January 20, 2007), Brian Holcomb, review of *Extras: Season Two.**

# Beth Goobie

## ■ Personal

Born 1959, in Guelph, Ontario, Canada. *Education:* University of Winnipeg, B.A., 1983; attended University of Alberta, 1986-88.

## ■ Addresses

*Home*—Saskatoon, Saskatchewan, Canada.

## ■ Career

Writer.

## ■ Awards, Honors

*Edmonton Journal* literary competitions, first prize for a long poem, 1987, for "just after i knew," and first prize for short fiction, 1990, for "Answers"; winner of radio writing contest, Canadian Broadcasting Corporation and Alberta Foundation for the Arts, 1991, for the radio play "Continuum"; prose poem award, *Grain* magazine, 1994, for "Permission"; R. Ross Annet Award for best children's book in Alberta, Writers Guild of Alberta, 1995, for *Mis-* *sion Impossible;* Pat Lowther Memorial Award for best book of poetry by a Canadian woman, League of Canadian Poets, 1995, for *Scars of Light;* Our Choice citations, Canadian Children's Book Centre, 1995, for *Mission Impossible,* 1998, for *The Good, the Bad, and the Suicidal,* 1999, for *The Colours of Carol Molev,* 2000, for *The Dream Where the Losers Go,* 2001, for *Before Wings,* 2002, for *Sticks and Stones,* 2003, for *Kicked Out,* 2004, for *Who Owns Kelly Paddik?,* 2005, for *Flux,* and 2007 for *The Dream Where the Losers Go* and *Hello, Groin;* Joseph S. Stauffer Award for Literature, Canada Council, 1999; Saskatchewan Children's Literature Award, 2000, Young Adult Book Award, Canadian Library Association (CLA), 2001, Governor General's Literary Award, 2001, Michael L. Printz Award nominee, American Library Association (ALA), 2001, Saskatchewan Book Award, 2001, Mr. Christie's Book Award, 2001, and Best Books for Young Adults selection, ALA, 2002, all for *Before Wings;* Amelia Bloomer List, ALA, and Young Adult Book Award nominee, CLA, both 2003, both for *Sticks and Stones;* Quick Picks for Reluctant Readers selection, ALA, 2003, for *Sticks and Stones,* 2004, for *Kicked Out,* and 2006, for *Something Girl;* Saskatchewan Children's Literature Awards, 2004, for *Flux,* and 2005, for *Fixed;* Books for the Teen Age selection, New York Public Library, 2005, for *Flux;* White Ravens List, International Youth Library, Munich, Germany, 2007, and Young Adult Book Award nominee, CLA, 2007, both for *Hello, Groin;* 2007 Best Books for Young Adults selection, ALA, Books for the Teen Age selection, New York Public Library, both 2007, both for *The Dream Where the Losers Go;* Stellar Award, 2008, for *Something Girl.*

## ■ Writings

*Could I Have My Body Back Now, Please?* (poetry and short stories), NeWest (Edmonton, Alberta, Canada), 1991.

*Continuum* (radio play), Canadian Broadcasting Corporation, 1992.

*Dandelion Moon* (two-act play), produced in Edmonton, Alberta, Canada, at Catalyst Theatre, 1992.

*Scars of Light* (poetry), NeWest (Edmonton, Alberta, Canada), 1994.

*Black Angels* (screenplay), Cynthia Wells Productions (Edmonton, Alberta, Canada), 1996.

*Janine Fowler Did It* (one-act play), produced in Guelph, Ontario, Canada, at Guelph Collegiate Vocational Institute, 1997.

*The Only-Good Heart* (novel), Pedlar Press (Toronto, Ontario, Canada), 1998.

*The Face Is the Place* (one-act play; first produced in Guelph, Ontario, Canada, at Guelph Collegiate Vocational Institute, 1998), Blizzard Publishing (Winnipeg, Manitoba, Canada), 2000.

*The Girls Who Dream Me* (poetry), Pedlar Press (Toronto, Ontario, Canada), 1999.

Work represented in anthologies, including *Under NeWest Eyes*, Thistledown Press (Saskatoon, Saskatchewan, Canada), 1996; *Vintage 1997-1998*, League of Canadian Poets (Toronto, Ontario, Canada), 1998; *Ice: New Writing on Hockey*, Spotted Cow (Edmonton, Alberta, Canada), 1999; *A Long Life of Making: Poems from the Pat Lowther Memorial Award Winners*, Gynergy Books (Charlottetown, Prince Edward Island, Canada), 2000; and *2000% Cracked Wheat*, Coteau Books (Regina, Saskatchewan, Canada), 2000. Contributor of poetry, short stories, and articles to periodicals, including *Fireweed, Prairie Fire, Secrets from the Orange Couch, Canadian Woman Studies, Capilano Review, Descant, Fiddlehead, Malahat Review, Prism International,* and *Canadian Review.*

*YOUNG ADULT NOVELS*

*Group Homes from Outer Space*, Maxwell Macmillan Canada (Toronto, Ontario, Canada), 1992, published as *Something Girl*, Orca Book Publishers (Victoria, British Columbia, Canada), 2005.

*Who Owns Kelly Paddik?*, Maxwell Macmillan Canada (Toronto, Ontario, Canada), 1993, Orca Book Publishers (Victoria, British Columbia, Canada), 2003.

*Hit and Run*, Maxwell Macmillan Canada (Toronto, Ontario, Canada), 1994.

*Sticks and Stones*, Maxwell Macmillan Canada (Toronto, Ontario, Canada), 1994.

*Mission Impossible*, Red Deer College Press (Red Deer, Alberta, Canada), 1994.

*Kicked Out*, Prentice-Hall (Englewood Cliffs, NJ), 1995.

*I'm Not Convinced*, Red Deer College Press (Red Deer, Alberta, Canada), 1997.

*The Good, the Bad, and the Suicidal*, Roussan (Montreal, Quebec, Canada), 1997.

*The Colours of Carol Molev*, Roussan (Montreal, Quebec, Canada), 1998.

*The Dream Where the Losers Go*, Roussan (Montreal, Quebec, Canada), 1999, Orca Book Publishers (Victoria, British Columbia, Canada), 2005.

*Before Wings*, Orca Book Publishers (Victoria, British Columbia, Canada), 2001.

*The Lottery*, Orca Book Publishers (Victoria, British Columbia, Canada), 2002.

*Flux*, Orca Book Publishers (Victoria, British Columbia, Canada), 2004.

*Fixed*, Orca Book Publishers (Victoria, British Columbia, Canada), 2005.

*Hello, Groin*, Orca Book Publishers (Victoria, British Columbia, Canada), 2006.

## ■ Sidelights

Beth Goobie is an award-winning Canadian writer who has produced poetry and fiction for both adult and young adult readers. Since 2000, she has concentrated primarily on novels for younger readers that tackle difficult and often controversial issues. Child abuse, sexual promiscuity, overcoming life-threatening illnesses, and teen suicide are just some of the weighty themes Goobie has taken on in her young adult works. "Goobie's protagonists are outsiders, cast into 'special' roles by no wish of their own," Amy Jo Ehman wrote in the *Quill & Quire*. "They are typically on the cusp of great change—both physically and emotionally. They learn that it is more important to be self-aware than to be understood. They are not cute. Their stories are both unfamiliar and unsettling."

### Of Poetry and Prose

In her first book, *Could I Have My Body Back Now, Please?*, Goobie presents both poems and short stories in which physical distortion and, in some cases, dismemberment figure as recurring motifs. In one work, an irate woman's wagging finger separates from her hand. In another tale, a male character repeatedly loses his sex organ. Still another work includes a child whose ears stretch and slide under closed doors to hear conversations. Joan Thomas, writing in *Books in Canada,* called *Could I Have My Body Back Now, Please?* a volume "of startling originality," describing it as "a noteworthy first collection." Another reviewer, Aritha Van Herk, called Goobie's book, in a *University of Toronto Quarterly* assessment, "a pleasure to read," and a *Bloomsbury Review* critic described it as a "cohesive collection."

Goobie's subsequent books of poetry include *Scars of Light,* in which, as Rhea Tregerov reported in the *University of Toronto Quarterly,* she "tells the story of the physical, emotional, and sexual abuse that occurred within her apparently 'ordinary' family." Tregerov acknowledged *Scars of Light* as "chillingly powerful." *Books in Canada* reviewer Marlene Cook-shaw also found favor with the book, which she described as a "harrowing journey . . . into the details of [Goobie's] abusive childhood." Lisa A. Dickson wrote in the *Canadian Book Review Annual 1994* that *Scars of Light* "offers us no platitudes, and demands none."

The poetry collection *The Girls Who Dream Me* deals, like *Scars of Light,* with Goobie's earlier abuses, but shows evidence of healing. "The book does talk about the difficult stuff," Goobie noted in a *Saskatoon Star Phoenix* article, "but it's also very much about the joy in the recovery of the ability to have sensual experiences. . . . Writing is healing for me." In her collection, Goobie challenges the adult condemnation of teenage sexual exploration, as well as many of the moral assumptions defined by Christianity. A contributor to *Letters in Canada* wrote of Goobie's poetry, "Her long lines nearly spill off the page, reaching to the margins with an insistence, an energetic arcing, that pulls poetry towards prose, prose towards poetry."

Goobie also chronicles abuse in *The Only-Good Heart,* a novel about a woman's grim experiences in a cult, including prostitution and murder. *Quill & Quire* reviewer Suzanne Methot summarized the novel as "a complex, multilayered exploration into suffering and survival," and she deemed it "a brave rendering of one woman's struggle to heal." *Suite101.com* contributor Kirman, meanwhile, observed that *The Only-Good Heart* is "drawn partially [Goobie's] own experiences." In the same *Suite101.com* article, Goobie expressed hope that *The Only-Good Heart* "would create a greater awareness in general for people in terms of cults and what they are doing." While calling the novel "Goobie's most difficult and challenging work," Thomas S. Woods of the Toronto *Globe and Mail* did not consider this a criticism; as he stated, "I know of no young writer in Canada capable of crafting subtle imagery and delicate phrasing to compare with that found in Goobie's

arresting poetry and prose. . . . Goobie's work is . . . starkly, almost self-consciously, original, strewn here and there with the telling detritus (much of it human) of modern popular culture."

## Turns to Young Adult Novels

Goobie's publications for young adult readers include *Group Homes from Outer Space* (later published as *Something Girl*), which centers on a teen who lives in fear of her abusive father. Edith Parsons, writing in the *Canadian Review of Materials,* described this work as a "fast-paced, well-told story," and a *Quill & Quire* reviewer Anne Louise Mahoney found the book "rewarding." *Who Owns*

In Goobie's novel *Sticks and Stones,* a girl's reputation suffers at the hands of her vengeful classmates. (Orca Book Publishers, 2002. Reproduced by permission.)

*Kelly Paddik?* relates the struggles of a teenage girl running from her sexually abusive father. Patty Lawlor, writing in *Quill & Quire*, called this book "a solid . . . offering."

Another young adult volume, *Hit and Run*, features a teen heroine who is plagued with guilt after she commits a horrific driving offense while drunk. *Sticks and Stones* presents a girl who is unfairly regarded as promiscuous by her classmates. Darlene R. Golke, reviewing both *Hit and Run* and *Sticks and Stones* in the *Canadian Book Review Annual 1994*, noted that "the plots of both books develop quickly." But Fred Boer, assessing both works in *Quill & Quire*, favored *Sticks and Stones*, which he singled out for its "hard-hitting, effective ending."

*Mission Impossible* relates the problems that ensue when a student protests against a school pageant by refusing to shave her legs. Mary Beaty, in her *Quill & Quire* critique, called *Mission Impossible* "an intelligent book," and Dean E. Lyons, in the *Kliatt*, described the book as "tough yet sensitive." Jean Free summarized the volume in a *Canadian Book Review Annual 1994* analysis as "clever, witty, often satirical, and humorous." Another work, *I'm Not Convinced*, concerns the relationship between a disabled Cree native and a teenage girl who was physically abused by her uncle. Harriet Zaidman wrote on the *University of Manitoba* Web site, "Beth Goobie has written a very warm and useful book for teens who need encouragement to find their inner strength and face their problems head on."

*The Good, the Bad, and the Suicidal* centers on a high school where the students are divided into three groups: the Jocks, the Irregulars, and the Leftovers. The Jocks and the Irregulars are rival gangs—the former composed of teenagers with money, the latter of teenagers without. Dariel, the narrator, is a Leftover—one of those not affiliated with either gang—who classifies herself as SWFF: "Single White Fat Female." Dariel finds herself becoming involved in the fight against a citywide curfew imposed on the local teenagers, which draws the attention of the leaders of both gangs. *Quill & Quire* reviewer Theresa Toten characterized the heroine as "straight up and hilarious" and noted the "entertainment value of spending some time with [her] and her small world." Steve Pitt described Goobie's tale in the *Canadian Book Review Annual 1997* as a "gritty book." Jacolyn Caton of the *Regina Sun* noted, "Strong characterization and plot are two of the trademarks of [Goobie's] writing." Sarah Ellis also praised the work in *Horn Book*, writing, "*The Good, the Bad, and the Suicidal* is a splendid book."

## Troubled Teens, Difficult Solutions

In *The Colours of Carol Molev*, a teenage girl discovers the presence of colorful energy zones that render her capable of extraordinary insights. Through her relationship with Rev, who can read minds, Carol learns how to use her own abilities to confront the powers of darkness. Bridget Donald wrote in *Quill & Quire* that *The Colours of Carol Molev* lacked sufficient "depth and consistency," but Susannah D. Ketchum, in a *Canadian Book Review Annual 1998* appraisal, deemed the book "worthwhile."

Goobie's next young adult novel, *The Dream Where the Losers Go*, focuses on a troubled adolescent. Skey Mitchell, the main character, is a sixteen-year-old sent to a lockup for adolescent girls after she tries to kill herself. Through the others she meets while incarcerated, Skey begins to redefine the world she once knew so well, and she also begins to understand the importance of having someone to turn to for support. "Although there is a tough side of life in this book," Sandra Vincent wrote in the *Canadian Review of Materials*, "the resolution is believable and not without hope."

In 2000 Goobie published the award-winning novel *Before Wings*, the story of fifteen-year-old Adrien, who suffered a brain aneurysm when she was thirteen. A second episode would be fatal, and now, practically smothered by her over-protective parents, Adrien simply waits to die. Then, during a working vacation at her aunt's summer camp, Adrien sees the spirits of five girls dancing on a lake and meets Paul, a boy who is haunted by premonitions that he will die, and she begins to understand how important it is to simply enjoy her life. Diana Masla, writing for *Voice of Youth Advocates*, stated, "On the surface, this book is an entertaining adolescent read. . . . The deeper message, the whole-hearted grasping of love and life, surely will resonate with many teens." Mara Alpert, writing in *School Library Journal*, explained, "This could have been a terribly bleak and depressing book, but it isn't. Its engaging characters, realistic setting, and upbeat ending will satisfy teen readers." A *Horn Book* reviewer called *Before Wings* "the best kind of romance," and Brenda Dillon, writing for *Resource Links*, praised, "This book is good. Very, very good. Buy it, read it, recommend it."

A sinister clique at a high school is the subject of Goobie's *The Lottery*. The group, known as the Shadow Council, is able to control other students through psychological manipulation. Each year the club holds a lottery to see which student will be their "victim." This unfortunate becomes a pariah to other students while forced to do errands for the Council and play tricks on other students. But when fifteen-year-old Sal is chosen, she figures it is only one more bit of misfortune to add to her troubled spirit, as she already feels guilty about her father's death in an automobile accident. Sal's brother as well as a male member of the Council try to protect her, but it is Sal herself who ultimately discovers how not be a victim any longer. For *Booklist* contributor Michael Cart, this novel, with its echoes of Shirley Jackson and Robert Cormier, "lacks freshness." However, Cart went on to praise the "vividly drawn character" of Sal. *Kliatt* reviewer Paula Rohrlick had a more positive assessment of the same work, calling *The Lottery* "a gripping and powerful narrative"

### Fantastic Tales

In *Flux* and *Fixed,* Goobie paints a dystopian alternate world and follows an adolescent protagonist who tries to navigate it. Nellie, twelve years old, is at the center of the action in this pair of novels, changing her level of existence at will while avoiding the evil machinations of the Interior, minions of which have killed her mother. She teams up with a boy named Deller whose brother, Fen, has also been taken by operatives from the Interior. In *Flux,* Nellie helps Deller in his search for Fen and also tries to learn the secrets of her own past. Reviewing *Flux* in *Kliatt,* Claire Rosser found it a "a harsh story," but one that makes the reader "care about [the characters] and look forward to the sequel." For *Resource Links* contributor K.V. Johansen, *Flux* "takes place in a thoroughly-imagined, well-created world."

Nellie's adventures continue in *Fixed.* Here, she and her twin, also called Nellie, are students in an underworld where they are subjected to the mind control of a religious cult anxious to dispose violently of their opponents. Nellie and her twin ultimately come together to battle the power of this cult. Reviewing this second novel in the series for *School Library Journal,* Sarah Couri felt that "Goobie's world building is fascinating and faultless" Rosser, writing for *Kliatt,* termed this novel "difficult, dark, complicated, and brilliant," and a book that "demands a lot from a reader." And *Booklist* reviewer Jennifer Mattson commented, "Goobie's mind-bending setup provides enough momentum to propel [readers] to the end."

In her 2006 novel, *Hello, Groin,* Goobie focuses on teenage homosexuality. Dylan is a sixteen-year-old high school student and desperately wants to seem normal despite the fact that she knows she is homosexual. She feels no attraction toward her boyfriend and ends up kissing another girl at a dance. When she finally comes out, her family is understanding; her old best friend from grade school has also discovered her sexual orientation and the two become lovers. Sheilah Kosco, writing for *School Library Journal,* felt that the story feels a "little too fairy-talelike," with so much understanding, but also observed that "Goobie stresses the value of all individuals, and their right to their own space in this world." Higher praise came from *Resource Links* contributor Linda Irvine, who called *Hello, Groin* "an important novel." Irvine further remarked, "Through Dylan, other teens may realize they are not alone in homosexual or even bisexual attractions." Similarly, *Canadian Review of Materials* contributor Jennifer Caldwell observed, "Goobie sensitively portrays a variety of perspectives regarding homosexuality." Caldwell concluded, "This story is about being true to oneself despite peer pressure, which is something all teens can relate to."

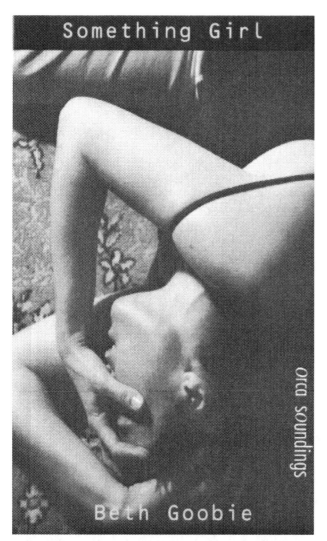

**A haunting tale of abuse and neglect,** *Something Girl* **centers on the strong bond between two friends.** (Orca Book Publishers, 2005. Reproduced by permission.)

If you enjoy the works of Beth Goobie, you may also want to check out the following books:

Cynthia Voight, *When She Hollers*, 1994.

Julie Anne Peters, *Keeping You a Secret*, 2003.

Neal Shusterman, *Unwind*, 2007.

---

Goobie once remarked: "My writing is a search for meaning, beauty, love, an integration of my lost parts." She added, "Creativity . . . is ultimately about healing, a recognition of the deeply human core ability to love and change that I encountered so often in children and adults trapped in similar circumstances." In her works, Goobie remarked to Ehman in *Quill & Quire*, she attempts to give her readers a feeling of hope and a sense of acceptance. "I think there are a lot of negative messages given to children and teenagers in our society, and I try to reverse that as much as possible in my books." The author concluded, "One of the messages that I'm trying to give teenagers more than anything is the need for self-love and self-trust. How infinitely valuable every individual is."

## ■ Biographical and Critical Sources

### BOOKS

*Canadian Book Review Annual 1994*, Canadian Book Review Annual (Toronto, Ontario, Canada), 1995.

*Canadian Book Review Annual 1997*, Canadian Book Review Annual (Toronto, Ontario, Canada), 1998.

*Canadian Book Review Annual 1998*, Canadian Book Review Annual (Toronto, Ontario, Canada), 1999.

### PERIODICALS

*Bloomsbury Review*, September, 1992, review of *Could I Have My Body Back Now, Please?*, p. 20.

*Booklist*, March 15, 2001, Frances Bradburn, review of *Before Wings*, p. 1391; January 1, 2003, Michael Cart, review of *The Lottery*, p. 870; April 15, 2005, Jennifer Mattson, review of *Fixed*, p. 1463.

*Books in Canada*, March, 1992, Joan Thomas, "Feelings in the Bone," p. 40; April, 1995, Marlene Cookshaw, "Patterns of Truth," pp. 55-56.

*Canadian Review of Materials*, October, 1992, Edith Parsons, review of *Group Homes from Outer Space*, p. 272; April 28, 2000, Sandra Vincent, review of *The Dream Where the Losers Go*; September 15, 2006, Jennifer Caldwell, review of *Hello, Groin*.

*Globe and Mail* (Toronto, Ontario, Canada), May, 1998, Thomas S. Woods, "Unconquerable Spirit Shines through Tale of Abuse."

*Horn Book*, November-December, 1998, Sarah Ellis, review of *The Good, the Bad, and the Suicidal*, pp. 773-774; March-April, 2001, review of *Before Wings*, p. 205.

*Kliatt*, January, 1996, Dean E. Lyons, review of *Mission Impossible*, p. 8; November, 2002, Paula Rohrlick, review of *The Lottery*, p. 10; July, 2004, Claire Rosser, review of *Flux*, p. 7; May, 2005, Claire Rosser, review of *Fixed*, p. 30.

*Letters in Canada*, 1998, review of *The Girls Who Dream Me*, pp. 216-218.

*Publishers Weekly*, October 28, 2002, review of *The Lottery*, p. 73.

*Quill & Quire*, June, 1992, Anne Louise Mahoney, review of *Group Homes from Outer Space*, p. 36; June, 1993, Patty Lawlor, review of *Who Owns Kelly Paddik?*, p. 37; February, 1995, Mary Beaty, review of *Mission Impossible*, p. 36; March, 1995, Fred Boer, reviews of *Hit and Run* and *Sticks and Stones*, p. 79; April, 1997, Janet McNaughton, review of *I'm Not Convinced*, pp. 37-38; October, 1997, Theresa Toten, review of *The Good, the Bad, and the Suicidal*, pp. 37-38; May, 1998, Suzanne Methot, review of *The Only-Good Heart*, p. 30; October, 1998, Bridget Donald, review of *The Colours of Carol Molev*, pp. 43-44; May, 2004, Amy Jo Ehman, "Beth Goobie's Otherworldy Views."

*Regina Sun* (Regina, Saskatchewan, Canada), June 14, 1998, Jacolyn Caton, "Real Teens; Real Problems."

*Resource Links*, December, 2000, Brenda Dillon, review of *Before Wings*, p. 28; June, 2004, K.V. Johansen, review of *Flux*, p. 25; June, 2005, Gail de Vos, review of *Fixed*, p. 30; December, 2006, Linda Irvine, review of *Hello, Groin*, p. 31.

*Saskatoon Star Phoenix* (Saskatoon, Saskatchewan, Canada), January, 2000, Verne Clemence, "Teenage Soul Explored."

*School Library Journal*, April, 2001, Mara Alpert, review of *Before Wings*, p. 140; March, 2003, Joel Shoemaker, review of *The Lottery*, p. 232; September, 2004, Susan W. Hunter, review of *Flux*, p. 206;

August, 2005, Sarah Couri, review of *Fixed*, p. 127; December, 2006, Sheilah Kosco, review of *Hello, Groin*, p. 140.

*University of Toronto Quarterly*, fall, 1992, Aritha Van Herk, review of *Could I Have My Body Back Now, Please?*, pp. 19-20; winter, 1995, Rhea Tregerov, review of *Scars of Light*, pp. 66-67; winter, 2000, Marnie Parsons, review of *The Girls Who Dream Me*.

*Voice of Youth Advocates*, April, 2001, Diane Masla, review of *Before Wings*.

ONLINE

*Stellar Book Award Web site*, http://www.stellar award.ca/ (January 23, 2010), "Beth Goobie."

*Suite101.com*, http://www.suite101.com/ (March 17-24, 2000), Paula E. Kirman, "Beth Goobie: Power and Survival."

*University of Manitoba Web site*, http://www. umanitoba.ca/ (October 17, 1997), Harriet Zaidman, review of *I'm Not Convinced.*\*

(Photograph by Tim Cathersal. Reproduced by permission.)

# Brent Hartinger

## ■ Personal

Born 1964, in WA; son of Harold (an attorney) and Mary Anne (a homemaker) Hartinger; partner of Michael Jensen (a writer). *Ethnicity:* "Caucasian." *Education:* Gonzaga University, B.S., 1986. *Politics:* Democrat. *Hobbies and other interests:* Reading, playing computer games, traveling, attending movies and plays.

## ■ Addresses

*Home*—Tacoma, WA. *Agent*—Jennifer DeChiara Literary Agency, 254 Park Ave. S., Ste. 2L, New York, NY 10010. *E-mail*—brentsbrain@harbornet.com.

## ■ Career

Novelist, playwright, and educator. Guest columnist, *News Tribune*, Tacoma, WA. Vermont College, Montpelier, writing instructor in M.F.A. Program in Creative Writing for Children and Young Adults.

Also worked as a counselor in a group home for troubled adolescents. Cofounder of Oasis (support group for gay and lesbian young people).

## ■ Member

Society of Children's Book Writers and Illustrators, Dramatists' Guild, Authors Supporting Intellectual Freedom (cofounder).

## ■ Awards, Honors

Audience Award, Dayton Playhouse Futurefest Festival of New Plays, and runner-up, Festival of Emerging American Theatre Award, both for *The Starfish Scream*; Popular Paperback selection, American Library Association (ALA), and Books for the Teen Age selection, New York Public Library, both for *Geography Club*; Popular Paperback selection and Quick Pick for Reluctant Readers selection, both ALA, both for *The Last Chance Texaco*; Fort Lauderdale Film Festival Screenwriting-in-the-Sun Award; Judy Blume grant for best young adult novel, Society of Children's Book Writers and Illustrators; Seattle Arts Commission Tacoma Artists Initiative grant and Development of a New Work grant; University of Southwestern Louisiana Young Adult Fiction Prize; Lambda Book Award, National Best Book Award, 2007, and Books for the Teenage selection, New York Public Library, 2008, all for *Split Screen*; Gay & Lesbian Alliance Against Defamation (GLAAD) Media Award, 2010, for Outstanding Digital Journalism Article.

## ■ Writings

*Geography Club*, HarperTempest (New York, NY), 2003.

*The Last Chance Texaco*, HarperTempest (New York, NY), 2004.

*The Order of the Poison Oak*, (sequel to *Geography Club*), HarperTempest (New York, NY), 2005.

*Grand & Humble*, HarperTempest (New York, NY), 2006.

*Dreamquest: Tales of Slumberia*, Tor/Starscape (New York, NY), 2007.

*Split Screen: Attack of the Soul-Sucking Brain Zombies/ Bride of the Soul-Sucking Brain Zombies* (sequel to *Geography Club*), HarperTempest (New York, NY), 2007.

*Project Sweet Life*, HarperTeen (New York, NY), 2009.

Also author of plays, including *The Starfish Scream* (for young adults), produced at Dayton Playhouse Futurefest Festival of New Plays, a stage adaptation of *Geography Club*, produced in Seattle, WA, a stage adaptation of *Grand & Humble*, and others. Editor of *TheTorchOnline.com*, a Web site devoted to fantasy. Contributor of more than four hundred essays, articles, cartoons, and stories to periodicals, including *Omni*, *Boy's Life*, *Plays*, *Emmy*, *Seattle Weekly*, *Genre*, *San Francisco Bay Guardian*, *Noise*, and *Advocate*. Contributor to anthologies, including *Rush Hour*, edited by Michael Cart, Random House, and *Young Warriors*, edited by Tamora Pierce and Josepha Sherman, Random House.

## ■ Sidelights

Brent Hartinger entered the vanguard of a sub-genre in young adult literature with the publication of his first novel, *Geography Club*, in 2003. That work, published to both critical and popular acclaim, deals with teenage homosexuality in a straightforward, honest, and sometimes amusing manner. Explaining part of his motivation in writing the book to a contributor for the *National Coalition against Censorship* Web site, Hartinger remarked: "There is no greater underdog in the world than a gay or lesbian teenager. Depending on where they live, the whole world might be against: their families, their religion,

their teachers, even their friends sometimes!" Since the book debuted, Hartinger has gone on to write a number of sequels to *Geography Club*, and he has also branched out into fantasy, problem novels, and humorous adventures.

Despite his great success as a novelist and playwright, Hartinger never planned to become a writer. His artistic instincts were evident from the beginning, however. Hartinger involved himself in a number of creative activities as a youngster, including editing and publishing his own newspaper, the "Weekly Worm," and he frequently made movies, posters, and audio tapes with his two best friends. During that time, he noted on his home page, "I learned just how much fun it is to create—how satisfying it is to make something from nothing and to get swept up in the sheer joy of invention. Creating something you care about can be hard work, but because you care so much about it, it doesn't feel like work."

Hartinger's high school experiences were another matter entirely. "It was even worse than I'd expected," he reported. "I wasn't popular, which didn't really bug me since I've never liked being the center of attention. But while all of my friends . . . were discovering girls, I was discovering I was gay. I went to Catholic schools, which made things much worse—a fact that I'm still pretty bitter about. I think it's absolutely criminal that gay kids are still forced to spend their adolescent years feeling as lonely, and as freakish, as I felt then." After graduating from college, Hartinger drifted for a time, trying his hand at acting (he had trouble remembering his lines) before deciding to write. When his first attempts at selling a novel failed, he turned to penning stage dramas, a number of which were produced to critical acclaim.

### Breakthrough in Gay Fiction for Teens

Although for over a decade Hartinger had been successfully writing articles, plays, and screenplays, it was not until he had racked up eight unpublished novels, thousands of query letters, and seventeen rejections of his then-current manuscript that his young adult novel *Geography Club* found a home at HarperCollins. In the work, Hartinger tells the story of high school student Russel Middlebrook, who is convinced that he is the only homosexual person in his school. When Russel discovers differently, he and his new friends form the Geography Club, a secret support group. Unlike other publishers, HarperCollins decided to take a gamble on a book with possibly limited appeal, and the gamble paid off.

*Geography Club*, **Hartinger's highly regarded debut novel, concerns a homosexual teen who discreetly forms a support group for his gay classmates.** (HarperTempest, 2004. Cover art © 2003 by Howard Huang. Cover © 2004 by HarperCollins Publishers Inc. Used by permission of HarperCollins Children's Books, a division of HarperCollins Publishers.)

"At the time, everyone claimed there was no market for a gay teen novel," Hartinger recalled on his home page. "Of course, now that the book has gotten all these great reviews and is selling strongly, all these editors are coming to my agent and [complaining that] . . . she didn't send the manuscript to them!"

Hartinger based his first-person novel on many of his own experiences growing up, and many of the characters also reflect his friends and acquaintances. *Geography Club* "gave me a chance to rewrite my teenage years but give it a little more of a happy ending," he wrote at his home page. Another influence was ancient mythology. "I always saw Russel's journey as epic," he continued. "I think of him as a classic hero who, like Odysseus and so many other Greek and Norse champions, must experience being

both prince and outcast before he can claim his rightful 'crown' of true belonging." Despite the serious subject matter—acceptance—Hartinger wanted to employ a light touch, as he told Amanda Laughtland for the Tacoma *News Tribune.* "I wanted my book to be fun and funny—a fast read. Not broccoli, but dessert."

When it appeared in 2003, *Geography Club* attracted a readership among teens and adults alike, earning good reviews from a number of critics, despite sparking objections from others. For his part, Hartinger told *Publishers Weekly Online* interviewer Kevin Howell that the novel's publisher, HarperTempest, "is known for edgier teen fiction. I was never encouraged to tone anything down. It's not for younger readers but there's not anything that teenagers today would find too threatening."

Several reviewers commented on the verisimilitude in *Geography Club,* among them *Horn Book* reviewer Roger Sutton, who ranked the work highly among books portraying gay characters and noted that Russel's "agonies of ostracism (and first love) are truly conveyed." A *Publishers Weekly* contributor also commented that the novel "does a fine job of presenting many of the complex realities of gay teen life." Writing in *School Library Journal,* Robert Gray praised Hartinger's characterizations, calling them "excellent" and predicting that teens of all sexual preferences would "find this novel intriguing." Several critics were a little less generous in their appraisals, among them *Booklist* reviewer Hazel Rochman and a *Kirkus Reviews* contributor. Both reviewers cited the novel's plot as flawed, Rochman writing that the plot strands are "settled a little too neatly in the end." Even so, the critic considered Hartinger's first-person narrative voice, dialogue, and portrayal of prejudice accurate. Despite imperfections in the plot, the *Kirkus Reviews* writer found the book "provocative, insightful, and . . . comforting." As Hartinger noted on his home page, "many gay men like to read these books to relive their teenage years."

## Popular Work Spawns Sequels

Hoping to escape his image as the "gay kid," Russel Middlebrook takes a job at a summer camp for childhood burn survivors in *The Order of the Poison Oak,* a sequel to *Geography Club.* Along with friends Gunnar and Min, Russel heads to Camp Serenity, where he takes charge of a group of restless ten year olds. To bond with his charges, he forms the Order of the Poison Oak, a secret group for outsiders of all types. Working past "his initial sense of discomfort around the burn survivors, with their visible scars and disabilities," as *Kliatt* reviewer Kathryn Kulpa noted, "Russel, with his less-obvious scars, gains an understanding of the common ground they occupy." He also finds himself involved in an awkward love triangle with Min and another counselor and comes to rely on the steadying influence of Otto, a burn survivor who now works at the camp. In her review for *Booklist*, Rochman praised Hartinger for spinning an "honest, tender, funny, first-person narrative that brings close what it's like to have a crush and hate a friend," while a *Kirkus Reviews* critic stated that Hartinger "creates a . . . touching and realistic portrait of gay teens."

Russel returns in the company of best friend Min in the flip-book addition to the series, *Split Screen: Attack of the Soul-Sucking Brain Zombies/Bride of the Soul-Sucking Brain Zombies*. Here the two protago-nists take part in the filming of a zombie movie, and the same events are viewed from their very different perspectives. In fact, both Russel and Min's stories are told in the two books included under this one cover. "You might say it's *Rashomon* for teens," Hartinger explained to *AfterElton.com* Web site contributor Michael Jensen, "except the two books cover completely different events. It's not at all like reading the same book twice. That said, the two books definitely inform each other. You don't know the whole story until you read both books together." While serving as extras on the movie, which is being filmed in their hometown, Russel and Min still must navigate their private lives: Russel has to decide between two boyfriends, one long distance and one local, while Min learns to deal with her girlfriend's decision to keep her homosexuality private. Reviewing the work, *Lambda Book Report* contributor Bill Burleson called it an "enjoyable, compelling, and well-told story." Likewise, *School Library Journal* reviewer Kathleen E. Gruver thought that "there is a lot of humor in this book."

An imaginative fantasy tale, *Dreamquest* focuses on a young girl who learns that a character from her dreams threatens to take control of her waking life. (Cover illustration by August Hall. Starscape/Tom Doherty Associates Book, 2007. Reproduced by permission of the illustrator.)

## A Different Viewpoint

Hartinger's novel *The Last Chance Texaco* is based on his experiences working as a counselor in a group home for troubled adolescents. The work concerns fifteen-year-old Lucy Pitt, a foster child whose parents were killed in a car accident when Lucy was seven years old. After being shuttled from one foster family to another, Lucy arrives at Kindle Home, an aging mansion known to its residents as "The Last Chance Texaco." Lucy knows that if she fails at Kindle Home, she will be sent to a high-security facility nicknamed Eat-Their-Young Island. Though Lucy is tested early and often by the other teen residents, she finds Kindle Home unlike any other place she has lived and is determined to stay. After a series of car fires in the neighborhood cast suspicion on the residents of the foster home, Lucy decides to investigate with the help of a new friend. "Hartinger clearly knows the culture, and Lucy speaks movingly (if occasionally too therapeutically) about her anger and grief," observed *Booklist* critic Rochman. Faith Brautigan, reviewing the novel in *School Library Journal*, similarly noted that "Hartinger excels at giving readers an insider's view of the subculture, with its myriad unspoken rules created by the kids, not the system."

A pair of seventeen-year-old boys from disparate backgrounds are haunted by strange premonitions in *Grand & Humble*. Told in alternating chapters, the work focuses on Harlan, a popular athlete whose father is a U.S. senator, and Manny, a sensitive

Three friends devise a series of complicated but futile get-rich-quick schemes in the humorous *Project Sweet Life*. (HarperTeen, 2009. Jacket photo © 2009 Fancy Photography/Veer, Inc. Used by permission of HarperCollins Children's Books, a division of HarperCollins Publishers.)

while she sleeps, venturing into the land of Slumberia where she discovers her dreams are scripted. When one of the denizens of this land escapes from Slumberia, she causes havoc in Julie's waking life. The *Publishers Weekly* contributor further felt that this "winning pairing of a sincere message with hyperbolic humor should resonate with readers." Further praise for *Dreamquest* came from *School Library Journal* contributor Robyn Gioia, who noted that readers in search of "a fun but edgy book will enjoy stepping into this unusual world with its grim circumstances and adventure." And a *Kirkus Reviews* writer concluded, "Julie's entertaining and humorous quest leads to a satisfying conclusion."

Three teenage buddies devise an elaborate strategy to avoid working while on summer vacation in Hartinger's 2009 book, *Project Sweet Life*. Planning to spend their time swimming, bike riding, and spelunking, a trio of fifteen year olds, Dave, Victor, and Curtis, are shocked when their parents demand that they get summer jobs. Instead of scouring the want ads, however, they lie to their fathers, telling them they have found employment, and the teens then busy themselves on a number of schemes to earn as much money as they can with as little effort as possible. Of course, their ill-advised plans only lead to chaos, resulting in "a hilarious story filled with mishaps, close calls, and outrageous adventures," according to Sarah K. Allen writing for *School Library Journal*. Reviewing the same work for *Booklist*, Lynn Rutan also found it "an amusing story with great teen appeal."

theater geek whose own father must work hard to make ends meet. As both teens struggle to make sense of their terrifying nightmares, frequently containing visions connected to the intersection of Grand and Humble streets in their town, they begin to question their pasts and discover that a tragic event that occurred fourteen years earlier will forever link their fates. "Parallels and double meanings abound in this tricky, but satisfying, double narrative," noted a *Kirkus Reviews* critic, and Paula Rohrlick wrote in *Kliatt* that Hartinger's "taut and clever thriller . . . will appeal to mystery and suspense fans."

With the 2007 title *Dreamquest: Tales of Slumberia*, Hartinger "deftly moves into the realm of fantasy," according to a *Publishers Weekly* reviewer. Hartinger also focuses on a younger protagonist in this outing, relating the story of eleven-year-old Julie whose dreams are troubled by the friction between her parents. One night she enters into another reality

### Advice for Aspiring Writers

Becoming a writer means being an avid reader, Hartinger maintained on his home page. "I read constantly—hundreds of books a year, and several newspapers a day," he noted. "And when I'm not reading, I go to movies and plays, and play computer games," all activities that involve a creative activity. Along with reading widely, Hartinger recommends that writers outline their works-to-be. "I know that while character and beautiful language are important, story is what keeps readers turning the pages. But story is all about structure, and structure almost never just 'happens.'"

"Finally," Hartinger wrote, "don't get discouraged. Because good writing is personal, it's hard not to take rejections personally. But being a sane writer means having an ego of granite with a Teflon coating. And being a successful writer means being very, very, very, very persistent."

If you enjoy the works of Brent Hartinger, you may also want to check out the following books:

Alex Sanchez, *Rainbow Boys*, 2001.
Neal Shusterman, *Everlost*, 2006.
Todd Strasser, *Boot Camp*, 2007.

## ■ Biographical and Critical Sources

*PERIODICALS*

*Booklist*, April 1, 2003, Hazel Rochman, review of *Geography Club*, p. 1387; January 1, 2004, Hazel Rochman, review of *The Last Chance Texaco*, p. 844; January 1, 2005, Hazel Rochman, review of *The Order of the Poison Oak*, p. 845; January 1, 2006, Hazel Rochman, review of *Grand & Humble*, pp. 83-84; October 1, 2008, Lynn Rutan, review of *Project Sweet Life*, p. 38.

*Childhood Education*, winter, 2004, Ann Pohl, review of *The Last Chance Texaco*, p. 107.

*Horn Book*, March-April, 2003, Roger Sutton, review of *Geography Club*, pp. 209-211.

*Kirkus Reviews*, December 15, 2002, review of *Geography Club*, p. 1850; March 1, 2004, review of *The Last Chance Texaco*, p. 223; January 15, 2005, review of *The Order of the Poison Oak*, p. 120; December 15, 2005, review of *Grand & Humble*, p. 1322; April 15, 2007, review of *Dreamquest: Tales of Slumberia*; January 1, 2009, review of *Project Sweet Life*.

*Kliatt*, March, 2004, Claire Rosser, review of *The Last Chance Texaco*, p. 11; January, 2006, Paula Rohrlick, review of *Grand & Humble*, p. 8; March, 2006, Kathryn Kulpa, review of *The Order of the Poison Oak*, p. 22.

*Lambda Book Report*, fall, 2008, Bill Burleson, interview with Hartinger and review of *Split Screen Split Screen: Attack of the Soul-Sucking Brain Zombies/Bride of the Soul-Sucking Brain Zombies*, p. 38.

*Public Libraries*, July-August, 2006, "Geography of a Writer," p. 27.

*Publishers Weekly*, February 3, 2003, review of *Geography Club*, pp. 76-77; January 26, 2004, review of *The Last Chance Texaco*, p. 255; February 13, 2006, review of *Grand & Humble*, p. 90; May 21, 2007, review of *Dreamquest*, p. 55.

*School Library Journal*, February, 2003, Robert Gray, review of *Geography Club*, pp. 141-142; March, 2004, Faith Brautigan, review of *The Last Chance Texaco*, pp. 212-213; April, 2005, Hillias J. Martin, review of *The Order of the Poison Oak*, p. 134; February, 2006, Suzanne Gordon, review of *Grand & Humble*, p. 132; April, 2006, Brent Hartinger, Nancy Reeder, and Trev Jones, "Censorship or Information?," pp. 13-14; March, 2007, Kathleen E. Gruver, review of *Split Screen*, p. 210; February, 2008, Robyn Gioia, review of *Dreamquest*, p. 116; April, 2009, Sarah K. Allen, review of *Project Sweet Life*, p. 135.

*Voice of Youth Advocates*, February, 2006, Melissa Potter, review of *Grand & Humble*, pp. 485-486.

*ONLINE*

*AfterElton.com*, http://www.afterelton.com/ (February 5, 2007), Michael Jensen, "Attack of the Gay Teen Zombies."

*Brent's Brain: The Brent Hartinger Home Page*, http://www.brenthartinger.com (January 24, 2010).

*Debbi Michiko Florence Web site*, http://debbimichikoflorence.com/ (October 2, 2006), interview with Hartinger.

*National Coalition against Censorship Web site*, http://www.ncac.org/ (June 19, 2009), "Kids' Right to Read Project: Interview with Brent Hartinger."

*News Tribune Online* (Tacoma, WA), http://www.Tribnet.com/ (March 2, 2003), Amanda Laughtland, "Gay Teen Novel Fills a Void."

*Publishers Weekly Online*, http://www.publishersweekly.com/ (March 21, 2003), Kevin Howell, "Gay YA Novel, *Geography Club*, Goes to the Head of the Class."

*Teenreads.com*, http://www.teenreads.com/ (April 12, 2005), Carlie Webber, interview with Hartinger.*

(Photograph courtesy of Evan Agostini/Getty Images.)

## ■ Personal

Full name, Charles Martin Jones; born September 21, 1912, in Spokane, WA; died of congestive heart failure, February 22, 2002, in Corona del Mar, CA; son of Charles Adams and Mabel Jones; married Dorothy Webster, January 31, 1935 (died, 1978); married Marian Dern (a writer), January 14, 1983; children: Linda Jones Clough. *Education:* Chouinard Art Institute (now California Institute of the Arts), diploma, 1930. *Politics:* Democrat. *Religion:* Unitarian-Universalist.

## ■ Career

Animator and director. Began career working as a seaman and portrait painter, among other positions; worked as cel washer and cel painter for Ub Iwerks, 1931; also worked at Charles Mintz Screen Gems Studio and for Walter Lantz at Universal Studios, 1932; Leon Schlesinger Studio (later acquired by Warner Brothers), Hollywood, CA, animator, 1933-38, director of animated films, 1938-63, including "Night Watchman," 1938, "Fast and Furry-ous," 1949, "For Scenti-Mental Reasons," 1949, "Rabbit of Seville," 1950, "Rabbit Fire," 1951, "Feed the Kitty,"

# Chuck Jones

1952, "Duck Dodgers in the 24 1/2 Century," 1953, "Duck Amuck," 1953, "One Froggy Evening," 1955, and "What's Opera, Doc?," 1957; founder of Chuck Jones Enterprises (film company), 1962; Metro-Goldwyn-Mayer, Hollywood, CA, producer of "Tom and Jerry" cartoon series, beginning in 1963, head of animation department, beginning in 1966; founder of Tower Twelve Productions, 1965; American Broadcasting Companies (ABC-TV), vice president of children's programming, beginning in 1970, and creator of the program *The Curiosity Shop,* 1971-73; co-producer, writer, and director of *The Bugs Bunny Show* for ABC-TV, 1960-62, and *The Bugs Bunny/Road Runner Hour* for Columbia Broadcasting System (CBS-TV), 1968-71; television specials include *How the Grinch Stole Christmas,* 1966, and *The Cricket in Times Square,* 1973, both for ABC-TV, and the CBS-TV specials *Rikki-Tikki-Tavi,* 1975, *A Connecticut Rabbit in King Arthur's Court,* 1978, *Raggedy Ann and Andy in the Great Santa Claus Caper,* 1978, and *The Pumpkin Who Couldn't Smile,* 1979; animator for *Gremlins,* 1984, *Gremlins 2,* 1990, and animation consultant, *Who Framed Roger Rabbit?,* 1988. Cofounder of Chuck Jones Film Productions (animation production company), Hollywood, CA, 1993; founder of Chuck Jones Foundation, 2000; teacher and lecturer at colleges and universities in the United States and abroad. *Exhibitions:* Work exhibited at Gallery Lainzberg and Circle Fine Art Galleries; film retrospectives at Museum of Modern Art, British Film Institute, American Film Institute, New York Cultural Center, Harvard University, Ottawa Art Center, London Film School, Filmex Festival, Deauville Festival of American Films,

Moscow Film Festival, and Montreal Film Festival. *Military service:* U.S. Army, worked on training films during World War II.

## ■ Member

Academy of Motion Picture Arts and Sciences, Screen Writers Guild, Academy of Television Arts and Sciences, National Council on Children and Television, Screen Actors Guild.

## ■ Awards, Honors

Award for the best animated cartoon of the year, Newsreel Theatre, 1940, for "Old Glory"; Academy Award, Academy of Motion Picture Arts and Sciences, 1950, for best animated cartoon "For Sentimental Reasons" 1950, for best documentary short subject *So Much for So Little,* and 1965, for best animated cartoon *The Dot and the Line;* CINE Eagle Certificates for animated films, Council on International Non-Theatrical Events, 1966, for *The Dot and the Line,* 1973, for *The Cricket in Times Square,* 1976, for *Rikki-Tikki-Tavi* and *The White Seal,* and 1977, for *Mowgli's Brothers;* Peabody Award for Television Programming Excellence, 1971, for *How the Grinch Stole Christmas* and *Horton Hears a Who;* tributes from American Film Institute, 1975 and 1980, and British Film Institute and New York Film Institute, both 1979; Best Educational Film Award from Columbus Film Festival (Columbus, Ohio), 1976; first prize from Tehran Festival of Films for Children, 1977; Parents' Choice Award for videos from Parents' Choice Foundation, 1985, for *Rikki-Tikki-Tavi* and *Mowgli's Brothers;* Great Director Award from U.S. Film Festival, 1986; inducted into Academy of Achievement, 1990; awarded star on Hollywood Walk of Fame, 1995; Academy Award for lifetime achievement, Academy of Motion Pictures Arts and Sciences, 1996; inducted into Animation Hall of Fame, 2001; received honorary lifetime membership from Directors Guild of America; the cartoons "What's Opera, Doc?" and "Duck Amuck" have been inducted into the Library of Congress's National Film Registry.

## ■ Writings

(And producer and director) *Gay Purr-ee* (screenplay), United Producers of America, 1962.

(Coauthor; and producer and director) *The Phantom Tollbooth* (screenplay), Metro-Goldwyn-Mayer, 1971.

*Chuck Amuck: The Life and Times of an Animated Cartoonist* (autobiography), with foreword by Steven Spielberg, Farrar, Straus (New York, NY), 1989, paperback edition with preface by Matt Groening, 1999.

*Chuck Jones: A Flurry of Drawings,* University of California Press (Berkeley, CA), 1994.

*Chuck Reducks: Drawings from the Fun Side of Life,* with foreword by Robin Williams, Warner (New York, NY), 1996.

*Chuck Jones: Conversations,* edited by Maureen Furniss, University Press of Mississippi (Jackson, MS), 2005.

*Stroke of Genius: A Collection of Paintings and Musings on Life, Love and Art,* Linda Jones Enterprises, 2007.

Creator of syndicated comic strip "Crawford," beginning in 1978. Author of preface, *Bugs Bunny: Fifty Years and Only One Grey Hare,* by Joe Adamson, Holt (New York, NY), 1990; author of foreword, *Serious Business: Cartoons and America from Betty Boop to Toy Story,* by Stefan Kanfer, Scribner (New York, NY), 1997. Contributor to periodicals.

*FOR CHILDREN*

(Illustrator) Rudyard Kipling, *Chuck Jones' Rikki-Tikki-Tavi,* Ideals Publishing (Nashville, TN), 1982.

(Illustrator) Rudyard Kipling, *Chuck Jones' The White Seal,* Ideals Publishing (Nashville, TN), 1982.

(Illustrator) George Selden, *The Cricket in Times Square,* Ideals Publishing (Nashville, TN), 1984.

(Illustrator) Rudyard Kipling, *Chuck Jones' Mowgli's Brothers,* Ideals Publishing (Nashville, TN), 1985.

(Self-illustrated) *William the Backwards Skunk,* Crown (New York, NY), 1987.

(Illustrator) George Daugherty and Janis Diamond, *Chuck Jones' Peter and the Wolf,* Warner Books (New York, NY), 1994.

(Self-illustrated) *Daffy Duck for President,* Worldwide Publishing (Burbank, CA), 1997.

## ■ Sidelights

Chuck Jones was considered one of the most gifted studio cartoonists of Hollywood's "Golden Age" of animated shorts, with a name eclipsed only by that of Walt Disney. "Calling Chuck Jones an animator is like calling Gregor Mendel a pea farmer: It hardly tells the whole story," commented Scott Brown in *Entertainment Weekly*. During his seven-decade-long career, Jones either created or gave verve to such classic characters as Bugs Bunny, Daffy Duck, Porky the Pig, Elmer Fudd, the Road Runner, Wile E. Coyote, and Pepé Le Pew, all of which have become essential assets of American pop culture. Jones did some of his best work between 1938 and 1962, when he made shorts starring these characters for Warner Brothers. According to Maureen Furniss, in her introduction to *Chuck Jones: Conversations,* the cartoonist "was a multi-faceted artist who not only helped to elevate the status of animation worldwide but also assured his own place in history through his talent, energy, and business sense."

After leaving Warner in the early 1960s, Jones worked on the Tom and Jerry series for Metro Goldwyn-Mayer, but also began to explore the emerging medium of television as a vehicle for his creative energies. He worked with longtime friend Theodore Geisel, also known as Dr. Seuss, on the animated children's specials *Horton Hears a Who* and *How the Grinch Stole Christmas.* He also directed the Oscar-winning animated short *The Dot and the Line* and founded his own production company, Chuck Jones Enterprises, which produced several animated specials for television.

## An Artist Is Born

Jones was born Charles Martin Jones on September 21, 1912, in Spokane, Washington. When he was

**During his long career, Jones helped develop such beloved cartoon characters as Bugs Bunny, Daffy Duck, Porky Pig, Wile E. Coyote, and the Roadrunner.** (Photograph courtesy of Don Perdue/Getty Images.)

around six, his family moved to southern California, where his father hoped to make his fortune. Jones was the third of four children of Charles Adams Jones and Mabel Martin Jones, and the family lived in a series of rented homes, some of them pleasantly close to the ocean. But Charles Jones's entrepreneurial schemes usually failed spectacularly. He published a book titled *Fifty Ways to Serve Avocados*, owned a vineyard during Prohibition, and once tried to start a geranium farm on a parcel of land near Long Beach called Signal Hill; frustrated, he sold it, and the land was later discovered to be rich in crude oil. As a result, there were reams of unused business stationery in the Jones house, which the children were heartily encouraged to use for drawing paper. They were even forbidden to use both sides of a sheet of paper to draw, so that the letterhead might disappear all the more quickly. Jones

In 1966 Jones teamed with celebrated author Dr. Seuss to produce the classic holiday special *How the Grinch Stole Christmas*. (Photograph courtesy of MGM TV/The Kobal Collection/The Picture Desk, Inc.)

loved to draw from an early age, and his first character studies were made of the family cat, Johnson, who liked to swim and had an inexplicable passion for grapefruit. The cat would tear an entire one apart and eat it, which sometimes left him with a helmet of rind on his head. "And so Johnson's first lesson to me as a future animator was this: Eschew the ordinary, disdain the commonplace," Jones wrote in his richly illustrated 1989 autobiography, *Chuck Amuck: The Life and Times of an Animated Cartoonist*.

Jones grew up in a literary household, and he picked up a fascination for the coyote from reading Mark Twain's book *Roughing It*. "The coyote is a living, breathing allegory of Want," Jones quoted the book in his autobiography. "He is *always* hungry. He is always poor, out of luck and friendless." Later, he would recall this description in creating one of his most memorable cartoon characters, the Road Runner's omnipresent predator. Jones was also an avid filmgoer, and loved the silent films of the era from comics like Buster Keaton and Charlie Chaplin. Some of the film studios were near his home, and he even appeared in a few himself as an extra for director Mack Sennett. "Years later at Warner Brothers," observed *New York Times* contributor John Canemaker, "Mr. Jones's observations of comic timing, the effective staging of gags, and the expression of personality through body language and movement were transferred to Bugs, Daffy, Roadrunner, et al., making them the true inheritors of the great tradition of physical comedy in film."

As a teen, Jones was an indifferent student, and his poor grades frustrated his father to the point where he was taken out of high school and enrolled in the Chouinard Art Institute, now California Institute of the Arts. He graduated in 1930, hoping to move to Paris to paint, but the Great Depression thwarted his plans. After looking for work as a janitor, the nearly indigent Jones found work in 1931 as a cel-washer at an animation studio owned by Ub Iwerks, a former Disney associate. Cel-washing was the lowliest job in animation, and involved wiping the drawings off hundreds of sheets of celluloid so they could be re-used. He eventually moved up to the status of in-betweener, the artist who drew the hundreds of small frames that, when filmed, actually "animated" the character. As Jones said about his career in the interview with Canemaker, "I just kind of fell uphill."

### Entering the Looney Bin

Jones credited his wife, Dorothy Webster, for finding him a job with the Leon Schlesinger Studio (later acquired by Warner Brothers) around 1933. Jones

**Jones adapted a famous tale by Mark Twain for his 1978 cartoon special** *A Connecticut Rabbit in King Arthur's Court.*
(Photograph courtesy of Warner Brothers/Everett Collection.)

soon felt at home among the jocular animation staff, and began to find his own style. His first credit was for the 1934 Friz Freleng short "The Miller's Daughter." By 1936, he was working for famed director Tex Avery, whose animated shorts were known for their verve and flawless comic timing. "If Disney was like Charlie Chaplin, spinning reality into magic," remarked Eric P. Nash in the *New York Times Magazine*, "Chuck Jones and the Warner Brothers crew were Buster Keaton-like anarchists, attacking the rules of time, space and gravity. Where Disney had a top-down management, with Walt getting all the credit, Warner Brothers animators were rampant individualists, each stamping the product with his own style."

Jones and his colleagues were involved with some of the early Porky the Pig shorts, and then helped create two of the most timeless cartoon anti-heroes, Daffy Duck and Bugs Bunny, in the late 1930s. Daffy was a hapless black duck who could never succeed.

"Daffy was Jones's richest subject," declared Pope Brock in *People.* "Originally a flat-out wacko, hopping around a lake on his head, the duck became in Jones's hands a resilient, greedy, insecure dynamo with big plans. Jones often cast him in heroic roles, like the Scarlet Pumpernickel, for which the duck considered himself fabulously well suited. Greeting each challenge with a volcanic surge of ego, he suffered endless humiliations."

Jones borrowed Daffy's catchword, "despicable," from recollections of his father's ire over President Warren G. Harding's mangling of the English language in his speeches. But Jones and his colleagues gave Daffy a raspy lisp in imitation of the arrogant Leon Schlesinger, whom they detested. "What we forgot," Jones recalled in a *People* interview with Brock, "was that Leon would have to see it. We figured when he heard his own voice coming out of this screwball duck, we'd all get fired. Leon came in and sat on the gold-painted throne that he'd probably stolen from some Theda Bara picture. We rolled it, praying. At the end he jumped up in the air and cried, 'Jethuth Chritht, where'd you get that great voith?'"

All of the Schlesinger studio shorts were created for the big screen, as part of a program of short features played before the billed film. Daffy Duck and his travails were an instant hit, and Jones began directing his own shorts. Bugs Bunny, another character that also came alive under Jones's direction, had been created by a man named Charles Thorson from an idea of an animator, Ben "Bugs" Hardaway, and the rabbit's wisecracking Brooklynite personality was the work of Tex Avery. But when Jones began directing the Bugs shorts, he gave the rabbit a very distinct personality. "His movements give the sense that he has real mass and inertia, that he weighs something, and Jones has frankly borrowed for him gestures from the great silent comedians (Keaton's eye movements, Chaplin's one-legged hopping turn)," noted Lloyd Rose in the *Atlantic*. "His Bugs also has sophistication—he is less the loudmouthed wise guy, more the gentleman anarchist." The dimwit rabbit hunter Elmer Fudd became a staple of the Bugs shorts, and in others, Daffy and Bugs would do battle with one another. "Some of his funniest cartoons result from matching the unflappable and ironic Bugs with the desperate and treacherous Daffy," declared Rose. "Daffy plots against Bugs; Bugs eludes him with lazy ease. Daffy, through greed, falls into trouble; Bugs, sighing, rescues him."

In the late 1940s—after a stint as a cartoonist making military training films for the U.S. Army, where he worked with Geisel—Jones and a gag writer named Michael Maltese created the classic Road Runner cartoons. Both had worked at the Schlesinger studio, which was sold to Warner Brothers outright in 1944, and wanted to make an animated short with no dialogue. What emerged from Jones's drawing board was the determined Road Runner, a creature constantly on the run from his nemesis, Wile E. Coyote. *People* journalist Brock described the Coyote as "the luckless predator who defines failure, whether he is raising a forlorn umbrella in the spreading shade of an incoming boulder or falling victim to Acme products through his own ineptness."

The first Road Runner cartoon was 1949's "Fast and Furry-ous," and was set in the southwestern United States desert. Studio executives at Warner didn't like it, primarily because it had no dialogue, and they were already paying Mel Blanc to do the voices for the cartoons; the Road-runner said only "Beep, beep." But when they learned that U.S. Navy pilots liked to call this out to each other over their radios, they changed their mind, and Jones and Maltese were given the go-ahead. According to Dave Kehr, writing in the *International Herald Tribune,* the cartoon "pushed an already abstract genre into something approaching formalism. The geometric purity of the desert landscapes, the elemental conflict between hunter (the desperate, ravenous coyote) and hunted (the insouciant, omnipotent road runner), the relentless rhythm of the simple, black-out gags all combine to create a kind of comic fable that is both modern and classical, situated somewhere between Sisyphus and Sartre." Jones and Maltese made twenty-six cartoons in the series, all set in a bleak landscape devoid of anything save desert sand, a road, some train tracks, a tunnel, and the inevitable cliff. There was usually a mailbox, which the Coyote used to send away for products from the Acme Company with which he might capture his prey. The "Acme" name served as homage to the maker of their camera crane at the studio.

## A Lovable Menagerie

Bugs, Daffy, Elmer, and other members of the madcap crew that Jones helped transform into

In 1995 the famed animator was honored with a star on the Hollywood Walk of Fame. (Photograph courtesy of Hal Garb/AFP/ Getty Images.)

cultural icons have retained their popularity over the decades, thanks in large part to the animator's ability to invest his creations with remarkably human emotions and behaviors. "I never had to leave home to develop any character I ever developed or help develop," Jones wrote in *Chuck Amuck.* "All I had to do was reach down inside my own self, and there lurking was the essence of Daffy Duck, the Coyote or Elmer or [Marvin] Martian. It was simply a matter of bringing it to the surface." "They all share certain characteristics: high energy, expressive eyes, exquisite comic timing, and the ability to surprise us," commented Rose in the *Atlantic* article that called Jones "our greatest invisible actor."

Jones went on to make numerous other short animated works outside of the character-centered series. Like his Road Runner cartoons, others without dialogue are termed especially brilliant by critics. In 1952's "Feed the Kitty," a large bulldog becomes unnaturally attached to the tiny kitten in his household, and allows it to ride on his back. One day, he mistakenly thinks it has been baked, and "The sight of the distraught bulldog, eyes red and cheeks tear-stained, carrying a cat-shaped cookie on his back, is both touching and absurd," declared Canemaker in the *New York Times.* In "One Froggy Evening," a 1955 cartoon, Jones offers a parable of avarice. "Jones has been described as the Michelangelo of cartoonists," Ian Johns stated in the London *Times.* "If so then 'One Froggy Evening' is his Pieta. On the surface it is a shaggy-dog story about a singing, dancing amphibian named Michigan J. Frog who performs brilliantly, but only for his present owner. But the cartoon also manages to plumb the mysteries of greed, human nature and fate, all in six minutes." Jones also won praise for the 1957 short "What's Opera, Doc?," that reduces nineteenth-century German Romantic composer Richard Wagner's sixteen-hour *Der Ring des Nibelungen* cycle to a six-minute musical confrontation between Bugs Bunny and Elmer Fudd.

### An Enduring Legacy

Warner closed its animation studio in 1963, and Jones and many of his team went to Metro Goldwyn-Mayer, where they created shorts for the "Tom and Jerry" series. Then Jones began finding work in a new medium—television. With Geisel, he collaborated on the 1966 holiday classic, *How the Grinch Stole Christmas,* and 1971's *Horton Hears a Who.* He also directed animated TV specials like 1975's *The White Seal,* based on a Rudyard Kipling tale. Even in his sixties, Jones continued to work, for he never earned more from his Warner days than the contractual salary he was paid as an animator

or director. He even won two Oscars for best animated short—the first in 1940 for "Old Glory," and again a decade later with the Pepé Le Pew vehicle "For Scentimental Reasons," but the producers accepted both and took them home. The studios kept all royalties when such works found a new generation of fans via television, and Jones and his colleagues were also left out of the lucrative licensing deals that Warner and MGM signed for merchandise.

Still, by the 1980s Jones's art was highly regarded and exhibited at galleries and museums around the world. Jones also lectured at a number of colleges and universities in the United States and abroad, and in 1996 he received a lifetime achievement award from the Academy of Motion Pictures Arts and Sciences. "I'm still astonished that somebody would offer me a job and pay me to do what I wanted to do. And to this day, that's been the astonishment of my life, and delight of my life and the wonder of my life," the cartoonist told an *Academy of Achievement* interviewer.

---

If you enjoy the works of Chuck Jones, you may also want to check out the following:

The works of pioneering animators such as Tex Avery (1908-1980), Friz Freleng (1906-1995), and Bob Clampett (1913-1984), as well as contemporary animators such as John Lasseter and Genndy Tartakovsky.

---

Jones was making new drawings until a month before his death, which came in Corona del Mar, California, on February 22, 2002. "If influence is measured in the intelligent pleasure given to a huge audience over more than a half-century, then Jones was the Einstein of modern comedy," Richard Corliss stated in *Time.* "After all, just one little letter separates the cosmic from the comic. And Chuck Jones' cartoons proved that those two words, those two worlds, could be one."

## ■ Biographical and Critical Sources

BOOKS

*Contemporary Theatre, Film, and Television,* Volume 6, Gale (Detroit, MI), 1988.

**Jones, who directed some of his most popular cartoons while at Warner Brothers, appeared at the opening of the Warner Bros. Museum in 1996.** (Photograph courtesy of Kim Kulish/Sygma/Corbis.)

Furniss, Maureen, editor, *Chuck Jones: Conversations,* University Press of Mississippi (Jackson, MS), 2005.

*International Dictionary of Films and Filmmakers,* Volume 4: *Writers and Production Artists,* St. James Press (Detroit, MI), 1996.

Jones, Chuck, *Chuck Amuck: The Life and Times of an Animated Cartoonist,* with foreword by Steven Spielberg, Farrar, Straus (New York, NY), 1989.

Jones, Chuck, *Chuck Reducks: Drawings from the Fun Side of Life,* with foreword by Robin Williams, Warner (New York, NY), 1996.

Jones, Chuck, *Stroke of Genius: A Collection of Paintings and Musings on Life, Love and Art,* Linda Jones Enterprises, 2007.

Kenner, Hugh, *Chuck Jones: A Flurry of Drawings,* University of California Press (Berkeley, CA), 1994.

Peary, Danny, and Gerald Peary, editors, *The American Animated Cartoon,* Dutton (New York, NY), 1980.

*PERIODICALS*

*American Film,* July-August, 1985, Leonard Maltin, "What's Up, Doc?"

*Animation Journal,* fall, 1996, Ken O'Brien, "Chuck Jones and MGM: Reevaluating Tom and Jerry"; spring, 1997, David R. Williams, "The Mouse that Chuck Built."

*Atlantic,* December, 1984, Lloyd Rose, "Our Greatest Invisible Actor," p. 124.

*Cinema Journal,* spring, 1969, Robert Benayoun, "The Road Runner and Other Characters."

*Classic Film Collector,* summer, 1976, Jay Rubin, interview with Jones.

*Film Comment,* January-February, 1975, Greg Ford and Richard Thompson, interview with Jones, and Richard Thompson, "Duck Amuck."

*Filmfax,* August-September, 1992, Gregory J.M. Catsos, "A Master of Animated Art: Chuck Jones."

*Filmmakers Newsletter,* April, 1974, John Canemaker, "The Hollywood Cartoon."

*Films and Filming,* September, 1982, John Lewell, The Art of Chuck Jones."

*Funnyworld,* spring, 1971, Michael Barrier, interview with Jones.

*Globe and Mail* (Toronto, Ontario, Canada), December 30, 1994, Geoff Pevere, "What's Up, Doc," p. C3.

*Houston Chronicle,* April 15, 1979, Jeff Millar, "The Biggest Laugh."

*International Herald Tribune,* December 18, 2003, Dave Kehr, "Bugs and Daffy and Greek Myth Movies," p. 20.

*Investor's Business Daily,* December 27, 2002, Curt Schleier, "The Art of Success: Chuck Jones Found Inspiration in the World around Him," p. A4.

*Los Angeles Herald Examiner,* January 21, 1985, "Animator Chuck Jones in Conversation with David Colker and Chris Gulker."

*Los Angeles Times,* August 27, 1978, Wayne Warga, "Chuck Jones—Director behind the Animated Stars."

*Millimeter,* November, 1976, Chuck Jones, "Friz Freleng and How I Grew."

*Newsweek,* October 21, 1985, Ron Givens, "Honoring a Daffy Auteur."

*New York Times,* October 7, 1979, A. Ward, "Master Animator Chuck Jones: The Movement's the Thing"; November 19, 2000, John Canemaker, "A Master of Laughter in Motion," p. 37.

*New York Times Magazine,* December 29, 2002, Eric P. Nash, "His Inner Critter," p. 55.

*Observer* (London, England), April 8, 1979, William Scobie, "Animal Crackers."

*People,* November 13, 1989, Pope Brock, "Chuck Jones," p. 103.

*Publishers Weekly,* August 12, 1996, review of *Chuck Reducks: Drawing from the Fun Side of Life,* p. 71.

*Take One,* September, 1978, Chuck Jones, "Confessions of a Cel Washer."

*Time,* December 17, 1973, Jay Cocks, "The World That Jones Made."

*Times* (London, England), November 29, 2003, Ian Johns, "Return of the Toon Army," p. 20.

ONLINE

*Academy of Achievement Web site,* http://www.achievement.org/ (February 12, 2008), "Chuck Jones: Animation Pioneer."

*Chuck Jones Home Page,* http://www.chuckjones.com (April 1, 2010).

OTHER

*Chuck Jones: Extremes and In-Betweens, A Life in Animation,* (documentary), PBS, 2000.

■ **Obituaries**

PERIODICALS

*Dallas Morning News,* February 23, 2002, Jane Sumner, "Animator Chuck Jones Dies at 89; Leaving Trail of Original Cartoon Characters."

*Entertainment Weekly,* March 8, 2002, Scott Brown, "Drawing Strength: Remembering Chuck Jones, the Genius Who Helped Make Warner Bros. 'Toons Looney," p. 22.

*Hollywood Reporter,* February 25, 2002, "Animator Jones Remembered as 'Wacky' Genius," p. 4.

*New York Times,* February 24, 2002, David M. Herszenson, "Chuck Jones, Animator of Bugs and Daffy, Dies at 89," p. 34.

*People,* March 11, 2002, ""That's All, Folks: Chuck Jones, Whose Wily Pen Begot Bugs Bunny, Led a Truly Animated Life," p. 88.

*Time,* March 4, 2002, Richard Corliss, "Chuck Reducks: Chuck Jones Just Made Cartoons," p. 80.

*Variety,* March 4, 2002, Richard Natale, obituary of Jones, p. 62.*

# Elia Kazan

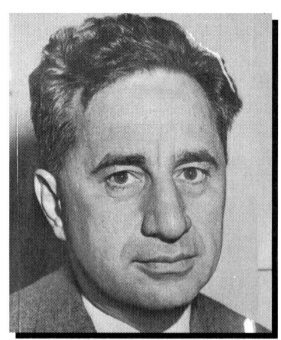

(Photograph courtesy of The Library of Congress.)

## ■ Personal

Born Elia Kazanjioglou, September 7, 1909, in Constantinople (now Istanbul), Turkey; died September 28, 2003, in New York, NY; son of George (a rug dealer) and Athena (Shismanoglou) Kazan; married Molly Day Thacher (a playwright), December 2, 1932 (died December 14, 1963); married Barbara Loden (an actress), June 5, 1967 (died September 5, 1980); married Frances Rudge, June 28, 1982; children: (first marriage) Judy, Chris, Nick, Katharine; (second marriage) Leo. *Education:* Williams College, A.B., 1930; Yale University School of Drama, graduate study, 1930-32; Group Theatre, apprentice to Lee Strasberg and Harold Clurman, 1932-33.

## ■ Career

Theatrical director, film director, actor, and author. Co-founder of Actor's Studio, 1947. Actor, 1932-41; made his Broadway debut as Louis in *Chrysalis* (also assistant stage manager), Martin Beck Theatre, November 15, 1932; went on to appear in and/or act as stage manager for such Broadway productions as *Men in White, Gold-Eagle Guy, Till the Day I*

*Die, Waiting for Lefty, Paradise Lost,* and *Case of Clyde Griffiths.* Member of Group Theatre, New York, NY, 1936-41; productions included *Johnny Johnson* and *Golden Boy.* Made London debut in *Golden Boy,* 1938. Actor in movies *City for Conquest,* 1941, and *Blues in the Night,* 1941. Radio performer on *The Philip Morris Hour, The Kate Smith Hour,* and *The Group Theatre Radio Program.*

Director of stage plays, including (with Alfred Saxe) *The Young Go First,* 1935, *Casey Jones,* 1938, *Thunder Rock,* 1939, *Five Alarm Waltz,* 1941, *Café Crown,* 1942, *The Skin of Our Teeth,* 1942, *Harriet,* 1943, *One Touch of Venus,* 1943, *Jacobowsky and the Colonel,* 1944, *Deep Are the Roots,* 1945, *Dunnigan's Daughter,* 1945, *All My Sons,* 1947, *A Streetcar Named Desire,* 1947, *Sundown Beach,* 1948, *Love Life,* 1948, (and producer) *Death of a Salesman,* 1949, *Camino Real,* 1953, *Tea and Sympathy,* 1953, *Cat on a Hot Tin Roof,* 1955, (and producer) *The Dark at the Top of the Stairs,* 1957, *J.B.,* 1958, *Sweet Bird of Youth,* 1959, *After the Fall,* 1964, *But for Whom Charlie,* 1964, and *The Changeling,* 1964. Also involved with, but not director of, *Marco Millions* and *Incident at Vichy.*

Director of films, including *A Tree Grows in Brooklyn,* 1945, *Boomerang,* 1947, *Gentleman's Agreement,* 1947, *Pinky,* 1949, *Panic in the Streets,* 1950, *A Streetcar Named Desire,* 1951, *Viva Zapata!,* 1953, *Man on a Tightrope,* 1953, *On the Waterfront,* 1954, *East of Eden,* 1955, *Baby Doll,* 1956, *A Face in the Crowd,* 1957, *Wild River,* 1960, *Splendor in the Grass,* 1961, (and producer) *America, America,* 1963, (and producer) *The Arrangement,* 1969, *The Visitors,* 1972, and *The Last Tycoon,* 1976.

## ■ Member

Screen Directors Guild of America, Screen Writers Guild, Phi Beta Kappa.

## ■ Awards, Honors

*Variety*-New York Drama Critics Poll, 1943, for direction of *The Skin of Our Teeth*, 1947, for *All My Sons*, 1949, for *Death of a Salesman*, and 1959, for *Sweet Bird of Youth*; Antoinette Perry (Tony) Award for direction, 1947, for *All My Sons*, 1949, for *Death of a Salesman*, and 1959, for *J.B.*; Academy Award (Oscar), Academy of Motion Picture Arts and Sciences, and Golden Globe Award for direction, both 1947, both for *Gentleman's Agreement*; Donaldson Award for direction, 1947, for *All My Sons*, 1948, for *A Streetcar Named Desire*, 1949, for *Death of a Salesman*, 1954, for *Tea and Sympathy*, and 1955, for *Cat on a Hot Tin Roof*; National Board of Review, Venice Film Festival Award, 1951, for *A Streetcar Named Desire*; Academy Award for best director, Academy of Motion Picture Arts and Sciences, Directors Guild of America Award for outstanding directorial achievement, and Golden Globe Award for best director, all 1955, all for *On the Waterfront*; D.Litt., Wesleyan University, 1954; Golden Globe Award for best director, 1957, for *Baby Doll*, and 1964, for *America, America*; D.Litt., Carnegie Institute of Technology (now Carnegie-Mellon University), 1962; Handel Medallion, New York City's Cultural Award, 1972, for forty-year contribution to the arts; D.W. Griffith Award, Directors Guild of America, 1987, for body of work; honored by American Museum of the Moving Image, 1987; National Board of Review special citation for lifetime achievement, 1996; Academy Award for lifetime achievement, Academy of Motion Picture Arts and Sciences, 1999.

## ■ Writings

*America, America* (novel; also see below), Stein & Day (New York, NY), 1962, reprinted, 1984.

(And director and co-producer) *America, America* (screenplay based on his novel; released in Great Britain as *The Anatolian Smile*), Warner Bros., 1963.

*The Arrangement* (novel; also see below), Stein & Day (New York, NY), 1967.

(And director and co-producer) *The Arrangement* (screenplay based on his novel), Warner Bros., 1969.

*The Assassins* (novel), Stein & Day (New York, NY), 1972.

*The Understudy* (novel), Stein & Day (New York, NY), 1974.

*A Kazan Reader*, Stein & Day (New York, NY), 1977.

*Acts of Love* (novel), Knopf (New York, NY), 1978.

*The Anatolian* (novel), Knopf (New York, NY), 1982.

*Une Odyssée Américaine*, Calmann-Lévy (Paris, France), 1987, translation by Michel Ciment published as *An American Odyssey*, St. Martin's Press (New York, NY), 1989.

*Elia Kazan: A Life*, (autobiography), Knopf (New York, NY), 1988.

*Beyond the Aegean* (novel), Knopf (New York, NY), 1994.

(With Jeff Young) *Kazan: The Master Director Discusses His Films: Interviews with Elia Kazan*, Newmarket Press (New York, NY), 1999, published in Britain as *Kazan on Kazan*, Faber & Faber (London, England), 1999.

*Elia Kazan: Interviews*, edited by William Baer, University Press of Mississippi (Jackson, MS), 2000.

*Kazan on Directing*, preface by Martin Scorsese, Knopf (New York, NY), 2009.

Also author, with Cheryl Crawford, of stage play *The Chain*.

## ■ Adaptations

The play *The Really Big Once* was produced in New York City in 2009 and incorporates Kazan's production notes, memoirs, and letters in telling the story of Kazan's 1953 production of Tennessee Williams's *Camino Real*.

## ■ Sidelights

Director Elia Kazan was associated with some of the greatest productions of theatre and film of the twentieth century, earning two Oscars, three Tony Awards, and four Golden Globes for direction in just over twenty years. In New York, he oversaw the premieres of such Pulitzer Prize-winning stage classics as Thornton Wilder's *The Skin of Our Teeth*, Arthur Miller's *Death of a Salesman*, Tennessee Williams's *A Streetcar Named Desire* and *Cat on a Hot Tin Roof*, and Archibald MacLeish's *J.B.* He also ushered several classic films to the screen, including *Gentleman's Agreement*, *On the Waterfront*, *East of Eden*, and

A legendary director of stage and screen, Kazan played an important role in bringing to life some of America's most treasured plays and movies. (Photograph courtesy of The Kobal Collection/The Picture Desk, Inc.)

*A Face in the Crowd,* and discovered such stars as Marlon Brando, James Dean, and Warren Beatty. During his career Kazan brought an emphasis on psychological realism to American drama, forever changing the art of acting. As Oscar-winning director Martin Scorsese wrote in *Entertainment Weekly:* "Kazan's films had an enormous impact on the way movies were made, I think. They extended the limits of what was emotionally and psychologically possible. They represented the beginnings of what you could call the modern style of American movie-making, and they led the way to . . . the independent movement of today."

Born in Istanbul, Turkey, to parents of Greek descent, Kazan was only four years old when his family immigrated to the United States in 1913. The family settled in New York City, where the elder Kazan joined his brother in running a rug store. In his autobiography *Elia Kazan: A Life,* the director recalled feeling like an outsider, struggling against his father's strictness and searching for a way to fit in. His high school years were forgettable; what he remembered from those years was his pursuit of

stories: "I spent afternoons after school in the stacks of the New Rochelle Public Library, reading books that might explain the intimate problems of my life. Or in the movie houses. Movies became my passion. They were dreams, like my dreams."

Kazan's father expected him to join the family business; instead Kazan entered Williams College, a private liberal arts college in Massachusetts that was filled with wealthy sons of prominent families. Kazan again felt like an outsider, especially since he had to support himself by waiting on tables in fraternities that wouldn't admit him as a member. Again, books "were the solution to my life," he wrote in his memoir. "I lived along with the authors of the great novels; by the light of their stories, I understood the drama of my own life." His alienating college experiences gave him skills he would later use as a director, teaching him how "to be a zealous listener, observe people sharply, form a private opinion—at that time often hostile and envious—but keep it all concealed. I learned the art of the masked observer in a waiter's white coat at the Zeta Psi fraternity house."

## The Theater Beckons

After graduation from Williams College, Kazan enrolled at the Yale School of Drama. Unsatisfied with their unemotional approach to the theater, he left Yale before finishing his degree, but not before meeting his first wife, Molly Day Thacher, an aspiring playwright who would advise him on scripts throughout his career. Kazan then became involved with the avant-garde Group Theatre, a socially conscious company of actors whose political loyalties leaned firmly to the left. There he served an apprenticeship with the renowned acting coaches Lee Strasberg and Harold Clurman and acquired the nickname "Gadget" for his willingness to take on any job, including set building and stage managing. He took small roles as an actor in Group productions and had success in two works by Clifford Odets, the 1935 strike play *Waiting for Lefty* and the 1937 hit drama *Golden Boy.* On the strength of his role in the latter as a gangster, he was cast in similar roles in two Hollywood films, and he later earned the lead in the 1940 Group production of Odets's *Night Music.* That was one of the Group's last productions, however, and Kazan decided that "being an actor in our time and place was a humiliating profession," as he wrote in his autobiography. From then on he would focus on directing.

Kazan had occasionally directed small theater productions throughout the late 1930s and early 1940s and finally had his first hit with Hy S. Kraft's

1942 comedy *Café Crown*. That led to a job directing *The Skin of Our Teeth*, the latest play by Thornton Wilder, already a Pulitzer winner for *Our Town*. Kazan took a play with potentially challenging staging—an immortal family encounters disasters throughout five thousand years—and turned it into a hit. The play earned Wilder another Pulitzer Prize for drama, while Kazan won the New York Drama Critics Award for direction. He followed that up with the 1944 hit *Jacobowsky and the Colonel*, S.N. Behrman's comedy about a Polish Jew escaping the Nazis with the help of an unwitting military man. It would run for almost a year, and cemented Kazan's reputation as a "boy wonder."

Hollywood had taken notice of Kazan as well, and in 1945 he directed his first feature film, *A Tree Grows in Brooklyn*. Based on Betty Smith's best-selling novel, the film recounted the struggle of Francie Smith, the young daughter of Irish immigrants, to escape from poverty and make something of herself. Kazan shot on location in Brooklyn—something unusual for the time—and took advantage of his actors' background and experiences to elicit specific emotions from them, a technique he would frequently use. The film was a hit and earned good reviews; *New York Times* critic Bosley Crowther noted that "Kazan has directed this picture, his first, with an easy naturalness that has brought out all the tone of real experience in a vastly affecting film."

Kazan returned to the theater to work on *All My Sons*, a play by the then-unknown writer Arthur Miller. The two men had a common background: both were sons of salesman who had fallen on hard times during the Depression, and both grew up in

**A reporter goes undercover to expose anti-Semitism in Kazan's 1947 film** *Gentleman's Agreement*, **featuring Gregory Peck.** (Photograph courtesy of 20th Century Fox/The Kobal Collection/The Picture Desk, Inc.)

**Vivien Leigh and Marlon Brando starred in Kazan's 1951 film adaptation of Tennessee Williams's *A Streetcar Named Desire*.** (Photograph courtesy of Warner Bros/The Kobal Collection/The Picture Desk, Inc.)

lower-middle-class New York City neighborhoods. *All My Sons* dealt with the tragic personal consequences that result when a businessman lies about delivering a batch of defective parts to the Air Force, causing the deaths of twenty-one airmen. The play became a hit, running for over a year, and earned Tony Awards for both Kazan and Miller. *New York Times* critic Brooks Atkinson noted that "it is always gratifying to see old hands succeed in the theatre. But there is something uncommonly exhilarating in the spectacle of a new writer bringing unusual gifts to the theatre under the sponsorship of a director with taste and enthusiasm." The critic credited much of the play's success to Kazan's work with the actors, none of whom were stars and thus open to the director's emphasis on psychological realism, with actors bringing real emotion to their roles. The same year that Kazan ushered *All My Sons* to suc-cess, he and two former Group Theatre associates, Cheryl Crawford and Robert Lewis, founded the Actors' Studio to teach this new style of acting.

## Directs Powerful Dramas

The year 1947 would also bring Kazan acclaim as a filmmaker with his adaptation of Laura Z. Hobson's best-selling novel *Gentleman's Agreement*. The film examined the way anti-Semitism thrived in postwar America. A writer (Gregory Peck) poses as Jewish in order to expose the constant slights and subtle discrimination prevalent in both big cities and small towns, and discovers unforeseen consequences on his own personal relationships. *Variety* critic Hobe Morrison's reaction was typical of many critics; he called the film "an improvement over the novel" because it "provides an almost overwhelming emotional experience and thus is not only highly topical, but truly universal." The critic concluded that Kazan's direction "establishes him in the top rank of Hollywood." The film earned three Academy Awards, including Best Picture and Best Director for Kazan.

Kazan returned to Broadway in late 1947 with the first of several collaborations with playwright Tennessee Williams. At the time Williams had enjoyed modest success with *The Glass Menagerie*, but Kazan's hit production of Williams's *A Streetcar Named Desire* would help bring him to prominence as one of the country's best dramatists. Part of the credit was due to Kazan's casting of then-unknown Marlon Brando as Stanley Kowalski, a brute of a man whose turbulent but steady relationship with his wife Stella is upset by the arrival of her sister, Blanche. Brando's passionate performance stunned audiences, who made the show a hit. "People in New York knew that [Kazan], too, had achieved something new, not quite like anything he or anyone else had done before," Richard Schickel noted in *Elia Kazan: A Biography.* The play earned Williams a Pulitzer Prize, and Kazan's 1951 film adaptation of the work would also become a classic, earning twelve Oscar nominations, including Best Director.

Kazan's second collaboration with playwright Arthur Miller led to another enduring American stage classic. *Death of a Salesman* premiered in 1949 and opens with salesman Willy Loman returning home after another less-than-successful sales trip. Through a series of flashbacks, the audience sees that Willy has continually overestimated his abilities, and why his current efforts to find a job closer

**The classic 1954 film *On the Waterfront* garnered eight Academy Awards, including one for Kazan for best director.**
(Photograph courtesy of Columbia/The Kobal Collection/The Picture Desk, Inc.)

to home are doomed to failure. His hopes for his two sons have been similarly disappointing, and the play ends with Willy's suicide. The play earned rave reviews and eventually a Tony Award and Pulitzer Prize. Kazan earned his second Tony Award for direction as well; as a *Time* reviewer noted, "a brilliant director, Elia Kazan, gives the whole thing edge and shape. Thanks to Kazan, a deeply human story catches the special resonance of the stage."

## A Controversial Decision

By 1952 Kazan had reached the pinnacle of success in both theater and films, and had developed a reputation as a left-leaning social critic. In fact, Kazan had been a member of the Communist Party during mid-1930s, although he resigned after less than two years, disgusted with how the Party had tried to take over the Group Theatre. The director "never surrendered his social zeal," screenwriter Budd Schulberg wrote in an *American Film* article on Kazan. "The identification with the oppressed that brought him into the Communist Party during the depths of the Depression was to stay with him all his life, and would inspire and inform much of his best work." Thus it surprised many colleagues when Kazan agreed to testify before the House Un-American Activities Committee (HUAC) in 1952. HUAC's efforts to identify Communists working in Hollywood had already led to the blacklisting of ten screenwriters and directors, and the witch hunt now had Kazan in their sights. Threatened with the blacklist, Kazan agreed to name members of the Communist Party he had known in the Group Theatre. "Rightly or wrongly, at that stage of his artistic life Kazan desperately wanted to continue making films," Dan Georgakas noted in *Cineaste*. "He did not want to return to the theater and he did not wish to become an expatriate."

To the end of his life, Kazan publicly stated that he never regretted his political actions. "If I had my life to live over," he said in a *U.S. News and World Report* interview with Alvin P. Sanoff, "I wouldn't do anything differently. I did exactly what I wanted. It doesn't bother me that I testified . . . and provided [the HUAC] with names. New York intellectuals who had not been in the Communist Party, who only had been to a meeting or two, had no goddamn business making judgments of the actions of people who had been in the party, as I had. How can you say anything unless you've been there?" And yet, as a passage from his autobiography attests, Kazan was profoundly affected by the events surrounding his HUAC testimony. "No one who did what I did, whatever his reasons, came out of it unchanged," he wrote. "Here I am, thirty-five years later, still worrying over it."

Despite being shunned by some former friends and colleagues, Kazan returned to work on new projects on both stage and screen. In 1953 he directed productions of Williams's *Camino Real* and Robert Anderson's *Tea and Sympathy*; the latter play ran for over 700 performances. He also began working with screenwriter Budd Schulberg, another former Communist Party member who had testified before HUAC. The resulting project, 1954's *On the Waterfront*, was named best picture of by the Academy of Motion Picture Arts and Sciences. According to Pauline Kael in her book *I Lost It at the Movies*, "The subject matter of *On the Waterfront* is alienation at the lowest social level." Protagonist Terry Malloy, played by Marlon Brando, is a dockside stevedore who uncovers union corruption, then agonizes over the decision whether or not to expose the wrongdoers. A "political allegory cast in the form of a morality play," as Peter Biskind described it in *Film Quarterly*, *On the Waterfront* presents a quandary "in which informing on criminal associates is the only honorable course of action for a just man. The injunction against informing on friends and colleagues is axiomatic in most societies where the state does not exercise overwhelming moral authority, but the film's dialogue repeatedly defines squealing not as an absolute but a relative matter. It depends on where you stand."

Although many contemporary reviewers only considered the film as a realistic crime drama, some faulted Kazan and Schulberg for using the drama to make excuses for their own political past. In a *Sight and Sound* review, Lindsay Anderson called the film "essentially an extremely artful conjuring trick; underneath its brilliant technical surface, essential conclusions are evaded and replaced by a personal drama whose implications are entirely different." Such mixed feelings about the movie did not prevent *On the Waterfront* from becoming a popular and critical success. It earned eight Oscars, including best film and best director, and as *New York Times* critic A.H. Weiler remarked, "Despite its happy ending, its preachments and a somewhat slick approach to some of the facets of dockside strife and tribulations, *On the Waterfront* is moviemaking of a rare and high order." The drama is still considered one of the finest American films ever made. As Roger Ebert of the *Chicago Sun-Times* concluded in reviewing the film 45 years later: "The acting and the best dialogue passages have an impact that has not dimmed; it is still possible to feel the power of the film and of Brando and Kazan, who changed American movie acting forever."

## One Success after Another

Kazan had made a triumphant return to filmmaking and returned to New York to prove himself once again on Broadway. During the late 1950s he worked with some of the stage's most important playwrights. He directed Williams's *Cat on a Hot Tin Roof* in 1955 and *Sweet Bird of Youth* in 1959, and William Inge's *The Dark at the Top of the Stairs* in 1957, earning Tony nominations for all three works. In 1958 he debuted Archibald MacLeish's *J.B.*, a modern reworking of the Biblical story of Job told in verse. Despite the challenging subject, Kazan's version became a hit, earning a Pulitzer Prize and Tony Award. It also brought Kazan his third Tony for best director.

Despite these Broadway successes, the late 1950s are better known for Kazan's films. *East of Eden* appeared in 1955 and was adapted from John Steinbeck's novel about two brothers competing for the approval of their strict father, a California rancher. Today the film is a cult classic, best remembered for introducing actor James Dean to audiences, but it

actually received mixed reviews on its first run. *New York Times* critic Crowther, for instance, regarded *East of Eden* as a work full of "energy and intensity but little clarity and emotion. It is like a great, green iceberg, mammoth and imposing but very cold." Andrew Sarris, in a *Film Culture* piece, said the work was "the deepest film Kazan has ever made and, in many respects, the best," though he also warned that the movie "has serious structural flaws. . . . Puzzling shifts in feeling in the main characters are unexplained." The film was also notable for being "Kazan's first color film and his first CinemaScope production," as Sean Axmaker noted on the *Turner Classic Movies* Web site. "He handles both magnificently. He shoots in longer takes, which gives the film the slower pace of an older age and draws the eye to Dean's restlessness and nervous spontaneity, which stands out against the calm and control of the rest of cast."

**Iconic actor James Dean (left) made his big-screen debut in 1955 in Kazan's *East of Eden*, based on John Steinbeck's novel.** (Photograph courtesy of Warner Bros./The Kobal Collection/The Picture Desk, Inc.)

Kazan once again worked with Williams for 1956's *Baby Doll,* a film he both produced and directed. Highly controversial because of its steamy sexual nature, the film took Williams's story of one man's obsession with a half-witted Southern nymphet and turned it into "just possibly the dirtiest American-made motion picture that has ever been legally exhibited," according to a *Time* reviewer. While the critic noted that the film's intent was to "arouse disgust" for the characters, "the moviegoer can hardly help wondering if the sociological study has not degenerated into the prurient peep." The film was condemned by the Catholic Legion of Decency, limiting its run, but the Hollywood Foreign Press Association awarded Kazan a best director Golden Globe Award for the comic film. To the late French director Francois Truffaut, in his book *The Films in My Life,* the movie's appeal outweighed its flaws. "We know . . . that Elia Kazan has nothing more to say to us than what his screenplay writers have written for him, and at the same time that he [knows] best of all how to reveal actors to themselves. The second time we see *Baby Doll,* we discover a second film which is still richer. Whether it is a work of genius or mere talent, whether decadent or generous, profound or brilliant, *Baby Doll* is fascinating."

A second collaboration with screenwriter Budd Schulberg, 1957's *A Face in the Crowd,* covered a topic still debated today: whether television plays too important a role in politics. The film shows how a media-created monster, the hillbilly singer "Lonesome" Rhodes (played by comic Andy Griffith in his first dramatic role), overdoses on political power and runs amok through the American consciousness. Though criticized in its time for its often over-the-top pacing and imagery, *A Face in the Crowd* has since achieved cult status as a satiric cautionary tale. "*A Face in the Crowd* peered into a glass darkly at the prospect of a mob mentality that might rise from the mud and follow the tune of a malignant Pied Piper," James Wolcott wrote in *Vanity Fair* on the occasion of the film's fiftieth anniversary. "While contemporary reviewers scoffed at the prospect of a hayseed fireball like Lonesome Rhodes becoming a national sensation, Kazan-Schulberg's depiction of the packaging and marketing of fake authenticity now looks prophetic, if a trifle overcooked." *A.V. Club* reviewer Noel Murray noted that "Kazan varies his shooting style, alternating between portraiture, expressionism, and docu-realism for a look and rhythm that's about 15 years ahead of its time." The result, *New York Times* critic A.O. Scott concluded, is that "more than 50 years after its first release *A Face in the Crowd,* Elia Kazan and Budd Schulberg's furious fable of media populism run amok, has lost surprisingly little resonance."

Kazan worked with another Pulitzer Prize-winner in filming William Inge's original screenplay for 1961's *Splendor in the Grass.* The film introduced future star Warren Beatty, who played one of two young lovers struggling against parental and social expectations during the 1930s. "*Splendor* covers territory that Kazan knows well: the self and how he or she negotiates the social world, and, more particularly, the psychic, emotional, and economic damage that this world can impose on the individual, and how she or he can—or cannot—withstand those pressures," Carole Zucker remarked in *Cineaste.* The critic added that "with the benefit of time and a general reappraisal of Kazan's oeuvre, *Splendor* looks considerably more accomplished as a portrait of the dark side of Americana." The film would be Kazan's last commercial success as a filmmaker.

### Kazan's Literary Career

Increasingly, the director was considering creating his own material to direct. When he had difficulty securing financing for a screenplay based on his uncle's journey from Turkey to America, he published it as a novel, 1962's *America, America.* He eventually created a film version, which debuted in 1963 under the same title. The film was shot in black-and-white (to give it a documentary feel) and lasted nearly three hours in telling the epic story of an immigrant's journey to America. It was not a box office hit but earned generally favorable reviews. It earned Kazan Oscar nominations for best picture, best writing, and best direction, as well as a Golden Globe for best director. Critic Schickel considered it one of the director's finest efforts, writing in his biography that *America, America* was "a striking film, one that was not quite like anything a major American director had ever accomplished. More than any of his films it achieves that simple and rather artless realism that was at the heart of his aesthetic."

Kazan directed a few plays during the early 1960s, most notably Arthur Miller's *After the Fall.* The 1964 production marked the first time the two men had worked together since Kazan's HUAC testimony, the first production of the Repertory Theatre of Lincoln Center—which had been founded under the direction of Kazan and producer Robert Whitehead—and the first major role for Kazan's then-mistress and future second wife, Barbara Loden. The autobiographical play, based on Miller's relationship with his late ex-wife, actress Marilyn Monroe, was a hit and earned Loden a Tony Award for best actress. But Kazan never had another hit production with the Lincoln Center company, perhaps because his style was not suited to the classic plays that were the company's mission, and he left stage directing behind after the 1964-65 season.

Instead, Kazan returned to novels and the occasional film. His second book, 1967's *The Arrangement,* was a surprise best seller, selling nearly four million copies. The story was a thinly veiled version of Kazan's own romantic history, presenting an advertising executive trying to balance both a wife and a mistress, and eventually abandoning his career and simplifying his life. It captured something about the social changes of the 1960s; as *New York Times* critic Eliot Fremont-Smith noted, "it does deal with feelings and fantasies that are serious, contemporary and not uncommon . . . stirring up from the bottom of his cauldron tasty rewards—nice, subtle surprises of observation." Kazan turned the book into a film in 1969, but it was not as successful as the novel.

Although Kazan would make two more films during his lifetime—1972's *The Visitors,* based on his son Chris's script, and 1976's *The Last Tycoon,* based on the F. Scott Fitzgerald novel—he would have more success as a novelist during the remainder of his life. While his 1972 novel *The Assassins* dealt with the murder of a drug dealer on an Air Force base, the rest of his novels—*The Understudy* (1974), *Acts of Love* (1978), and *America, America* sequels *The Anatolian* (1982) and *Beyond the Aegean* (1994)—once again drew on autobiographical subjects. Most of these novels were moderate successes, earning critical attention and hitting best seller lists.

With his willingness to draw on his own life in his fiction, it surprised few people when Kazan produced an extremely frank memoir in 1988, *Elia Kazan: A Life.* He described details of his three marriages and numerous liaisons with a zeal that surprised some. "No serious writer has made such free use of the now widely accepted (even expected) tell-all confessional mode in an autobiography," remarked *Washington Post Book World* contributor Bruce Cook. "It's not simply a matter of kiss-and-tell, but rather of spilling everything. He has fed off women—love, sex—drawing nourishment for his ego and art, regretting only the inconvenient duplicity made necessary by his marriages." In a *New York Review of Books* piece on the autobiography, David Denby saw Kazan's work this way: "Absurdly garrulous, and often coarse to the point of moral unconsciousness, [the author] tells so much—airing other people's critical opinions of his behavior as well as his own self-explanations and doubts—that he almost asks us to catch him fibbing, evading. He may be an egotist, but he is not vain, and his autobiography, for all its loutish demand on our patience, is also a soulful portrait of a man flailing about in a thicket of desire and guilt."

Kazan was just as open in sharing his thoughts on the art of directing. He donated all his script notes, journals, and papers to Wesleyan University, and the 2009 book *Kazan on Directing* was drawn from these materials. "This book is a lot of things," John Simon remarked in *New Criterion.* "It is a fascinating account of how a master director works, much of it in detailed passages too long to quote. It offers abundant insight into the unique psyche and mentality of a genius. It affords often shocking revelations of the prudishness and parochialism of yesterday's Hollywood. It sheds light on well-known actors. It is also, quite simply, a good read."

**A Lasting Legacy**

Kazan had one last turn in the limelight in 1999, when the Academy of Motion Picture Arts and Sciences decided to bestow him an honorary award for

In 1999 Kazan, who had been vilified for cooperating with the House Un-American Activities Committee decades earlier, received a controversial Academy Award for his lifetime contribution to film. (Photograph courtesy of Timothy A. Clary/AFP/Getty Images.)

lifetime achievement. The decision brought up his old history with HUAC, as many in the film community felt that someone who had named names should not be so honored. (In fact, groups such as the American Film Institute had already voted to deny Kazan recognition based on his political past.) There were protests at the ceremony, and some actors and filmmakers in the audience refused to stand or even applaud his award. Kazan refused to apologize for his past actions or even acknowledge the controversy; instead he responded to the award by saying, "Thank you, and now I can just fade away."

---

If you enjoy the works of Elia Kazan, you may also want to check out the following films:

*How Green Was My Valley,* directed by John Ford, 1941.

*Angela's Ashes,* directed by Alan Parker, 1999.

*Atonement,* starring Keira Knightley and James McAvoy, 2007.

---

Kazan died in 2003, and while most obituaries commented on the ongoing controversy that surrounded him, they all acknowledged his stellar career as a director. During his career, actors under his direction received twenty-one Academy Award nominations, with nine picking up the Oscar. He was also an innovator in the use of location shooting. "*On the Waterfront, East of Eden, Baby Doll,* and *Wild River* make wonderful use of on location shooting, displaying a strong response to the interplay between environment, actor and characterization," Richard Lippe observed in *CineAction.* "Kazan also made expert use of deep focus photography and understood the importance time and space have for the medium." As film critic and former director John Foote concluded on the *In Contention* Web site: "Kazan directed some of the greatest films of all time, superb studies of life in America as real as he could make them at that time in history. His films were gritty and authentic, filled with characters we felt we knew or had encountered in life, populated with brilliant performances. Like him, hate him, admire him, despise him, it cannot be denied his work had an extraordinary impact on so many to follow."

## ■ Biographical and Critical Sources

*BOOKS*

*Contemporary Literary Criticism,* Gale (Detroit, MI), Volume 6, 1976, Volume 16, 1981, Volume 63, 1991.

Baer, William, editor, *Elia Kazan: Interviews,* University Press of Mississippi (Jackson, MS), 2000.

Guernsey, Otis L., Jr., editor, *Broadway Song and Story: Playwrights/Lyricists/Composers Discuss Their Hits,* Dodd, Mead (New York, NY), 1986.

*International Dictionary of Films and Filmmakers,* Volume 2: *Directors,* St. James Press (Detroit, MI), 1991.

Jones, David Richard, *Great Directors at Work,* University of California Press (Berkeley, CA), 1986.

Kael, Pauline, *I Lost It at the Movies,* Little, Brown (Boston, MA), 1965.

Kazan, Elia, *America, America,* Stein & Day (New York, NY), 1962, reprinted, 1984.

Kazan, Elia, *A Kazan Reader,* Stein & Day (New York, NY), 1977.

Kazan, Elia, *Elia Kazan: A Life,* Knopf (New York, NY), 1988.

Kazan, Elia, *Kazan on Directing,* preface by Martin Scorsese, Knopf (New York, NY), 2009.

Kazan, Elia, and Jeff Young, *Kazan: The Master Director Discusses His Films: Interviews with Elia Kazan,* Newmarket Press (New York, NY), 1999, published in Britain as *Kazan on Kazan,* Faber & Faber (London, England), 1999.

Murphy, Brenda, *Tennessee Williams and Elia Kazan: A Collaboration in the Theatre,* Cambridge University Press (New York, NY), 1992.

Schickel, Richard, *Elia Kazan: A Biography,* HarperCollins (New York, NY), 2005.

*Shots in the Dark: A Collection of Reviewers' Opinions of Some of the Leading Films Released between January 1949 and February 1951,* Allen Wingate (London, England), 1951.

Truffaut, Francois, *The Films in My Life,* Simon & Schuster (New York, NY), 1978.

*PERIODICALS*

*American Film,* July-August, 1988, Budd Schulberg, review of *Elia Kazan: A Life,* p. 55.

*Chicago Sun-Times,* March 21, 1999, Roger Ebert, review of *On the Waterfront,* p. 5.

*CineAction,* winter, 2010, Richard Lippe, "Elia Kazan: 1909-2009 A Man in Conflict," p. 6.

*Cineaste,* fall, 2006, Carole Zucker, "Love Hurts: Performance in Elia Kazan's *Splendor in the Grass,*" p. 18; winter, 2009, Dan Georgakas, "Elia Kazan: The Cinema of an American Outsider," p. 77.

*Entertainment Weekly,* December 26, 2003, Martin Scorsese, "Farewell: Martin Scorsese Pays Tribute to Elia Kazan."

*Film Culture,* May-June, 1955, Andrew Sarris, review of *East of Eden.*

*Film Quarterly,* fall, 1975, Peter Biskind, "The Politics of Power in *On the Waterfront.*"

*New Criterion,* September, 2009, John Simon, "A Director's Notes," p. 18.

*New York Review of Books,* May, 1988, David Denby, review of *Elia Kazan: A Life.*

*New York Times,* March 1, 1945, Bosley Crowther, review of *A Tree Grows in Brooklyn;* Feb. 9, 1947, Brooks Atkinson, "Welcome, Stranger," review of *All My Sons;* November 12, 1947, Bosley Crowther, review of *Gentleman's Agreement;* July 29, 1954, A.H. Weiler, review of *On the Waterfront;* March 10, 1955, Bosley Crowther, review of *East of Eden;* February 21, 1967, Eliot Fremont-Smith, "All About Eddie"; March 2, 2008, A.O. Scott, review of *A Face in the Crowd,* p. 3; January 7, 2010, Joseph Berger, "A New Look at an Old Quarrel Over *On the Waterfront,*" p. A28.

*Sight and Sound,* January-March, 1955, Lindsay Anderson, "The Last Sequence of *On the Water-front.*"

*Time,* February 21, 1949, review of *Death of a Salesman;* December 24, 1956, review of *Baby Doll.*

*U.S. News and World Report,* June 6, 1988, Alvin P. Sanoff, "'I'm Not Afraid of Anything,'" p. 55.

*Vanity Fair,* March, 2007, James Wolcott, "An Unforgettable Face," p. 228.

*Variety,* November 12, 1947, Hobe Morrison, review of *Gentleman's Agreement.*

*Washington Post Book World,* May 8, 1988, Bruce Cook, review of *Elia Kazan: A Life.*

*ONLINE*

*A.V. Club,* http://www.avclub.com/ (May 17, 2005), Noel Murray, "Controversial Classics."

*In Contention,* http://incontention.com/ (June 5, 2009), John Foote, "Elia Kazan Sparks Renewed Interest."

*Turner Classic Movies,* http://www.tcm.com/ (April 4, 2010), Sean Axmaker, review of *East of Eden.*

*OTHER*

Epstein, Michael, "Arthur Miller, Elia Kazan and the Blacklist: None without Sin," *American Masters Series,* PBS, 2003.

■ **Obituaries**

*PERIODICALS*

*Chicago Tribune,* September 29, 2003, Section 2, pp. 1, 6.

*Los Angeles Times,* September 29, 2003, pp. A1, A20.

*New York Times,* September 29, 2003, pp. A1, A20.

*Washington Post,* September 29, 2003, pp. A1, A29.*

# Nikos Kazantzakis

## ■ Personal

Surname also transliterated "Kazantzakes" and "Kazantzake"; born February 18, 1883, in Heraklion (one source says Candia), Crete; died of complications of leukemia, October 26, 1957, in Freiburg, West Germany; buried in Heraklion, Crete; son of Michael (a farmer) and Maria Kazantzakis; married first wife, 1911 (divorced); married Eleni (Helen) Samios, 1945. *Education:* Attended French School of the Holy Cross (Naxos, Crete), 1897-1899, and Gymnasium (Heraklion, Crete), 1899-1902; received law degree from University of Athens, 1906; further study in Paris, Germany, and Italy, 1906-1910.

## ■ Career

Writer and traveler. Held various posts in the Greek government, c. 1919-46, including director general in the Ministry of Public Welfare, 1919-27, minister of state, 1945, and minister of national education, c. 1945-46; served in Antibes, France, as director of UNESCO's Bureau of Translations of the Classics, 1947-48.

## ■ Member

Greek Writers Society (president, beginning in 1950).

## ■ Awards, Honors

Received Lenin Peace Prize from the Soviet Union, 1957; nominated several times for Nobel Prize for literature.

## ■ Writings

*FICTION*

*Ophis kai krinos* (novella), [Athens, Greece], 1906, translation with introduction and notes by Theodora Vasils published as *Serpent and Lily: A Novella With a Manifesto* (includes essay "The Sickness of the Age"), University of California Press (Berkeley, CA), 1980.

*Toda-Raba: Moscou a Crie* (novel; originally written in French), [Paris, France], 1934, reprinted, Plon (Paris, France), 1962, translation by Amy Mims published as *Toda Raba,* Simon & Schuster (New York, NY), 1964.

*Le Jardin des rochers* (novel; originally written in French), [Amsterdam, Netherlands], 1936, reprinted, Plon (Paris, France), 1959, translation by Richard Howard published as *The Rock Garden* (includes passages from *The Saviors of God* [also see below]), Simon & Schuster (New York, NY), 1963.

*Bios kai politeia tou Alexi Zorba* (novel), first published in 1946, reprinted, Diphros (Athens, Greece), 1957, translation by Carl Wildman published as *Zorba the Greek,* introduction by Ian Scott-Kilvert, J. Lehmann, Simon & Schuster (New York, NY), 1953.

*Ho Kapetan Michales* (novel), first published in 1953, reprinted, Diphros (Athens, Greece), 1957, translation by Jonathan Griffin published as *Freedom or Death*, preface by A. Den Doolaard, Simon & Schuster (New York, NY), 1956, reprinted, 1983, published as *Freedom and Death*, Faber (London, England), 1956.

*Ho Christos xanastavronetai* (novel), first published in 1954, reprinted, Diphros (Athens, Greece), 1957, translation by Jonathan Griffin published as *The Greek Passion*, Simon & Schuster (New York, NY), 1954, published as *Christ Recrucified*, Cassirer (London, England), 1954.

*Ho teleftaios peirasmos* (novel), first published in 1955, reprinted, Diphros (Athens, Greece), 1959, translation with afterword by P.A. Bien published as *The Last Temptation of Christ*, Simon & Schuster (New York, NY), 1960, published as *The Last Temptation*, Cassirer (London, England), 1961.

*Ho phtochoules tou Theou* (novel), Diphros (Athens, Greece), 1956, translation by P.A. Bien published as *Saint Francis*, Simon & Schuster (New York, NY), 1962, published as *God's Pauper: St. Francis of Assisi*, Cassirer (London, England), 1962.

*Hoi aderphophades* (novel), first published in 1963, translation by Athena Gianakas Dallas published as *The Fratricides*, Simon & Schuster (New York, NY), 1964, reprinted, 1984.

*Megas Alexandros* (juvenile), first published in 1979, translation by Theodora Vasils published as *Alexander the Great*, Ohio University Press (Athens, OH), 1982.

*Sta palatia tes Knosou: Historiko mythistorema gia paidia* (juvenile), Ekdoseis Kazantzake, 1981, abridged and edited translation by Themi and Theodora Vasils published as *At the Palaces of Knossos*, Ohio University Press (Athens, OH), 1988.

### POETRY

*Odysseia*, first published in 1938, reprinted, Diphros (Athens, Greece), 1960, translation with synopsis and notes by Kimon Friar published as *The Odyssey: A Modern Sequel*, Simon & Schuster (New York, NY), 1958, reprinted, 1985.

*Tertsines*, [Athens, Greece], 1960.

*Symposion*, first published in 1971, translation by Theodora and Themi Vasils published as *Symposium*, Crowell (New York, NY), 1973.

Poetry represented in anthologies, including *Synchronoi kretikoi poietes*, Barmpounakes, 1983.

### TRAVEL

*Te eida set Rousia*, two volumes, first published in 1928, 2nd edition published as *Taxideuontas: Rousia*, Diphros (Athens, Greece), 1956, translation by

Michael Antonakes and Thanasis Maskaleris published as *Russia: A Chronicle of Three Journeys in the Aftermath of the Revolution*, Creative Arts Book Company (Berkeley, CA), 1989.

*Ho Morias*, first published in 1937, translation by F.A. Reed published as *Journey to the Morea*, Simon & Schuster (New York, NY), 1965, published as *Travels in Greece*, Cassirer (London, England), 1966.

*Ispania*, first published in 1937, reprinted, Diphros (Athens, Greece), 1957, translation by Amy Mims published as *Spain*, Simon & Schuster (New York, NY), 1963, reprinted, Creative Arts Book Company (Berkeley, CA), 1983.

*Iaponia-Kina*, first published in 1938, reprinted, Diphros (Athens, Greece), 1956, translation by George C. Pappgeotes published as *Japan, China*, epilogue by Helen Kazantzakis, Simon & Schuster (New York, NY), 1963, published as *Travels in China and Japan*, Cassirer (London, England), 1964.

*Anglia*, first published in 1941, reprinted, Diphros (Athens, Greece), 1958, translation published as *England: A Travel Journal*, Simon & Schuster (New York, NY), 1965.

*Italia, Aigyptos, Sina, Hierousalem, Kypros, ho Morias*, [Athens, Greece], 1961, translation by Themi and Theodora Vasils published as *Journeying: Travels in Italy, Egypt, Sinai, Jerusalem, and Cyprus*, Little, Brown (Boston, MA), 1975.

*Voyages, Russie*, Plon (Paris, France), 1977.

*Russia: A Chronicle of Three Journeys in the Aftermath of the Revolution*, Creative Arts Book Company (Berkeley, CA), 1989.

Travel works published in six-volume collection titled *Taxideuontas*.

### PLAYS

*Theatro tragodies me Byzantina themata*, three volumes, Diphros (Athens, Greece), 1955–1956.

*Theatro tragodies me diaphora themata* (title means "Theatrical Tragedies With Different Themes"), Diphros (Athens, Greece), 1956.

*Three Plays* (contains *Christopher Columbus, Melissa*, and *Kouros*), translated by Athena Gianakas Dallas, Simon & Schuster (New York, NY), 1969.

*Christopher Columbus* (four-act), Allen Press (Kentfield, CA), 1972.

*Two Plays* (contains *Sodom and Gomorrah* and *Comedy: A Tragedy in One Act*), translated by Kimon Friar and P.A. Bien, North Central Publishing (St. Paul, MN), 1982.

*Buddha*, translated by Kimon Friar and Athena Dallis-Damis, Avant Books (San Diego, CA), 1983.

Also author of plays *O Protomastoras*, 1910, *Niceforos Fokas*, 1927, *Christos* and *Odysseas*, both 1928, and *Ioulianos*, 1945.

CORRESPONDENCE

*Epistoles pros te Galateia*, Diphros (Athens, Greece), 1958, translation by Philip Ramp and Katerina Anghelaki Rooke published as *The Suffering God: Selected Letters to Galatia and to Papastephanou*, Caratzas Brothers (New Rochelle, NY), 1979.

Selected letters also published in *Tetrakosia grammata tou Kazantzakis ston Prebelaki*, three volumes, 1965, and in *Kazantzakes*, 1975.

OTHER

*Salvatores Dei* (essay), first published in 1927, revised edition published as *Salvatores Dei: Astetiki*, Sympan, c. 1960, translation with introduction by Kimon Friar published as *The Saviors of God: Spiritual Exercises*, Simon & Schuster (New York, NY), 1960.

*Historia tes Rosikes logotechnias* (history and criticism), two volumes, first published in 1930, reprinted, Ekdoseis Kazantzake, 1965.

*Anaphora ston Gkreko* (autobiography), first published in 1961, reprinted, Ekdoseis Kazantzake, 1962, translation by P.A. Bien published as *Report to Greco*, Simon & Schuster (New York, NY), 1965.

Translator of works by Dante Alighieri, Wolfgang Johann von Goethe, Homer, Friedrich Nietzsche, Machiavelli, Charles Darwin, Charles Dickens, Harriet Beecher Stowe, William James, Johann Peter Eckermann, and Henri Bergson.

## ■ Adaptations

*The Greek Passion* was adapted for film; *Zorba the Greek* was adapted for a Broadway musical with book by Joe Stein, lyrics by Fred Ebb, and first performed in New York City at the Imperial Theater, November 17, 1968; *Zorba the Greek* was also made into a motion picture featuring Anthony Quinn in the title role by Twentieth Century-Fox in 1964; *The Last Temptation of Christ* was released by Universal as a movie starring Willem Dafoe in 1988.

## ■ Sidelights

Nikos Kazantzakis is often paired in the minds of many Western readers with one of his more lasting fictional creations, the bigger than life, blustery Al-

exis Zorba, an "Everyman with a Greek accent," as a reviewer for *Time* magazine described the character. "He is Sinbad crossed with Sancho Panza. He is the Shavian Life Force poured into a long, lean, fierce-mustached Greek whose 65 years in the Mediterranean sun have neither dimmed his hawk eyes nor dulled his pagan laughter." And for many, he is Anthony Quinn, who portrayed this Rabelaisian protagonist in the movie version of the novel. Life-affirming, hard-drinking, and womanizing, Zorba has crept into the international psyche as a symbol of the free-spirited life, as the ultimate in carpe diem symbolism. Yet his creator, Kazantzakis, was anything but a free spirit. He wrote patriotic novels of the history and culture of his homeland, Crete, and also novels tracing the connection between man and God.

After losing the Nobel Prize in 1957, he wrote to his wife Helen, as noted in her *Nikos Kazantzakis: A Biography Based on His Letters*, that he intended to redouble his literary efforts: "There lay the battlefield suited to my temperament. I wanted to make my novels the extension of my own father's struggle for liberty. But gradually, as I kept deepening my responsibility as a writer, the human problem came to overshadow political and social questions. All the political, social, and economic improvements, all the technical progress cannot have any regenerating significance, so long as our inner life remains as it is at present. The more the intelligence unveils and violates the secrets of Nature, he more the danger increases and the heart shrinks."

Deeply philosophical and spiritual and even somewhat psychically tormented, Kazantzakis is regarded as the most important and controversial writer in twentieth-century Greek literature. The widely translated author of poetry, plays, travel books, and novels, Kazantzakis spent most of his life traveling and studying, seeking to define the purpose of man's existence. In novels such as *Ho teleftaios peirasmos* (*The Last Temptation of Christ*) and *Bios kai politeia tou Alexi Zorba* (*Zorba the Greek*), Kazantzakis probes the conflicts between man's physical, intellectual, and spiritual natures. "My principal anguish and the source of all my joys and sorrows from my youth onward," he wrote in his prologue to *The Last Temptation of Christ*, "has been the incessant, merciless battle between the spirit and the flesh."

Kazantzakis's writing is often appraised as a single body that reveals the author's philosophical and spiritual values; most critics agree that his writings are in this sense autobiographical. But although Kazantzakis's works seek to reconcile the dualities of human nature—mind and body, affirmation and despair, even life and death—some critics have suggested that the author's ultimate concern lies more in striving to overcome inherent human conflicts than in resolving them. "Every one of Kazantzakis' major works can be read as a portrayal of Man's seeking reintegration," explained C.N. Stavrou in the *Colorado Quarterly*. "Some succeed, some enjoy a partial success, some fail, others are completely indifferent or find integration by a repudiation rather than a reconciliation of the eternal duality. But there is never any question that in Kazantzakis' eyes the *desideratum* was the conciliation, not the subjugation of the opposing selves in the human psyche. . . . In his works more importance attaches to the struggle to arrive than to the fact of arrival itself."

While Kazantzakis's stature as a unique voice in modern literature is uncontested, critical opinion about the literary quality of his individual works is frequently divided. Many hold the view that Kazantzakis subordinated his artistic concerns to the philosophical ideas he wanted to express. But some critics admire what they consider the passionate poetic voice in which the author communicates with his readers, and others appreciate the realistic descriptions, metaphors, and profuse imagery that comprise Kazantzakis's writing style.

Kazantzakis remained relatively unknown as a writer for much of his career, finally achieving popularity during the last decade of his life with the 1946 publication of *Zorba the Greek*, his story of the friendship between a bookish intellectual and an unsophisticated peasant. Kazantzakis's fame was intensified by the controversy surrounding several of his subsequent works, beginning with his description of modern Christianity as an ineffective, power-hungry institution in the novel *Ho Christos xanastavronetai* (*The Greek Passion*). Further notoriety ensued with the publication of *The Last Temptation of Christ*, Kazantzakis's 1955 portrayal of an uncertain, emotional Christ troubled by the temptation to renounce his calling and live as an ordinary man. The furor raised by Kazantzakis's work, however, brought the author worldwide notice and established his reputation as a significant writer.

## A Writer Comes of Age

Kazantzakis was born in Heraklion, Crete, in 1883. The son of a peasant farmer and feed dealer, Kazantzakis grew up in a rustic community of shepherds, farmers, and fishermen. His Cretan roots—his love for the peasantry and his early exposure to the Cretans' fervent patriotic desire to overthrow

their Turkish oppressors—would exert a large influence on his writings. Several of his novels take place in Crete, and one of them, *Ho Kapetan Michales* (*Freedom or Death*), depicts the Cretan fight for independence. Several critics suggest that Kazantzakis's peasant heritage manifests itself in the Demotic Greek—the language of ordinary people—which he used instead of the traditional literary Atticistic Greek. Although Kazantzakis's use of the language met with criticism from the intellectual community, contemporary critics seem to agree that the coarse, more concrete language of the common man enhanced his literary style. Perhaps most importantly, Crete provided Kazantzakis with an outlook from which he could embrace various viewpoints that ultimately provided the foundation for his thematic concerns. Kazantzakis came to characterize himself in his autobiography *Anaphora ston Gkreko* (*Report to Greco*) as the possessor of a "Cretan glance," a way of seeing that encompassed seemingly incompatible philosophies and perspectives. This ability to blend opposing attitudes, Kazantzakis believed, arose from both the geographical and cultural orientation of his Mediterranean homeland, equidistant from what he saw as the more passive spirituality of Eastern religion and the materialism of the West.

After witnessing increasing tension on his native island throughout his childhood, Kazantzakis was sent as a teenager to the Greek island of Naxos when the Cretan people rose in violence against the Turks in 1897. On Naxos, Kazantzakis attended school at a Franciscan monastery, where he learned French and Italian, studied Western philosophy, and became exposed to the mysteries of Christianity as taught by the monks. In 1906, after he received his law degree from the University of Athens, Kazantzakis moved to France and became the pupil of the French philosopher Henri Bergson. He wrote a dissertation on the works of German philosopher Friedrich Nietzsche and then studied for four years in Germany and Italy. It was at this time that Kazantzakis began his writing career, translating the works of Western scientists and thinkers, composing verse dramas, and completing the novella *Ophis kai krinos* (*Serpent and Lily*), the first of his books to be published.

Commentators suggest that Nietzsche and Bergson strongly influenced Kazantzakis's thought. The author was especially interested in the concepts Nietzsche outlined in *The Birth of Tragedy*, wherein Nietzsche postulated that the primary tension in human nature exists between man's physical drives and his intellectual and spiritual impulses; this idea is central to Kazantzakis's themes. The author was also profoundly interested in Bergson's concept of progressive spiritual development as man's attempt

**Anthony Quinn's memorable portrayal of Kazantzakis's free spirit Alexis Zorba highlighted the popular 1964 film** *Zorba the Greek.* (Photograph courtesy of 20th Century Fox/The Kobal Collection.)

to escape the constraints of his physical and social existence and unite with what Bergson termed the *elan vital,* the universal creative force. Both *Serpent and Lily,* about a young man's struggle to balance the physical and spiritual elements of his love for a woman, and *Salvatores Dei: Asketiki* (*The Saviors of God: Spiritual Exercises*), an essay in which the author explains his early philosophical concerns, display these influences, as do many of Kazantzakis's subsequent works.

### From Civil Servant to Author

In 1919 Kazantzakis accepted a position as director general in Greece's Ministry of Public Welfare, marking the beginning of his association with the Greek government. He spent the following years coordinating the rescue and feeding of nearly 150,000 Greeks affected by civil war in the Caucasus region of the southern Soviet Union. During the rest of the decade he continued to study and traveled widely in Europe and Asia. After visiting the devastation in Germany following World War I, Kazantzakis became attracted to the principles of social change furthered by communist leader Vladimir Lenin. He subscribed to Marxist philosophy for the next several years and visited the Soviet Union several times before 1927, when he resigned his position in the Ministry of Public Welfare to concentrate on bringing about greater understanding between the people of different cultures through his travel and writing. Kazantzakis remained a continual traveler for his entire life, accepting numerous invitations from foreign governments to visit and write about their nations. He published books discussing his impressions and thoughts about his journeys through countries such as Japan, China, England, Spain, Italy, the Soviet Union, and Greece.

During the 1930s Kazantzakis worked as a translator and author, concentrating primarily on his epic poem *Odysseia* (*The Odyssey: A Modern Sequel*), which he based on the Greek poet Homer's classic epic of the same title. Kazantzakis wrote several drafts of the Demotic poem before publishing it in 1938. Critics consider the poem an autobiographical work that presents a psychological portrait of Kazantzakis—in the mythic character Odysseus—after the author became disillusioned by what he saw as communism's inability to fulfill man's spiritual needs. According to Andreas K. Poulakidas's *Comparative Literature Studies* article, "It was toward the end of his Russian experience that Kazantzakis realized he was like Odysseus, a man of many philosophies and personalities. Like Odysseus, he had been a homeless, rootless, but robust wanderer. . . . Thus, Odysseus is the best symbol for his philosophy, and *The Odyssey: A Modern Sequel* . . . is able to give us an interpretive account of Kazantzakis' psychic state at the time he had this realization." Considering the poem to be his most important work, Kazantzakis confirmed his identification with Odysseus's journey in *Report to Greco*. "I created [Odysseus] in order to face the abyss calmly," he was quoted by Kimon Friar in *Saturday Review*, "and in creating him I strove to resemble him. I myself was being created. I entrusted all my yearning to this Odysseus."

### A Modern Odyssey

*The Odyssey* begins at the point in Homer's epic where Odysseus returns to his native Ithaca, and it narrates the hero's continued adventures around the Mediterranean. Odysseus arrives home and slays his wife's suitors, but he becomes disenchanted with his life and begins a quest for self-understanding and fulfillment that takes him to Sparta, Crete, and Egypt. After unsuccessfully battling an Egyptian pharaoh, he sails inland, dreaming of establishing an ideal community. Odysseus confers directly with God, builds his utopia, and institutes a social order based on spiritual laws, but at the society's dedication, the city is completely destroyed by a massive eruption of the earth, whereupon Odysseus renounces all personal and social ties. He wanders to the southern tip of Africa, where he builds a boat and sails for the South Pole to die alone.

Critics assert that *The Odyssey* functions at an allegorical as well as autobiographical level. As explained by John Ciardi in *Saturday Review*, each episode in the poem is "an allegory of a stage of the soul, and all are threaded together on a series of mythic themes." Odysseus progresses, according to the reviewer, through seven stages of "Bestiality, Battle-Hunger, Lust, Pure Intellect, Despair, Detachment, and finally, Pure Soul." Critics disagree, however, in their interpretations of the poem's ending. Some regard Odysseus's solitary death as Kazantzakis's comment on life's ultimate meaninglessness, while others construe Odysseus's withdrawal as the triumph of man's soul over both his physical existence and the random disasters that endanger it.

Although critics in Greece reportedly reacted negatively to Kazantzakis's use of Demotic language, reception of the work in English translation was generally favorable, with some reviewers admiring the quality of the poetry itself. "The literary achievement of Kazantzakis's *Odyssey* lies in his rich and sonorous language and vivid and original imagery," asserted C.A. Trypanis, for example, in the *Manchester Guardian*. But some critics found the poem outdated and unoriginal. "There is something oddly old-fashioned about this poem. . . . Not a new departure nor a daring experiment, but simply a kind of nostalgia for the days of the grand style and the picaresque epic," noted *Poetry* contributor L.O. Coxe. Still other reviewers were highly enthusiastic in their praise, hailing the epic as a masterpiece. Adonis Decavalles, for instance, in another *Poetry* review, lauded *The Odyssey* as "undoubtedly the greatest long poem of our time, a colossal achievement in art and substance. It is the mature product of Kazantzakis' deep familiarity with the best in world literature and thought, of intense living, traveling, and thinking."

### Finds Popularity with Zorba

The 1940s saw the publication of perhaps Kazantzakis's best-known novel, *Zorba the Greek*. Kazantzakis wrote the autobiographical work during the early part of the decade as a tribute to his close friend George Zorba, with whom he had undertaken a mining venture in Crete in 1917. The author, as quoted by George T. Karnezis in the *Carnegie Series in English: A Modern Miscellany*, professed a deep admiration for Zorba, whom he felt "possessed 'the broadest soul, the soundest body, and the freest cry I have known in my life.'" The novel's narrator is accepted by critics as Kazantzakis's self-portrait as an artist and philosopher.

A tale of the friendship between two men with sharply contrasting personalities and outlooks, *Zorba the Greek* is arguably Kazantzakis's most concrete illustration of his preoccupation with the split between man's physical and intellectual natures.

The book's narrator is an inhibited scholar referred to only as "the boss," who describes himself as having "fallen so low that, if I had to choose between falling in love with a woman and reading a book about love, I should have chosen the book." He decides to participate more fully in life by leaving his studies and reopening his inactive lignite mine in Crete. While awaiting passage to the island from Greece, he meets Zorba, an earthy, uneducated man who seeks experience rather than understanding. Taken with Zorba's vibrant nature and his impulsive offer to accompany him to Crete, the boss hires Zorba as his foreman and personal cook; the remainder of *Zorba the Greek* is a record of how Zorba challenges his employer's outlook. Assuming at first that Zorba is naive, the boss continually misinterprets Zorba's motives. But by the end of the novel, the boss develops a deep reverence for the workman's love for life, which Zorba demonstrates in his ability to dance, work, love, and fight—intensely and wholeheartedly. The boss has come to see him, as quoted by Karnezis, as "a man with warm blood . . . who lets real tears run down his cheeks when he is suffering; and when he is happy he does not spoil the freshness of his joy by running it through the fine sieve of metaphysics."

*Zorba the Greek* met with a favorable reception, although a few critics faulted Kazantzakis for sacrificing the novel's literary aspects—such as a strong plot and individualistic characters—to its philosophical ideas. Other reviewers, however, were enthusiastic, commending the symbolism embodied in Kazantzakis's characterizations of both himself and Zorba. Representing both views was *New Republic* contributor Kimon Friar, who commented, "If read on a literal plane alone, Zorba may be said to have no plot worthy of the name, to be deficient in complexity of characterization, [and] to lack motivation. . . . [But] once the point of view is established, the plan is easily grasped in its magnificent boldness and simplicity, the characters and their actions take on symbolic universality."

Some critics, focusing on Zorba as a literary creation, admired Kazantzakis's success in presenting Zorba's joyful and vital character. "Zorba . . . is funny, ferocious, ingenious, unscrupulous, indomitable, bawdy, sacrilegious and frenzied. Above all, he is terrifyingly, disconcertingly alive," Edmund Fuller asserted in the *New York Times*. "It is in the life force of Zorba himself that [the novel's] uniqueness rests." G.D. Painter offered a similar assessment in the *New Statesman and Nation*, proclaiming *Zorba the Greek* "a novel sweet and elate with sunlight, friendship and happiness, with a life full of both sensations and thoughts; . . . and Zorba, one feels, is among the significant and permanent characters in modern fiction."

## Continues Work in Government and Writing

After completing *Zorba the Greek* Kazantzakis worked in several capacities as a public servant. In 1945 he became the Greek government's minister of state, and he tried for nearly a year to resolve political differences dividing the government before resigning without success. He also served briefly as minister of education during the ensuing civil war before accepting a post in France in 1947 as director of UNESCO's Translation Bureau, which he held until 1948.

The years from 1948 until Kazantzakis's death in 1957 were the most prolific of his career. During this period he published travel essays, plays, and several novels that explored Christian themes, including *Ho Christos xanastavronetai* (*The Greek Passion*), *The Last Temptation of Christ*, *Ho phtochoules tou Theou* (*St. Francis*), and *Hoi aderphophades* (*The Fratricides*). *The Greek Passion*, Kazantzakis's first novel to probe the nature and meaning of Christ's crucifixion, is not one of the author's best-known fictions, but critics consider it among his most powerful and finely crafted. *The Greek Passion* concerns the inhabitants of Lycovrissi, a Greek village under the domination of the Turks in the 1920s. The novel opens with the village elders casting the townspeople in their roles for the following year's enactment of the crucifixion in the annual passion play, and then successfully encouraging the citizens to turn away a group of Greeks seeking refuge from violent Turkish aggression. After the parts have been distributed, however, the actors begin to assume the identities of their characters, and, as a result, crime, hypocrisy, and prostitution in the village begin to decline. Protagonist Manolios, chosen to play the role of Jesus, offers to sacrifice himself as the murderer of the Turkish ruler's son. Further, when the now-starving refugees return, again asking for protection, Manolios accommodates them in Christian fashion by sharing his land and possessions with them. Manolios's deeds infuriate the village priest, who deems him a heretic and incites the residents to demand that the Turkish officials sentence him to death. The villagers, with the aid of the priest, eventually murder Manolios, thereby creating their own twentieth-century version of Christ's martyrdom.

*The Greek Passion*'s negative portrayal of a modern church more concerned with protecting its power than with following Christ's teachings incurred a negative response from the Greek Orthodox Church; Kazantzakis was nearly excommunicated. Reaction to the English translation was mixed, with some critics admiring the passion displayed by the book's characters, message, and presentation, and others panning the novel's violence and complaining that the work's philosophical content diminishes its dramatic effect. Kazantzakis again faced severe criticism from his compatriots with the publication of *Freedom or Death* in 1954. A nonpartisan rendering of Crete's unsuccessful revolt against Turkish rule in 1889, *Freedom or Death* depicts, according to critic and translator P.A. Bien in his afterword to *The Last Temptation of Christ,* "both the good and bad sides of Greek heroism." For his unemotional portrayal, newspapers reportedly labeled Kazantzakis a traitor to Crete and to Greece.

## Most Controversial Novel

A year later, Kazantzakis followed *Freedom or Death* with his most controversial novel, *The Last Temptation of Christ.* Kazantzakis described his work on the book, as quoted by Theodore Ziolkowski in *Fictional Transfigurations of Jesus,* as "a laborious, sacred, creative endeavor to reincarnate the essence of Christ, setting aside the dross, falsehood and pettiness which all the churches and all the cassocked representatives of Christianity have heaped upon this figure, thereby distorting it." A surrealistic fictional biography of Christ, whom Kazantzakis considered to be the supreme embodiment of man's battle to overcome his sensual desires in pursuit of a spiritual existence, the novel focuses on what Kazantzakis imagines as the psychological aspects of Jesus's character and how Christ overcomes his human limitations to unite with God. "In order to mount to the Cross, the summit of sacrifice, and to God, the summit of immateriality, Christ passed through all the stages which the man who struggles passes through," Kazantzakis stated in his prologue to the novel. "That is why his suffering is so familiar to us; that is why we share it, and why his final victory seems to us so much our own future victory. . . . If he had not within him this warm human element, he would never be able to touch our hearts with such assurance and tenderness."

*The Last Temptation of Christ* offers, according to *Atlantic* contributor Phoebe Adams, "the life story of Jesus of Nazareth,. . . the human events from which the worshipful Gospel account was derived and their meaning to the people who experienced

**Acclaimed director Martin Scorsese brought Kazantzakis's controversial novel** *The Last Temptation of Christ* **to the screen in 1988.** (Photograph courtesy of Universal/The Kobal Collection/The Picture Desk, Inc.)

them." The novel—which repeatedly departs from *New Testament* accounts . . . opens with Jesus working as a cross-builder for the ruling Romans in an attempt to repudiate his divinity. The story follows Jesus's struggle to accept God's will, his increasing strength through his realization that he is the Messiah, the gathering of disciples, his preaching and working miracles, his entry into Jerusalem, and ultimately, his crucifixion, during which he experiences his strongest temptation to abandon his commitment to God. Hanging on the cross, Jesus dreams that a guardian angel rescues him and allows him to reject his role as God's representative on earth and live instead as an ordinary carpenter, husband, and father. In his dream he experiences, according to Nancie Matthews in the *New York Times Book Review,* "erotic bliss and a worldly life." Later, however, Judas Iscariot, whom Jesus had ordered to betray him, appears. Angry that Jesus has not carried out the saving of mankind, Judas accuses Jesus of succumbing to Satan, at which point Jesus awakens and affirms his role as Christ.

Angered by *The Last Temptation of Christ*'s presentation of Christ's humanity, the Greek Orthodox Church branded Kazantzakis a heretic and again threatened to excommunicate him. The book was also placed on the Roman Catholic Index of Forbidden Books, most probably because of its depiction of Jesus's desire to marry and beget children. Criticism of the English translation, like that for *Zorba the Greek,* ranged from the disapproving to the highly laudatory. *Christian Century*'s Kyle Haselden expressed disappointment with Christ's characterization, maintaining that Kazantzakis "writes divinely of that which is human. . . . But in depicting that which is divine the novelist is reduced to the human touch." Adams assessed *The Last Temptation*'s Jesus as a literary figure, noting that "this Jesus is not the assured son of God following a pre-accepted path, but a man who, in God's service, . . . assumes something of the character of those epic heroes who choose their deaths—Achilles sailing for Troy under the shadow of the prophecy, or Cuchulainn riding on to battle when he knows his magical luck has left him." More impressed was Matthews, who described *The Last Temptation of Christ* as a "mosaic of all the highlights of the Gospel story, vividly colored by . . . extravagant imagery, which is always richly overflowing but at times is distasteful, too." She concluded, "If the book can be read without prejudice, this will be found a powerfully moving story of a great spiritual victory."

## Final Days of a Peripatetic Writer

Undaunted by *The Last Temptation of Christ*'s fiery reception, Kazantzakis spent his last years traveling and writing. He died from complications of leuke-

mia in 1957 while returning from a visit to China. Because his conflicts with the church resulted in its refusal to conduct a traditional public funeral mass in Greece, the author was buried quietly in Crete. Several more works, including *St. Francis,* a fictional rendering of the life of St. Francis of Assisi, and *The Fratricides,* an incomplete novel about an elderly priest in civil-war-torn Greece, were published posthumously, along with the autobiographical *Report to Greco* and several works for children.

Among his works for younger readers was *Sta palatia tes Knosou: Historiko mythistorema gia paidia* (*At the Palaces of Knossos*), set in the waning days of Minoan power on Crete. Kazantzakis blends myth and history in this tale of the spreading influence of civilized Athens, which supplants the primitive and pagan culture of ancient Crete. Reviewing this young adult novel in *Publishers Weekly,* John Mutter felt that Kazantzakis "paints a dreamlike tapestry of the Cretan magnificence, power, and cruelty."

Discussing Kazantzakis's significance as a writer, Bien noted in his *Nikos Kazantzakis:* "Those who read only sparingly will most likely find Kazantzakis appealing because of the opinions which he promulgated in everything he wrote—more accurately, because of the way he made these ideas incandescent. For some, the ideas themselves will seem less important than the sincerity . . . with which he wrote them. Others, however, will find that he speaks directly to their own needs. . . ." Bien added, "It is doubtful whether future generations will suddenly consider him a superb thinker or craftsman; they may, however, consider him a superb man."

Even in death, Kazantzakis has continued to inspire strong opinions. The 1988 film adaptation of his *The Last Temptation of Christ,* by Martin Scorsese, brought protests from many Christian groups, and even the opening of the Heraklion airport, named in honor of the author, brought protests from homeowners who complained of the noise. Operas have been adapted from his work and his beloved Zorba received a Broadway revival as recently as 2007.

"It is now more than forty years since the death of Nikos Kazantzakis, yet his philosophical and theological views still remain subject to debate," wrote Lewis Owens in a 1998 volume of the *Journal of Modern Greek Studies.* "Dominated by the search for his own idiosyncratic God, Kazantzakis drew upon the many influences that touched his life, particularly Nietzsche, Bergson, Buddha, Lenin, and Christ. His writings show him struggling to give meaning to human existence—in other words, to speak of 'God' in the face of suffering, injustice, and Nietzsche's vehement attack on metaphysics."

If you enjoy the works of Nikos Kazantzakis, you may also want to check out the
following books:

Flannery O'Connor, *Wise Blood,* 1952.
José Saramago, *The Gospel According to
Jesus Christ,* 1991.
Mary Doria Russell, *A Thread of Grace,*
2005.

## ■ Biographical and Critical Sources

*BOOKS*

Bien, Peter, *Nikos Kazantzakis,* Columbia Essays on
Modern Writers Pamphlet No. 62, Columbia
University Press (New York, NY), 1972.
Bien, Peter, *Kazantzakis: Politics of the Spirit,* two
volumes, Princeton University Press (Princeton,
NJ), 2007.
Dombrowski, Daniel A., *Kazantzakis and God,* State
University of New York Press (Albany, NY), 1997.
Kazantzakis, Helen, *Nikos Kazantzakis: A Biography
Based on His Letters,* translated from the French by
Amy Mims, Simon & Schuster (New York, NY),
1968.
Kazantzakis, Nikos, *Zorba the Greek,* translated by
Carl Wildman, Simon & Schuster (New York, NY),
1953.
Kazantzakis, Nikos, *The Last Temptation of Christ,*
translated with afterword by P.A. Bien, Simon &
Schuster (New York, NY), 1960.
Kazantzakis, Nikos, *Report to Greco,* translated by
P.A. Bien, Simon & Schuster (New York, NY),
1965.
Middleton, Darren J.N., and Peter Bien, *God's Strug-
gler: Religion in the Writings of Nikos Kazantzakis,*
Mercer University Press (Macon, GA), 1996.
Prevalakis, Pandelis, *Nikos Kazantzakis and His Odys-
sey: A Study of the Poet and the Poem,* translated by
Philip Sherrard, Simon & Schuster (New York,
NY), 1961.
*Twentieth-Century Literary Criticism,* Gale (Detroit,
MI), Volume 2, 1974, Volume 5, 1976, Volume 33,
1985, Volume 181, 2007.

Ziolkowski, Theodore, *Fictional Transfigurations of
Jesus,* Princeton University Press (Princeton, NJ),
1982.

*PERIODICALS*

*Atlantic,* September, 1960, Phoebe Adams, review of
*The Last Temptation of Christ.*
*Carnegie Series in English: A Modern Miscellany,*
Volume X, 1970, George T. Karnezis, profile of Ni-
kos Kazantzakis.
*Christian Century,* October 5, 1960, Kyle Haselden,
review of *The Last Temptation of Christ.*
*Colorado Quarterly,* spring, 1964, C.N. Stavrou,
profile of Kazantzakis.
*Comparative Literature Studies,* June, 1969, Andreas
K. Poulakidas, profile of Kazantzakis.
*Journal of Modern Greek Studies,* October, 1998, Lewis
Owens, profile of Kazantzakis, pp. 331-348.
*Journal of Modern Literature: Nikos Kazantzakis Special
Number 2,* number 2, 1971-72.
*Manchester Guardian,* March 20, 1959, C.A. Trypanis,
review of *The Odyssey: A Modern Sequel.*
*New Republic,* April 27, 1953, Kimon Friar, review of
*Zorba the Greek.*
*New Statesman and Nation,* September 6, 1952, G.D.
Painter, review of *Zorba the Greek.*
*New York Times,* April 19, 1953, Edmund Fuller,
review of *Zorba the Greek.*
*New York Times Book Review,* August 7, 1960, Nancie
Matthews, review of *The Last Temptation of Christ.*
*Poetry,* December, 1959, Adonis Decavalles, review
of *The Odyssey,* p. 175, and L.O. Coxe, review of
*The Odyssey,* p. 179.
*Publishers Weekly,* November 27, 1987, John Mutter,
review of *At the Palaces of Knossos,* p. 77.
*Saturday Review,* December 13, 1958, John Ciardi,
review of *The Odyssey;* February 6, 1965, review
of *The Fratricides,* p. 37; May 29, 1965, Kimon Friar,
review of *Journey to the Morea,* p. 37; August 14,
1965, review of *Report to Greco,* p. 34.
*Time,* April 20, 1953, review of *Zorba the Greek.*

*ONLINE*

*Nikos Kazantzakis Files,* http://www.historical-
museum.gr/ (January 25, 2010).*

# Margo Lanagan

(Photograph courtesy of Amy Sussman/Contributor/Getty Images Entertainment/Getty Images.)

## ■ Personal

Born 1960, in Newcastle, New South Wales, Australia; children: two sons. *Education:* Studied history at universities in Perth and Sydney, Australia.

## ■ Addresses

*Home*—Sydney, New South Wales, Australia.

## ■ Career

Freelance book editor, technical writer, and author. Has also worked as a secretary and a kitchen hand at a roadhouse.

## ■ Awards, Honors

Writing grant, Literature Board of the Australia Council; Best Book for Young Adults selection, American Library Association (ALA), and Books for the Teen Age list, New York Public Library, both for *White Time;* World Fantasy Award for Best Short Fiction, 2005, for "Singing My Sister Down"; Bram Stoker Award nomination, Horror Writers of America, World Fantasy Award for Best Collection, 2005, Michael L. Printz Award Honor Book, ALA, 2006, Victorian Premier's Literary Awards Prize for Young Adult Fiction, and Golden Aurealis Award for Best Young Adult Short Story, all for *Black Juice;* Older Readers' Book of the Year, Children's Book Council of Australia, 2007, for *Red Spikes;* Michael L. Printz Award Honor Book, ALA, 2009, for *Tender Morsels.*

## ■ Writings

*FICTION*

*Wildgame,* Allen & Unwin (North Sydney, New South Wales, Australia), 1991.

*The Tankermen,* Allen & Unwin (North Sydney, New South Wales, Australia), 1992.

*The Best Thing,* Allen & Unwin (St. Leonards, New South Wales, Australia), 1995.

*Touching Earth Lightly,* Allen & Unwin (St. Leonards, New South Wales, Australia), 1996.

*Walking through Albert,* Allen & Unwin (St. Leonards, New South Wales, Australia), 1998.

*White Time* (short stories), Allen & Unwin (Crows Nest, New South Wales, Australia), 2000, Eos (New York, NY), 2006.

*Treasure Hunters of Quentaris*, Lothian Books (South Melbourne, New South Wales, Australia), 2004.

*Black Juice* (short stories), Allen & Unwin (Crows Nest, New South Wales, Australia), 2004, Eos (New York, NY), 2005.

*Red Spikes* (short stories), Allen & Unwin (Crows Nest, New South Wales, Australia), 2006, Alfred A. Knopf (New York, NY), 2007.

*The Lost Shimmaron 1: Seacastle*, ABC Books (Sydney, New South Wales, Australia), 2007.

*The Lost Shimmaron 2: The Singing Stones*, ABC Books (Sydney, New South Wales, Australia), 2007.

*Tender Morsels*, Alfred A. Knopf (New York, NY), 2008.

Has also written young adult romances under a pseudonym. Contributor to anthologies, including *Click*, Scholastic (New York, NY), 2007, and *Firebirds Soaring: An Anthology of Original Speculative Fiction*, Penguin (New York, NY), 2008.

**Lanagan's *White Time* contains ten imaginative tales of speculative fiction.** (Eos/HarperCollins, 2006. Jacket art © 2000 by Laura Siotos. Reproduced by permission of HarperCollins Publishers Inc.)

■ **Adaptations**

*Tender Morsels* was adapted as an audio book, Brilliance Audio, 2008.

■ **Sidelights**

Margo Lanagan is an Australian writer of novels and short stories targeted at a young adult reading audience. A two-time Michael L. Printz Award Honor Book designee, Lanagan is recognized for the range of her storytelling material—from fantasy to stark realism to retelling of fairy tales—as well as the emotional intensity of her stories. She is best known in the United States for her short story collections *White Time*, *Black Juice*, and *Red Spikes*, and for her teen novel *Tender Morsels*, loosely based on the tale of Snow White.

Lanagan was born in 1960 in Newcastle, New South Wales, Australia, and grew up in the Hunter Valley. As a teenager, she moved to Melbourne, Australia, and then in her twenties she traveled extensively and studied history at universities in Perth and Sydney. The insight and experiences gained from her travels and her education have provided the inspiration for Lanagan's middle-grade and young adult novels as well as her short story collections.

Lanagan's ability to bend genres is a hallmark of her writing. Pushing boundaries, she told *SF Site* interviewer Trent Walters, "is just the way my mind works. I can't say I know the fantasy genre so well that I could consciously go about blurring the boundaries. I only know that the balance of the real and unreal in my stories is pretty much how I see the world. Some weird small thing in the real world strikes me (like misreading a magazine title *Modern Bride* as *Wooden Bride*, out of the corner of my eye) and my mind just builds and builds on it until there's a whole other world there, full of wooden brides!"

Lanagan's first work for young readers, the 1991 title *Wildgame*, announced the author's vivid imagination and genre-crossing abilities. As Macka plays a computer game, an animal jumps out of the screen and onto her lap. Lanagan's fantasy takes on adventuresome overtones when the youngster is confronted with how to get the animal back into the game and its natural habitat before its entire species is imperiled. Similarly, in early novels such as *The Tankermen* and *Walking through Albert*, Lanagan mixes fantasy and adventure with dashes of humor.

**Black Juice, a collection of surrealistic fantasy stories, earned a World Fantasy Award.** (Eos/HarperCollins, 2004. Jacket art © 2005 by Amy Ryan. Reproduced by permission of HarperCollins Publishers Inc.)

### Gains an International Audience

Lanagan's first breakthrough into the U.S. market came with the short story collection *Black Juice,* which includes the stories "Earthly Uses," "Singing My Sister Down," "House of the Many," and "Sweet Pippit." It was described by *Kliatt* contributor Sherry Hoy as "a powerful, evocative collection" that is "not for faint-hearted readers." In *School Library Journal* Sarah Couri wrote that each of the book's ten stories "is strange and startling," providing readers with "a glimpse into weird, wondrous, and sometimes terrifying worlds." The collection was also praised for containing "memorable characters a-plenty" by a *Kirkus Reviews* contributor. Frances Bradburn, writing in *Booklist,* further commented that these fantasy tales are "peopled with empathetic characters who battle nature, individuals, and events." And *Horn Book* contributor Joanna Rudge Long found the stories in the collection "mesmerizing." The volume was awarded the 2006 Michael L. Printz Award Honor Book designation following its publication in the United States.

*White Time,* though published after *Black Juice* in the United States, appeared first in the author's native Australia. *White Time* is another "magical, wondrous collection" that weaves speculative fiction and fantasy into stories that resonate with universal human themes, according to Amy Fiske in the *Journal of Adolescent and Adult Literacy.* Writing for *Booklist,* Holly Koelling also commended this volume, noting that it displays the author's "mastery of the craft," and further noting that "each story underscores Lanagan's talent for inspiring curiosity, disturbing sensibilities, and provoking thought." Reviewing the same book in *School Library Journal,* Alison Follos observed, "Lanagan's themes range from reckoning to healing, and her conflicts tackle eating disorders, terrorists, and self-empowerment." A *Kirkus Reviews* contributor thought that "each compelling entry is rich in imaginative twists and details," and Long, writing for *Horn Book* concluded, "Taut, vivid, original: another winner."

Lanagan's short-story collection *Red Spikes,* which weaves such disparate elements as monkeys, gods, and a changeling, coalesces through the author's "searing prose and bizarre, whimsical vision," according to a *Kirkus Reviews* writer. Containing ten stories, *Red Spikes* presents the stuff of nightmares in a text that features what *Horn Book* reviewer Deirdre F. Baker characterized as "a mixture of earthly dialect and inventiveness" that makes *Red Spikes* "mesmerizing, sometimes horrifying, and occasionally funny." Further praise came from *School Library Journal* reviewer Christi Voth, who felt that Lanagan's "writing is haunting, evocative, and thought-provoking." Likewise, *Booklist* contributor Jennifer Mattson felt that this "razor-sharp assemblage thrusts readers . . . into alien, hermetic environments and uncompromisingly idiomatic points of view." A *Publishers Weekly* contributor called Lanagan's stories "gritty, dark and sometimes very nasty," and, "at their best, worthy of comparison to the fairy tales of Angela Carter."

Remarking on her explorations of the short narrative form, Lanagan remarked to *Journal of Adolescent and Adult Literacy* contributor Fiske that "the short stories that I like to read and write are the sort that gather a whole society and geographical region into a nice tidy incident with a few defined characters, so that there is a feeling of there being lots of detail and interest just beyond the borders of the story. To make a story-world seem real, you have to give the impression of its being complex and as many-layered as the real one(s)." Lanagan added that she likes to create a sense of "disorder" for her audience, telling Fiske, "I want readers, usually, to be inside the main characters' heads, feeling as stressed as they do; I like to watch the way thoughts, under stress, worriedly jump around or circle, how people try to reassure themselves, and sometimes succeed and sometimes make themselves even more fearful."

### Return to the Novel

A longer work of fiction, *Tender Morsels* is a young adult novel in which Lanagan draws from the story "Snow White and Rose Red." The story focuses on two sisters, Branza and Urdda, who live in isolation with their victimized mother, Liga, deep in the forest, until a wild bear and a dwarf draw them out and force each sister to decide between isolation

**A Michael L. Printz Award Honor Book,** *Tender Morsels* **offers Lanagan's take on the Grimm Brothers's "Snow White and Rose Red."** (Alfred A. Knopf, 2008. Book cover copyright © 2008 by Knopf Children. Used by permission of Alfred A. Knopf, an imprint of Random House Children's Books, a division of Random House, Inc.)

*Red Spikes* **presents a variety of dark, evocative stories featuring sophisticated prose and thought-provoking concepts.** (Alfred A. Knopf, 2007. Jacket art copyright © 2006 Knopf Children. Reproduced by permission of Alfred A. Knopf, an imprint of Random House Children's Books, a division of Random House, Inc.)

and the risks of human society. The author told Jeff VanderMeer of *Clarkesworld Magazine* Web site, "I always wanted the story to feel like a fairytale, and the main third-person narration I wanted to have the weird combination of privileged knowledge and slight distance, slight hovering-over the subjects' lives and stories, slight objectivity, that traditional oral-based stories often have."

While noting the novel's complexities, *School Library Journal* contributor Carolyn Lehman assured her readers that Lanagan's text is "beautifully written and surprising" in its exploration of "what it means to be human." The author's "trademark linguistic gyrations bring to life" her "utterly fresh take" on the classic Brothers Grimm story, according to a *Kirkus Reviews* writer, and she "offers up difficult truths . . . that are as sobering as they are triumphant," according to Baker in *Horn Book*. Similarly,

*Booklist* contributor Ian Chipman termed the novel "a marvel to read and [a book that] will only further solidify Lanagan's place at the very razor's edge of YA speculative fiction." Likewise, a *Publishers Weekly* reviewer found the work "extraordinary and often dark," while another *Horn Book* contributor commended its "mythic imagery and masterful prose." *Tender Morsels* was named a 2009 Michael L. Printz Award Honor Book.

Discussing her transition between writing novels and short fiction with Fiske, Lanagan explained: "Short stories are more instantly gratifying to write. Even when they don't work, you know soon whether a story idea is going to work on its own, or require some other idea and more time to animate it. Also, it doesn't take a lot of work to hold the story in its entirety in my head, which means that I can fit short stories into the rest of my life more easily. Writing novels, you really have to put aside good slabs of weeks to keep the thing operational."

---

If you enjoy the works of Margo Lanagan, you may also want to check out the following books:

Kelly Link, *Stranger Things Happen,* 2001.
Nancy Werlin, *Impossible,* 2008.
Maggie Stiefvater, *Shiver,* 2009.

---

Speaking with VanderMeer of *Clarkesworld Magazine* Web site, Lanagan expounded on her decision to become an author: "I write because, when I was pushing thirty, I decided that, as I had no burning ambition to do anything in particular, I needed to choose an activity to focus on that I could possibly develop into a career, but that was also rewarding in itself. I think perhaps I concentrated too hard on the career-development aspect for a while; these days it's primarily the reward-in-itself that I try to keep foremost in my mind as I write." "Inspiration is pretty much everywhere," Lanagan noted in an essay on the *Allen & Unwin Web site.* "I get it from reading both good and bad writing, from watching and listening to people, from landscapes and cityscapes, from wildlife documentaries and building sites and classrooms and music."

## ■ Biographical and Critical Sources

PERIODICALS

*Australian Book Review,* October, 1995, review of *The Best Thing,* p. 58; November, 1996, review of *Touching Earth Lightly,* p. 57; November, 2000, review of *White Time,* p. 57.

*Booklist,* April 15, 2005, Frances Bradburn, review of *Black Juice,* p. 1463; August 1, 2006, Holly Koelling, review of *White Time,* p. 75; October 1, 2007, Jennifer Mattson, review of *Red Spikes,* p. 58; August 1, 2008, Ian Chipman, review of *Tender Morsels,* p. 69.

*Horn Book,* May-June, 2005, Joanna Rudge Long, review of *Black Juice,* p. 330; January-February, 2006, review of *Black Juice,* p. 11; July-August, 2006, Joanna Rudge Long, review of *White Time,* p. 445; November-December, 2007, Deirdre F. Baker, review of *Red Spikes,* p. 683; September-October, 2008, Deirdre F. Baker, review of *Tender Morsels,* p. 590; January-February, 2009, review of *Tender Morsels,* p. 11.

*Journal of Adolescent and Adult Literature,* March, 2007, Amy Fiske, review of *White Time* and interview with Lanagan, pp. 506-508.

*Kirkus Reviews,* February 1, 2005, review of *Black Juice,* p. 178; July 15, 2006, review of *White Time,* p. 725; October 1, 2007, review of *Red Spikes;* September 15, 2008, review of *Tender Morsels.*

*Kliatt,* July, 2006, Sherry Hoy, review of *Black Juice,* p. 24.

*Magpies,* July, 1992, review of *Wildgame,* p. 21; July, 1993, review of *The Tankermen,* p. 35; March, 1998, review of *Walking through Albert,* p. 33; July, 2000, review of *The Best Thing,* p. 18; November, 2000, review of *White Time,* p. 40; March, 2004, Alison Gregg, review of *Black Juice,* p. 20; November, 2006, Ben Gilholme, review of *Red Spikes,* p. 42; November, 2008, Lyn Linning, review of *Tender Morsels,* p. 43.

*Publishers Weekly,* October 1, 2007, review of *Red Spikes,* p. 59; September 8, 2008, review of *Tender Morsels,* p. 51.

*School Library Journal,* March, 2005, Sarah Couri, review of *Black Juice,* p. 213; November, 2006, Alison Follos, review of *White Time,* p. 139; October, 2007, Christi Voth, review of *Red Spikes,* p. 156; November, 2008, Carolyn Lehman, review of *Tender Morsels,* p. 126; April, 2009, review of *Tender Morsels,* p. S56.

ONLINE

*Allen & Unwin Web site,* http://www.allenandunwin.com/ (January 28, 2010), "Margo on Writing."

*Clarkesworld Magazine,* http://clarkesworldmagazine.com/ (January 28, 2010), Jeff VanderMeer, "Margo Lanagan and *Tender Morsels.*"

*Margo Lanagan Web log,* http://amongamidwhile.blogspot.com/ (April 1, 2010).

*SF Site,* http://www.sfsite.com/ (August, 2003), Trent Walters, interview with Margo Lanagan.*.

# *Laura Lippman*

(Photograph courtesy of Robert Pitts/Landov Media.)

## ■ Personal

Born January 31, 1959, in Atlanta, GA; daughter of Theo (a journalist) and Madeline (a children's librarian) Lippman, Jr.; married John Roll (divorced); married David Simon (a screenwriter and producer). *Education:* Studied journalism at Northwestern University. *Hobbies and other interests:* Eating, drinking, socializing with family and friends, exercise.

## ■ Addresses

*Home*—Baltimore, MD. *E-mail*—laura@lauralipp man.com.

## ■ Career

Journalist and author. *Tribune-Herald,* Waco, TX, reporter, 1981-83; *San Antonio Light,* San Antonio, TX, reporter, 1983-89; *Evening Sun,* Baltimore, MD, reporter and features writer, 1989-2001; full-time novelist, 2001—.

## ■ Awards, Honors

Edgar Award and Shamus Award, both for best paperback original novel, both 1997, both for *Charm City;* Agatha Award for best novel, and Anthony Award for best paperback original, both 1998, both for *Butchers Hill;* Anthony Award and Shamus Award, both 1999, both for *In Big Trouble;* Nero Wolfe Award, 2000, for *The Sugar House;* best local *Sun* report, *Baltimore* magazine, 2001; Anthony Award and Barry Award, both 2003, both for *Every Secret Thing;* Romantic Times Award for best PI novel, 2004, for *By a Spider's Thread;* Gumshoe Award for best novel, 2005, for *To the Power of Three;* Anthony Award, 2006, for *No Good Deeds;* Anthony Award, Barry Award, Macavity Award, and Quill Award in mystery/suspense category, 2007, all for *What the Dead Know;* Anthony Award, for short story "Hardly Knew Her"; Baltimore (MD) Mayor's Award for Literary Excellence; named Author of the Year, Maryland Library Association.

## ■ Writings

*NOVELS*

*Every Secret Thing,* Morrow (New York, NY), 2003.
*To the Power of Three,* Morrow (New York, NY), 2005.
*What the Dead Know,* Morrow (New York, NY), 2007.
*Life Sentences,* Morrow (New York, NY), 2009.

*"TESS MONAGHAN" SERIES; MYSTERY NOVELS*

*Baltimore Blues,* Avon (New York, NY), 1997.
*Charm City,* Avon (New York, NY), 1997.
*Butchers Hill,* Avon (New York, NY), 1998.
*In Big Trouble,* Avon (New York, NY), 1999.
*The Sugar House,* Morrow (New York, NY), 2000.
*In a Strange City,* Morrow (New York, NY), 2001.
*The Last Place,* Morrow (New York, NY), 2002.
*By a Spider's Thread,* Morrow (New York, NY), 2004.
*No Good Deeds,* Morrow (New York, NY), 2006.
*Another Thing to Fall,* Morrow (New York, NY), 2008.

*OTHER*

(Editor, author of introduction, and contributor) *Baltimore Noir* (short stories), Akashic Books (New York, NY), 2006.
*Hardly Knew Her* (short stories), Morrow (New York, NY), 2008.

Also contributor to Otto Penzler's *Murderer's Row.*

### ■ Adaptations

*To the Power of Three* was adapted as an audiobook.

### ■ Sidelights

The city of Baltimore, Maryland, is the setting for Laura Lippman's popular series featuring Tess Monaghan, a gutsy and savvy reporter turned private investigator. The series has been well-received by readers and critics alike, earning such prestigious prizes as the Edgar Award, the Shamus Award, and the Agatha Award. Elizabeth Pincus, writing in the *Voice Literary Supplement,* called Monaghan "a dame with the old-fashioned hubris of Phillip Marlowe and a thoroughly modern, unruly mind." The critic added: "There's a pulpy little thrill in finding the best mystery writing around within the gaudy, palm-sized pages of a mass market release."

In addition to her "Tess Monaghan" series, Lippman has also written a number of popular standalone novels, including *What the Dead Know.* In her works, Lippman often employs her intimate knowledge of Baltimore, where most of them are set. As the author told *Spinetingler* contributor Sandra Ruttan, "I'm in love with Baltimore. I don't know why

and I've stopped trying to analyze it, as there's not a lot of logic to it." Lippman continued, "It can be crude and rude and messy, but it also seems to be missing a veneer that some other cities try to slap on. It's a city with a multitude of faces, which is probably part of the reason it's never boring."

### Journalistic Roots

Lippman was born in Atlanta, Georgia, in 1959, the daughter of Theo Lippman Jr. and his wife Madeline. Her father worked as a newspaper editorial writer while her mother was a school librarian. Lippman attempted to write her first novel at a young age; she used her father's typewriter when she was just four years old to compose her book knowing only how to spell one word: pig. When she was five years old, her father took a job at the Baltimore *Evening Sun* and later the Baltimore *Sun.* Lippman was raised primarily in Baltimore but eventually graduated from high school in Columbia, Maryland.

After graduating from high school, Lippman attended Northwestern University's Medill School of Journalism, then worked as a reporter and journalist for several years in Texas. "I've done just about every beat possible at a newspaper," she remarked to a *Bookreporter.com* interviewer. While living in San Antonio, Lippman was already considering writing fiction. To that end, she drove to Austin to take fiction-writing workshops with author Sandra Cisneros, whom she had profiled for a newspaper piece. Lippman noted in her interview that Cisneros "gave me a lot of encouragement, urging me to send my stories to literary magazines."

In 1989, Lippman returned to Baltimore and took a job at the Baltimore *Evening Sun.* In 1991, she became a features writer at the Baltimore *Sun* when the papers merged. Lippman turned to writing novels in the early 1990s, working on her fiction a few hours each morning before heading to the newspaper. Her "Tess Monaghan" series "started with a chance encounter," she related to Tracy Cochran in *Publishers Weekly.* "Somebody's boss was really rude to me and I said to my friend, 'Your boss is so rude, some day somebody is going to kill him and there will be way too many suspects for anybody to ever figure out who did it.' We began batting the story around and I realized that it was a story I really could write."

### Enter Tess Monaghan

The first book in the series, *Baltimore Blues,* introduces Tess, a reporter who has been downsized from her most recent newspaper job. When not working at Aunt Kitty's bookstore, Tess works out by rowing in the Patapsco River. After Rocky, a rowing buddy, pays her a huge sum of money to follow his fiancé, a murder ensues and Rocky becomes the chief suspect. A *Publishers Weekly* contributor noted that in Lippman's debut effort, "hometown and newspaper backgrounds are alive from page one," but the critic felt that the characters were not sufficiently developed throughout the book.

In the second Monaghan book, *Charm City*, Tess investigates the suicide of local celebrity and tycoon "Wink" Wynkowsky. However, as she uncovers deep corruption in the baseball stadium project that Wynkowsky championed, she soon finds out that Wynkowsky's demise might not have been self-

Lippman garnered Edgar and Shamus Awards for *Charm City*, the second work in her popular "Tess Monaghan" series. (Avon Books/HarperCollins, 1997. Reproduced by permission of HarperCollins Publishers Inc.)

inflicted. She also must figure out how the recent mugging of her Uncle Spike, which left the man in a coma, is related to Wynkowsky's death. The book offers "shrewd observation, on-target descriptions, believable characters and hilarious one-liners," noted a *Publishers Weekly* critic.

*Butchers Hill* is based on an experience Lippman had as a reporter when she covered the murder of an eleven-year-old boy. The novel, which concerns a vigilante killing, looks at racial violence in Baltimore. As in her other works, Lippman's "dialogue is on the mark," a *Publishers Weekly* reviewer asserted. Lippman takes Monaghan out of Baltimore and into Texas for *In Big Trouble*. While searching the Lone Star State for her ex-boyfriend Crow, Tess uncovers a number of long-buried secrets. A host of eccentric characters "add amusement to this gripping mystery," observed a contributor in *Publishers Weekly*. In *The Sugar House*, family loyalties and betrayals come into play as Tess looks into the murder of a Jane Doe for her father. According to *Library Journal* critic Wilda Williams, the novel's Baltimore setting "is as memorable and sassy a character as Tess Monaghan herself." *In a Strange City* focuses on one of Baltimore's most famous phenomena, the annual appearance of the mysterious "Poe Toaster," who leaves cognac and three red roses on Edgar Allan Poe's grave on the author's birthday every January. The appearance of a second Poe Toaster, and the death of one, complicates the literary tradition. *Booklist* contributor Jenny McLarin noted that audiences will be drawn to the series protagonist "who, like one of Baltimore's famous stone crabs, sports a tough shell that hides a sweet center."

Asked by *MysteryNet.com* contributor Ellen Healy about the similarities between Tess and herself, Lippman commented: "She's the person I might have been if I had lost my job in my 20s—a rougher exterior, but a much softer interior, full of self doubts. Like many fictional characters, she gets to say the rude/funny things I would never dare to say out loud. She is brave and principled, two things I like to think I am, but perhaps not to the extent Tess is." The author further explained to Mel Gussow in the *New York Times*, "In many ways, Tess is intended to be something I'm not, which is a quintessential Baltimorean. I've been there for almost 40 years, but I'm still a newcomer to the real old-timers. But I'd be lying if I didn't say that intellectually, temperamentally, we are very much alike. I have better impulse control by far, but people with good impulse control are not much fun to write novels about."

For the thriller *Butchers Hill,* Lippman drew from her experiences as a reporter in Baltimore. (Harper, 1998. Reproduced by permission of HarperCollins Publishers Inc.)

### Tess to the Rescue

Lippman's journalism background adds verisimilitude to the tales of Monaghan. "During her 20 years as a reporter," Gussow stated in the *New York Times,* "she covered politics, the Police Department, social services and juvenile justice and occasionally interviewed authors like Sue Grafton, George Pelicanos and Walter Mosley, which fortified her expertise when she became a private detective novelist." In a *ReadersRead.com* interview, the author stated, "The primary advantage to being a newspaper reporter is that it really demystifies research. If I don't know something, I know how to find it out. And I know that truth is stranger than fiction, that the real test for my novels is making them credible."

In a 2002 installment of the series, *The Last Place,* Tess clashes with a predator who prowls the Internet looking for young girls to seduce. At the same time, she takes on the task of reinvestigating several apparently unrelated murder cases, triggering events that place her own life in danger. "Lippman deftly juggles a sense of foreboding with quotidian details as she spins an engrossing tale," noted Michele Leber in *Library Journal.* "The hallmark of Lippman's finely crafted mystery series has been her acute ability to deliver sturdy tales that push the edges of the traditional private eye novel," noted Oline H. Cogdill in the *South Florida Sun-Sentinel,* and in this one, she "takes an unconventional look at the anger and maliciousness behind domestic violence."

*By a Spider's Thread,* the next book in the "Tess Monaghan" series, centers on Mark Rubin, a local furrier, who approaches Tess because his wife and children have vanished. Although there is no evidence that they have been kidnapped, neither was there any reason for Rubin's wife to take the children and leave him without word of their whereabouts. The author "spins another taut, masterly tale full of complex characters," Leber wrote. Andi Shechter, reviewing *By a Spider's Thread* for the *Bookreporter.com* Web site, commented on the gradual maturation that Tess has exhibited over the course of the series, concluding that "Lippman writes real characters; you don't always like them and you may not always sympathize with them—they're flawed and they're human."

The title of Lippman's ninth Monaghan book, *No Good Deeds,* refers to the old saying that "no good deed goes unpunished." The good deed that begins the narrative occurs when Tess's live-in boyfriend, Crow, brings home an African-American teenager, Lloyd Jupiter, who tried to hustle him in a minor scam. Tess is not pleased, but as it turns out, Lloyd may know more than he is letting on about the circumstances surrounding the death of federal prosecutor Gregory Youssef. She turns over Lloyd's information to the press, assured that her source will remain confidential—only to find herself hounded by federal investigators. There is "nail-biting suspense" in the story, remarked Stephanie Zvirin in a review for *Booklist.*

In *Another Thing to Fall,* Tess is hired to protect twenty-year-old Selene Waites, one of the stars of a television show that has come to film in town. Selene is supposedly being threatened by a stalker, but it soon appears that she is not the one who is in the most immediate danger. When a director's assistant is brutally beaten to death, Tess begins an investigation, attempting to determine who killed the assistant and why—and if anyone else on the cast or crew is at risk. In a review in *Booklist,* Zvirin remarked that "plenty of red herrings and personality clashes make this a delightfully quick, satisfying read." A contributor for *Kirkus Reviews* declared that

"Tess's latest leaves you fully satisfied but looking forward to next time," and a reviewer for *Publishers Weekly* concluded that "fans will appreciate the author's usual authentic local color and intricate plotting."

Lippman said in an interview with *Books 'n' Bytes* contributor Jon Jordan that she enjoys setting her novels in the town where she lives: "I know parts of Baltimore well, but it's an extremely complicated city. I'd be skeptical of anyone who claimed to master all its cultures and subcultures, not to mention its history. It's like a really good song, a standard that a lot of people have covered over the years . . . say, 'My Funny Valentine.' I have my version, and it's authentic, but not authentic." Noah Adams, on the National Public Radio (NPR) program *Morning Edition,* noting the importance of setting for Lippman, wrote that the author "is so focused on the authenticity of the place that she often gets into a dispute with her editors over whether to spell row house (Baltimore is well-known for the narrow brick structures) as one or two words."

### Stand-Alone Fiction

Lippman is also the author of several novels outside the "Tess Monaghan" series. In *Every Secret Thing,* two young girls, Alice Manning and Ronnie Fuller, spot an unattended baby carriage and decide they must rescue the baby. The infant is killed while in their care, however, and the two are sent to prison. Released after seven years, Alice and Ronnie return home to the neighborhood where they committed the deed. As they try to readjust to normal life, a toddler mysteriously disappears, placing the duo under intense scrutiny. A *Kirkus Reviews* critic called the book "lucid, tight, and compelling," and a *Publishers Weekly* reviewer concluded that Lippman's "deft handling of this disturbing material is sure to increase the breadth of her readership."

*To the Power of Three* concerns a deadly school shooting. Kat, Josie, and Perri are high school students who have been best friends since childhood. One morning, however, the school and the city is rocked when the three suffer violence in a restroom: Kat is dead, Perri is seriously injured and in a coma, and Josie—the only eyewitness—is deeply traumatized. Although the evidence suggests that Perri was the shooter, police officers do not believe Josie's story, and their investigation leads them to a troublesome conclusion. "In swift prose, Lippman . . . builds believable characters and palpable suspense," Amy Brozio-Andrews noted in *Library Journal.* "Some of the scenes are wonderfully well told, and Lippman, as always,

neatly skewers people in power," commented a *Publishers Weekly* reviewer. Cogdill concluded that with this book, "Lippman shows the power of strong characters who richly control the story, and resolutions are often as messy as life."

The novel *What the Dead Know,* according to *Detroit Free Press* reviewer Marta Salij, "heralds a leap forward" in Lippman's work "from very good to great." The story begins when a woman flees a hit-and-run accident near Baltimore. After the police find her, she claims to be one of two sisters who were abducted from the city as teenagers thirty years earlier and presumed murdered. The detec-

**A chilling mystery involving a woman who reappears thirty years after her abduction is the focus of *What the Dead Know.*** (Harper, 2008. Reproduced by permission of HarperCollins Publishers Inc.)

tive investigating the incident can't decide how much to trust this woman and must try to find out the truth about her past. The result, Salij wrote, is a thrilling and engrossing novel that shows that "Lippman's grasp of the mysteries on the page and in human hearts is absolutely sure." Comparing the novel's narrative structure to that of film director Akira Kurosawa in *Rashomon,* Simon King observed in a *Bookreporter.com* review that "Lippman has shown once again why she wins countless awards for her consummate writing and satisfies eager fans with every new release." In the *New York Times,* Janet Maslin hailed *What the Dead Know* as an "uncommonly clever" novel that is "doubly satisfying. You read it once just to move breathlessly toward the finale. Then you revisit it to marvel at how well Ms. Lippman pulled the wool over your eyes."

With *Hardly Knew Her,* Lippman branched out from her popular novels to produce a collection of short fiction. Each story is a self-contained mystery that shows the darker side of the female psyche. In this collection, Lippman's killers are soccer moms and college students, women selling real estate in the suburbs and seemingly normal teenagers. These women kill for passionate reasons—because a man has cheated on them or taken them for granted—or simply because they have been insulted passed bearing. Donna Seaman, in a review for *Booklist,* opined that "Lippman is a class act and a potent storyteller in these elegant, furious, and blues-blasting dispatches." A reviewer for *Publishers Weekly* declared of Lippman that the "selections in her first short story collection are as intricate and witty as her novels."

Lippman returns to longer fiction with her 2009 title *Life Sentences.* The work centers on a successful Baltimore memoirist, Cassandra Fallows, who decides to write a book about her former classmate and felon Calliope Jenkins. Accused of murdering her son, Jenkins spent seven years in prison without saying a word about the boy's disappearance. In the course of her researches, Cassandra discovers that her own life is the biggest mystery, for she has completely misunderstood key events from her past. In the work, Lippman examines a number of themes, from the fragility and fallibility of memory to an insider view on publishing, with the mystery of the missing boy at its heart.

*Life Sentences* received praise from many quarters. Writing for *People,* Sue Corbett felt that the work "succeeds brilliantly on several levels." Similarly, *Booklist* contributor Seaman termed *Life Sentences* "an ensnaring and revelatory mystery of the human heart masterfully told." A *Publishers Weekly* reviewer also commended the book, calling it "a rich, complex journey from self-deception to self-discovery." And a *Kirkus Reviews* contributor concluded, "Lipp-

man's writing is powerful and her gaze unflinching as she invokes a world in which no one is either entirely guilty or truly innocent."

Discussing her career as a novelist with Cochran in *Publishers Weekly,* Lippman stated, "I want to write books that work on two levels. I want people who like crime fiction to come to my books and be satisfied, but I would also like to write books that stay with people—where one scene, one moment, one line lingers with someone. After that, the dream would be to get one person, literally one, to think about things differently. I know I've said this many, many times but I'm proud to be a crime writer."

If you enjoy the works of Laura Lippman, you may also want to check out the following books:

Lisa Scottoline, *Mistaken Identity,* 1999.
Marcia Muller's "Sharon McCone" mystery series, including *Vanishing Point,* 2006.
Harlan Coben, *The Woods,* 2007.

Reflecting on her legacy as a writer with *Shots Ezine* contributor Ayo Onatade, Lippman noted that "the real battle in literature is to write something that outlasts you—you have no say in the matter. There is not enough money in the world. You could be a billionaire and you could endow your own library and make it carry your books for the next three centuries but no one gets to determine what future generations are going to read, what's going to have staying power. That's outside our control. You just hope that you have created something that will be remembered."

## ■ Biographical and Critical Sources

*PERIODICALS*

*Booklist,* May 1, 2001, Jenny McLarin, review of *In a Strange City,* p. 1635; September 1, 2002, Connie Fletcher, review of *The Last Place,* p. 63; July, 2003, Connie Fletcher, review of *Every Secret Thing,* p. 1846; March 1, 2005, Stephanie Zvirin, review of *By a Spider's Thread,* p. 1213; May 1, 2006, Stephanie Zvirin, review of *No Good Deeds,* p. 34;

March 1, 2007, Allison Block, review of *What the Dead Know*, p. 68; March 15, 2008, Stephanie Zvirin, review of *Another Thing to Fall*, p. 4; September 1, 2008, Donna Seaman, review of *Hardly Knew Her*, p. 55; January 1, 2009, Donna Seaman, review of *Life Sentences*, p. 22.

*Detroit Free Press*, April 25, 2007, Marta Salij, "Truth Enslaves in a Riveting *What the Dead Know*."

*Economist*, May 12, 2001, "Damn Yankees; Two Hot Talents in Detective Fiction," review of *The Sugar House*, p. 1.

*Entertainment Weekly*, September 5, 2003, Caroline Kepnes, review of *Every Secret Thing*, p. 80; March 16, 2007, Jennifer Reese, review of *What the Dead Know*, p. 72.

*Kirkus Reviews*, August 1, 2002, review of *The Last Place*, p. 1080; July 1, 2003, review of *Every Secret Thing*, p. 878; February 1, 2007, review of *What the Dead Know*, p. 103; January 15, 2008, review of *Another Thing to Fall*; February 1, 2009, review of *Life Sentences*.

*Kliatt*, November, 2003, Nola Theiss, review of *The Sugar House*, p. 53; May, 2005, Francine Levitov, review of *By a Spider's Thread*, p. 52; September 1, 2006, Francine Levitov, review of *No Good Deeds*, p. 55.

*Library Journal*, September 15, 2000, Wilda Williams, review of *The Sugar House*, p. 119; September 15, 2002, Michele Leber, review of *The Last Place*, p. 97; July, 2003, Michele Leber, review of *Every Secret Thing*, p. 123; August, 2004, Michele Leber, review of *By a Spider's Thread*, p. 60; July 1, 2005, Amy Brozio-Andrews, review of *To the Power of Three*, p. 69; March 1, 2007, B. Allison Gray, review of *No Good Deeds*, p. 122; March 15, 2007, Amy Brozio, review of *What the Dead Know*, p. 61; September 1, 2009, Joyce Kessel, review of *Life Sentences*, p. 78.

*New York Times*, August 21, 2004, Mel Gussow, "As Gumshoes Squish In Streets of Baltimore," p. B7; June 26, 2005, Marilyn Stasio, "Mean Girls"; April 5, 2007, Janet Maslin, review of *What the Dead Know*.

*Orlando Sentinel* (Orlando, FL), October 17, 2003, Nancy Pate, review of *The Last Place*.

*People*, March 23, 2009, Sue Corbett, review of *Life Sentences*, p. 57.

*Publishers Weekly*, December 30, 1996, review of *Baltimore Blues*, p. 64; August 18, 1997, review of *Charm City*, p. 89; June 1, 1998, review of *Butchers Hill*, p. B48; July 26, 1999, review of *In Big Trouble*, p. 88; November 29, 1999, Judy Quinn, "No Mystery to Laura Lippman's Leap," p. 32; August 7, 2000, review of *The Sugar House*, p. 79; September 23, 2002, review of *The Last Place*, p. 54; July 7, 2003, review of *Every Secret Thing*, p. 49; July 5, 2004, Tracy Cochran, "The Baltimore Beat: Charmed City Scribe Laura Lippman Covers

Crime in Her Own Way," p. 29; May 16, 2005, review of *To the Power of Three*, p. 35; March 6, 2006, review of *Baltimore Noir*, p. 49; May 15, 2006, review of *No Good Deeds*, p. 49; June 5, 2006, Suzanne Fox, "Topical Crimes," p. 30; January 22, 2007, review of *What the Dead Know*, p. 156; May 28, 2007, review of *What the Dead Know*, p. 57; January 14, 2008, review of *Another Thing to Fall*, p. 37; February 11, 2008, Sara Nelson, "Lady Baltimore," p. 46; August 25, 2008, review of *Hardly Knew Her*, p. 50; January 19, 2009, review of *Life Sentences*, p. 37.

*School Library Journal*, May 1, 2007, Jenny Gasset, review of *What the Dead Know*, p. 174.

*South Florida Sun-Sentinel* (Fort Lauderdale, FL), September 21, 2001, Oline H. Cogdill, review of *In a Strange City*; October 25, 2002, Oline H. Cogdill, review of *The Last Place*; June 29, 2005, Oline H. Cogdill, review of *To the Power of Three*.

*Voice Literary Supplement*, October-November, 1999, Elizabeth Pincus, "The Lonesome Star," p. 135.

*Washington Post*, August 16, 2009, Laura Lippman, "The Writing Life."


ONLINE

*BookPage*, http://www.bookpage.com/ (July 20, 2007), Jay MacDonald, "Reality Check: Flawed Characters Keep Laura Lippman Honest."

*Bookreporter.com*, http://www.bookreporter.com/ (September 5, 2003), interview with Lippman; (April 1, 2010), Ava Dianne Day, reviews of *The Last Place* and *Every Secret Thing*; Andi Schechter, reviews of *By a Spider's Thread* and *To the Power of Three*; Simon King, review of *What the Dead Know*.

*Books 'n' Bytes*, http://www.booksnbytes.com/ (April 4, 2003), Jon Jordan, "Interview with Laura Lippman."

*Laura Lippman Home Page*, http://www.lauralippman.com (April 1, 2010).

*MysteryNet.com*, http://www.mysterynet.com/ (February 3, 2000), Ellen Healy, "Meet the Author: In Big Trouble with Baltimore Mystery Author Laura Lippman."

*National Public Radio Web site*, http://www.npr.org/ (August 23, 2007), Noah Adams, "Laura Lippman's Baltimore: Loving a Flawed Place."

*ReadersRead.com*, http://www.readersread.com/ (January 28, 2010), "Interview with Laura Lippman."

*Shots Ezine*, http://www.shotsmag.co.uk/ (July 20, 2007), Ayo Onatade, "Interview with Laura Lippman."

*Spinetingler*, http://www.spinetinglermag.com/ (July 20, 2007), Sandra Ruttan, "On Baltimore and Books: A Discussion with Laura Lippman."*

# Geraldine McCaughrean

(Photograph courtesy of Shaun Curry/AFP/Getty Images.)

## ■ Personal

Surname is pronounced "Mc-CORK-ran"; born June 6, 1951, in London, England; daughter of Leslie Arthur (a firefighter) and Ethel (a teacher) Jones; married John McCaughrean; children: Ailsa. *Education:* Attended Southgate Technical College, Middlesex, England, 1969-70; Christ Church College, Canterbury, B.Ed. (with honors), 1977.

## ■ Addresses

*Home*—Berkshire, England. *E-mail*—mccaughrean@btinternet.com.

## ■ Career

Author. Thames Television, London, England, secretary, 1970-73; Marshall Cavendish Ltd., London, assistant editor, 1977-80, subeditor, 1978-79, staff writer, 1982-88; Carreras-Rothman Ltd., Aylesbury, England, editorial assistant, 1980-81; writer, 1981—.

## ■ Awards, Honors

Winner in short-story category, All-London Literary Competition, Wandsworth Borough Council, 1979, for "The Pike"; Whitbread Award, 1987, for *A Little Lower Than the Angels*; Carnegie Medal, British Library Association, and London *Guardian* Award, both 1989, for *A Pack of Lies*; Katholischen Kinderbuchpreis (Germany), 1991, for *Gabriel und der Meisterspieler* (German translation of *A Little Lower Than the Angels*); Whitbread Award, 1994, for *Gold Dust*; Bronze Award, Nestle Smarties Book Prize, 1996, for *Plundering Paradise*; UK Reading Association Children's Book Award, 1998, for *Forever X*; *Newsweek* Best Picture Book citation, 1999, for *Grandma Chickenlegs*; Blue Peter Book of the Year Award, 2000, for *Pilgrim's Progress*; Independent Publisher Book Award, 2000, for *Grandma Chickenlegs*; Blue Peter Book Award for Best Book to Keep Forever, 2001, for *The Kite Rider*; Carnegie Medal, 2001, for *Stop the Train!*; Nestle Smarties Bronze Medal, 2001, for *The Kite Rider*, 2002, for *Stop the Train!*, and 2004, for *Smile!*; Best Book for Young Adults selection, American Library Association (ALA), 2003, for *The Kite Rider*; Notable Books for Children selection, ALA, 2004, for *Stop the Train!*; Whitbread Award, 2004, for *Not the End of the World*; Michael L. Printz Award, ALA, 2008, for *The White Darkness*.

## ■ Writings

YOUNG ADULT NOVELS

*A Little Lower Than the Angels,* Oxford University Press (Oxford, England), 1987.

*A Pack of Lies,* Oxford University Press (Oxford, England), 1988.

*Gold Dust,* Oxford University Press (Oxford, England), 1993.

*Plundering Paradise,* Oxford University Press (Oxford, England), 1996, published as *The Pirate's Son,* Scholastic (New York, NY), 1998.

*Forever X,* Oxford University Press (Oxford, England), 1997.

*The Kite Rider,* HarperCollins (New York, NY), 2002.

*Stop the Train!,* HarperCollins (New York, NY), 2003.

*Showstopper,* Oxford University Press (Oxford, England), 2003.

*Not the End of the World,* Oxford University Press (Oxford, England), 2003, HarperTempest (New York, NY), 2005.

*Peter Pan in Scarlet,* illustrated by David Wyatt, Oxford University Press (Oxford, England), 2006, illustrated by Scott M. Fischer, Simon & Schuster (New York, NY), 2006.

*The White Darkness,* HarperTempest (New York, NY), 2007.

*Tamburlaine's Elephants,* Usborne Children's Books, 2007.

*The Death Defying Pepper Roux,* Oxford University Press (Oxford, England), 2009, HarperCollins (New York, NY), 2010.

*FOR CHILDREN; RETELLER*

*One Thousand and One Arabian Nights,* illustrated by Stephen Lavis, Oxford University Press (Oxford, England), 1982, illustrated by Rosamund Fowler, 1999.

*The Canterbury Tales,* illustrated by Victor Ambrus, Oxford University Press (Oxford, England), 1984, Rand McNally (Skokie, IL), 1985.

*The Story of Noah and the Ark,* illustrated by Helen Ward, Templar (Dorking, England), 1987.

*The Story of Christmas,* illustrated by Helen Ward, Templar (Dorking, England), 1988.

*Saint George and the Dragon,* illustrated by Nicki Palin, Doubleday (New York, NY), 1989.

*El Cid,* Oxford University Press (Oxford, England), 1989.

*The Orchard Book of Greek Myths,* illustrated by Emma Chichester Clark, Orchard (London, England), 1992, published as *Greek Myths,* Margaret K. McElderry Books (New York, NY), 1993.

*The Odyssey,* illustrated by Victor Ambrus, Oxford University Press (Oxford, England), 1993.

*Stories from Shakespeare,* illustrated by Antony Maitland, Orion Children's Books (London, England), 1994.

*The Orchard Book of Stories from the Ballet,* illustrated by Angela Barrett, Orchard (London, England), 1994, published as *The Random House Book of Stories from the Ballet,* Random House (New York, NY), 1995.

*The Golden Hoard: Myths and Legends of the World,* illustrated by Bee Willey, Margaret K. McElderry Books (New York, NY), 1996.

*God's People: Stories from the Old Testament,* illustrated by Anna C. Leplar, Margaret K. McElderry Books (New York, NY), 1997.

*The Silver Treasure: Myths and Legends of the World,,* illustrated by Bee Willey, Margaret K. McElderry Books (New York, NY), 1997.

*The Bronze Cauldron,* illustrated by Bee Willey, Orion Children's Books (London, England), 1997, Margaret K. McElderry Books (New York, NY), 1998.

*Perseus and the Gorgon Medusa,* illustrated by Tony Ross, Orchard (London, England), 1997.

*Daedalus and Icarus,* illustrated by Tony Ross, Orchard (London, England), 1997.

*The Wooden Horse,* illustrated by Tony Ross, Orchard (London, England), 1997.

*The Orchard Book of Greek Gods and Goddesses,* illustrated by Emma Chichester Clark, Orchard (London, England), 1997, published as *Greek Gods and Goddesses,* Margaret K. McElderry Books (New York, NY), 1998.

*The Story of the Nativity,* illustrated by Ruth Wickings, Bantam (New York, NY), 1998.

*Casting the Gods Adrift: A Tale of Ancient Egypt,* illustrated by Patricia D. Ludlow, A&C Black (London, England), 1998, Cricket Books (Chicago, IL), 2002.

*The Crystal Pool: Myths and Legends of the World,* illustrated by Bee Willey, Margaret K. McElderry Books (New York, NY), 1999.

*God's Kingdom: Stories from the New Testament,* illustrated by Anna C. Leplar, Margaret K. McElderry Books (New York, NY), 1999.

*The Orchard Book of Roman Myths,* illustrated by Emma Chichester Clark, Orchard (London, England), 1999, published as *Roman Myths,* Margaret K. McElderry Books (New York, NY), 2001.

*Beauty and the Beast,* illustrated by Gary Blythe, Carolrhoda Books (Minneapolis, MN), 2000.

*Starry Tales,* illustrated by Sophy Williams, Margaret K. McElderry Books (New York, NY), 2000.

*Oxford Treasury of Fairy Tales,* illustrated by Sophy Williams, Oxford University Press (Oxford, England), 2003.

*Gilgamesh the Hero,* illustrated by David Parkins, Eerdmans (Grand Rapids, MI), 2003.

*Odysseus,* Oxford University Press (Oxford, England), 2003, illustrated by Tom Kidd, Cricket Books (Chicago, IL), 2004.

*Hercules,* Oxford University Press (Oxford, England), 2003, Cricket Books (Chicago, IL), 2005.

*Theseus,* Oxford University Press (Oxford, England), 2003, Cricket Books (Chicago, IL), 2005.

*Perseus,* Oxford University Press (Oxford, England), 2003, illustrated by Tom Kidd, Cricket Books (Chicago, IL), 2005.

*Questing Knights of the Faerie Queen,* illustrated by Jackson Cockcroft, Hodder Children's Books (London, England), 2006.

*Greek Heroes,* Oxford University Press (Oxford, England), 2007.

Also author of *Athena and the Olive Tree and Other Greek Myths* and *Zeus Conquers the Titans and Other Greek Myths,* both illustrated by Tony Ross.

*FOR CHILDREN*

*Seaside Adventure,* illustrated by Chrissie Wells, Hamlyn (London, England), 1986.

*Tell the Time,* illustrated by Chrissie Wells, Hamlyn (London, England), 1986.

(Adapter) Michel Tilde, *Who's That Knocking at My Door?,* Oxford University Press (Oxford, England), 1986.

*My First Space Pop-up Book,* illustrated by Mike Peterkin, Little Simon (New York, NY), 1989.

*My First Earth Pop-up Book,* illustrated by Mike Peterkin, Little Simon (New York, NY), 1990.

(Adapter) *The Snow Country Prince,* Knopf (New York, NY), 1991.

(Adapter) Daisaku Ikeda, *The Princess and the Moon,* Knopf (New York, NY), 1991.

(Adapter) Daisaku Ikeda, *The Cherry Tree,* illustrated by Brian Wildsmith, Knopf (New York, NY), 1992.

(Adapter) Daisaku Ikeda, *Over the Deep Blue Sea,* illustrated by Brian Wildsmith, Knopf (New York, NY), 1993.

*Blue Moon Mountain,* illustrated by Nicki Palin, Golden (London, England), 1994, Simply Read Books (Vancouver, British Columbia, Canada), 2006.

*Blue Moo,* illustrated by Colin Smithson, Longman (Harlow, England), 1994.

*How the Reindeer Got Their Antlers,* illustrated by Debi Gliori, Orchard (London, England), 1995, illustrated by Heather Holland, Holiday House (New York, NY), 2000.

*On the Day the World Began,* illustrated by Norman Bancroft-Hunt, Longman (Harlow, England), 1995.

*The Quest of Isis,* illustrated by David Sim, Longman (Harlow, England), 1995.

*Wizziwig and the Crazy Cooker,* Orchard (London, England), 1995.

*Wizziwig and the Singing Chair,* Orchard (London, England), 1995.

*Wizziwig and the Sweet Machine,* Orchard (London, England), 1995.

*Wizziwig and the Wacky Weather Machine,* Orchard (London, England), 1995.

*Cowboy Jess,* Dolphin/Orion (London, England), 1997.

*Cowboy Jess Saddles Up,* Dolphin/Orion (London, England), 1997.

*Unicorns! Unicorns!,* illustrated by Sophie Windham, Holiday House (New York, NY), 1997.

*My First Oxford Book of Stories,* illustrated by Ruby Green, Oxford University Press (Oxford, England), 1999.

*Too Big!,* illustrated by Peter Bailey, Corgi Pup (London England), 1999.

*Noah and Nelly,* illustrated by Anthony Lewis, Orchard Books (London, England), 1999.

*The Stones Are Hatching,* HarperCollins (New York, NY), 2000.

*Grandma Chickenlegs,* illustrated by Moira Kemp, Carolrhoda Books (Minneapolis, MN), 2000.

*Six Storey House,* illustrated by Ross Collins, Hodder Children's (London, England), 2002.

*One Bright Penny,* illustrated by Paul Howard, Viking (New York, NY), 2002.

*My Grandmother's Clock,* illustrated by Stephen Lambert, Clarion (New York, NY), 2002.

*The Jesse Tree,* illustrated by Bee Willey, Eerdmans (Grand Rapids, MI), 2003.

*Doctor Quack,* illustrated by Ross Collins, Hodder Children's (London, England), 2003.

*Dog Days,* Hodder Children's (London, England), 2003.

*Jalopy: A Car's Story in Five Drivers,* illustrated by Ross Collins, Orchard (London, England), 2003.

*Dancing the Night Away,* illustrated by Carolyn King, Oxford University Press (Oxford, England), 2003.

*Smile!,* illustrated by Ian McCaughrean, Oxford University Press (Oxford, England), 2004, Random House (New York, NY), 2006.

*Sky Ship and Other Stories,* A&C Black (London, England), 2004.

*Fig's Giant,* illustrated by Jago, Oxford University Press (Oxford, England), 2005.

*Think Again,* illustrated by Bee Willey, Collins (London, England), 2005.

*Father and Son: A Nativity Story,* Hyperion Books for Children (New York, NY), 2006.

*Mo,* illustrated by Ross Collins, Hodder Children's Books (London, England), 2006.

*Wenceslas,* illustrated by Christian Birmingham, Transworld Publishers (London, England), 2007.

*Noisy Neighbors,* Oxford University Press (Oxford, England), 2008.

*The Nativity Story,* illustrated by Sophy Williams, Lion (London, England), 2008.

Also author of elementary-grade readers for Oxford University Press.

Author's works have been translated into other languages, including Welsh.

### OTHER

(Under name Geraldine Jones) *Adventure in New York* (textbook), illustrated by Cynthia Back, Oxford University Press (Oxford, England), 1979.

(Under name Geraldine Jones) *Raise the Titanic* (textbook), Oxford University Press (Oxford, England), 1980.

(Under name Geraldine Jones) *Modesty Blaise* (textbook), Oxford University Press (Oxford, England), 1981.

*The Maypole* (adult novel), Secker & Warburg (London, England), 1989.

*Fires' Astonishment* (adult novel), Secker & Warburg (London, England), 1990.

*Vainglory* (adult novel), J. Cape (London, England), 1991.

*Lovesong* (adult novel), Richard Cohen Books (London, England), 1994.

*The Ideal Wife* (adult novel), Richard Cohen Books (London, England), 1997.

*Cyrano,* Oxford University Press (Oxford, England), 2006.

*Doktor Faustus* (play), Oxford University Press (Oxford, England), 2006.

Editor, *Banbury Focus,* 1981-82; subeditor and writer of stories for *Storyteller* and *Great Composers.*

## ■ Adaptations

*Not the End of the World* has been adapted for the stage. Film rights to *Peter Pan in Scarlet* have been sold to Headline Pictures, BBC Films, and the United Kingdom Film Council. Many of McCaughrean's books have been adapted as audiobooks, among them *The Kite Rider,* Full Cast, 2004; *A Pack of Lies,* BBC Audio, 2005; and *Stop the Train!,* Full Cast, 2005.

## ■ Sidelights

British novelist, editor, and reteller Geraldine McCaughrean is the award-winning author of over 150 books for young readers. A three-time recipient of England's prestigious Whitbread Children's Book Award, McCaughrean has also won the Carnegie Medal, and in 2008 she received the Michael L. Printz Award from the American Library Association for her young adult novel, *The White Darkness.* "McCaughrean does not write 'typical' contemporary books," noted Elizabeth O'Reilly on the *British Council* Web site. "Her novels often have historical settings or take place in different cultures . . . . She therefore encourages her readers to expand their horizons and explore far beyond their familiar environment. Moreover, her use of language—rich, eloquent and full of vivid metaphors—requires the child-reader to work quite hard, while offering a rewarding, thought-provoking experience to those who make the effort."

During her long career, McCaughrean has penned novels for young adults as well as stories and picture books for young children. She has also adapted tales, myths, and legends from various cultures and written adult fiction and textbooks. Whatever her subject, McCaughrean brings a flair for intricate prose and exciting storytelling to her writing. "Reading McCaughrean," Eileen Dunlop asserted in *Twentieth-Century Children's Writers,* "reinforces the belief that a good book is for everyone capable of reading it, regardless of its intended primary audience." Among her most popular works for young adults are the novels *Stop the Train!, Not the End of the World,* and the award-winning *The Kite Rider* and *The White Darkness.* The author's highly regarded retellings include *One Thousand and One Arabian Nights* and classical myths about Theseus, Perseus, and Odysseus, as well as an anthology of fairy tales and works less-familiar to Western readers, such as *Casting the Gods Adrift: A Tale of Ancient Egypt.*

### From Editor to Author

Born in North London in 1951, McCaughrean was brought up by her mother, a teacher, and her father, who was a firefighter. Though she did not excel in school ("I was shy and not very bright," she noted on her home page), she developed a passion for literature. After leaving school, McCaughrean became a secretary at Thames Television. Then her boss sent her to college at Christ Church, Canterbury, where she studied theater. She was particularly interested in Shakespeare, a passion that would someday lead her to write original versions of his plays. After college, McCaughrean worked for a time as a teacher, then was a writer and an editor for various British publishers for a decade, writing in her spare time and even on her way to and from work.

**McCaughrean's debut title, a retelling of _One Thousand and One Arabian Nights_, appeared in 1982.** (Copyright © 1982 Oxford University Press. Reproduced by permission of Oxford University Press.)

McCaughrean started her career as a children's author with her retelling of _One Thousand and One Arabian Nights,_ a series of tales told by the legendary Shahrazad to her royal husband as a way to postpone the woman's execution. McCaughrean was immediately praised for her inspired storytelling and her ability to make the familiar stories of Sinbad, Aladdin, and Ali Baba seem exciting and original. Marcus Crouch commented in _Junior Bookshelf_ that with _One Thousand and One Arabian Nights,_ McCaughrean achieves a "brilliant tour de force in what is not so much a translation as a thorough reworking of the tales," and that she uses "the original as the starting point of a piece of individual creative enterprise."

In _The Canterbury Tales,_ McCaughrean takes fourteenth-century writer Geoffrey Chaucer's classic story collection and focuses on the pilgrimage to Canterbury itself. She tones down the content of some of the more ribald tales, and then, "in colorful style and language, . . . creatively reconstructs and adds conversation, event and detail, in keeping with

the medieval times, to stitch the tales together," as Ruth M. McConnell described it in _School Library Journal._ While he felt that some of the tales lose something in the retelling, _Times Educational Supplement_ contributor Terry Jones noted that "McCaughrean's real achievement is the way she has succeeded in turning the whole pilgrimage itself into a story, and has brought that far-off medieval expedition to life in a quite remarkable way." In _Junior Bookshelf,_ Crouch concluded that in _The Canterbury Tales,_ McCaughrean "captures most beautifully the mood of the pilgrimage, the high spirits, the smell of the countryside and the muddy road."

## Turns to Young Adult Novels

McCaughrean's first novel, _A Little Lower Than the Angels,_ won the coveted Whitbread Children's Novel Award in 1987. It is a complex, multilevel drama set in medieval England during the time when traveling players performed Mystery plays in towns and villages throughout the British countryside. The story revolves around Gabriel, a stonemason's apprentice who runs away from his cruel master to join a troupe of players. The boy's flowing blond curls make him a natural to play the part of the angel Gabriel. Then the superficially benevolent playmaster Garvey, seizing a chance to increase the troupe's wealth and popularity, convinces the boy to play an off-stage role as a miracle healer. Gabriel soon starts to believe in his own power, but he questions the rightness of his actions when he is asked for help by townspeople dying of the plague and desperate for a miracle. McCaughrean "has triumphed in her first novel in presenting the lives of ordinary people of the past, in direct, present-day language, with just a few archaisms to set the scene, and relevant historical information," Jessica Yates wrote in _British Book News Children's Books._ As Crouch similarly concluded in _Junior Bookshelf, A Little Lower Than the Angels_ "is a very good novel, rich in uncluttered historical detail, written with sensitive fluency, and with a gallery of memorable characters."

McCaughrean's Carnegie Medal-winning novel _A Pack of Lies_ demonstrates several different approaches to storytelling. Ailsa Povey and her mother eke out a living selling antiques out of their dilapidated shop. One day, Ailsa meets a mysterious young man named MCC Berkshire, who offers to help in the shop in exchange for room and board. He is spectacularly successful, as he weaves elaborate stories about each item in the shop, enthralling customers into making purchases. Every tale displays his—and, according to several critics, McCaughrean's—brilliance as a storyteller, as each one reflects a different literary style. "Each is an utterly convincing example of its kind, enthralling the reader in a web of make-believe," Valerie Caless observed in the *School Librarian*. A reviewer in *Publishers Weekly* similarly hailed the author's "leaps from genre to genre, in the writing equivalent of sleight of hand," and added that McCaughrean "pulls off each meta-fictional complexity with finesse and humor."

*A Pack of Lies* is more than just a collection of stories, however, as the ending reveals. MCC does not stay around the shop for long, and after his departure, the disconsolate Ailsa picks up a book and finds herself a character in a story about MCC, their meeting, and his time in the shop. As Caless asked: "Who, then, is the fiction and who the liar telling it? Is Ailsa a figment of MCC's imagination or he of hers?" As Stephanie Nettell concluded in *Books for Keeps*: "More than anything, *A Pack of Lies* is an exuberant celebration of fiction's spell, a smiling

surrender to the grip of the unruly imagination, a playful introduction to the riches of style that lie waiting in books."

## Imaginative Historical Novels

McCaughrean again shows the depth of her imagination in the historical novels *Gold Dust, The Kite Rider,* and *Stop the Train!*, *Gold Dust* is set in a poor mining town in Brazil. The effects of uncontrolled greed caused by the discovery of gold are seen through the eyes of Inez de Souza and her brother Maro, who watch as their town is slowly destroyed and its inhabitants corrupted by a gold rush. "Sharp observations on a kaleidoscope of topics enliven every page, often underlined by ironic humour, whether understated . . . or sharper," Brian Slough wrote in the *Times Educational Supplement*. As Crouch commented in his *Junior Bookshelf* review, with its "sparkling" language and "wonderfully inventive, consistent and hideously convincing" plot, *Gold Dust* is "an engrossing, funny, tragic blockbuster of a story."

In her award-winning book *The Kite Rider*, McCaughrean takes readers back in time to the thirteenth century, as twelve-year-old Hanoyou agrees to work aboard the ship of his late father as a kite rider, one who tests the winds and the will of the gods by sailing above the masts tied to a large kite. While working to prevent his recently widowed mother's marriage to an evil ship's mate, Hanoyou travels with his older cousin, the wise and beautiful Mipeng, and amazes audiences with his skill at riding a kite up into the heavens, where he pretends to commune with the spirits of the dead. The cousins are then approached by the charismatic Miao Je, who asks the pair to join his traveling circus. The group soon journeys to the court of famed Mongol leader Kublai Khan, the conqueror of China. As her characters wrestle with love, revenge, racism, trust, duty, and honor, McCaughrean spins a story that *Kliatt* reviewer Claire Rosser praised as "truly marvelous" and "amazingly imaginative, exotic, and challenging."

Moving even further back in time, *Not the End of the World* concerns those fortunate enough to be given a place on Noah's famed ark and saved from the deadly flood that covered the earth. Narrated by animals as well as by Noah's family members, the book "raises thought-provoking questions in its expansion and exploration of an ancient tale," according to *School Library Journal* contributor Kathy Piehl. Portraying Noah as a zealot, McCaughrean brings life to this biblical character and the members

*A Pack of Lies,* a celebration of storytelling, earned Mc-Caughrean the prestigious Carnegie Medal. (Copyright © Geraldine McCaughrean 1988. Reproduced by permission of Oxford University Press.)

of his family. In what *Booklist* reviewer Ilene Cooper called "a powerfully crafted, uneasy read," the author describes a voyage that is trying due to the filthy conditions and the deprivations suffered by those afloat for the forty long days it took the waters to recede. As a *Publishers Weekly* reviewer noted, McCaughrean "masterfully transforms the famous biblical story" in what the critic dubbed a "provocative retelling."

"The literary equivalent of a grand old western movie," according to a *Publishers Weekly* critic, *Stop the Train!* takes place in the early twentieth century and focuses on a group of settlers making a new home in the wilds of Oklahoma. The settlers have such pride in their new town, which they name Florence, that they refuse to sell their land when a powerful railroad tycoon makes them an offer. Angered, the railroad owner refuses to build a station in Florence, thus threatening the life of the struggling community until residents can devise a way to get passing trains to stop. Grounded by a "strong sense of community spirit," the story paints a "busy panorama that's just exaggerated enough to ward off . . . picky questions of historical accuracy," noted *Horn Book* contributor Peter D. Sieruta. In a *School Library Journal* review, Bruce Anne Shook deemed the story a "rollicking tale" featuring "eccentric but lovable characters and their unusual exploits."

### Retellings and Myths

In addition to writing fiction, McCaughrean has produced numerous retellings and adaptations, among them *Saint George and the Dragon*, her version of the story of England's patron saint. Traveling across the countryside, George of Lydda comes across Sabra, the king's daughter, who has been tied to the stake as a sacrifice to the dragon—a slimy, lizard-like creature called Wickedness, whose father is Evil and whose mother is Darkness. In *El Cid*, McCaughrean retells the story of one of Spain's most famous heroes, Rodrigo Diaz, who was exiled from Castile only to become a brilliant warrior who recaptured territory from the invading Moors. "McCaughrean shows herself a grand storyteller," a *Kirkus Reviews* critic remarked of *El Cid*; "she presents this prototypical chivalric knight in a lively narrative sparked with humor, drama, and her hero's daring trickery."

McCaughrean later rewrote ten well-known Shakespearean plays and titled the collection *Stories From Shakespeare*. Reviewing the work, Maxine Kumin of the *New York Times Book Review* pointed out that

*Stories From Shakespeare* is "useful and enjoyable. . . ." Furthermore, Crouch, in a review for *Junior Bookshelf*, explained that McCaughrean uses an accessible writing style and a solid understanding of Shakespeare to produce a work that children can comprehend and appreciate. Above all, he stated, McCaughrean "aims her book at children who are only just coming to Shakespeare, and she gives them an excellent start, showing that the plays are great entertainment and hinting at the depths to which they can in time be explored."

McCaughrean also wrote her own version of the classic novel *Moby Dick* by Herman Melville. Considered one of the greatest works in the canon of American literature, *Moby Dick* follows the vengeful Captain Ahab's pursuit of a great white whale. Elaine Moss, in an article in *Books for Keeps*, stated her belief that young readers should wait until they are old enough to take on the classics in their original form. However, she made an exception for McCaughrean, remarking, "despite my misgivings about the retellings of the classics I must go on record as saying that if anyone is to retell *Moby Dick* (and I still think nobody should) that person is Geraldine McCaughrean." Moss cited McCaughrean's skill as a writer as her saving grace, believing that the author had captured the excitement of Melville's novel. Hazel Townson wrote in *School Librarian* that McCaughrean's *Moby Dick* "combines power and beauty with a clarity" which would prove appealing to adolescent readers.

In *The Odyssey* and *The Orchard Book of Greek Myths* (published in the United States as *Greek Myths*), McCaughrean uses humor to create interest and excitement for younger readers. Janet Tayler, reviewing *The Odyssey* for the *School Librarian*, noted that here the adventures of Odysseus are retold in a "lively, rather tongue-in-cheek manner," while Hazel Rochman wrote in *Booklist* that the stories in *Greek Myths* are "direct, robust, and gleeful." While Pauline Long noted that *Greek Myths* is not intended as a reference tool, she added in the *School Librarian* that "its real purpose is to delight and entertain—and this it does in flamboyant style." Rochman commented that McCaughrean's stories have the "dramatic immediacy" of familiar legends: "'Long ago, when fortune-tellers told the truth, there lived a very frightened man.' How can you not read on?"

McCaughrean profiles four of the most well-known ancient heroes in the books *Theseus, Odysseus, Hercules,* and *Perseus.* "Those who wonder why the ancient heroes are worth knowing will be richly answered," a *Kirkus Reviews* writer noted of *Theseus*, which follows the story of the son whose coming was foretold to King Aegeus at the Oracle of Delphi.

Ultimately banished from his family after bringing tragedy to his father's home, Theseus goes on to encounter the Minotaur, Amazonian Queen Hippolyta, and Procrustes, among other characters. The hero of *Perseus* confronts Medusa, whose look turns the unwary into stone, and saves the beautiful Andromeda. Citing McCaughrean's ability to blend "the colloquial and contemporary," Rochman commented in *Booklist* that, with *Perseus*, the author's "rhythmic storytelling of the gruesome and the heroic . . . will grab kids." Other ancient heroes are brought to life by McCaughrean in books such as *Gilgamesh the Hero*, which retells the oldest recorded story in human history.

In *Greek Gods and Goddesses*, McCaughrean recounts fifteen myths from ancient Greece and its pantheon of gods and goddesses. This 1998 title was followed in 2001 with *Roman Myths*, which also features illustrations by Emma Chichester Clark. Here McCaughrean explains that the Romans—rivals of Greece in ancient times—adapted the Greek gods and myths for their own use. In contrast to the Greek stories, which often impart a lesson about human folly, the Roman tales stress the role of fate in life. Myths recounted here include that of Aeneas and the founding of Rome, and the stories of Sibyl, Jupiter, and Diana. McCaughrean includes some lesser-known Roman legends as well, such as the tragedy of Erisychthon, who destroyed an ancient sacred forest, and that of Tarquin, a despotic ruler. A *Horn Book* reviewer found that a "mix of cynicism (on the part of Roman mythology's perpetrators) and credulity (by the populace) makes McCaughrean's ironic, light-hearted tone especially appropriate." *School Library Journal* reviewer Nina Lindsay also weighed in with a positive assessment, noting that McCaughrean "has accomplished an appealing and approachable introduction to Roman mythology that will make readers want to seek out more."

McCaughrean turns to the stories of the Bible with *God's Kingdom: Stories from the New Testament*. The tales included here, most of which recount events from the life of Christ, bring figures such as Lazarus and John the Baptist into greater focus. "McCaughrean also does a good job with the more complicated parables, writing them in a way that makes them understandable," remarked *Booklist* contributor Ilene Cooper. *School Library Journal* reviewer Patricia Pearl Dole noted that McCaughrean's "text flows smoothly from incident to miracle to parable, often using explanatory bridging matter to clarify the meaning."

Drawing upon pirate lore, McCaughrean spins a fictional tale of a young boy who must find his own way in the world in *The Pirate's Son*. The story, intended for younger readers, is set in the 1700s, and focuses on Tamo White, the son of a pirate and a woman from Madagascar, an island in the Indian Ocean. Tamo has been sent to England for schooling, but he returns to Madagascar with two friends, ferried there aboard a ship captained by the seemingly friendly Sheller. The seaman proves unreliable, however, when he tries to sell Tamo's friend Maud into slavery. On Madagascar, Tamo finds that his mother has wed King Samson, another pirate, and he must extricate himself and his friends from danger. "The writing lacks only Technicolor, bringing both the exotic locale and its equally exotic pillagers to riotous life," asserted a *Kirkus Reviews* contributor. *School Library Journal* reviewer Steven Engelfried also commended the book. "The conclusion is satisfying and convincing," Engelfried noted, adding that the story "develops into a vivid picture of a time and a place new to most youngsters."

## A Master Storyteller for Many Audiences

Among her other books for young adult readers, McCaughrean won critical praise for *The Stones Are Hatching*. Based on an old Celtic tale, the story blends elements from other cultures in its tale of Phelim Green and his unusual adventures. The youngster lives in England in 1919, where he is belittled daily by his vicious sister. One day the shy and reclusive eleven year old wakes and finds the house wrecked. A spirit called the Domovoy—a house guardian borrowed from Slavic folklore—tells him to rescue the world from the Hatchlings of the Stoor Worm. Phelim thinks the Domovoy is mistaken and has inadvertently selected the wrong person for the hero's job, but he sets out anyway. Along the way he meets animals and a witch who join him on his journey to the mouth of the Stoor Worm. They learn that the massive artillery of World War I has awakened this beast from centuries of sleep, and eggs of stone are now hatching horrendous creatures near its snout. There is much adventure along the way, including Phelim's escape from a determined, ambulatory sack of digestive organs. "While it may be too violent for some, this evocative and sometimes profound fantasy distinguishes itself by way of vivid imagery, compelling action and often Siren-like lyricism," noted a *Publishers Weekly* contributor. Other reviews of *The Stones Are Hatching* were similarly laudatory. "With lyrical language, pieces of old songs and poetry, and wondrous imagery, McCaughrean has created a story of amazing depth and breadth," remarked Martha Walke in *Horn Book*. *School Library Journal* contributor Susan L. Rogers especially noted the way that McCaughrean interweaves lessons about loyalty and the human spirit into her tale, and wrote that this approach illustrates to readers "that the horrors of war and the loss of a friend are worse than all of the monsters Phelim encounters."

As a testament to her writing talent and wide-ranging popularity, McCaughrean was selected from among hundreds of writers who entered a competition sponsored by the Great Ormond Street Hospital for Children to write a sequel to *Peter Pan,* the children's classic penned by Scottish novelist J.M. Barrie. First published as a stage play in 1904, the book's rights were bequeathed to the London hospital in 1929, six years before Barrie's death. McCaughrean's sequel, titled *Peter Pan in Scarlet,* was translated into over thirty languages and published in 2006. "Only the most stony-hearted, dyed-in-the-wool Peter Pan fan could fail to be charmed by Geraldine McCaughrean's lightness of touch, sureness of writing and sparkling imagination," wrote Philip Ardagh of the novel in his review for the London *Guardian.* McCaughrean's sequel follows Barrie's original text, allowing Wendy and the Lost Boys to age, transforming some characters in surprising ways, and turning the whole into what Ardagh described as "an extraordinary achievement" that will appeal to both adults and children.

Commenting on the challenge of writing a sequel to such a classic and frequently adapted tale as *Peter Pan,* the author stated in the *Guardian* that she strove to be faithful to Barrie's original work, but added: "I also wanted to create something distinctly my own. So what I attempted was a literary counterpart—the matching bookend—same world, but somewhat reversed," as she did not share all of Barrie's dark views on adults and the inevitability of their happiness.

The author retold another classic in terms accessible to young, modern audiences with *Cyrano,* her adaptation of Edmond Rostrand's play *Cyrano de Bergerac.* McCaughrean's version of the story of the witty, intelligent man with the huge, ugly nose, who writes love letters for a handsome, inarticulate friend, is "eloquent and spirited," stated a *Publishers Weekly* reviewer. Praise also came from Sharon Morrison in *School Library Journal;* she called the author's writing "entertaining and tender." That same year also saw the publication of *Father and Son: A Nativity Story,* in which McCaughrean offers readers a "provocatively imagined tale" that evokes the feelings and doubts experienced by Joseph, the foster father of Jesus. Looking at the infant and knowing him to be the incarnation of God, Joseph wonders how he can ever teach him anything. According to Nancy Menaldi-Scanlan, who reviewed the book in *School Library Journal,* the book is a good compliment to the traditional story, "especially for older children, who can appreciate some of the subtleties of the man's concerns."

GERALDINE McCAUGHREAN

The White Darkness

A bookish teen's obsession with Antarctica leads to intrigue and danger in the award-winning *The White Darkness.* (HarperTeen, 2009. Used by permission HarperCollins Children's Books, a division of HarperCollins Publishers.)

*The White Darkness,* published in 2006, is another young adult novel by McCaughrean. This unusual tale focuses on Symone Wates, a fourteen-year-old girl who has become obsessed with the continent of Antarctica since the death of her father. In fact, Sym imagines herself holding conversations with explorer Titus Oates, who lost his life on Robert Scott's ill-fated expedition to the South Pole. When her Uncle Victor makes it possible for her to visit Antarctica, the sensitive teen experiences "White Darkness," the polar summer in which the sun never sets. What Sym does not realize, however, is that Victor has his own agenda, and she soon finds herself caught up in a web of secrets and manipulation.

Reviewers also had high praise for *The White Darkness.* A contributor for *Publishers Weekly* termed it "a girl's adventure yarn of the first order," and *Booklist* reviewer Jennifer Hubert similarly noted that "this imaginative, intellectually demanding novel offers plenty of action." For a *Kirkus Reviews* contributor, the same novel is an "intense, inwardly focused survival tale" *Horn Book* reviewer Martha V. Parravano found *The White Darkness* many books in one. Not only is it a "quirky" coming-of-age tale, but also "a page-turning survival thriller; a love story; and not least a scintillatingly observed, unsentimental portrait of Antarctica." Speaking with *Booklist* contributor Stephanie Zvirin, McCaughrean called *The White Darkness* not only her favorite work but "the most autobiographical, too—not that I ever got dragged off to Antarctica by a mad uncle—but, like Sym, I feel the need of an imaginary world where I like myself more."

In her 2009 novel *The Death-Defying Pepper Roux*, McCaughrean sets the action in France in the early years of the twentieth century in a "wildly improbable but thoroughly entertaining" tale, according to a *Horn Book* contributor Jonathan Hunt. Young Pepper Roux has an aunt of villainous and vindictive proportions who prophesies that the poor child will die by the age of fourteen. Yet when he awakens on his fourteenth birthday still extant, he decides to hit the road, or the seas, and continue cheating death. His adventures find him taking on many different personas, from ship's captain to journalist to member of the French Foreign Legion. Hunt felt that this book demonstrates that McCaughrean is "one of the more remarkable novelists writing for children today." Further praise came from *Booklist* reviewer Ian Chipman, who noted, "McCaughrean's exuberant prose and whirling humor animate an unforgettable cast of characters." Likewise, a *Kirkus Reviews* contributor termed the work a "poignant, odd, wonderfully composed and vastly entertaining novel."

---

If you enjoy the works of Geraldine Mc-Caughrean, you may also want to check out the following books:

Garth Nix, *Sabriel*, 1995.
Cornelia Funke, *Inkheart*, 2003.
Rick Riordan, *The Battle of the Labyrinth*, 2008.

---

In an author statement for the *British Council* Web site, McCaughrean expounded on her motivation for writing: "I write for much the same reasons as I did when I was a child of eight, forever scribbling stories in an exercise book for no-one's benefit but my own: I like to go somewhere else and become someone else." The versatile and prolific McCaughrean has yet to reach all her writer's goals, as she explained on her home page: "I'd like to write more plays—for stage and radio and schools. Maybe Peter Pan will give me the chance. I'd like to get on a train or Tube or bus and see the passenger opposite reading a book of mine. One day!"

■ **Biographical and Critical Sources**

*BOOKS*

*Children's Literature Review*, Volume 38, Gale (Detroit, MI), 1996.
*Twentieth-Century Children's Writers*, 4th edition, St. James Press (Detroit, MI), 1995.

*PERIODICALS*

*Booklist*, February 1, 1993, Hazel Rochman, review of *Greek Myths*, p. 982; July, 1995, Chris Sherman, review of *The Odyssey*, p. 1873; October 1, 1995, April Judge, review of *The Random House Book of Stories from the Ballet*, p. 310; May 1, 1996, Hazel Rochman, review of *The Golden Hoard: Myths and Legends of the World*, p. 1501; April 15, 1997, Karen Morgan, review of *The Silver Treasure: Myths and Legends of the World*, p. 1424; November 15, 1997, Carolyn Phelan, review of *Unicorns! Unicorns!*, p. 566; March 1, 1998, Susan Dove Lempke, review of *God's People: Stories from the Old Testament*, p. 1130; April 15, 1998, Wilma Longstreet, review of *The Silver Treasure*, p. 1460; May 15, 1998, John Peters, review of *The Bronze Cauldron: Myths and Legends of the World*, p. 1624; August, 1998, GraceAnne A. DeCandido, review of *The Pirate's Son*, p. 2000; October 1, 1998, Ilene Cooper, review of *God's People*, p. 343; November 15, 1998, Susan Dove Lempke, review of *Greek Gods and Goddesses*, p. 584; May 15, 1999, John Peters, review of *The Crystal Pool: Myths and Legends of the World*, p. 1694; October 15, 1999, GraceAnne A. DeCandido, review of *Grandma Chickenlegs*, p. 449; January 1, 2000, Ilene Cooper, review of *God's Kingdom: Stories from the New Testament*, p. 914; July, 2000, GraceAnne A. DeCandido, review of *My First Oxford Book of Stories*, p. 2037; September 1, 2000, GraceAnne A. DeCandido, review of *How the Reindeer Got Their Antlers*, p. 134; February 15, 2001, Karen Hutt, review of *Starry Tales*, p. 1136; September 1, 2001, Susan Dove Lempke, review of *Roman Myths*, p. 101; December 1, 2001, Anna

Rich, review of *The Stones Are Hatching*, p. 664; November 1, 2002, Connie Fletcher, review of *One Bright Penny*, p. 509; August, 2003, GraceAnne A. DeCandido, review of *Stop the Train!*, p. 1981; September 1, 2003, GraceAnne A. DeCandido, review of *Gilgamesh the Hero*, p. 77; October 15, 2003, Linda Perkins, review of *Casting the Gods Adrift: A Tale of Ancient Egypt*, p. 412; December 15, 2004, Hazel Rochman, review of *Odysseus*, p. 739; April 15, 2005, Hazel Rochman, review of *Perseus*, p. 1452; August, 2005, Ilene Cooper, review of *Not the End of the World*, p. 2015; October 1, 2005, Jennifer Mattson, review of *The Jesse Tree*, p. 70; September 15, 2006, Hazel Rochman, review of *Cyrano*, p. 71; October 15, 2006, Carolyn Phelan, review of *Father and Son: A Nativity Story*, p. 54; November 15, 2006, Gillian Engberg, review of *Peter Pan in Scarlet*, p. 42; December 1, 2006, Jennifer Hubert, review of *The White Darkness*, p. 45; March 15, 2007, GraceAnne A. DeCandido, review of *Blue Moon Mountain*, p. 54; March 1, 2008, Stephanie Zvirin, "The Booklist Printz Interview: Geraldine McCaughrean," p. 65; November 1, 2009, Ian Chipman, review of *The Death-Defying Pepper Roux*, p. 34.

*Books for Keeps*, May, 1989, Stephanie Nettell, review of *A Pack of Lies*, p. 25; July, 1997, Elaine Moss, "Classic Cuts," pp. 4-5.

*British Book News Children's Books*, June, 1987, Jessica Yates, review of *A Little Lower Than the Angels*, p. 30.

*Guardian* (London, England), October 7, 2006, Philip Ardagh, review of *Peter Pan in Scarlet*.

*Horn Book*, May-June, 1996, Maria B. Salvadore, review of *The Golden Hoard*, p. 342; November, 1998, Ann A. Flowers, review of *The Pirate's Son*, p. 735, and Kristi Beavin, review of *The Silver Treasure*, p. 767; January, 2000, review of *Grandma Chickenlegs*, p. 88; July, 2000, Martha Walke, review of *The Stones Are Hatching*, p. 462; July, 2001, review of *Roman Myths*, p. 464; July-August, 2003, Peter D. Sieruta, review of *Stop the Train!*, p. 462; September-October, 2003, Joanna Rudge Long, review of *Gilgamesh the Hero*, p. 622; July-August, 2005, Joanna Rudge Long, review of *Not the End of the World*, p. 473; September-October, 2006, Kristi Elle Jemtegaard, review of *Smile!*, p. 610; November-December, 2006, Joanna Rudge Long, review of *Cyrano*, p. 720; March-April, 2007, Martha V. Parravano, review of *The White Darkness*, p. 198; January-February, 2010, Jonathan Hunt, review of *The Death-Defying Pepper Roux*, p. 88.

*Junior Bookshelf*, February, 1983, Marcus Crouch, review of *One Thousand and One Arabian Nights*, p. 44; February, 1985, Marcus Crouch, review of *The Canterbury Tales*, pp. 41-42; June, 1987, Marcus Crouch, review of *A Little Lower Than the Angels*,

p. 135; August, 1989, pp. 159-160; February, 1994, Marcus Crouch, review of *Gold Dust*, pp. 34-35; February, 1995, Marcus Crouch, review of *Stories from Shakespeare*, pp. 38-39.

*Kirkus Reviews*, October 15, 1989, review of *El Cid*, p. 1532; April 1, 1992, review of *The Cherry Tree*, p. 466; May 15, 1993, review of *Over the Deep Blue Sea*; August 1, 1998, review of *The Pirate's Son*, p. 1121; May 1, 2001, review of *Roman Myths*, p. 664; June 1, 2003, review of *Casting the Gods Adrift*, p. 808; September 15, 2003, review of *Gilgamesh the Hero*, p. 1178; November 15, 2004, review of *Odysseus*, p. 1091; April 15, 2005, review of *Perseus*, p. 478; June 15, 2005, review of *Not the End of the World*, p. 687; October 1, 2005, review of *Theseus*, p. 1084; September 1, 2006, review of *Smile!*, p. 908; September 15, 2006, review of *Cyrano*, p. 961; November 1, 2006, review of *Father and Son*, p. 1132; December 1, 2006, review of *The White Darkness*, p. 1223; December 15, 2009, review of *The Death-Defying Pepper Roux*.

*Kliatt*, November, 2003, Claire Rosser, review of *The Kite Rider*, p. 17; July, 2005, Claire Rosser, review of *Not the End of the World*, p. 13, and Phyllis LaMontagne, review of *Stop the Train!*, p. 23; January 1, 2007, Claire Rosser, review of *The White Darkness*, p. 16; March 1, 2007, Nola Theiss, review of *The White Darkness*, p. 52.

*Magpies*, March, 1997, review of *The Silver Treasure*, p. 18; March, 1998, review of *God's People*, pp. 22-23; March, 2001, review of *Gold Dust*, p. 34.

*New York Times Book Review*, April 23, 1995, Maxine Kumin, review of *Stories from Shakespeare*, p. 27.

*Publishers Weekly*, April 28, 1989, review of *A Pack of Lies*, p. 82; April 15, 1996, review of *The Golden Hoard*, p. 69; August 25, 1997, review of *Unicorns! Unicorns!*, p. 71; May 11, 1998, review of *The Bronze Cauldron*, p. 68; September 7, 1998, review of *The Pirate's Son*, p. 96; May 10, 1999, review of *The Crystal Pool*, p. 69; August 16, 1999, review of *The Pirate's Son*, p. 87; October 25, 1999, review of *Grandma Chickenlegs*, p. 80; December 20, 1999, review of *God's Kingdom*, p. 78; May 29, 2000, reviews of *The Stones Are Hatching*, p. 83; September 25, 2000, review of *How the Reindeer Got Their Antlers*, p. 72; March 19, 2001, review of *Starry Tales*, p. 101; August 20, 2001, review of *Roman Myths*, p. 82; May 26, 2003, review of *Stop the Train!*, p. 71; July 7, 2003, review of *Casting the Gods Adrift*, p. 72; November 10, 2003, review of *Stop the Train!*, p. 37; December 13, 2004, review of *Odysseus*, p. 69; July 25, 2005, review of *Not the End of the World*, p. 78; August 29, 2005, review of *The Jesse Tree*, p. 60; September 25, 2006, review of *Father and Son*, p. 70; October 9, 2006, review of *Cyrano*, p. 57; January 22, 2007, review of *The White Darkness*, p. 185; December 7, 2009, review of *The Death-Defying Pepper Roux*, p. 49.

*Resource Links,* April, 2007, Tanya Boudreau, review of *Blue Moon Mountain,* p. 6.

*School Librarian,* February, 1989, Valerie Caless, review of *A Pack of Lies,* p. 31; February, 1993, Pauline Long, review of *The Orchard Book of Greek Myths,* p. 22; May, 1994, Janet Tayler, review of *The Odyssey,* p. 62; May, 1997, Hazel Townson, review of *Moby Dick,* p. 89; winter, 1999, review of *Beauty and the Beast,* p. 213.

*School Library Journal,* February, 1986, Ruth M. McConnell, review of *The Canterbury Tales,* p. 82; December, 1995, Kay McPherson, review of *The Random House Book of Stories from the Ballet,* p. 120; March, 1996, Cheri Estes, review of *The Golden Hoard,* pp. 211-212; April, 1997, Patricia Lothrop-Green, review of *The Silver Treasure,* p. 153; March, 1998, Patricia Pearl Dole, review of *God's People,* p. 198; July, 1998, Angela J. Reynolds, review of *The Bronze Cauldron,* p. 108; October, 1998, Angela J. Reynolds, review of *Greek Gods and Goddesses,* p. 157; November, 1998, Steven Engelfried, review of *The Pirate's Son,* p. 124; August, 1999, Angela J. Reynolds, review of *The Crystal Pool,* p. 174; October, 1999, Lisa Falk, review of *The Nutcracker,* p. 68; April, 2000, Patricia Pearl Dole, review of *God's Kingdom,* p. 122; June, 2000, Susan L. Rogers, review of *The Stones Are Hatching,* p. 150; September, 2000, M. Lang Budin, review of *My First Oxford Book of Stories,* p. 220; October, 2000, review of *How the Reindeer Got Their Antlers,* p. 61; December, 2000, Susan Scheps, review of *Beauty and the Beast,* p. 134; July, 2001, Nina Lindsay, review of *Roman Myths,* p. 96; December, 2001, Suzanne Libra, review of *The Stones Are Hatching,* p. 76; August, 2003, Angela J. Reynolds, review of *Casting the Gods Adrift,* p. 162, and Bruce Anne Shook, review of *Stop the Train!,* p. 163; December, 2003, Patricia D. Lothrop, review of *Gilgamesh the Hero,* p. 171; December, 2004, Angela J. Reynolds, review of *Odysseus,* p. 163; August, 2005, Kathy Piehl, review of *Not the End of the World,* p. 130, and M. Lang Budin, review of *Perseus,* p. 146; October, 2005, review of *Odysseus,* p. 52; January, 2006, Linda L. Walkins, review of *The Jesse Tree,* p. 106, and M. Lang Budin, review of *Hercules,* p. 158; August, 2006, Casey Rondini, review of *Smile!,* p. 56; October, 2006, Nancy Menaldi-Scanlan, review of *Father and Son,* p. 98, and Sharon Morrison, review of *Cyrano,* p. 161; December, 2006, Jayne Damron, review of *Smile!,* p. 150; April, 2007, Jayne Damron, review of *Blue Moon Mountain,* p. 112, and Christi Voth, review of *The White Darkness,* p. 142; January, 2010, Connie Tyrrell Burns, review of *The Death-Defying Pepper Roux,* p. 108.

*Teacher Librarian,* June, 2000, Jessica Higgs, reviews of *Greek Gods and Goddesses, Myths and Legends of the World,* and *The Crystal Pool,* pp. 54-55; February, 2003, Liza Graybill, review of *One Bright Penny,* p. 115.

*Time,* September 4, 2006, Michael Brunton, "Return to Neverland," p. 53.

*Times Educational Supplement,* February 1, 1985, Terry Jones, "Pilgrim's Way," p. 27; November 12, 1993, Brian Slough, "Gold Fever," p. 3; April 23, 1999, Geraldine Brennan, review of *Roman Myths and Legends,* p. 11; December 24, 1999, review of *A Pack of Lies,* p. 27.

*Voice of Youth Advocates,* August, 1997, Roxy Ekstrom, review of *The Silver Treasure,* p. 204.

*Washington Post Book World,* July 10, 2005, Elizabeth Ward, review of *Not the End of the World,* p. 12.

ONLINE

*British Council Web site,* http://www.contemporarywriters.com/ (February 1, 2010), Elizabeth O'Reilly, "Contemporary Writers: Geraldine McCaughrean."

*Geraldine McCaughrean Home Page,* http://www.geraldinemccaughrean.co.uk (February 1, 2010).*

(Photograph courtesy of David Livingston/Getty Images.)

# Larry McMurtry

## ■ Personal

Born June 3, 1936, in Wichita Falls, TX; son of William Jefferson (a rancher) and Hazel Ruth McMurtry; married Josephine Ballard, July 15, 1959 (divorced, 1966); children: James Lawrence. *Education:* North Texas State College (now University), B.A., 1958; Rice University, M.A., 1960; additional study at Stanford University, 1960.

## ■ Addresses

*Home*—Archer City, TX. *Office*—Booked Up, Box 1286, 216 South Center, Archer City, TX 76351.

## ■ Career

Novelist, screenwriter, essayist, and bookseller. *Houston Post,* Houston, TX, reviewer, 1960s; Texas Christian University, Fort Worth, TX, instructor, 1961-62; Rice University, Houston, TX, lecturer in English and creative writing, 1963-69; *Washington Post,* Washington, DC, reviewer; George Mason College, Fairfax, VA, visiting professor, 1970; American University, Washington, DC, visiting professor, 1970-71. Booked Up Book Store, Archer City, TX, owner, 1970—; has also owned book stores in Washington, DC, Houston, TX, and Tucson, AZ; also worked as a rare book scout and a dealer for book stores in Texas and California.

## ■ Member

PEN American Center (president, 1989-91), Texas Institute of Letters.

## ■ Awards, Honors

Wallace Stegner fellowship, 1960; Jesse H. Jones Award, Texas Institute of Letters, 1962, for *Horseman, Pass By;* Guggenheim fellowship, 1964; Academy Award (Oscar) for best screenplay based on material from another medium, Academy of Motion Picture Arts and Sciences, 1972, for *The Last Picture Show;* Barbara McCombs/Lon Tinkle Award for continuing excellence in Texas letters, Texas Institute of Letters, 1986; Pulitzer Prize for fiction, Spur Award, Western Writers of America, and Texas Literary Award, Southwestern Booksellers Association, all 1986, all for *Lonesome Dove;* Robert Kirsch Award, *Los Angeles Times,* 2003, for McMurtry's body of work that "grows out of and reflects brilliantly upon the myth and reality of the American West in all of its infinite variety"; Golden Globe award for Best Screenplay, 2005, Academy Award for best adapted screenplay, 2005, and BAFTA award for Best Adapted Screenplay, British Academy of Film and Television Arts, 2006, all for *Brokeback Mountain*; *Lonesome Dove* was selected Best TV Western Miniseries/Movie of all time, Western Writers of America, 2009; inducted into Texas Trail of Fame, 2009.

## ■ Writings

### NOVELS

*Horseman, Pass By*, Harper (New York, NY), 1961, Texas A & M University Press (College Station, TX), 1988, published as *Hud*, Popular Library (New York, NY), 1961.

*Leaving Cheyenne*, Harper (New York, NY), 1963, Texas A & M University Press (College Station, TX), 1986.

*The Last Picture Show* (also see below), Dial (New York, NY), 1966, Simon & Schuster (New York, NY), 1989.

*Moving On*, Simon & Schuster (New York, NY), 1970, Pocket Books (New York, NY), 1988.

*All My Friends Are Going to Be Strangers*, Simon & Schuster (New York, NY), 1972, published with a preface by the author and afterword by Raymond L. Neinstein, Scribner Paperback Fiction (New York, NY), 2002.

*Terms of Endearment*, Simon & Schuster (New York, NY), 1975, reprinted with new preface, Scribner (New York, NY), 1999.

*Somebody's Darling*, Simon & Schuster (New York, NY), 1978.

*Cadillac Jack*, Simon & Schuster (New York, NY), 1982.

*The Desert Rose*, Simon & Schuster (New York, NY), 1983.

*Lonesome Dove*, Simon & Schuster (New York, NY), 1985, reprinted, Simon & Schuster, 2000.

*Texasville* (sequel to *The Last Picture Show*; also see below), Simon & Schuster (New York, NY), 1987.

*Anything for Billy*, Simon & Schuster (New York, NY), 1988.

*Some Can Whistle* (sequel to *All My Friends Are Going to Be Strangers*), Simon & Schuster (New York, NY), 1989.

*Buffalo Girls*, Simon & Schuster (New York, NY), 1990.

*The Evening Star* (sequel to *Terms of Endearment*), Simon & Schuster (New York, NY), 1992.

*Streets of Laredo* (sequel to *Lonesome Dove*), Simon & Schuster (New York, NY), 1993.

(With Diana Ossana) *Pretty Boy Floyd*, Simon & Schuster (New York, NY), 1994.

*Three Bestselling Novels* (contains *Lonesome Dove*, *Leaving Cheyenne*, and *The Last Picture Show*) Wings Books (New York, NY), 1994.

*Dead Man's Walk* (prequel to *Lonesome Dove*), Simon & Schuster (New York, NY), 1995.

*The Late Child*, Simon & Schuster (New York, NY), 1995.

(With Diana Ossana) *Zeke and Ned*, Simon & Schuster (New York, NY), 1997.

*Comanche Moon* (prequel to *Lonesome Dove*), Simon & Schuster (New York, NY), 1997.

*Duane's Depressed* (sequel to *Texasville*), Simon & Schuster (New York, NY), 1999.

*Sin Killer: The Berrybender Narratives, Book One*, Simon & Schuster (New York, NY), 2002.

*The Wandering Hill: The Berrybender Narratives, Book Two*, Simon & Schuster (New York, NY), 2003.

*By Sorrow's River: The Berrybender Narratives, Book Three*, Simon & Schuster (New York, NY), 2003.

*Folly and Golly: The Berrybender Narratives, Book Four*, Simon & Schuster (New York, NY), 2004.

*Loop Group*, Simon & Schuster (New York, NY), 2005.

*Telegraph Days*, Simon & Schuster (New York, NY), 2006.

*When the Light Goes* (sequel to *Duane's Depressed*), Simon & Schuster (New York, NY), 2007.

*Rhino Ranch* (sequel to *When the Light Goes*), Simon & Schuster (New York, NY), 2009.

### ESSAYS

*In a Narrow Grave: Essays on Texas*, Encino Press (Austin, TX), 1968, Simon & Schuster (New York, NY), 1989.

*It's Always We Rambled: An Essay on Rodeo*, Frank Hallman (New York, NY), 1974.

*Film Flam: Essays on Hollywood*, Simon & Schuster (New York, NY), 1987.

*Sacagewea's Nickname: Essays on the American West*, New York Review of Books (New York, NY), 2001.

### SCRIPTS

(With Peter Bogdanovich) *The Last Picture Show* (screenplay; based on McMurtry's novel of same title; produced by Columbia, 1971), B.B.S. Productions, 1970.

*Montana* (teleplay), Turner Network Television, 1990.

*Falling from Grace* (screenplay), Columbia, 1992.

(With Cybill Shepherd) *Memphis* (teleplay; based on a novel by Shelby Foote), Turner Home Entertainment, 1992.

(With Diana Ossana) *Streets of Laredo* (teleplay; based on McMurtry's novel of the same title), CBS, 1995.

(With Diana Ossana) *Dead Man's Walk* (teleplay; based on McMurtry's novel of the same title), ABC, 1996.

(With Diana Ossana) *Johnson County War* (teleplay; based on the novel *Riders of Judgement* by Frederick Manfred), Hallmark Channel, 2002.

(With Diana Ossana) *Brokeback Mountain* (based on the short story by Annie Proulx), Focus Features, 2005.

(With Diana Ossana) *Comanche Moon* (teleplay; based on McMurtry's novel of the same title), CBS, 2008.

*OTHER*

(Author of foreword) Frederick L. Olmsted, *Journey through Texas: or, A Saddle-Trip on the Southwestern Frontier,* University of Texas Press (Austin, TX), 1978.

(Author of foreword) John R. Erickson, *Panhandle Cowboy,* University of Nebraska Press (Lincoln, NE), 1980.

(Author of introduction) Dan Flores, *Canyon Visions: Photographs and Pastels of the Texas Plains,* Texas Tech University Press (Lubbock, TX), 1989.

(Author of introduction) Donna A. Demac, *Liberty Denied: The Current Rise of Censorship in America,* Rutgers University Press (New Brunswick, NJ), 1990.

(Author of foreword) Clarus Backes, editor, *Growing up Western,* Knopf (New York, NY), 1990.

*Crazy Horse* (biography), Viking (New York, NY), 1999.

*Walter Benjamin at the Dairy Queen: Reflections at Sixty and Beyond* (memoir), Simon & Schuster (New York, NY), 1999.

(Editor) *Still Wild: Short Fiction of the American West, 1950 to the Present,* Simon & Schuster (New York, NY), 2000.

*Roads, Driving America's Great Highways* (memoir), Simon & Schuster (New York, NY), 2000.

*Boone's Lick* (stories), Simon & Schuster (New York, NY), 2000.

*Paradise* (memoir), Simon & Schuster (New York, NY), 2001.

*Oh What a Slaughter: Massacres in the American West, 1846-1890,* Simon & Schuster (New York, NY), 2005.

*The Colonel and Little Missie: Buffalo Bill, Annie Oakley, and the Beginnings of Superstardom in America,* Simon & Schuster (New York, NY), 2005.

(With Annie Proulx and Diana Ossana) *Brokeback Mountain: Story to Screenplay,* Scribner (New York, NY), 2006.

(Author of foreword) Bill Wittliff, *A Book of Photographs from Lonesome Dove,* University of Texas Press (Austin, TX), 2007.

*Books: A Memoir,* Simon & Schuster (New York, NY), 2008.

*Literary Life: A Second Memoir,* Simon & Schuster (New York, NY), 2009.

Also contributor to *Texas in Transition,* Lyndon Baines Johnson School of Public Affairs, 1986, and *Rodeo: No Guts No Glory,* Aperture (New York, NY), 1994. Contributor of numerous articles, essays, and book reviews for magazines and newspapers, including *Atlantic Monthly, Gentleman's Quarterly, New York Times, Saturday Review,* and *Washington Post.* Contributing editor of *American Film,* 1975-92.

## ■ Adaptations

*Hud,* a motion picture starring Paul Newman, Patricia Neal, and Melvyn Douglas and based on *Horseman, Pass By,* was produced by Paramount, 1962; *Lovin' Molly,* based on *Leaving Cheyenne,* was produced by Columbia, 1974; *Terms of Endearment,* based on the novel of the same title, was produced by Paramount, 1983; *Lonesome Dove,* based on the novel of the same title, was produced as a television miniseries, CBS, 1989; *Texasville,* based on the novel of the same title, was produced by Columbia, 1990; *Return to Lonesome Dove,* based on characters from *Lonesome Dove,* was produced as a television miniseries, CBS, 1993; *The Evening Star,* based on the novel of the same title, was produced by Paramount, 1996; *The Desert Rose* was adapted for film by Columbia Pictures from a script by Nora and Delia Ephron.

## ■ Sidelights

In the decades since he published his first novel, Larry McMurtry has emerged as one of America's most prominent fiction writers. His landscape is his native Texas; the author frequently examines the uneasy interaction between that state's mythic past and its problematic, ongoing urbanization during the later decades of the twentieth century. His fiction is united by common themes, including nostalgia for the past and fear of the future, the importance of place, and rites of passage and initiation. In the words of Mark Busby, writing in the *Dictionary of Literary Biography*, "McMurtry's work is marked by his imaginative connections with the American West. Drawn to place, McMurtry demonstrates in his work the mythic pattern of escape and return to his 'blood's country,' his homeland."

The author's earliest works, such as the critically acclaimed *Horseman, Pass By* and *The Last Picture Show*, expose the bleak prospects for adolescents on the rural ranches or in the small towns of west Texas, while his novels written in the 1970s, including *Terms of Endearment*, trace Texas characters drawn into the urban milieus of Houston, Hollywood, and Washington, D.C. His 1986 Pulitzer Prize-winning novel, *Lonesome Dove*, received high praise for its realistic detailing of a cattle drive from the late nineteenth century, a transformation into fiction of a part of Texas history the author previously approached in his essays on cowboys, ranching, and rodeos. As Si Dunn noted in the *Dallas News*, McMurtry's readers find him "a writer who has made living in Texas a literary experience."

As a spokesman for the status of modern Texas letters, McMurtry has been known to criticize some Texas writers for their tendency to overlook the potentially rich material to be found in that state's modern, industrialized society and growing urban areas. In *In a Narrow Grave: Essays on Texas*, he concluded: "Texas writers are sometimes so anxious to avoid the accusation of provincialism that they will hardly condescend to render the particularities of their own place, though it ought to be clear that literature thrives on particulars. The material is here, and it has barely been touched." He added, "Literature has coped fairly well with the physical circumstances of life in Texas, but our emotional experience remains largely unexplored, and therein lie the drama, poems, and novels."

In *The Ghost Country: A Study of the Novels of Larry McMurtry*, Raymond L. Neinstein expressed the belief that McMurtry "has journeyed from an old-fashioned regionalism to a kind of 'neo-regionalism,' his characters, and the novels themselves, turning from the land as the locus of their values to an imaginary, fictive 'place.' But they, characters and novels both, are finally not able to manage there, at least not comfortably. McMurtry clearly does not trust 'living in the head'; the pull of the old myth is still strong." Indeed, much of McMurtry's fiction reflects his home state's struggle to reconcile its frontier past with its urbanized future. "Being a writer and a Texan is an amusing fate, one that gets

**McMurtry shared screenwriting credits with Peter Bogdanovich on** *The Last Picture Show*, **the film adaptation of his 1966 novel about life in small-town Texas.** (Photograph courtesy of Columbia/The Kobal Collection/The Picture Desk, Inc.)

funnier as one's sense of humor darkens," the author continued in *In a Narrow Grave*. "The transition that is taking place is very difficult, and the situations it creates are very intense. Living here consciously uses a great deal of one's blood; it involves one at once in a birth, a death, and a bitter love affair."

## Lone Star Roots

The son and grandson of cattle ranchers, McMurtry grew up in sparsely populated Archer County in north central Texas. From childhood he was more interested in reading than ranching, but the family stories he heard as a youth exerted an enormous influence on his sense of identity. He wrote in *In a Narrow Grave*: "It is indeed a complex distance from those traildrivers who made my father and my uncles determined to be cowboys to the mechanical horse that helps convince my son that he is a cowboy, as he takes a vertical ride in front of a laundrymat." If he felt pride and nostalgia for the ranching way of life which was vanishing even as he came of age, McMurtry was far less enthusiastic about tiny Archer City, where he attended high school as an honor student. He found little to nourish his imagination within the confines of the town, noting in *In a Narrow Grave:* "I grew up in a bookless town, in a bookless part of the state—when I stepped into a university library, at age eighteen, the whole of the world's literature lay before me unread, a country as vast, as promising, and, so far as I knew, as trackless as the West must have seemed to the first white men who looked upon it."

Interestingly, in creating his own fiction, McMurtry has drawn many of his themes from his bookless, "blood's country" of Texas. His early works portray a fictional town and countryside with a strong resemblance to Archer County. In *Horseman, Pass By,* his first novel, McMurtry introduces the adolescent narrator Lonnie Bannon, who describes a series of tragic events that occur on his grandfather's ranch when an epidemic of hoof-and-mouth disease is discovered. Nearing manhood himself, the orphaned Lonnie is confronted with several role models whose behavior he must evaluate: his step-uncle Hud, an egotistic and ruthless hedonist; his grandfather's hired hand Jesse, a storytelling drifter; and his grandfather, Homer, who, Charles D. Peavy stated in his *Larry McMurtry,* "epitomizes all the rugged virtues of a pioneer ethic." Lonnie's frustration is additionally fanned by the presence of Halmea, the black housekeeper who Peavy suggested is both "love object and mother surrogate" to the young man. John Gerlach noted in the *Dictionary of Literary Biography* that the relationship between Lonnie and Halmea, based on "tenderness, lack of fulfillment, and separation due here to differences in age and race," marks "the beginning of what becomes an essential theme in [McMurtry's] later works—people's needs do not match their circumstances." Peavy saw *Horseman, Pass By* as the first chronicle of another recurring McMurtry theme: "the initiation into manhood and its inevitable corollaries—loneliness and loss of innocence."

*Horseman, Pass By* was published when its author was twenty-five. While not an immediate commercial success, it established McMurtry's reputation within the Western genre. In an article in *Regional Perspectives: An Examination of America's Literary Heritage,* Larry Goodwyn called McMurtry "one of the most interesting young novelists in the Southwest—and certainly the most embattled in terms of frontier heritage." While McMurtry claimed in *In a Narrow Grave* that "the world quietly overlooked" *Horseman, Pass By,* and that he himself viewed it in retrospect an immature work, the book was not only significant enough to warrant an Academy Award-winning movie adaptation, but also of sufficient literary merit to garner McMurtry a 1964 Guggenheim award for creative writing. Peavy quoted a letter critic John Howard Griffin wrote to McMurtry's agent after reading *Horseman, Pass By:* "This is probably the starkest, most truthful, most terrible and yet beautiful treatment of [ranching country] I've seen. It will offend many, who prefer the glamour treatment—but it is a true portrait of the loneliness and pervading melancholy of cowboying; and of its compensations in nature, in human relationships."

*Leaving Cheyenne,* McMurtry's second novel, is also set in ranching country. The story revolves around Molly Taylor and the two men she loves throughout her lifetime: Gid, a rancher, and Johnny, a cowboy. Each of the three central characters narrates a section of the book; their intertwined lives are traced from youth to death. "McMurtry is psychologically precise in tracing this three-sided relationship," wrote Walter Clemons in the *New York Times Book Review.* "Odd as the roots of this friendship may seem, there's enduring consideration and feeling in it. The story takes so many years to tell because feelings that last a lifetime are the subject." Gerlach noted that *Leaving Cheyenne* explores a new aspect of the theme of "mismatching and the isolation it brings. . . . The expanded time scheme and number of narrators enrich the themes of the novel." Clemons, who called McMurtry "one of the two best writers to come out of Texas in the [1960s]," claimed that *Leaving Cheyenne* is "a rarity among second novels in its exhilarating ease, assurance and openness of feeling."

When evaluating McMurtry's early works, critics tend to group *Horseman, Pass By* and *Leaving Cheyenne* together due to their similarities of setting and theme. According to Goodwyn, "McMurtry's first two novels . . . were promising efforts to put the materials of frontier culture to serious literary use . . . . [Both books] are in-the-grain novels of people striving to live by the cultural values of the legend. . . . McMurtry speaks through a narrator who is frontiersman enough to move with ease through the tall-in-the-saddle milieu, but sensitive enough to note the ritualized energy and directionless fury surrounding him. . . . Relying . . . on the literary device of the provincial narrator, McMurtry found a voice that seemed to serve well as a strengthening connection between himself and his sources."

## Small-Town Blues

The fictional town of Thalia figures peripherally in both *Horseman, Pass By* and *Leaving Cheyenne.* In *The Last Picture Show,* McMurtry's third novel, Thalia becomes the primary setting and the debilitating monotony of small-town life one of the primary themes. Thomas Lask in the *New York Times* described McMurtry's Thalia: "A sorrier place would be hard to find. It is desiccated and shabby physically, mean and small-minded spiritually. Mr. McMurtry is expert in anatomizing its suffocating and dead-end character." The novel's action once again revolves around a group of late adolescents who are struggling to achieve adulthood in the town's confining atmosphere. Peavy wrote of McMurtry: "He examines the town's inhabitants—the oil rich, the roughnecks, the religious fanatics, the high school football stars, the love-starved women—with an eye that is at once sociological and satiric. For the first time he abandons the first-person narrative in his fiction, and the result is a dispassionate, cold look at the sordidness and hypocrisy that characterize the town."

When it was first published in 1966, *The Last Picture Show* raised some controversy in McMurtry's hometown of Archer City and elsewhere for its graphic detailing of teenage sexuality—including exhibitionism, bestiality, petting, masturbation, and homosexuality. "On the surface," Peavy noted, "McMurtry's treatment of small-town sexuality may seem quite sensational; actually, it is accurate. In the cloying confines of Thalia, the only outlet for frustrations, loneliness, boredom, even hatred—for both adolescents and adults—is sex. . . . Some of McMurtry's sexual scenes are highly symbolic, all are important thematically, and none should be taken as sensationalism." W.T. Jack expressed the same opinion in the *New York Times Book Review*: "Offensive? Miraculously, no. McMurtry is an alchemist who converts the basest materials to gold. The sexual encounters are sad, funny, touching, sometimes horrifying, but always honest, always human." Peavy felt, in fact, that "neither Updike nor Salinger has been as successful as McMurtry in describing the gnawing ache that accompanies adolescent sexuality."

Some critics felt that certain characterizations in *The Last Picture Show* approach stereotype. "McMurtry has said that part of the concern of *The Last Picture Show* is to portray how the town is emotionally centered in high school—in adolescence," stated Peavy. "As a result, the protagonist of the book is somewhat inadequately developed." According to Peavy, some of the difficulties in McMurtry's novel were surmounted in the film script of *The Last Picture Show* through the added perspective of director and co-writer Peter Bogdanovich. "The film script . . . is a much more sympathetic portrait of McMurtry's hometown than is the novel," Peavy

suggested. "The combination of the two young writers [McMurtry and Bogdanovich] was fortunate." Filmed in black and white on location in Archer City, *The Last Picture Show* was a commercial and critical success, winning three Academy Awards including an award for best screenplay based on material from another medium. In an *Atlantic Monthly* review, David Denby stated that the movie "reverses many of the sentimental assumptions about small towns that were prevalent in the movies of the forties, but it never becomes a cinematic exposé. It's a tough-minded, humorous, and delicate film—a rare combination in an American movie." Writing for *Newsweek*, Paul D. Zimmerman called the film "a masterpiece" with "a finely tuned screenplay." Zimmerman also claimed that *The Last Picture Show* "is not merely the best American movie of a rather dreary year; it is the most impressive work by a young American director since *Citizen Kane*."

### Examines Urban Life

McMurtry followed *The Last Picture Show* with what is sometimes referred to as his "urban trilogy": *Moving On, All My Friends Are Going to Be Strangers,* and *Terms of Endearment.* These novels represent a radical departure in setting and tone in detailing the lives of Houston urbanites, some of whom travel across the country in various, seemingly aimless pursuits. In her *Western American Literature* study on McMurtry's work, Janis P. Stout wrote of *Moving On* and *All My Friends Are Going to Be Strangers:* "None of the characters in these two novels has any sense of a usable past, and none is purposefully directed toward the future. They inhabit the burgeoning cities of Texas with no apparent means of orienting themselves and nothing to engage them but endless, unsatisfying motion—as the title *Moving On* well indicates." McMurtry uses a revolving set of characters as the cast for all three books. The supporting troupe in one novel may evolve to primary importance in another volume, as is the case with Emma Horton, who appears briefly in *Moving On* and *All My Friends Are Going to Be Strangers* before becoming the protagonist in *Terms of Endearment.* R.C. Reynolds noted in the *Southwest Review*: "Though time sequences often fall out of order in the three novels, key events and characters are repeated often enough to maintain a continuous theme which, not surprisingly, has three parts: sex and its frustrations, academics and its frustrations, and something like culture and its frustrations which McMurtry has branded *Ecch-Texas*."

Considered as a group, *Moving On, All My Friends Are Going to Be Strangers,* and *Terms of Endearment* did not achieve the favorable critical response that

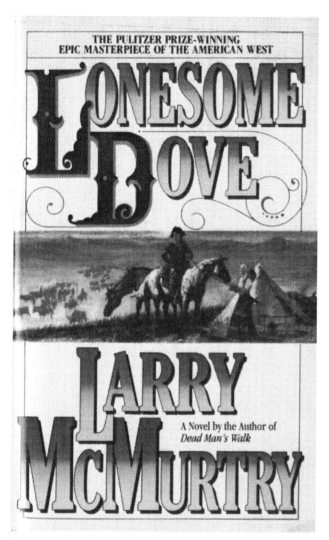

*Lonesome Dove,* **McMurtry's epic, Pulitzer Prize-winning novel, offers a richly detailed look at a nineteenth-century cattle drive.** (Pocket Books, 1986. Cover art copyright © 1986 Shannon Stirnweis. Reproduced by permission of Pocket Books, an imprint of Simon & Schuster Macmillan.)

quickly followed McMurtry's earlier books. Stout claimed that "the journey pattern so insistent in McMurtry's first three novels has in [*Moving On* and *All My Friends Are Going to Be Strangers*] become dominant, as the characters drive endlessly and pointlessly around the country chiefly between Texas and California. Not surprisingly, novels so constituted lack cohesive form; or rather, their forms may be described as being imitative to a radical and destructive degree. . . . Unfortunately, this expressive form, by its very nature, is destructive of the overall novelistic structure and renders the work a chronicle of tedium." Goodwyn sensed an ambiguity at work in the novels: "The frontier ethos, removed from the center of [McMurtry's] work,

continues to hover around the edges—it surfaces in minor characters who move with purpose through novels that do not."

Reviewers were not unanimously disappointed with the "urban trilogy," however. In a review of *Moving On* for the *New York Times,* John Leonard wrote: "McMurtry has a good ear: [the characters] talk the way people actually talk in Houston, at rodeos, in Hollywood. Mr. McMurtry also has a marvelous eye for locale: the Southwest is superbly evoked. It is a pleasure . . . to escape claustrophobic novels that rely on the excitation of the verbal glands instead of the exploration of social reality." "It is difficult to characterize a talent as outsized as McMurtry's," suggested Jim Harrison in the *New York Times Book Review.* "Often his work seems disproportionately violent, but these qualities in *All My Friends Are Going to Be Strangers* are tempered by his comic genius, his ability to render a sense of landscape and place, and an interior intellectual tension that resembles in intensity that of Saul Bellow's *Mr. Sammler's Planet.* McMurtry . . . has a sense of construction and proper velocity that always saves him." A *Times Literary Supplement* reviewer likewise concluded: "There are few books one remembers with a real sense of affection, but *All My Friends* is indisputably one of them. Mr. McMurtry's talent for characterization and the evocation of place—together with his ability to blend them convincingly, so that they seem almost to interdepend—makes [the protagonist's] near-indefinable yearnings for a past which seems close enough to grab at wholly understandable."

*Terms of Endearment,* first published in 1975, has since become the most popular segment of the "urban trilogy." The story concerns Aurora Greenway, a New England-born widow who lives in Houston, and her married daughter, Emma. The greater portion of the novel deals with Aurora's relationship with her several "suitors," including a retired armored corps commander and an oil millionaire, but the final chapter follows Emma through a deteriorating marriage to her ultimate death from cancer. *New York Times* critic Christopher Lehmann-Haupt observed that "maybe what keeps one entertained [with the book] is the sympathy with which Mr. McMurtry writes about these people. . . . One laughs at the slapstick, one weeps at the maudlin, and one likes all of Mr. McMurtry's characters, no matter how delicately or broadly they are drawn." Gerlach found Aurora "loveable because she can turn a phrase. . . . Her story has endless permutations but no motion; she is timeless." Though some critics felt that the tragic ending strikes a jarring note following the light comic adventures of Aurora, they nonetheless found the section moving. Robert Towers, writing in the *New York Times Book Review,* noted: "The final scenes between the dying Emma and her stricken boys are the most affecting in the book."

*Terms of Endearment,* according to McMurtry, marked a turning point in his fiction writing. As he told Dunn, "I lived in Texas quite a while, and for my own creative purposes had kind of exhausted it. Texas is not an inexhaustible region." Having himself moved from Houston to Washington, DC in 1970, McMurtry began to seek new regional settings for his books. The three novels McMurtry published between 1978 and 1983 all have primary settings outside of Texas. *Somebody's Darling* centers on the Hollywood career of a young female film director, *Cadillac Jack* follows the cross-country ramblings of an aging antiques dealer, and *The Desert Rose* provides a fictional portrait of a good-hearted Las Vegas showgirl. Critical appraisals of these works concentrate on McMurtry's ability to create appealing characters who are independent of his traditional regional setting. In a *Dictionary of Literary Biography Yearbook* essay, Brooks Landon suggested that *Somebody's Darling* contains "two of [McMurtry's] most mature and most fully realized characters." *Washington Post Book World* contributor Jonathan Yardley similarly stated of *Somebody's Darling:* "Mr. McMurtry's characters are real, believable and touching, his prose has life and immediacy and he is a very funny writer." Less successful, according to reviewers, is *Cadillac Jack,* a novel based in Washington, DC. Peter Prince wrote in *Nation* that the principal character "is the man to squelch everything down to the level of his own deep ordinariness," while Yardley stated in the *Washington Post* that "the city as it emerges in the novel is a mere caricature, like too many of the characters in it." Of the three books, *The Desert Rose* received the most commendation for its sympathetic

***Lonesome Dove*** **was adapted as a 1989 television mini-series featuring Angelica Huston and Robert Duvall.** (Photograph © CBS Photo Archive/Hulton Archive/Getty Images.)

characterization. Yardley claimed in the *Washington Post Book World:* "In her innocent, plucky, unaffected way [the protagonist] is as courageous a character as one could hope to meet." As Larry McCaffery observed in the *Los Angeles Times Book Review,* McMurtry "flirts with being unbearably cute . . . but his lack of condescension toward characters and situation makes his depictions ring true."

### Depicting the Real Wild West

McMurtry's ability to transcend caricature and present his characters as real, living people has earned him a reputation as a mythbreaker. Nowhere is this reputation better supported than in his triptych of historical westerns, *Lonesome Dove, Anything for Billy,* and *Buffalo Girls,* which together successfully debunk the myths of the Old West—with its hardy cowboys, ruthless gunslingers, and savage Indians—recasting them as the sad inhabitants of a dying era.

*Lonesome Dove,* McMurtry's 800-page, 1985 release, not only returns to the author's native state for its setting—a locale he had consciously avoided for five years—but also concerns the brief cattle drive era that has proven the focus of much of the Western romantic mystique. McMurtry told the *New York Times Book Review* that the novel "grew out of my sense of having heard my uncles talk about the extraordinary days when the range was open," a subject the author had previously addressed only in his nonfiction. According to the reviewers, a strong advantage to the book is the author's objective presentation of frontier life. As George Garrett explained in the *Chicago Tribune Book World, Lonesome Dove* contains "the authority of exact authenticity. You can easily believe that this is how it really was to be there, to live, to suffer and rejoice, then and there. And thus, the reader is most subtly led to see where the literary conventions of the Western came from, how they came to be in the first place, and which are true and which are false." *New York Times Book Review* contributor Nicholas Lemann also wrote of *Lonesome Dove:* "Everything about the book feels true; being anti-mythic is a great aid to accuracy about the lonely, ignorant, violent West." This anti-mythic foundation in the novel, according to Lemann, "works to reinforce the strength of the traditionally mythic parts . . . by making it far more credible than the old familiar horse operas."

*Lonesome Dove* achieved best-seller status within weeks of its release and was a critical success as well. "McMurtry is a storyteller who works hard to satisfy his audience's yearning for the familiar," stated R.Z. Sheppard in *Time.* "What, after all, are legends made of? The secret of his success is embellishment, the odd detail or colorful phrase that keeps the tale from slipping into a rut." *Newsweek's* Walter Clemons claimed that the novel "shows, early on, just about every symptom of American Epic except pretentiousness." Clemons concluded: "It's a pleasure . . . to be able to recommend a big popular novel that's amply imagined and crisply, lovingly written. I haven't enjoyed a book more this year." "The aspects of cowboying that we have found stirring for so long are, inevitably, the aspects that are stirring when given full-dress treatment by a first-rate novelist," explained Lemann. *Lonesome Dove* was awarded the Pulitzer Prize for fiction in 1986.

McMurtry's contrasting of the "popular" Old West to the "real" Old West is more heavy-handed in his 1988 novel *Anything for Billy.* Cast in the role of narrator is Benjamin Sippy, a depressed Easterner fascinated by the cowboy adventures he reads and writes about in such dime novels as *Orson Oxx, Man of Iron* and *Solemn Sam, the Sad Man from San Saba.* Fed up with his oppressive wife and his nine horrible daughters, Sippy heads west to live the life of an outlaw. The western plains that await him, though, are not those of his precious dime novels; there are more bugs than buffalo. After a disastrous attempt at train robbery, Sippy meets a buck-toothed simpleton named Billy Bone who, though never having pulled a trigger, has somehow built a reputation as a gunfighter—a reputation he is determined to live up to. With the help of Sippy's writing and a sawed-off shotgun, Billy Bone transforms himself into Billy the Kid.

McMurtry's retelling of the story of Billy the Kid is unique, a portrayal Julian Loose of the *Times Literary Supplement* warned "will certainly upset anyone nostalgic for Hollywood's version of the boy who never grew old." Missing from its pages is the Lincoln County war, mentor-turned-adversary John Chisum, or the traitorous Pat Garrett. The Kid himself is ugly, crude, and ignorant; he is afraid of thunder and lightning; possessing poor vision and bad aim, he compensates by shooting his victims at close range with an oversized gun, often without provocation. "There is nothing heroic or even accomplished about this Billy," lamented Loose, "yet he exudes an irresistible boyish charm" that "attracts followers and lovers who will do 'anything for Billy' but [who] cannot stop him wandering on to his premature and pointless doom."

The theme of *Anything for Billy* is age-old: Don't believe everything you read. By making Sippy both a writer and reader of pulp fiction, McMurtry points his finger at those who perpetuate the myths of the Old West. "The book's greatest strength," added *Village Voice*'s M. George Stevenson, "is in Sippy's accounts of how his dime novelist's expectations of the West were either too grand or too mundane." Robert Gish, reviewing *Anything for Billy* in the *Los Angeles Times Book Review*, proclaimed the novel "a tall tale that outdoes any previous telling about Billy the *bandito* boy of old New Mexico," and which forces readers to "think again about the real and the imagined West and the rendering of them in words."

As with *Anything for Billy*, 1990's *Buffalo Girls* features a cast of historical characters: Calamity Jane, Wild Bill Hickok, Buffalo Bill Cody, and Sitting Bull. Unlike young Billy Bone, though, the characters in *Buffalo Girls* are depicted at the end of their careers; tired, old and drunk, they travel together in Buffalo Bill's Wild West Show, emulating the adventures that made them into legends. The dwindling lives of McMurtry's characters mirror the approaching demise of the Wild West itself: the once-untamable land is now settled, the animals slaughtered, the bloodthirsty Indians relegated to small parcels of land. "Almost everyone in *Buffalo Girls* knows himself and his world to be on the verge of extinction," Susan Fromberg Schaeffer observed in the *New York Times Book Review*. "They begin to understand that they have outlived their time. The question then becomes whether they can find a new way to live, or at least a new meaning that will justify their lives. That most of them fail to do so should be no surprise, because the Wild West, as Mr. McMurtry seems to conceive it [is] the childhood of our country and, like all childhoods, it must pass."

In his historical Westerns, *New York Times Book Review* critic Jack Butler maintained that McMurtry alternates "the Old Wild West with the West of the present or near-present" in order to counterpoint the overly romanticized myths that permeate American literature. "I'm a critic of the myth of the cowboy," McMurtry explained to Mervyn Rothstein in the *New York Times*. "I don't feel that it's a myth that pertains, and since it's a part of my heritage I feel it's a legitimate task to criticize it." The reason for the popularity of the cowboy myth—that of the tough-but-fair rogue who adheres to the "code of the West"—is, he believes, rooted in the American psyche. "If you actually read the biography of any of the famous gunfighters . . . they led very drab, mostly very repetitive, not very exciting lives. But people cherish a certain vision, because it fulfills psychological needs. People need to believe that cowboys are simple, strong and free, and not twisted, fascistic and dumb, as many cowboys I've known have been."

Though McMurtry told Rothstein that he is "simply having fun reinventing" the myth of the Wild West, critics have found greater significance in his historical novels. Schaeffer described *Buffalo Girls* as "a work of resurrection, a book that rescues an important era of our country's saga both from that taxidermist, the history book, and from that waxwork beautifier, the myth machine." Butler, too, praised McMurtry's efforts as "doing something with the American West that is very much like what William Faulkner did with Mississippi. He is re-(not de-) mythologizing it. . . . None of this would matter if he were not a poet, a resonant scene-setter and a master of voice, but he is; and since the West figures so strongly in our vision of what it means to be American, Mr. McMurtry's labor is, I think, essential literature."

Perhaps because of the success of such films as *The Last Picture Show* and *Terms of Endearment*, as well as the television miniseries *Lonesome Dove*, during the late 1980s McMurtry became known more for his screenplays and the cinematic adaptations of his novels than as a novelist. Reviewers often criticized his books in Hollywood terms, as if they had already been translated to the screen; *The Evening Star*, for example, was panned by Mark Starr of *Newsweek* as "more script than novel," and Robert Plunkett of the *New York Times Book Review* attributed the popularity of the novel's main character, Aurora Greenway, to the performance of Shirley MacLaine in *Terms of Endearment*.

## Returns to Familiar Ground

A number of McMurtry's later works—including *Texasville, Some Can Whistle, The Evening Star, The Streets of Laredo*, and *The Late Child*—are sequels to earlier novels. McMurtry also penned a sequel to *Texasville*, titled *Duane's Depressed*. "More than any other writer I know of, McMurtry is inclined to return to his earlier books and spin off sequels," observed H.H. Harriman in the *Detroit News*. "It is hard to say exactly what the motivation is here— genuine and fond nostalgia, what could pass for a genuine preoccupation with unfinished business, or more darkly, the less than genuine and never gentle persuasion of a publisher's greed." McMurtry also wrote two prequels to *Lonesome Dove: Dead Man's Walk* and *Comanche Moon*.

Of his sequels, one that weathered the critical storm is *Texasville*. Though it reintroduces the city of Thalia, Texas, and the characters of *The Last Picture Show*, its tone is far different from that of its predecessor. Set thirty years after the events of the first novel,

*Texasville* shows Thalia's residents as middle-aged men and women who, having made their fortunes during the oil boom of the 1970s, are now systematically going bankrupt. The town is as stifling and monotonous as ever, but the once-idealistic adolescents of *The Last Picture Show* have ceased to struggle against it. "They have stopped having thoughts," wrote Louise Erdrich in the *New York Times Book Review*. "They simply act out their emotions by destroying things. . . . Waste is celebrated." While the observations of *Texasville*'s main character render the decline of Thalia in a humorous light, it is humor of the darkest, most cynical variety. "If Thalia . . . can stand for modern America," John Clute opined in the *Times Literary Supplement*, "then for Larry McMurtry modern America is terrifyingly like hell."

As the townspeople grow more irrational and irresponsible, they once again turn to sex—and lots of it—to keep their minds off their moral and financial deterioration. "But there's something sadder and more irrevocable" about the promiscuity in *Texasville*, according to Michiko Kakutani in the *New York Times*. "Everyone is older now, sinking into the disappointments and weariness of middle age, and for most of them, familial security and enduring love are no longer dreamed-of possibilities but lost opportunities, consigned to a receding past." Erdrich, too, noted the difference between the two novels' use of frequent sex: "In *The Last Picture Show*, the quest was not only for sex, but sex linked to tenderness and mystery, to love. In *Texasville*, sex is just sex. It happens everywhere and often."

Though *Texasville* is universally regarded as a very different book from its predecessor, it was still considered by many critics to be a literary success. "While [*Texasville*] lacks the ambition and epic resonance of *Lonesome Dove*, it shows off the author at his popular storytelling best, and it attests, again, to his sure feeling for people and place," lauded Kakutani.

With *Duane's Depressed*, McMurtry returned to the denizens of Thalia, this time centering on sixty-two-year-old Duane Moore. Oil rich and disillusioned with his life, family, and friends, Duane's dissatisfaction begins to manifest itself in eccentric behavior. He parks his pickup truck and begins walking everywhere. He moves out of his house and chooses to live in a cabin in the woods. Although never of a literary bent, Duane discovers the works of Henry David Thoreau and decides to take the philosopher's advice and "live deliberately." Eventually Duane is persuaded to see a psychiatrist, the lesbian Honor Carmichael, with whom he falls hopelessly in love, and who introduces him to Mar-

cel Proust. Discussing the book in the *New York Times Book Review*, Robert Houston observed: "By the book's end, Duane's beginning a fresh, untried kind of trip, one that is both literal and symbolic. He's on a plane to the Pyramids of Egypt, old passions confronted, the unknown ahead." While considering the plot at times forced and the character of Honor Carmichael "a bit too saintly, a bit too wise," Houston nevertheless concluded that "*Duane's Depressed* is a worthwhile end to an important trilogy, one that captures vividly and movingly nearly half a century of life in a great swath of America." A reviewer for *Publishers Weekly* added: "Using barren landscapes and drab interiors to emphasize the subtle, potent drama of Duane's search for himself, McMurtry shines as he examines the issues of alienation, grief and the confrontation with personal mortality."

Unlike his sprawling "urban trilogy," McMurtry's sequels are more static, their characters less prone to travel and external relationships. Receiving mixed reviews were *Some Can Whistle* and *The Evening Star*, each of which reprises a popular set of characters who, now older, attempt to reconcile with their families and, eventually, themselves. While both novels are rife with dark humor and sudden, jarring tragedy, Kakutani considered the combination "contrived and melodramatic," although adding that it is executed successfully through the author's "fluency and poise as a writer." His penchant for sequels has furthered the criticism of McMurtry as a "cinematic writer," *Time* reviewer Paul Gray noting of *Some Can Whistle*: "Everything and everyone in the tale reeks of Hollywood." Still, his books remain popular among loyal readers. "While utterly satisfying on their own, [these sequels] also give the longtime reader the pleasure of seeing a character mature through the decades," Kakutani explained. "The result is not unlike growing old in the company of a favorite relative or friend."

If *Texasville* has fared the best among McMurtry's sequels, *Streets of Laredo* has probably fared the worst, with several critics questioning the wisdom of continuing a tale as well-constructed as *Lonesome Dove*. "Part of the very bittersweet pleasure of finishing reading a great book is that its story and characters are *finite*," Harriman commented. "In that respect, they 'die,' only to live on in our memories. Sequels then are a kind of exhumation, a dishonor to the memory of the dead." In *Streets of Laredo*, Harriman concluded, "the tried and true caveats about the built-in, inevitable disappointments of sequels have been overlooked, and a Pulitzer Prize-winner has been reduced to pandering."

Not all reviewers disliked *Streets of Laredo*. *Detroit Free Press* contributor Martin F. Kohn lauded the way McMurtry "depicts the wild West on its last legs—more vicious than ever, as if enraged by its own coming demise at the hands of railroads, growing towns and other constructs of civilization." Kohn called the novel "a delicious, though vividly violent, read," wherein "verbal stands of color are planted at many a turn . . . relieving the brutal landscape of the main narrative. . . . As a purveyor of time, place, plot and character [McMurtry] remains our novelist laureate of the old West." *New York Times Book Review* critic Noel Perrin suggested that, while on many pages *Streets of Laredo* "is the full equal of *Lonesome Dove*, there are also many [pages] on which Mr. McMurtry makes you wish he had left the characters of *Lonesome Dove* in peace."

critical opinion was again somewhat mixed for *Dead Man's Walk*, a prequel to *Lonesome Dove*. The novel finds teens Gus McCrae and Woodrow Call joining their first mission as Texas Rangers under a self-declared colonel. On the mission they are dogged by merciless Indians, saved by a noblewoman in a leper colony, and endure a 200-mile "dead man's walk" across New Mexico. Observed Thomas Flanaghan in the *New York Times Book Review,* "It is a stranger and a more ambitious book than [*Lonesome Dove*], ruthless in its disposition of characters, sparse and vivid in its creation of the inhuman landscapes of New Mexico and the plains." According to some critics, the novel provides no new insight into the development of the central characters, and the plot is preposterous because so many of the facts on which the story is based have been greatly exaggerated. "It's one thing to demystify Rangers and quite another to invent a comic-book past," remarked Noel Perrin in the *Washington Post Book World.* "If *Dead Man's Walk* were not a prequel [to *Lonesome Dove*]," wrote John Skow in *Time,* "it would be worth only glancing notice. As things are, it is a satisfactory foothill, with the grand old mountain in view."

In the story chronology of the "Lonesome Dove" series, *Comanche Moon* follows *Dean Man's Walk* and precedes *Lonesome Dove*, filling the twenty-year gap between the end of one book and the beginning of the other. McCrae and Call fight to advance the American frontier in the face of hostile Comanches led first by Buffalo Hump, and later his son Blue Duck. The narrative also explores the love affairs of the protagonists, Gus with a local shopkeeper who marries another man, and Woodrow with a prostitute who gives birth to his child. Discussing the novel, a *Kirkus Reviews* critic noted that McMurtry "delivers a generally fine tableau of western life, full of imaginative exploits, convincing historical background, and characters who are alive." Barbara Perkins of *Library Journal* wrote: "McMurtry is at his best with a host of characters and painting on this large canvas."

## An Eclectic Oeuvre

In 2002 McMurtry published *Sin Killer*, the first book in his four-volume series known as "The Berrybender Narratives." Set in the untamed American West during the 1830s, the darkly comic series follows the exploits of Lord Berrybender, a bumbling, pompous English aristocrat, and his large, ever-changing entourage of family members and servants. According to *New York Times Book Review* critic David Willis McCullough, "The Berrybenders may seem boorish, cruel and exceptionally unpleasant, but they follow a definite literary tradition—that grotesque behavior exhibited by people with first names like Albany, Bobbety, and Buffum often leads to comedy, or at least entertaining eccentricity." *Sin Killer* was followed by *The Wandering Hill, By Sorrow's River*, and *Folly and Glory*. "As always," observed Verlyn Klinkenborg in the *New York Times Book Review*, "McMurtry is a natural creator of incident. He knots and unknots stories as easily as can be, and if you went looking for the literary sources of the Berrybender narratives you'd find them not only in the western potboilers of an earlier era but in the yarning that one imagines took place at a rendezvous of trappers and mountain men."

*Telegraph Days* looks at the waning days of the Old West through the eyes of Nellie Courtright, a feisty young woman who, after penning a best-selling dime novel about her brother's heroic exploits, improbably ends up managing the Wild West Show, fending off a robbery attempt by Jesse James, and witnessing the Gunfight at the O.K. Corral. "This rollicking epic is filled with excitement and humor, tinged with sadness and a longing for the past," noted *Booklist* contributor Jay Freeman, and *Texas Monthly* contributor Mike Shea described the work as "filled with telling historical detail and atmospheric with choking dust and whiskey-breathed cowhands." "McMurtry could not be more clear in his conviction that the Western ethos must be abandoned as an actual way of life," noted Cheryl Miller, writing in *Policy Review*. "But he still recognizes the nobility of Western myth. Thus, *Telegraph Days*, even with its merciless skewering of the Old West, celebrates the beauty of the Western dream—as a dream that never was a reality."

McMurtry returned to a contemporary setting for *Loop Group*, "a quirky but enjoyable buddy story," stated Freeman. After a hysterectomy has left her feeling low, sixty-year-old widow Maggie Clary, the owner of a small film dubbing company, invites her best friend Connie to accompany her on a road trip to visit Maggie's aunt in the Texas panhandle. Along the way, the women encounter a host of eccentric characters, including a professional hitchhiker and a

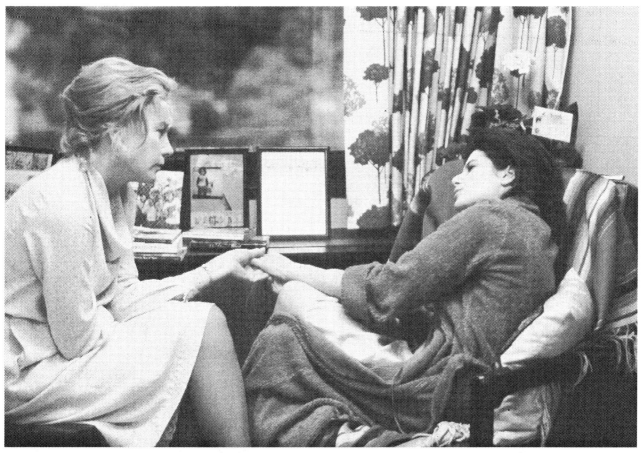

**Shirley MacLaine (left) and Debra Winger starred in the film version of McMurtry's moving family drama *Terms of Endearment*.** (Photograph courtesy of Paramount/The Kobal Collection/Rosenthal, Zade/The Picture Desk, Inc.)

polite car thief. According to a *Kirkus Reviews* critic, "there's something here for everyone: An affectionate peek at the workers clinging to Hollywood's lowest rung; campy sex; drama on the highway; and canny insights into the dynamics of family and friendship."

Eight years after the publication of *Duane's Depressed*, McMurtry resurrected the character of Duane Moore for *When the Light Goes*, a "piquantly comic celebration of the absurdity of aging," observed Shea. Now widowed, impotent, and in need of a triple bypass, Duane falls for twenty-six-year-old Ann Cameron, the flirtatious new employee of his oil company, competently managed by his son, Dickie. He also enters an affair with Carmichael, whose own lover has recently passed away. "Muddle is what Duane and his male peers do best, aided by Viagra, sexual instruction videos and forgiving women," noted John Leland in the *New York Times Book Review*. "At 64, Duane is no longer much help to his children or family business. That women fall into his lap is a happy accident. They're

a Wild West he doesn't have to tame, just survive." Despite the critical success of McMurtry's previous works about Thalia, *When the Light Goes* received decidedly mixed reviews. A contributor in *Publishers Weekly* noted that "this slim novel reads like a short story," and Jerry Eberle, writing in *Booklist*, remarked that "it's nice to know what ultimately becomes of old Duane—even if it isn't particularly enthralling."

McMurtry completed his cycle of novels featuring Duane Moore with *Rhino Ranch* "a top-shelf blend of wit and insight, sharply defined characters and to-the-point prose," according to a contributor in *Publishers Weekly*. A prosperous, widowed retiree in his late 60s, Duane finds himself depressed and directionless, circumstances shared by friends Boyd Cotton, an aging cowboy, and Bobby Lee Baxter, his former employee. Duane's interest is soon piqued, however, when billionaire heiress K.K. Slater moves to Thalia, announcing plans to build a sanctuary for African black rhinos. "McMurtry, as always, treats his characters with humor, affection, and respect,"

Freeman noted in *Booklist,* and a critic in *Kirkus Reviews* observed that the novel "closes lyrically with ineluctable sadness, life being in the end a succession of small tragedies and occasional triumphs."

In addition to his many novels, McMurtry has also published the short story collection *Boone's Lick,* the memoirs *Walter Benjamin at the Dairy Queen: Reflections at Sixty and Beyond* and *Paradise,* the biographies *Crazy Horse* and *The Colonel and Little Missie: Buffalo Bill, Annie Oakley, and the Beginnings of Superstardom in America,* as well as essay collections, nonfiction, and screenplays. In *Paradise,* the author ruminates on his parent's difficult marriage before moving forward in time to the period of his mother's death in Archer City, a period during which McMurtry was traveling the South Sea Islands. The book—part travelogue, part memoir—includes "some characteristically wonderful passages that only McMurtry could write," maintained *Book* contributor Don McLeese, while still expressing disappointment over the brevity of the volume. More enthusiastically, a reviewer for *Publishers*

*Weekly* commented that "Readers of this excellent travelogue, abounding with literary references from Henry James to [Jack] Kerouac, will likely return to the book often to reread . . . favorite passages of McMurtry's meditative prose." Calling McMurtry "such a pro he could make laundry seem interesting," *Booklist* contributor Donna Seaman characterized his approach as "a magnetic blend of irascibility and grace."

In *Walter Benjamin at the Dairy Queen,* McMurtry combines essay with personal reminiscence to demonstrate, as Richard Bernstein of the *New York Times* put it, "how he abandoned the cowboy life in Texas where he grew up, and became . . . a herder of words." The "Walter Benjamin" of the title refers to a German-Jewish literary critic and essayist whom McMurtry first read while at the Dairy Queen in Archer City. The material here is wide ranging, including McMurtry's childhood memories of his parents' ranch, discussion of writers as diverse as Susan Sontag and Miguel Cervantes, a description of McMurtry's 1991 heart attack, and a

**With cowriter Diana Ossana, McMurtry received a 2006 Academy Award for best adapted screenplay for** *Brokeback Mountain,* **based on a story by Annie Proulx.** (Photograph courtesy of Focus Features/The Kobal Collection/The Picture Desk, Inc.)

lament concerning the decline of storytelling in everyday life. For Bernstein, this "memoir is not easy to get a bead on. It meanders: it picks up themes and then picks up other themes, but it often doesn't get to a point. . . . it leaves the reader longing for a stronger theme, great narrative punch." Thomas Mallon voiced a similar sentiment in the *New York Times Book Review* when he stated that the book "reads tantalizingly like the notes toward" an autobiography; "a reader does become frustrated with certain gaps and discontinuities." In contrast, Mike Shea wrote in *Texas Monthly* that McMurtry's "dry and gentle humor makes the essays read like his best fiction," while a *Publishers Weekly* reviewer called *Walter Benjamin at the Dairy Queen* "a thoughtful, elegant retrospective on Texas, his [McMurtry's] work and the meaning of reading by an author who has the range to write with intelligence about both Proust and the bathos of a Holiday Inn marquee."

Reviewing *Crazy Horse* for *Library Journal,* Stephen H. Peters credited McMurtry with "constructing a thoughtful discussion of Sioux culture around the known facts to show how Crazy Horse was shaped by his society and how he reacted to its destruction as whites spread onto the Great Plains." In *The Colonel and Little Missie,* McMurtry examines the lives of Buffalo Bill Cody, the Army scout, buffalo hunter, and entertainer, and Oakley, the legendary sharpshooter who became the star attraction of Cody's Wild West Show. According to a critic in *Publishers Weekly,* "the book's aim, to separate fact from folklore, is beautifully accomplished."

In 2005 McMurtry received the Academy Award for his screenplay for *Brokeback Mountain*, coauthored with Diana Ossana, his close friend and collaborator who helped nurse him back to health after his heart attack and subsequent struggle with depression. Based on the short story by Annie Proulx, *Brokeback Mountain* concerns the decades-long relationship between Ennis Del Mar and Jack Twist, a pair of Wyoming ranch hands who meet in the summer of 1963 while tending sheep. Alone on Brokeback Mountain, the men stave off boredom and loneliness by swapping stories and drinking whiskey; one night, Jack invites Ennis into his tent and initiates a sexual encounter. After going their separate ways, Ennis and Jack both marry and have children, yet their connection remains strong and they periodically reunite over the years. "They're men who have fallen in love without quite realizing that's what's happened to them," observed *Entertainment Weekly* reviewer Owen Gleiberman, "and the glory of *Brokeback Mountain* is that in tracing their fates, treating their passion as something unprecedented—a force so powerful it can scarcely be named—the movie makes love seem as ineffable as it really is." According to Alonso Duralde, writing in the *Advocate,* McMurtry and Ossana "have crafted a haunting and practically perfect romance," and *Newsweek* contributor Sean Smith commented, "No American film before has portrayed love between two men as something this pure and sacred. As such, it has the potential to change the national conversation and to challenge people's ideas about the value and validity of same-sex relationships."

## A Life Devoted to Literature

In addition to his writing, McMurtry spends time overseeing the operations of "Booked Up," an antiquarian bookstore he founded. "I began to realize that with real estate as it is now in urban centers, the only way you could have a giant bookstore is to have it in a small town," he explained to *New York Times Magazine* contributor Mark Horowitz. "I've watched it in my own time: the giant bookstores died in Boston, in Philadelphia, in Washington, D.C., in Long Beach, in Cincinnati, in Chicago. I just love the possibilities of really big used bookstores— vast repositories of knowledge—and the only hope of preserving them for another generation is to build one in a small town." In 1989 McMurtry was chosen president of the PEN American Center, a prestigious writers' organization with affiliates around the world. He was the first non-New Yorker to head the American branch since Indiana's Booth Tarkington, who founded it in 1922.

In his autobiographical 2008 work, *Books: A Memoir,* McMurtry reflects on his life as a book scout, seller, and collector, and reminisces about his encounters with a host of eccentric book dealers. "With remarkable clarity, he gives his readers a glimpse into the world of a bookman," Anthony Pucci stated in *Library Journal,* and a *Publishers Weekly* reviewer asserted that "McMurtry is at his best when he uses his considerable skills as a writer to recreate moments from his personal past." The author focuses on his career as a novelist, screenwriter, and essayist, as well as his relationships with other writers, in *Literary Life: A Second Memoir.* "McMurtry's understated style is charming and deceptively sophisticated," a critic in *Publishers Weekly* maintained, and Freeman called the work "an enjoyable and revealing look at the thoughts and career of a great writer."

McMurtry describes his approach to his craft in peculiarly Texan terms. Writing, he claimed to Sheila Benson in the *Los Angeles Times,* is "the ultimate analogue to my herding tradition. I herd words, I herd them into sentences and then I herd them into

If you enjoy the works of Larry McMurtry, you may also want to check out the following books:

Loren D. Estleman, *This Old Bill*, 1984.
John Updike's "Rabbit" series, including *Rabbit at Rest*, 1990.
Cormac McCarthy, *The Crossing*, 1994.

paragraphs and then I herd these paragraphs into books." As Neinstein indicated, the region McMurtry has written about with such success is "a ghost country . . . a country of love and of blood-ties. When those ties break down, when the love is gone, when the inheritance or inheritability of that country is somehow thwarted and its traditions are no longer viable, then the poignancy of the country's neglected beauty, of the tradition's unusable force, and of the human life left to survive without that beauty, that tradition, that center, becomes the subject of McMurtry's powerful and nostalgic novels." These novels, McMurtry told a contributor in the *Los Angeles Times*, are not based on mere "notes of scandals of the neighborhood," but rather are built by essential flights of imagination. "I am more and more convinced," he declared, "that the essential reward of writing fiction is in the delight of seeing what you can make out of the sole tools of your imagination and your experience."

## ■ Biographical and Critical Sources

BOOKS

*Authors in the News*, Volume 2, Gale (Detroit, MI), 1976.
Bennett, Patrick, *Talking with Texas Writers: Twelve Interviews*, Texas A & M University Press (College Station, TX), 1980.
*Bestsellers 89*, Issue 2, Gale (Detroit, MI), 1989.
Bonner, Stayton, *The Bookman: A Story about Larry McMurtry's Other Day Job*, introduction by McMurtry, Three Dog Press (Archer City, TX), 2006.
Burke, John Gordon, editor, *Regional Perspectives: An Examination of America's Literary Heritage*, American Library Association (Chicago, IL), 1971.
Busby, Mark, *Larry McMurtry and the West: An Ambivalent Relationship*, University of North Texas Press (Denton, TX), 1995.
*Contemporary Literary Criticism*, Gale (Detroit, MI), Volume 2, 1974, Volume 3, 1975, Volume 7, 1977, Volume 11, 1979, Volume 27, 1984, Volume 44, 1987, Volume 127, 2000, Volume 250, 2008.

*Contemporary Novelists*, St. James Press (Detroit, MI), 2001.
*Dictionary of Literary Biography*, Gale (Detroit, MI), Volume 2: *American Novelists since World War II, First Series* 1978, Volume 143: *American Novelists since World War II, Third Series*, 1994, Volume 256: *Twentieth-Century American Western Writers, Third Series*, 2002.
*Dictionary of Literary Biography Yearbook*, Gale (Detroit, MI), *1979*, 1980, *1980*, 1981, *1986*, 1987, *1987*, 1988, *1993*, 1994.
Jones, Roger Walton, *Larry McMurtry and the Victorian Novel*, Texas A&M University Press (College Station, TX), 1994.
Landess, Thomas, *Larry McMurtry*, Steck-Vaughn (Austin, TX), 1969.
Lich, Lera Patrick Tyler, *Larry McMurtry's Texas: Evolution of the Myth*, Eakin Press (Austin, TX), 1987.
McCullough, David W., *People Books and Book People*, Harmony Books (New York, NY), 1981.
McMurtry, Larry, *In a Narrow Grave: Essays on Texas*, Encino Press (Austin, TX), 1968, Simon & Schuster (New York, NY), 1989.
McMurtry, Larry, *Walter Benjamin at the Dairy Queen: Reflections at Sixty and Beyond*, Simon & Schuster (New York, NY), 1999.
McMurtry, Larry, *Paradise*, Simon & Schuster (New York, NY), 2001.
McMurtry, Larry, *Books: A Memoir*, Simon & Schuster (New York, NY), 2008.
McMurtry, Larry, *Literary Life: A Second Memoir*, Simon & Schuster (New York, NY), 2009.
Neinstein, Raymond L., *The Ghost Country: A Study of the Novels of Larry McMurtry*, Creative Arts Book Company (Berkeley, CA), 1976.
*Newsmakers*, Issue 4, Gale (Detroit, MI), 2006.
*Pages: The World of Books, Writers, and Writing*, Gale (Detroit, MI), 1976.
Peavy, Charles D., *Larry McMurtry*, Twayne (Boston, MA), 1977.
Reilly, John M., *Larry McMurtry: A Critical Companion*, Greenwood Press (Westport, CT), 2000.
Reynolds, Clay, editor, *Taking Stock: A Larry McMurtry Casebook*, Southern Methodist University Press (Dallas, TX), 1989.
Schmidt, Dorey, editor, *Larry McMurtry: Unredeemed Dreams*, Pan American University (Edinburgh, TX), 1978.

PERIODICALS

*Advocate*, December 6, 2005, Alonso Duralde, review of *Brokeback Mountain*, p. 81; February 28, 2006, "*Brokeback*'s Big Secrets," p. 42.

*America,* March 5, 1983, review of *Cadillac Jack,* p. 179; April 29, 1995, Robert R. Burke, review of *Pretty Boy Floyd,* p. 32; November 18, 1995, Loren F. Schmidtberger, review of *The Late Child,* p. 28.

*American Heritage,* April-May, 2006, Allen Barra, "Larry McMurtry: Writing Westerns from *Hud* to *Brokeback Mountain,*" p. 18.

*Atlantic Monthly,* December, 1971, David Denby, review of *The Last Picture Show.*

*Book,* July, 2001, Don McLeese, review of *Paradise,* p. 72; May-June, 2002, Don McLeese, review of *Sin Killer,* p. 69.

*Booklist,* April 15, 2001, Donna Seaman, review of *Paradise,* p. 1506; April 1, 2002, Mary Frances Wilkens, review of *Sin Killer: The Berrybender Narratives, Book One,* p. 1283; March 15, 2003, Jay Freeman, review of *The Wandering Hill: The Berrybender Narratives, Book Two,* p. 1253; September 1, 2003, Jay Freeman, review of *By Sorrow's River: The Berrybender Narratives, Book Three,* p. 7; February 15, 2004, Jay Freeman, review of *Folly and Glory: The Berrybender Narratives, Book Four,* pp. 1003-1004; October 15, 2004, Jay Freeman, review of *Loop Group,* p. 363; March 1, 2006, Jay Freeman, review of *Telegraph Days,* p. 44; December 15, 2006, Jerry Eberle, review of *When the Light Goes,* p. 5; July 1, 2009, Jay Freeman, review of *Rhino Ranch,* p. 9; December 1, 2009, Jay Freeman, review of *Literary Life: A Second Memoir,* p. 11.

*Chicago Tribune Book World,* June 9, 1985, George Garrett, review of *Lonesome Dove,* p. 1.

*Dallas Morning News,* August 2, 2009, Michael Granberry, "Texan Author Larry McMurtry Thinks 30th Novel May Be His Last Page."

*Dallas News,* January 18, 1976, Si Dunn, "Larry McMurtry Moves On."

*Denver Post,* July 13, 2008, Elaine Margolin, "Git Along, Writer Nowadays, Author Larry McMurtry Is a Bookseller and Collector," p. E-11.

*Detroit Free Press,* July 25, 1993, Martin F. Kohn, review of *Streets of Laredo,* p. J6.

*Detroit News,* July 31, 1993, H.H. Harriman, review of *Streets of Laredo,* p. D14.

*Economist* (US), August 19, 2000, review of *Roads,* p. 75.

*Entertainment Weekly,* March 13, 1992, Owen Gleiberman, review of *Falling from Grace,* p. 34; August 26, 1994, Mark Harris, review of *Pretty Boy Floyd,* p. 105; November 28, 2003, Mary Kaye Schilling, "Lone Star," p. 82; December 9, 2005, Owen Gleiberman, "The Searchers," review of *Brokeback Mountain,* p. 59.

*Kirkus Reviews,* September 15, 1997, review of *Comanche Moon;* September 15, 2004, review of *Loop Group,* p. 886; July 1, 2009, review of *Rhino Ranch;* October 15, 2009, review of *Literary Life.*

*Library Journal,* November 15, 1998, Stephen H. Peters, review of *Crazy Horse,* p. 75; February 1, 2000, Barbara Perkins, review of *Comanche Moon,* p. 133; October 15, 2000, Thomas L. Kilpatrick, review of *Boone's Lick,* p. 102; July, 2001, Cynde Bloom Lahey, review of *Paradise,* p. 90; May 1, 2002, Joseph M. Eagan, review of *Sin Killer,* p. 134; August 1, 2008, Anthony Pucci, review of *Books: A Memoir,* p. 84; December, 2009, Nedra Crowe-Evers, review of *Literary Life,* p. 106.

*Los Angeles Times,* May 27, 1984, Garry Abrams, "A West Texas Literary Herdsman"; January 31, 1989, Charles Champlin, "McMurtry on the Trail of *Dove* Again"; July 3, 1989, David Lamb, "Small Texas Town's First Picture Show Won't Be Its Last Dose of Hollywood, Thanks to Resident Author"; September 28, 1990, Sheila Benson, "*Texasville:* Midlife Crises Film," p. F1.

*Los Angeles Times Book Review,* November 14, 1982, Carolyn See, review of *Cadillac Jack,* p. 1; September 4, 1983, Larry McCaffery, review of *The Desert Rose,* p. 7; June 9, 1985, John Horn, review of *Lonesome Dove,* p. 2; August 16, 1987, review of *Film Flam: Essays on Hollywood,* p. 12; October 30, 1988, Robert Gish, review of *Anything for Billy,* p. 1; October 22, 1989, review of *Some Can Whistle,* p. 2; June 7, 1992, review of *The Evening Star,* p. 4; June 4, 1995, review of *The Late Child,* p. 3.

*Nation,* February 3, 1979, Brina Caplan, review of *Somebody's Darling,* p. 121; November 20, 1982, Peter Prince, review of *Cadillac Jack,* p. 536.

*Newsweek,* October 1, 1971, Paul D. Zimmerman, review of *The Last Picture Show;* June 3, 1985, Walter Clemons, review of *Lonesome Dove,* p. 19; September 26, 1988, Walter Clemons, review of *Anything for Billy,* p. 76; June 8, 1992, Mark Starr, review of *The Evening Star,* p. 58; January 11, 1999, Malcolm Jones, "The Poet Lariat," p. 62; November 21, 2005, Sean Smith, "Forbidden Territory," review of *Brokeback Mountain,* p. 68.

*New York Review of Books,* August 13, 1992, Thomas R. Edwards, review of *The Evening Star,* p. 54.

*New York Times,* December 3, 1966, Thomas Lask, review of *The Last Picture Show,* p. 37; June 10, 1970, John Leonard, review of *Moving On,* p. 45; October 22, 1975, Christopher Lehmann-Haupt, review of *Terms of Endearment,* p. 43; December 20, 1978, Christopher Lehmann-Haupt, review of *Somebody's Darling,* p. C25; June 3, 1985, Christopher Lehmann-Haupt, review of *Lonesome Dove,* p. C20; April 8, 1987, Michiko Kakutani, review of *Texasville,* p. C24; June 27, 1987, Michiko Kakutani, review of *Film Flam,* p. C7; September 28, 1988, Michiko Kakutani, review of *Anything for Billy,* p. C24; November 1, 1988, Mervyn Rothstein, "A Texan Who Likes to Deflate The Legends of the Golden West," p. C17; October 16, 1990, Michiko Kakutani, review of *Buffalo Girls,* p. C17;

May 12, 1992, Michiko Kakutani, review of *The Evening Star,* p. C17; August 26, 1994, Michiko Kakutani, review of *Pretty Boy Floyd,* p. C28; June 28, 1995, Richard Bernstein, review of *The Late Child,* p. C19; December 13, 1999, Richard Bernstein, "An Author's Seminal Moment at a Texas Drive-In."

*New York Times Book Review,* November 13, 1966, W.T. Jack, review of *The Last Picture Show,* p. 68; July 26, 1970, review of *Moving On,* p. 16; August 15, 1971, Walter Clemons, reviews of *Leaving Cheyenne, Moving On,* and *In a Narrow Grave,* p. 39; March 19, 1972, Jim Harrison, review of *All My Friends Are Going To Be Strangers,* p. 5; October 19, 1975, Robert Towers, review of *Terms of Endearment,* p. 4; November 21, 1982, Eden Ross Lipson, review of *Cadillac Jack,* p. 13; October 23, 1983, Steve Tesich, review of *The Desert Rose,* p. 12; June 9, 1985, Nicholas Lemann, review of *Lonesome Dove,* p. 7; September 16, 1985, Edwin McDowell, "Western Novels Ride High Again," p. C13; April 19, 1987, Louise Erdrich, review of *Texasville,* p. 7; May 31, 1987, William Murray, review of *Film Flam,* p. 35; October 16, 1988, Jack Butler, review of *Anything for Billy,* p. 3; October 22, 1989, Barbara Kingsolver, review of *Some Can Whistle,* p. 8; October 7, 1990, Susan Fromberg Schaeffer, review of *Buffalo Girls,* p. 3; June 21, 1992, Robert Plunkett, review of *The Evening Star,* p. 12; July 25, 1993, Noel Perrin, review of *Streets of Laredo,* p. 9; October 16, 1994, Sidney Zion, review of *Pretty Boy Floyd,* p. 31; May 21, 1995, Verlyn Klinkenborg, review of *The Late Child,* p. 12; September 10, 1995, Thomas Flanagan, review of *Dead Man's Walk,* p. 33; February 21, 1999, Robert Houston, review of *Duane's Depressed;* November 21, 1999, Thomas Mallon, "Even Cowboys Get the Blues"; November 26, 2000, Karen Karbo, review of *Boone's Lick,* p. 16; November 26, 2000, Karen Karbo, review of *Boone's Lick,* p. 16; June 10, 2001, John Vernon, "Lonesome Son: When Larry McMurtry's Mother Was Dying, He Got as Far Away from the World as Possible," p. 19; May 26, 2002, Neil Gordon, "An Englishman Abroad," p. 8; June 1, 2003, David Willis McCullough, "Chaps in Chaps," p. 32; December 7, 2003, Verlyn Klinkenborg, "Plunging In," p. 48; June 18, 2006, Chelsea Cain, "Cowboys Are My Weakness," p. 11; March 18, 2007, John Leland, "Duane's Depraved," review of *When the Light Goes.*

*New York Times Magazine,* December 7, 1997, Mark Horowitz, "Larry McMurtry's Dream Job"; May 29, 2005, Deborah Solomon, "Cowboy Culture," p. 17.

*Policy Review,* February-March, 2007, Cheryl Miller, "Creating the American West," p. 88.

*Publishers Weekly,* December 2, 1996, review of *Zeke and Ned,* p. 40; November 16, 1998, review of *Crazy Horse,* p. 59; December 7, 1998, review of *Duane's Depressed,* p. 51; October 1, 1999, review of *Walter Benjamin at the Dairy Queen,* p. 87; May 21, 2001, review of *Paradise,* p. 92; October 22, 2001, review of *Sacagawea's Nickname: Essays on the American West,* p. 62; March 31, 2003, review of *The Wandering Hill,* pp. 38-39; August 25, 2003, review of *By Sorrow's River,* p. 35; November 8, 2004, Allison Block, "The Circle of Life," p. 34; May 2, 2005, review of *The Colonel and Little Missie: Buffalo Bill, Annie Oakley, and the Beginnings of Superstardom in America,* p. 186; October 10, 2005, review of *Oh What a Slaughter: Massacres in the American West, 1846-1890,* p. 47; December 18, 2006, review of *When the Light Goes,* p. 38; May 26, 2008, review of *Books,* p. 54; November 16, 2009, review of *Literary Life,* p. 47; June 22, 2009, review of *Rhino Ranch,* p. 29.

*Southwest Review,* winter, 1976, R.C. Reynolds, review of *Terms of Endearment,* p. 102.

*Texas Monthly,* November, 1999, Mike Shea, review of *Walter Benjamin at the Dairy Queen,* p. 30; May, 2003, Don Graham, "Not Moving On," pp. 84-86; September, 2004, Evan Smith, "Larry McMurtry," p. 102; June, 2006, Mike Shea, review of *Telegraph Days,* p. 50; March, 2007, Mike Shea, review of *When the Light Goes,* p. 66; July, 2008, Mike Shea, review of *Books,* p. 54; December, 2009, Mike Shea, review of *Literary Life,* p. 70

*Time,* June 10, 1985, R.Z. Sheppard, review of *Lonesome Dove,* p. 79; April 20, 1987, John Skow, review of *Texasville,* p. 71; October 24, 1988, R.Z. Sheppard, review of *Anything for Billy,* p. 92; October 16, 1989, Paul Gray, review of *Some Can Whistle,* p. 89; May 25, 1992, review of *The Evening Star,* p. 73; August 9, 1993, John Skow, review of *Streets of Laredo,* p. 59; September 19, 1994, John Skow, review of *Pretty Boy Floyd,* p. 82; September 4, 1995, John Skow, review of *Dead Man's Walk,* p. 65; November 28, 2005, Richard Schickel, "A Tender Cowpoke Love Story," p. 68; January 30, 2006, Josh Tyrangiel, "Capturing the Cowboys," p. 62.

*Times Literary Supplement,* March 23, 1973, review of *All My Friends Are Going To Be Strangers,* p. 313; September 11, 1987, John Clute, review of *Texasville,* p. 978; November 3, 1989, Julian Loose, review of *Anything for Billy,* p. 1217.

*Tribune Books* (Chicago, IL), April 5, 1987, review of *Texasville,* p. 1; October 9, 1988, review of *Anything for Billy,* p. 1; October 15, 1989, review of *Some Can Whistle,* p. 4; May 17, 1992, review of *The Evening Star,* p. 1; September 4, 1994, review of *Pretty Boy Floyd,* p. 3; September 10, 1995, review of *Dead Man's Walk,* p. 6.

*Variety,* September 12, 2005, Todd McCarthy, review of *Brokeback Mountain,* p. 63.

*Village Voice,* October 30, 1988, M. George Stevenson, review of *Anything for Billy,* p. 63.

*Washington Post*, October 13, 1982, Jonathan Yardley, review of *Cadillac Jack.*

*Washington Post Book World*, November 12, 1978, Jonathan Yardley, review of *Somebody's Darling,* p. E5; August 28, 1983, Jonathan Yardley, review of *The Desert Rose,* p. 1; June 9, 1985, review of *Lonesome Dove,* p. 1; April 12, 1987, review of *Texasville,* p. 3; October 9, 1988, review of *Anything for Billy,* p. 1; October 22, 1989, review of *Some Can Whistle,* p. 5; October 7, 1990, review of *Buffalo Girls,* p. 6; September 4, 1994, review of *Pretty Boy Floyd,* p. 9; August 27, 1995, Noel Perrin, review of *Dead Man's Walk,* p. 3.

*Western American Literature,* spring, 1976, Janis P. Stout, "Journeying as a Metaphor for Cultural Loss in the Novels of Larry McMurtry," pp. 37-50.

*Writer,* March, 2010, Steve Weinberg, "McMurtry Reflects on His Life in Books," p. 41.

ONLINE

*National Public Radio Web site,* http://www.npr.org/ (December 23, 2009), "McMurtry's *Literary Life:* Not Simple, But Practical."*

# Andre Norton

## ■ Personal

Born Alice Mary Norton; name legally changed, 1934; born February 17, 1912, in Cleveland, OH; died of congestive heart failure, March 17, 2005, in Murfreesboro, TN; daughter of Adalbert Freely and Bertha Norton. *Education:* Attended Flora Stone Mather College and Cleveland College, Western Reserve University (now Case Western Reserve University), 1930-32. *Politics:* Republican. *Religion:* Presbyterian. *Hobbies and other interests:* Collecting fantasy and cat figurines and paper dolls, needlework.

## ■ Career

Writer, editor, novelist, poet, and librarian. Cleveland Public Library, Cleveland, OH, children's librarian, 1930-41, 1942-51; worked as a special librarian for a citizenship project in Washington, DC, and at the Library of Congress, 1940-41; Mystery House (book store and lending library), Mount Ranier, MD, owner and manager, 1941; freelance writer, 1950-2005. Reader, Gnome Press, 1950-58; High Hallack Genre Writers' Research Library, Murfreesboro, TN, director, 1999-2004.

## ■ Member

Science Fiction Writers of America, Swordsmen and Sorcerers Association.

## ■ Awards, Honors

Award from Dutch government, 1946, for *The Sword Is Drawn;* Ohioana Juvenile Award honor book, 1950, for *Sword in Sheath;* Boys' Clubs of America Medal, 1951, for *Bullard of the Space Patrol;* Hugo Award nominations, World Science Fiction Convention, 1962, for *Star Hunter,* 1964, for *Witch World,* and 1968, for story "Wizard's World"; Headliner Award, Theta Sigma Phi, 1963; Invisible Little Man Award, Westercon XVI, 1963, for sustained excellence in science fiction; Boys' Clubs of America Certificate of Merit, 1965, for *Night of Masks;* Book of the Year award, Child Study Association, 1965, for *Steel Magic;* Phoenix Award, 1976, for overall achievement in science fiction; Gandalf Master of Fantasy Award, World Science Fiction Convention, 1977, for lifetime achievement; Scroll of Honour, Fantasy Gaming Hall of Fame, 1977; Andre Norton Award established, Women Writers of Science Fiction, 1978; Life Achievement Award, Orlando Science Fiction Society, 1978; Balrog Fantasy Award, 1979; Martha Kinney Cooper Ohioana Library Award, 1980, for body of work; named to Ohio Women's Hall of Fame, 1981; Fritz Leiber Award, 1983, for work in the field of fantasy; E.E. Smith Award, 1983; Nebula Grand Master Award, Science

Fiction Writers of America, 1984, for lifetime achievement; Jules Verne Award, 1984, for work in the field of science fiction; Daedalus Award, 1986, for lifetime achievement; Second Stage Lensman Award, 1987, for lifetime achievement; Howard Award, World Fantasy Convention, 1987; E.E. Evans Big Heart Award, 1988; Readers' Award, Science Fiction Book Club, 1991, for *The Elvenbane*; Scientificon Award, Fandom Hall of Fame, 1994; named to Science Fiction and Fantasy Writers Hall of Fame, 1996; Magic Carpet Con Award, 1997; Life Achievement Award, World Fantasy Convention, 1998; the Science Fiction and Fantasy Writers of America created the Andre Norton Award for young adult novels in her honor.

## ■ Writings

*FANTASY*

*Rogue Reynard* (juvenile), illustrated by Laura Bannon, Houghton (Boston, MA), 1947.

*Huon of the Horn* (juvenile), illustrated by Joe Krush, Harcourt (New York, NY), 1951.

*Steel Magic*, illustrated by Robin Jacques, World Publishing (Cleveland, OH), 1965, published as *Gray Magic*, Scholastic Book Service (New York, NY), 1967.

*Octagon Magic*, World Publishing (Cleveland, OH), 1967.

*Fur Magic*, World Publishing (Cleveland, OH), 1968.

*Dread Companion*, Harcourt Brace Jovanovich (New York, NY), 1970, published in omnibus *Dark Companion*, Baen (Riverdale, NY), 2005.

*High Sorcery* (stories), Ace (New York, NY), 1970.

*Dragon Magic*, Crowell (New York, NY), 1972.

*Garan the Eternal* (stories), Fantasy Publishing (Alhambra, CA), 1972.

*Lavender-Green Magic*, illustrated by Judith Gwyn Brown, Crowell (New York, NY), 1974.

*Merlin's Mirror*, DAW (New York, NY), 1975.

*Wraiths of Time*, Atheneum (New York, NY), 1976, published in omnibus *Gods and Androids*, Baen (Riverdale, NY), 2004.

*Red Hart Magic*, illustrated by Donna Diamond, Crowell (New York, NY), 1976.

*Yurth Burden*, DAW (New York, NY), 1978.

*Quag Keep*, Atheneum (New York, NY), 1978.

*Wheel of Stars*, Simon & Schuster (New York, NY), 1983.

*Were-Wrath*, illustrated by Judy King-Rieniets, Cheap Street (New Castle, VA), 1984.

*The Magic Books*, Signet (New York, NY), 1988.

*Moon Mirror*, Tor (New York, NY), 1988.

*Wizards' Worlds*, edited by Ingried Zierhut, Tor (New York, NY), 1989.

(With Susan M. Shwartz) *Imperial Lady: A Fantasy of Han China*, Tor (New York, NY), 1990.

(With Marion Zimmer Bradley and Julian May) *Black Trillium*, Doubleday (New York, NY), 1990.

(With Mercedes Lackey) *The Elvenbane: An Epic High Fantasy of the Halfblood Chronicles* ("Halfblood Chronicles" series), Tor (New York, NY), 1991.

*The Mark of the Cat*, Ace (New York, NY), 1992.

(With Susan M. Shwartz) *Empire of the Eagle*, Tor (New York, NY), 1993.

*Golden Trillium*, Bantam (New York, NY), 1993.

*The Hands of Lyr*, Morrow (New York, NY), 1994.

*Mirror of Destiny*, Morrow (New York, NY), 1995.

(With Mercedes Lackey) *Elvenblood: An Epic High Fantasy* ("Halfblood Chronicles" series), Tor (New York, NY), 1995.

*Scent of Magic*, Avon (New York, NY), 1998.

*Wind in the Stone*, Avon Eos (New York, NY), 1999.

(With Rosemary Edghill) *The Shadow of Albion* ("Carolus Rex" series), Tor (New York, NY), 1999.

(With Rosemary Edghill) *Leopard in Exile* ("Carolus Rex" series), Tor (New York, NY), 2001.

*Mark of the Cat/Year of the Rat*, Meisha Merlin (Atlanta, GA), 2001.

(With Mercedes Lackey) *Elvenborn: An Epic High Fantasy* ("Halfblood Chronicles" series), Tor (New York, NY), 2002.

*Three Hands for Scorpio*, Tor (New York, NY), 2005.

(With Jean Rabe) *A Taste of Magic*, Tor (New York, NY), 2006.

(With Jean Rabe) *Return to Quag Keep*, Tor (New York, NY), 2006.

(With Jean Rabe) *Dragon Mage*, Tor (New York, NY), 2008.

*SCIENCE FICTION*

*Star Man's Son, 2250 A.D.*, illustrated by Nicholas Mordvinoff, Harcourt (New York, NY), 1952, published as *Daybreak—2250 A.D.* (bound with *Beyond Earth's Gates*, by C.M. Kuttner), Ace (New York, NY), 1954.

*Star Rangers* ("Central Control" series), Harcourt (New York, NY), 1953, published as *The Last Planet*, Ace (New York, NY), 1955.

*The Stars Are Ours!* ("Astra" series), World Publishing (Cleveland, OH), 1954, published in omnibus *Star Flight*, Baen (Riverdale, NY), 2007.

*Star Guard* ("Central Control" series), Harcourt Brace (New York, NY), 1955.

*The Crossroads of Time* ("Time Travel" series), Ace (New York, NY), 1956, published in omnibus *Crosstime*, Baen (Riverdale, NY) 2008.

*Star Born* ("Astra" series), World Publishing (Cleveland, OH), 1957, published in omnibus *Star Flight*, Baen (Riverdale, NY) 2007.

*Sea Siege*, Harcourt Brace (New York, NY), 1957, published in omnibus *From the Sea to the Stars*, Baen (Riverdale, NY), 2008.

*Star Gate*, Harcourt Brace (New York, NY), 1958, published in omnibus *From the Sea to the Stars*, Baen (Riverdale, NY), 2008.

*The Sioux Spaceman*, Ace (New York, NY), 1960, published in omnibus *The Game of Stars and Comets*, Baen (Riverdale, NY), 2009.

*Storm over Warlock* ("Planet Warlock" series), World Publishing (Cleveland, OH), 1960.

*Star Hunter*, Ace (New York, NY), 1961.

*Catseye*, Harcourt Brace (New York, NY), 1961, published in omnibus *Masks of the Outcasts*, Baen (Riverdale, NY), 2005.

*Eye of the Monster*, Ace (New York, NY), 1962, published in omnibus *The Game of Stars and Comets*, Baen (Riverdale, NY), 2009.

*Judgment on Janus* ("Janus" series), Harcourt Brace (New York, NY), 1963.

*Ordeal in Otherwhere* ("Planet Warlock" series), World Publishing (Cleveland, OH), 1964.

*Night of Masks*, Harcourt Brace (New York, NY), 1964, published in omnibus *Masks of the Outcasts*, Baen (Riverdale, NY), 2005.

*Quest Crosstime* ("Time Travel" series), Viking Press (New York, NY), 1965, published as *Crosstime Agent*, Gollancz (London, England), 1975, published in omnibus *Crosstime*, Baen (Riverdale, NY), 2008.

*The X Factor*, Harcourt Brace (New York, NY), 1965, published in omnibus *The Game of Stars and Comets*, Baen (Riverdale, NY), 2009.

*Victory on Janus* ("Janus" series), Harcourt (New York, NY), 1966.

*Operation Time Search*, Harcourt Brace (New York, NY), 1967.

*Dark Piper*, Harcourt Brace (New York, NY), 1968, published in omnibus *Dark Companion*, Baen (Riverdale, NY), 2005.

*The Zero Stone* ("Zero Stone" series), Viking Press (New York, NY), 1968, published in omnibus *Search for the Star Stone*, Baen (Riverdale, NY), 2008.

*Uncharted Stars* ("Zero Stone" series), Viking Press (New York, NY), 1969, published in omnibus *Search for the Star Stone*, Baen (Riverdale, NY), 2008.

*Ice Crown*, Viking Press (New York, NY), 1970.

*Android at Arms*, Harcourt Brace Jovanovich (New York, NY), 1971, published in omnibus *Gods and Androids*, Baen (Riverdale, NY), 2004.

*Breed to Come*, Viking Press (New York, NY), 1972.

*Here Abide Monsters*, Atheneum (New York, NY), 1973.

*Forerunner Foray*, Viking Press (New York, NY), 1973.

*Iron Cage*, Viking Press (New York, NY), 1974.

*The Many Worlds of Andre Norton* (stories), edited by Roger Elwood, Chilton (Radnor, PA), 1974, published as *The Book of Andre Norton*, DAW (New York, NY), 1975.

*Outside*, illustrated by Bernard Colonna, Walker (New York, NY), 1975.

(With Michael Gilbert) *The Day of the Ness*, illustrated by Michael Gilbert, Walker (New York, NY), 1975.

*Knave of Dreams*, Viking Press (New York, NY), 1975.

*No Night without Stars*, Atheneum (New York, NY), 1975.

*Perilous Dreams* (stories), DAW (New York, NY), 1976.

*Voorloper*, illustrated by Alicia Austin, Ace (New York, NY), 1980, published in omnibus *The Game of Stars and Comets*, Baen (Riverdale, NY), 2009.

*Forerunner* ("Forerunner" series), Tor (New York, NY), 1981.

*Moon Called*, Simon & Schuster (New York, NY), 1982.

*Voodoo Planet* [and] *Star Hunter* (*Voodoo Planet* also under "Solar Queen" series) Ace (New York, NY), 1983.

*Forerunner: The Second Venture* ("Forerunner" series), Tor (New York, NY), 1985.

*Brother to Shadows*, Morrow (New York, NY), 1993.

*Star Soldiers* (contains edited versions of *Star Rangers* and *Star Guard*), Baen (Riverdale, NY), 2001.

*Janus* (contains edited versions of *Judgment on Janus* and *Victory on Janus*), Baen (Riverdale, NY), 2002.

*Warlock* (contains edited versions of *Storm over Warlock*, *Ordeal in Otherwhere*, and *Forerunner Foray*), Baen (Riverdale, NY), 2002.

*Darkness and Dawn* (contains edited versions of *Star Man's Son* and *No Night without Stars*), Baen (Riverdale, NY), 2003.

*Gods and Androids* (omnibus; contains *Android at Arms* and *Wraiths of Time*), Baen (Riverdale, NY), 2004.

*Dark Companion* (omnibus; contains *Dark Piper* and *Dread Companion*), Baen (Riverdale, NY), 2005.

*Masks of the Outcasts* (omnibus; contains *Catseye* and *Night of Masks*), Baen (Riverdale, NY), 2005.

*Star Flight* (omnibus; contains *The Stars Are Ours* and *Star Born*), Baen (Riverdale, NY) 2007.

*Search for the Star Stone* (omnibus; contains *The Zero Stone* and *Uncharted Stars*), Baen (Riverdale, NY), 2008.

*From the Sea to the Stars* (omnibus; contains *Sea Siege* and *Star Gate*), Baen (Riverdale, NY), 2008.

*Crosstime* (omnibus; contains *The Crossroads of Time* and *Quest Crosstime*), Baen (Riverdale, NY) 2008.

*The Game of Stars and Comets* (omnibus; contains *The X-Factor, The Sioux Spaceman, Eye of the Monster,* and *Voorloper*), Baen (Riverdale, NY), 2009.

*"SOLAR QUEEN" SERIES*

(Under pseudonym Andrew North) *Sargasso of Space* (also see below), Gnome Press (New York, NY), 1955, published under name Andre Norton, Gollancz (London, England), 1970, reprinted with a new introduction by Sandra Miesel, Gregg Press (Boston, MA), 1978.

(Under pseudonym Andrew North) *Plague Ship* (also see below), Gnome Press (New York, NY), 1956, published under name Andre Norton, Gollancz (London, England), 1971.

(Under pseudonym Andrew North) *Voodoo Planet,* Ace (New York, NY), 1959.

*Postmarked the Stars,* Harcourt (New York, NY), 1969, Fawcett (New York, NY), 1985.

(With Pauline Griffin) *Redline the Stars,* Tor (New York, NY), 1993.

(With Sherwood Smith) *Derelict for Trade,* Tor (New York, NY), 1997.

(With Sherwood Smith) *A Mind for Trade,* Tor (New York, NY), 1997.

*The Solar Queen* (contains *Sargosso of Space* and *Plague Ship*), Tor (New York, NY), 2003.

*"TIME TRADERS" SERIES*

*The Time Traders* (also see below), World Publishing (Cleveland, OH), 1958, revised edition, 1stworld Publications (Fairfield, IA), 2009.

*Galactic Derelict* (also see below), World Publishing (Cleveland, OH), 1959.

*The Defiant Agents* (also see below), World Publishing (Cleveland, OH), 1962.

*Key Out of Time* (also see below), World Publishing (Cleveland, OH), 1963.

(With Pauline Griffin) *Firehand,* Tor (New York, NY), 1994.

(With Sherwood Smith) *Echoes in Time: A New Time Traders Adventure,* Tor (New York, NY), 1999.

*Time Traders* (contains updated versions of *The Time Traders* and *Galactic Derelict*), Baen (Riverdale, NY), 2000.

*Time Traders II* (contains updated versions of *The Defiant Agents* and *Key out of Time*), Baen (Riverdale, NY), 2001.

(With Sherwood Smith) *Atlantis Endgame: A New Time Traders Adventure,* Tor (New York, NY), 2002.

*"BEAST MASTER" SERIES*

*Beast Master,* Harcourt Brace (New York, NY), 1959, published in omnibus *Beast Master's Planet,* Tor (New York, NY), 2005.

*Secret of the Lost Race,* Ace (New York, NY), 1959, published as *Wolfshead,* Hale (London, England), 1977.

*Lord of Thunder,* Harcourt Brace (New York, NY), 1962, published in omnibus *Beast Master's Planet,* Tor (New York, NY), 2005.

(With Lyn McConchie) *Beast Master's Ark,* Tor (New York, NY), 2002.

(With Lyn McConchie) *Beast Master's Circus,* Tor (New York, NY), 2004.

*Beast Master's Planet* (omnibus; contains *Beast Master* and *Lord of Thunder*), Tor (New York, NY), 2005.

(With Lyn McConchie) *Beast Master's Quest,* Tor (New York, NY), 2006.

*"WITCH WORLD" SERIES*

*Witch World* (also see below), Ace (New York, NY), 1963.

*Web of the Witch World,* Ace (New York, NY), 1964.

*Year of the Unicorn,* Ace (New York, NY), 1965.

*Three against the Witch World,* Ace (New York, NY), 1965.

*Warlock of the Witch World,* Ace (New York, NY), 1967.

*Sorceress of the Witch World,* Ace (New York, NY), 1968.

*Spell of the Witch World* (stories), DAW (New York, NY), 1972.

*The Crystal Gryphon* (first volume in "Gryphon" trilogy), Atheneum (New York, NY), 1972.

*The Jargoon Pard,* Atheneum (New York, NY), 1974.

*Trey of Swords* (stories), Ace (New York, NY), 1977.

*Zarsthor's Bane,* Ace (New York, NY), 1978.

*Lore of the Witch World* (stories), DAW (New York, NY), 1980.

*Gryphon in Glory* (second volume in "Gryphon" trilogy), Atheneum (New York, NY), 1981.

*Horn Crown,* DAW (New York, NY), 1981.

*'Ware Hawk,* Atheneum (New York, NY), 1983.

(With A.C. Crispin) *Gryphon's Eyrie* (third volume in "Gryphon" trilogy), Tor (New York, NY), 1984.

*The Gate of the Cat,* Ace (New York, NY), 1987.

(With others) *Tales of the Witch World,* Tor (New York, NY), 1987.

(With others) *Tales of the Witch World 2,* Tor (New York, NY), 1988.

*Four from the Witch World,* Tor (New York, NY), 1989.

(With others) *Tales of the Witch World 3,* Tor (New York, NY), 1990.

(With Pauline Griffin) *Storms of Victory* (first volume in *"The Turning"* trilogy), Tor (New York, NY), 1991.

(With A.C. Crispin) *Songsmith,* Tor (New York, NY), 1992.

(With Pauline Griffin and Mary Schaub) *Flight of Vengeance* (second volume in *"The Turning"* trilogy), Tor (New York, NY), 1992.

(With Patricia Mathews and Sasha Miller) *On Wings of Magic* (third volume in *"The Turning"* trilogy), Tor (New York, NY), 1994.

(With Lyn McConchie) *The Key of the Keplian,* Warner (New York, NY), 1995.

*The Warding of Witch World* (three novellas), Warner (New York, NY), 1996.

(With Lyn McConchie) *Ciara's Song: A Chronicle of the Witch World,* Warner Aspect (New York, NY), 1998.

*The Gates to Witch World* (contains *Witch World, Web of the Witch World,* and *Year of the Unicorn*), introduction by C.J. Cherryh, Tor (New York, NY), 2001.

*Lost Lands of Witch World,* introduction by Mercedes Lackey, Tor (New York, NY), 2004.

(With Lyn McConchie) *The Duke's Ballad,* Tor (New York, NY), 2005.

(With Lyn McConchie) *Silver May Tarnish,* Tor (New York, NY), 2005.

*"MOON MAGIC" SERIES*

*Moon of Three Rings,* Viking Press (New York, NY), 1966, published in omnibus *Moonsinger,* Baen (Riverdale, NY), 2006.

*Exiles of the Stars,* Viking Press (New York, NY), 1971, published in omnibus *Moonsinger,* Baen (Riverdale, NY), 2006.

*Flight in Yiktor,* Tor (New York, NY), 1986.

*Dare to Go A-Hunting,* Tor (New York, NY), 1990.

*Moonsinger* (omnibus; contains *Moon of Three Rings* and *Exiles of the Stars*), Baen (Riverdale, NY), 2006.

*"STAR KA'AT" SERIES*

(With Dorothy Madlee) *Star Ka'at,* illustrated by Bernard Colonna, Walker (New York, NY), 1976.

(With Dorothy Madlee) *Star Ka'at World,* illustrated by Jean Jenkins, Walker (New York, NY), 1978.

(With Dorothy Madlee) *Star Ka'ats and the Plant People,* illustrated by Jean Jenkins, Walker (New York, NY), 1979.

(With Dorothy Madlee) *Star Ka'ats and the Winged Warriors,* illustrated by Jean Jenkins, Walker (New York, NY), 1981.

*"BOOK OF THE OAK, YEW, ASH, AND ROWAN" SERIES*

(With Sasha Miller) *To the King a Daughter,* Tor (New York, NY), 2000.

(With Sasha Miller) *Knight or Knave,* Tor (New York, NY), 2001.

(With Sasha Miller) *A Crown Disowned,* Tor (New York, NY), 2002.

(With Sasha Miller) *Dragon Blade: The Book of the Rowan,* Tor (New York, NY), 2005.

(With Sasha Miller) *The Knight of the Red Beard,* Tor (New York, NY), 2008.

*HISTORICAL NOVELS*

*The Prince Commands,* Appleton-Century Company (New York, NY), 1934.

*Ralestone Luck,* Appleton-Century Company (New York, NY), 1938.

*Follow the Drum,* Penn Publishing (New York, NY), 1942.

*The Sword Is Drawn* (first volume of *"Swords"* trilogy), illustrated by Duncan Coburn, Houghton Mifflin (Cambridge, MA), 1944.

*Scarface,* illustrated by Lorence Bjorklund, Harcourt Brace (New York, NY), 1948.

*Sword in Sheath* (second volume of *"Swords"* trilogy), Harcourt (New York, NY), 1949.

*At Swords' Points* (third volume of *"Swords"* trilogy), Harcourt Brace (New York, NY), 1954.

*Yankee Privateer,* illustrated by Leonard Vosburgh, World Publishing (Cleveland, OH), 1955.

*Stand to Horse,* Harcourt Brace (New York, NY), 1956.

*Shadow Hawk,* Harcourt (New York, NY), 1960.

*Ride Proud, Rebel!,* World Publishing (Cleveland, OH), 1961.

*Rebel Spurs,* World Publishing (Cleveland, OH), 1962.

*EDITOR*

Malcolm Jameson, *Bullard of the Space Patrol* (science fiction), World Publishing (Cleveland, OH), 1951.

(And author of introduction and notes) *Space Service* (science fiction), World Publishing (Cleveland, OH), 1953.

*Space Pioneers* (science fiction), World Publishing (Cleveland, OH), 1954.

*Space Police* (science fiction), World Publishing (Cleveland, OH), 1956.

(With Ernestine Donaldy) *Gates to Tomorrow: An Introduction to Science Fiction* (science fiction), Atheneum (New York, NY), 1973.

*Small Shadows Creep*, Dutton (New York, NY), 1974.

*Baleful Beasts and Eerie Creatures*, Rand McNally, 1976.

(With Robert Adams) *Magic in Ithkar* (fantasy), four volumes, Tor (New York, NY), 1985–87.

(With Martin H. Greenberg) *Catfantastic* (fantasy), five volumes, DAW Books (New York, NY), 1989–94.

(With Ingrid Zierhut) *Grand Master's Choice* (science fiction), Tor (New York, NY), 1991.

(With Jean Rabe) *Renaissance Faire*, Daw Books (New York, NY), 2005.

*OTHER*

(With Grace Hogarth, under joint pseudonym Allen Weston) *Murder for Sale* (mystery novel), Hammond (London, England), 1954, published under names Hogarth and Norton as *Sneeze on Sunday*, Tor (New York, NY), 1992.

(With mother, Bertha Stemm Norton) *Bertie and May* (biography), illustrated by Fermin Rocker, World Publishing (New York, NY), 1969.

*The White Jade Fox* (gothic novel), Dutton (New York, NY), 1975.

*Velvet Shadows* (gothic novel), Fawcett (New York, NY), 1977.

*The Opal-Eyed Fan* (gothic novel), Dutton (New York, NY), 1977.

(With Phyllis Miller) *Seven Spells to Sunday* (juvenile), Atheneum (New York, NY), 1979.

*Snow Shadow* (mystery novel), Fawcett (New York, NY), 1979.

*Iron Butterflies* (historical gothic novel), Fawcett (New York, NY), 1980.

*Ten Mile Treasure* (juvenile mystery), Pocket Books (New York, NY), 1981.

(With Enid Cushing) *Caroline*, Pinnacle (New York, NY), 1982.

(With Phyllis Miller) *House of Shadows* (mystery novel), Atheneum (New York, NY), 1984.

*Stand and Deliver*, Tor (New York, NY), 1984.

(With Phyllis Miller) *Ride the Green Dragon* (mystery novel), Atheneum (New York, NY), 1985.

(With Robert Bloch) *The Jekyll Legacy* (horror novel), Tor (New York, NY), 1990.

(With Marion Zimmer Bradley and Mercedes Lackey) *Tiger Burning Bright*, Morrow (New York, NY), 1995.

*The Monster's Legacy* ("Dragonflight" series), illustrated by Jody A. Lee, Atheneum Books for Young Readers (New York, NY), 1996.

Contributor to numerous periodicals and anthologies.

## ■ Adaptations

Norton's novel *The Beast Master* was the inspiration for a 1982 film of the same name, its 1991 sequel *Beastmaster 2: Through the Portal of Time,* and the syndicated television series *The Beastmaster*, which ran from 1999 to 2002.

## ■ Sidelights

Andre Norton was a prolific author best known and admired for her works of science fiction and fantasy. Women writers were rare in those genres when she published *Star Man's Son, 2250 A.D.* in 1952, yet Norton quickly became a popular favorite, with many of her books hitting the bestseller lists. Despite frequent critical dismissal of her work as lacking complexity, Norton's fans and peers recognized her important contributions to science fiction. She was one of the few writers to be awarded both the Science Fiction Writers of America's Grand Master Award and science fiction fandom's equivalent, the Gandalf Award. Using universal themes such as the coming of age and the necessity of communication, Norton created adventures that drew readers into incredibly vivid and detailed new worlds. As Charlotte Spivack wrote of Norton in *Merlin's Daughters: Contemporary Women Writers of Fantasy:* "Not only does she succeed in holding her reader, but her cosmos lingers in the mind, with its unforgettable images of alien species, jewels and talismans resonant with psychic powers, and magical transcendence of time and space."

Born February 17, 1912, Alice Mary Norton was the second child of Bertha Stemm and Adalbert Norton, both descendants of pioneers. Books and reading were important elements of the Norton family life, with weekly family trips to the library a regular routine. Norton's mother had a keen interest in American history in particular, and nurtured Norton's own fascination with, as Norton described it in her essay "On Writing Fantasy" (from *The Many Worlds of Andre Norton*), "the kind of history which deals with daily life, the beliefs and aspirations of people long since dust." In later years, Norton's mother was to prove a valuable sounding board for ideas and half-written manuscripts.

During her teens Norton became interested in writing and joined the staff of her high school newspaper. She wrote her first novel as a high-school senior. (She later reworked this story, and it became her second published book, *Ralestone Luck.*) Intending to pursue a career as a history teacher, Norton entered Western Reserve University. However, the Depression hit during her freshman year, and Norton was forced to leave school in order to find a job. She found a position at the Cleveland Public Library, and, realizing she would not be able to continue her formal education, took various writing courses at night while continuing to write in her spare time.

As a librarian, Norton was assigned to the children's book section. One of her responsibilities was to find suitable material for the children's hour, leading Norton to become well-versed in both popular and classic children's literature. At this time she was

The Gates to Witch World **contains the first three works from Norton's acclaimed "Witch World" saga, which began in 1963.** (Orb, 2003. Reproduced by permission.)

already interested in writing science fiction, but the only market for the genre was magazines, and Norton found it difficult to write short stories. Instead she turned to children's historical fiction. During this time she wrote *The Prince Commands,* which was to become her first published novel—a sale that was made when Norton was just twenty years old. This was followed by several more juvenile adventure novels, including three spy novels about the Dutch underground in World War II (the "Sword" series) that earned Norton an award from the Netherlands government. Norton continued to work in this genre throughout the 1930s and 1940s, firmly establishing herself as a writer who could be counted on to provide older children with fast-paced and historically accurate entertainment.

### The Origins of Andre

For these early novels Norton adopted the pseudonym Andre Norton, which she later made her legal name. The use of a male-sounding pseudonym was deemed necessary by her publishers, who feared that her given name would turn off her potential readers, expected to be almost exclusively boys. The name change also served Norton well when she turned to writing science fiction in the 1950s, very much a male-dominated field at that time. By then she had left her library position to work as a freelance editor, a job that allowed her to pursue her own writing. Science fiction was enjoying a tremendous growth in readership and respectability, boosted in part by technological advances that suddenly made space travel an impending reality rather than just an incredible dream. As the public interest grew, the genre moved beyond the short stories found in pulp magazines and into the realm of "legitimate" hard cover publishing and novel-length works.

Norton's position as the editor of a World Publishing science fiction anthology provided her with an entree into the field, and her first science fiction novel, *Star Man's Son, 2250 A.D.,* was published in 1952. Like her earlier adventure novels, it was originally marketed as a book for older children and enjoyed considerable popular success as such. However, Donald Wollheim, then the editor of Ace Books, recognized that the book also had a potentially high appeal for adult readers. He acquired the paperback rights and published the novel with a new title, *Daybreak—2250 A.D.,* omitting from the cover all reference to the book as a story for young readers. As Wollheim wrote in his introduction to *The Many Worlds of Andre Norton:* "I presented it simply as a good novel for anyone who reads science fiction. It was so accepted and it has been selling steadily ever since."

A New Witch World Novel!

SONGSMITH

ANDRE NORTON AND A.C. CRISPIN

"Andre Norton and A.C. Crispin are giants in the field of fantasy, and SONGSMITH combines the best of their strengths." —George Alec Effinger

**A number of Norton's "Witch World" novels, including _Songsmith_, were done in collaboration with other writers.** (Tom Doherty Associates Book, 1992. Reproduced with permission of Palgrave Macmillan.)

The story of _Star Man's Son, 2250 A.D._ exemplifies one of Norton's most frequently visited themes: a young person's rite of passage into adulthood and self-realization. Fors is a young mutant who is scorned by a postwar society because of his differences. He embarks on a solo quest to fulfill his father's legacy, and in doing so he discovers his own self-worth. Throughout his adventures he is constantly tested, not only in terms of physical strength and mental agility, but also ethically. As Francis J. Molson wrote in the _Dictionary of Literary Biography,_ the book "speaks directly and forcefully . . . through its convincing story of a boy's passage from a questioning, unsure adolescence to confident, assured young manhood." Critic and biographer Elisa Kay Sparks believed that this theme figures prominently in Norton's work. In another _Dictionary_

_of Literary Biography_ essay, Sparks noted that Norton's writings frequently "center on the process by which a somehow displaced, exiled, or alienated hero or heroine finds a new home or sense of community. From the first to the last her books insist on the necessity of cooperation between equals."

The setting is different and the central character is female, but a similar process occurs in the 1970 novel _Ice Crown._ Roane, an orphan who has been raised by an uncle who shows her no love, undergoes her own rite of passage as she attempts to aid the aristocracy of a small kingdom on the planet Clio. Roane and her uncle have come to Clio, a closed planet whose inhabitants are still under the influence of a long-defunct mind-control experiment, on a mission to find archeological treasure. Roane is strictly forbidden to interfere with the destinies of the planet's inhabitants, but she cannot resist coming to the aid of the princess Ludorica, whom she stumbles upon while on a scouting trip. Roane is soon drawn into Ludorica's search for the "Ice Crown"—the source of Ludorica's family's power—and, in the process, begins to turn away from much that she has been taught by her own people. In the end, Roane's heroic actions help free Clio's people from the mind-control that has gripped them, and she, in turn, discovers a new life and identity among those she has chosen to befriend.

### Fantastic Coming-of-Age Stories

The novels of the "Halfblood Chronicles" fantasy series, written by Norton with Mercedes Lackey in the 1990s and early 2000s, similarly describe the heroic efforts of an alienated young girl who struggles to reconcile her individuality and to end the subjugation of humans in a world where they are enslaved by a merciless race of elves. In _The Elvenbane: An Epic High Fantasy of the Halfblood Chronicles,_ the first volume of the series, a human slave gives birth to Shana, a half-elven baby who is the feared "Elvenbane" of prophecy. Raised by a dragon in the desert, Shana masters her unique powers and leads the Elvenbane wizards in their struggle against the elven lords in the sequel, _Elvenblood: An Epic High Fantasy._ With her ability to determine the interconnected fate of the humans, elves, and dragons by her actions, Shana realizes her capacity to chart her own destiny and to fight injustice in the world around her. Reviewers cited this series as an example of how Norton created believable, compelling, character-driven fiction. Reviewing the third volume, _Elvenborn: An Epic High Fantasy,_ in _Booklist,_ Roland Green noted that "neither Norton nor Lackey could tell a really bad story if she tried."

This coming-of-age pattern is repeated throughout Norton's novels, be they science fiction or fantasy, with seemingly endless variations. In 1970's *Dread Companion,* a young governess follows her two charges to a nightmarish parallel world and must rely on her own courage and endurance—and the help of more than a little magic—to bring the children back to safety. In the 1973 novel *Here Abide Monsters,* Nick Shaw, a young man who has lost his mother and become alienated from his father, travels to a parallel world where he uses his developing mental powers to bring about the fall of a group that employs advanced technology to threaten the world's other inhabitants. The 1992 novel *The Mark of the Cat* follows Hynkkel, a disgraced young nobleman, as he embarks on a quest that leads to friendship with a race of intelligent sandcats, and, finally, to an emperor's throne.

In resolving this theme of self-fulfillment, Norton's work frequently expresses another idea of importance to her fiction: that to understand oneself, a person must come to understand and accept others. Norton's respect for individual diversity is clear in her staunchly anti-racist stance, both in creating character and story. Long before the practice was commonplace, Norton's casts of characters were multiracial. This is true in works as early as 1952's *Star Man's Son: 2250 A.D.,* which features a post-atomic war culture established by African-American Air Force veterans, and 1959's *The Beast Master,* whose protagonist is a young Native American. In the "Solar Queen" series, which began in 1955, Dane Thorson's best friend is black, while in *The Sioux Spaceman* (1960) a Native American works together with members of three other races as equals. In an introduction to the 1978 Gregg Press edition of *Sargasso of Space,* Sandra Miesel noted that for the most part, Norton "lets the situations speak for themselves," in these early novels, with the exception of a couple of rare, pointed comments. The author deals more directly with prejudice in later novels such as *Lavender-Green Magic* (1974) and *Wraiths of Time* (1976).

Interestingly, in Norton's early novels this egalitarian approach did not also apply to women. It is not that their worth was downgraded in these books, but rather that female characters were simply not included. The conspicuous absence of women was not a statement of Norton's personal belief regarding the worth of women, however. Before the publication of *Witch World* in 1963, Norton's editors had insisted that she omit female characters from her tales, since science fiction was considered to have a strictly masculine appeal. With the "Witch World" books female characters became increasingly more important in Norton's work, and she wrote about active, intelligent heroines in many of her other novels as well. *Year of the Unicorn, Moon of Three Rings, Dread Companion,* and *Forerunner Foray* all describe the maturation of young women, making it clear that Norton's concern for the individual extends to both sexes as well as to all races.

## Explores a Powerful Society

In what became her most popular series, "Witch World," the resolution of many of the books lies in the cooperation of male and female aspects. Roger C. Schlobin commented in *Andre Norton: A Primary and Secondary Bibliography* that Norton's "resolutions are androgynous: within themselves or in union with another, [Norton's characters] find the ideal combination of male and female characteristics. Most of all, they discover a sanctity of ideas and ethics, and they recognize their own places within the patterns and rhythms of elemental law and carry that recognition forward into a hopeful future." The Witch World includes a society of female witches who remain virginal as a means of sustaining their power; this rule is later shown to be unnecessary and even detrimental to the witches. Characters who reject such compromises make up a great number of Norton's antagonists, stated Sparks, who wrote that "Norton consistently associates evil with the denial of such bonds, or with a lack of appreciation for individuality and liberty; opportunism, willful destructiveness, and the urge to dominate through the imposition of mechanized forms of control are characteristic attributes of her villains."

Norton began her monumental saga in 1963 with *Witch World,* in which Simon Tregarth is transported to a parallel world where female magicians are battling against invaders from another universe who wish to subjugate humans with machinery. The series has grown to more than thirty volumes, a number of which are collaborations with several other authors. From the 1990s forward, most volumes were created in part or entirely by others under Norton's editorial aegis. Critical reception of these volumes was generally favorable, though some reviewers lamented Norton's limited role as the series creator and editor. Beginning with *Storms of Victory,* the novels are set in the aftermath of "The Turning," an apocalyptic battle that leaves the Witch World devastated. As in previous volumes, Norton and her collaborators examine the process of maturation and various conflicts between good and evil.

Another means by which Norton communicated her regard for the individual was through her obvious distrust of science and machines. Critics have observed that it is the mechanical, non-individualistic aspects of science that frequently provide the conflict in Norton's work. Miesel noted that this anti-science bent is evident in the "Solar Queen" series, where "the wages of technology is death. Machine-dominated civilizations turn into radioactive slag heaps. . . . High technology run amok may soon send humanity tumbling after the Forerunners into oblivion." This can also be seen in the "Witch World" series, where the super science of Kolder is the ultimate evil. "Though many of her novels are set in the future," remarked Schlobin, "she has no special affection for the technological and, in fact, science is most often the antagonist in her fiction." Rick Brooks similarly noted in *The Many Worlds of Andre Norton* that "in the battle between technology and nature, Miss Norton took a stand long before the great majority of us had any doubts. . . . Technology is a necessary evil [in her work] to get there for the adventure and to get some of the story to work. And the adventure is as much to mold her universe to her views as to entertain."

Norton revealed the reasons behind her distrust of technology to Charles Platt in *Dream Makers: The Uncommon Men and Women Who Write Science Fiction*, commenting: "I think the human race made a bad mistake at the beginning of the Industrial Revolution. We leaped for the mechanics, and threw aside things that were just as important. We made the transition too fast. I do not like mechanical things very much." Norton added: "And I don't like a lot of the modern ways of living. I prefer to do things with my hands; and I think everybody misses that. People need the use of their hands to feel creative." Brooks further noted that Norton "consistently views the future as one where the complexity of science and technology have reduced the value of the individual. . . . So Miss Norton is actually wrestling with the prime problem, that of human worth and purpose."

If Norton distrusts machines in general, her "special wrath is reserved for computers," as Miesel observed, noting that "in *Star Hunter* Lansor's inability to adapt to the 'mechanical life of a computer tender' is supposed to demonstrate his depth of sensitivity and intelligence." Computers programmed to do evil or that have somehow run amok are the villains in more than a few of her novels, among them, *Judgment on Janus*, *Victory on Janus*, *Ice Crown*, and *No Night without Stars*. This anti-science stance may seem odd for one of the major science fiction authors of the twentieth century. However, as John Rowe Townsend noted in *A Sense of Story: Essays on Contemporary Writers for Children*, Norton "is not much interested in science-for-science's sake." The critic explains that "Miss Norton handles her gadgetry with great

aplomb. She never draws special attention to it; it is simply there." As Schlobin explained in *The Feminine Eye*, "the major thrusts of Norton's science fiction must be grouped with those of other such luminaries as Frank Herbert, Ursula K. LeGuin, and Gene Wolfe. They all write what could be variously labeled as 'social,' 'humanistic,' or 'soft' science fiction. While all their works contain the extrapolated factual material characteristic of science fiction, they really focus on the future of humanity and its possible traits and societies."

## Places Faith in Nature

On the flip side of Norton's aversion for technology and science is her deep love of nature and animals, and a belief in humanity's need for a spiritual connection with the two. As Townsend maintained, "The value of the old ways of life, of the simple and natural against the sophisticated, artificial and ever-changing, is a frequent issue in Miss Norton's work. . . . There is a part of her . . . which is deeply aware of instinctual life, is conscious of the rooting of myth in the cycle of life and death, the turning of the seasons." Norton's belief in the benefits of renewing and maintaining humanity's ties to the natural world can be seen in her extensive use of magic in the "Witch World" series and in fantasies like *Moon Called*, *Dread Companion*, and one of her later novels, 1994's *The Hands of Lyr*. Jewels, talismans, and touchstones figure prominently in these stories, with psychic and other powers often conveyed through the use of these artifacts. As a *Times Literary Supplement* critic noted, in Norton's work, "power is generated by the obedience to the nature of things, by stones that have lain in earth or other talismanic objects." In the "Witch World" series in particular, female characters are often portrayed as possessing magical abilities that stem from their strong connections to the land, to being somehow plugged into a collective unconscious, and from their awareness of an intrinsic order of the cosmos.

Norton's desire for closer ties between humanity and the natural world can also be seen in the significant role animals play in many of her novels. Her protagonists are often telepathically linked with animals, such as Travis Fox and the mutant coyotes in *The Defiant Angels*, Maelen of *Moon of Three Rings* and the animals in her traveling show, Karara Trehern and the dolphins in *Key out of Time*, and, of course, Fors and Lura of *Star Man's Son, 2250 A.D.* Animals are also often portrayed as the intellectual equals of humans, and, not infrequently, as ethically and morally superior to humans, largely because of their stronger links to nature. For example, in both

*Breed to Come* and *Iron Cage*, the planets inhabited by intelligent animals must be defended against possible colonization by humans. In *Breed to Come*, Earth, devastated and then deserted by people, is the home of cats, dogs, and cattle that have evolved to human levels of sophistication. These animals band together to head off possible re-colonization of Earth by humans, who would undoubtedly destroy the planet's resources once again. Similarly, in *Iron Cage*, intelligent bears must resist an attempt by humans to dominate animals by caging them and using them for experiments. As Margery Fisher remarked in a *Growing Point* review of *The Jargoon Pard*, Norton seems concerned that "man is distancing himself from the animal kingdom in which so much of his ancestry and aptitude rests."

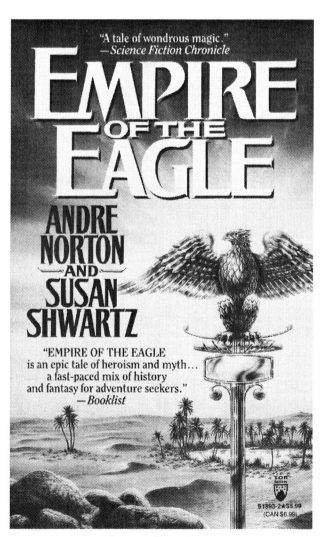

*Empire of the Eagle*, **a historical fantasy, is based on Battle of Carrhae, a stunning defeat for the Roman legions.** (Tor Books, 1993. Reproduced by permission.)

One of Norton's most notable series to feature human-animal cooperation is the saga started with 1959's *The Beast Master*. Hosteen Storm is a Native American exiled from Earth whose telepathic connection to an eagle, a meerkat, and a puma helps him defeat an invasion of his new home, the planet Arzor. Norton continued the series in collaboration with Lyn McConchie in 2002's *Beast Master's Ark*. After Earth has been destroyed by vicious Xik invaders, some of the remnants of Earth's population share the planet Arzor with the indigenous Nitri. A common enemy has emerged to terrify both races, and young Tani must overcome her distrust of strangers to acquire special abilities that could save her planet. A *Kirkus Reviews* critic called Norton's "Beast Master" saga "one of the better SF series going."

Norton was never afraid to revisit worlds she had created decades before, updating new editions or adding sequels. Begun in 1958, the "Time Traders" series featured one of science fiction's most enduring species of villains, the completely hairless Baldies. The Baldies are time-traveling aliens who consistently interfere in Earth history in order to drive humanity toward an unknown, but probably unpleasant, end. The protagonists of the books, Travis Fox and Ross Murdock, are members of the Time Patrol, human time-travelers who journey in time to investigate disasters, to encourage peace among alien races, and to foil mysterious plots by the inscrutable Baldies. Baen Books reissued all the previous "Time Traders" books beginning in 2000, printing them in pairs. Notably, Norton revised these volumes to update elements that might seem dated to readers in the early twenty-first century, but without fundamentally changing the nature of the stories she originally told. Her updates had to accommodate more than forty years of worldwide developments in social, technological, and political areas. Russian Communists became Russian imperialists, for example, and far-ranging advancements in communications, computers, and other technology were taken into consideration. "The characters' can-do attitude and Norton's magic with a story have survived two generations in fine style," commented Roland Green in a *Booklist* reviewer of the revised *Time Traders*. In a further review of *Time Traders II*, Green observed: "The books bear revamping better than most of their contemporaries might because they were better written in the first place by one of SF's hardy perennials."

Norton also added new works to her "Time Traders" series with *Firehand*, written with Pauline Griffin, and *Echoes in Time: A New Time Traders Adventure*, with Sherwood Smith. "Norton and Smith don't just send an old hero through familiar paces," noted a *Publishers Weekly* contributor. "Ross Murdock has now moved into the laptop era." Green, writing again in *Booklist*, commented that even though the novel is "sometimes slack in pace, the book compensates with its humane, intelligent, original development of nonhuman races." In *Atlantis Endgame*, written by Norton and Smith, the members of the Time Patrol discover that someone has tampered with the historical events surrounding the disappearance of the fabled continent of Atlantis. The book offers "plenty of adventure, a fair scattering of archeological trivia and some new twists on the alien-human relations that carry forward from the previous books," noted a *Publishers Weekly* contributor. This new addition to the "Time Traders" series "proves that skillful writing can keep a concept launched half-a-century ago afloat today," observed *Booklist*'s Green.

The "Solar Queen" series, which began in 1955 with the publication of *Sargasso in Space*, continued into the late 1990s with such titles as *Derelict for Trade* and *A Mind for Trade*. In reviewing *Derelict for Trade* in *Booklist*, Green wrote observed that Norton "was thirty years ahead of her time" when she first penned the series. A *Publishers Weekly* contributor reviewing *Derelict for Trade* called the book "very nearly a model of how to update a venerable series . . . bringing everything . . . into harmony with current expectations," and felt that the original characters and concept remained intact. Green, in another review for *Booklist*, noted that the plot of *A Mind for Trade* "is tight, the suspense and action are continuous, the characters are as engaging as ever." Discussing the success of the "Solar Queen" series, a *Publishers Weekly* reviewer remarked, "long may it ply the spaceways—and the bookstores."

### A Life Fulfilled

During her decades-long career, Norton was a consistent and vigorous supporter of upcoming writers, offering advice and encouragement that helped many fledgling authors achieve publication. In 1999 she established High Hallack, a retreat and research library for writers, which lasted until 2004, when the retreat was closed and the books auctioned off. She collaborated with both established and up-and-coming authors, helping to propel them toward greater achievements in their own careers. Much of Norton's own work throughout the late 1990s and early 2000s was done in collaboration with other writers, including the "Carolus Rex" series written with Rosemary Edghill (the pseudonym of Eluki Bes Shahar) and the "Book of the Oak, Yew, Ash, and Rowan" series, written with Sasha Miller. The former series, which includes *The Shadow of Albion* and *Leopard in Exile*, begins in an alternative version of the nineteenth century. There has been no

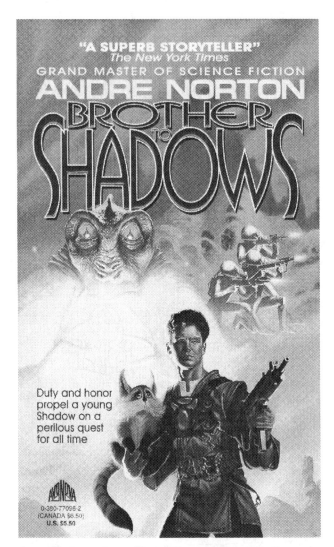

An exiled warrior and an alien scholar join forces in *Brother to Shadows*, a blend of science fiction, mystery, and adventure. (Avon Books, 1993. Reproduced by permission of HarperCollins Publishers Inc.)

Revolutionary War, and Thomas Jefferson is governing what is still the British colony of America, which is also populated by faeries. The latter series is also a fantasy, featuring a child of noble blood born in the swamps and raised by a witch healer, who is caught up in a power struggle between the houses of Oak, Yew, Ash, and Rowan. A *Publishers Weekly* writer said of Norton and Miller's second book, *Knight or Knave*, that "this cheerful, childlike, appealing fantasy blithely romps along after its predecessor . . . replete with whimsical sorcery, swordsmanship, and swampy creatures."

*Three Hands for Scorpio* was Norton's last solo novel, completed just before her death in March 2005. In the book, the daughters of a prominent border lord are kidnapped as part of a longstanding, acrimonious feud. Tamara, Drucilla, and Sabina, members of the Scorpys family, are forced into the forbidding Dismals, a dangerous and gloomy underground world that threatens their lives consistently, and from which few have emerged unharmed, or even alive. Living by their wits, the sisters meet a strange young man and his powerful, catlike companion, who may be either allies or another danger to overcome. As they interact, the sisters learn to trust him, and they discover a long-held secret that affects them all. The young man also offers them a way to escape to safety, as well as a means to defeat the enemies that plague their topside world. "This tale is told with all of Norton's charm and vigor," demonstrating how and why she "maintained her popularity for more than a half-century," remarked *Booklist* reviewer Frieda Murray. "Grand Master Norton's first solo novel in five years belongs in every library," asserted Jackie Cassada in the *Library Journal.*

Norton suffered from poor health all her long life, and died of congestive heart failure at the age of ninety-three. In a gesture symbolic of the work that bracketed her life, and of all the reading and writing in between, Norton requested that she be cremated along with copies of her first and last novels. She was consistently aware of the power and allure of writing, even in her final illness, especially for young readers. Shortly before her death, she approved plans for the Science Fiction and Fantasy Writers of America (SFWA) to establish the Andre Norton Award for young adult fiction, to be given in conjunction with the annual Nebula Awards. "Many adults today, myself included, were first introduced to science fiction and fantasy through her books and have gone on to become readers, fans, and authors themselves," stated author and SFWA president Catherine Asaro on the *Science Fiction and Fantasy Writers of America* Web site. "Andre Norton has done more to promote reading among young adults than anyone can measure."

For many years, Norton received little critical attention; science fiction critics overlooked her because of her past as a writer for young adults, while critics of children's literature dismissed her as a genre writer. Meanwhile, her fans and peers recognized her as a giant of science fiction and fantasy, a Grand Master who influenced countless followers—especially women—and whose skills in world-building were unmatched. As Brooks stated, "the chief value of Andre Norton's fiction may lie not in entertainment or social commentary, but in her 're-enchanting' us with her creations that renew our linkages to all life." Wollheim agreed, writing that "Andre Norton is at home telling wonder stories. She is telling us that people are marvelously

If you enjoy the works of Andre Norton, you may also want to check out the following books:

Mercedes Lackey's "Valdemar" series, including *Arrow's Flight*, 1987.
The "Acorna" series by Anne McCaffrey and Elizabeth A. Scarborough, including *Acorna's Triumph*, 2004.
Charles de Lint's "Newford" series, including *Widdershins*, 2006.

complex and marvelously fascinating. She is telling us that life is good and that the universe is vast and meant to enhance our life to infinity. She is weaving an endless tapestry of a cosmos no man will ever fully understand, but among whose threads we are meant to wander forever to our personal fulfillment. . . . Basically this is what science fiction has always been about." Wollheim continued: "Because she has always understood this, her audience will continue to be as ever-renewing and as nearly infinite as her subjects." Schlobin similarly concluded in *The Feminine Eye,* "Andre Norton, then, like all special writers, is more than just an author. She is a guide who leads us, the real human beings, to worlds and situations that we might very well expect to live in were we given extraordinary longevity . . . . The Norton future is an exciting realm alive with personal quests to be fulfilled and vital challenges to be overcome. Is it any wonder that millions upon millions of readers, spanning three generations, have chosen to go with her in her travels?"

### ■ Biographical and Critical Sources

*BOOKS*

Bankston, John, *Andre Norton*, Chelsea House (New York, NY), 2009.
*Contemporary Literary Criticism,* Gale (Detroit, MI), Volume 12, 1980, Volume 50, 1999.
*Dictionary of Literary Biography,* Gale (Detroit, MI), Volume 8: *Twentieth-Century American Science Fiction Writers,* 1981, Volume 52: *American Writers for Children since 1960: Fiction,* 1986.
Elwood, Roger, editor, *The Many Worlds of Andre Norton,* Chilton (Radnor, PA), 1974, published as *The Book of Andre Norton,* DAW (New York, NY), 1975.

Miesel, Sandra, introduction to *Sargasso of Space* by Andre Norton, Gregg Press (Boston, MA), 1978.

Platt, Charles, *Dream Makers: The Uncommon Men and Women Who Write Science Fiction*, Berkley Books (New York, NY), 1983.

*St. James Guide to Fantasy Writers*, St. James Press (Detroit, MI), 1996.

*St. James Guide to Science Fiction Writers*, St. James Press (Detroit, MI), 1996.

*St. James Guide to Young Adult Writers*, 2nd edition, St. James Press (Detroit, MI), 1999.

Schlobin, Roger C., *Andre Norton*, Gregg Press (Boston, MA), 1979.

Schlobin, Roger C., *Andre Norton: A Primary and Secondary Bibliography*, G.K. Hall (Boston, MA), 1980.

Shwartz, Susan, editor, *Moonsinger's Friends: An Anthology in Honor of Andre Norton*, Bluejay Books (New York, NY), 1985.

Spivack, Charlotte, *Merlin's Daughters: Contemporary Women Writers of Fantasy*, Greenwood Press (Westport, CT), 1987.

Staicar, Tom, editor, *The Feminine Eye: Science Fiction and the Women Who Write It*, Ungar (New York, NY), 1982.

Townsend, John Rowe, *A Sense of Story: Essays on Contemporary Writers for Children*, Lippincott (Philadelphia, PA), 1971.


*PERIODICALS*


*Analog Science Fiction & Fact*, March, 1999, Tom Easton, review of *Scent of Magic*, p. 132; April, 2000, Tom Easton, review of *Echoes in Time: A New Time Traders Adventure*, p. 135.

*Booklist*, October 15, 1993, Roland Green, review of *Brother to Shadows*, p. 422; January 1, 1994, review of *On Wings of Magic*, p. 1781; June 1, 1994, Roland Green, reviews of *Firehand* and *The Hands of Lyr*, p. 1781; April 1, 1996, Sally Estes, review of *The Monster's Legacy*, p. 1356; September 1, 1996, Roland Green, review of *The Warding of Witch World*, p. 69; February 1, 1997, Roland Green, review of *Derelict for Trade*, p. 929; October 1, 1997, Roland Green, review of *A Mind for Trade*, p. 312; June 1, 1998, Roland Green, review of *Ciara's Song: A Chronicle of the Witch World*, p. 1736; October 15, 1999, Roland Green, review of *Wind in the Stone*, p. 424; November 15, 1999, Roland Green, review of *Echoes in Time*, p. 609; November 1, 2000, Roland Green, review of *Time Traders*, p. 522; February 1, 2001, Roland Green, review of *Time Traders II*, p. 1042; May 15, 2002, Roland Green, review of *Beast Master's Ark*, p. 1583; October 1, 2002, Roland Green, review of *Elvenborn: An Epic High Fantasy*, p. 309; December 15, 2002, Roland Green, review of *Atlantis Endgame*, p. 740; February 1, 2004, Frieda Murray, review of *Beast Master's Circus*, p. 956; January 1, 2005, Frieda Murray, review of *The Duke's Ballad*, p. 834; April 15, 2005, Frieda Murray, review of *Three Hands for Scorpio*, p. 1445.

*Fantasy Review*, September, 1985, Carl B. Yoke, review of *Forerunner: The Second Venture*.

*Growing Point*, October, 1975, Margery Fisher, review of *The Jargoon Pard*.

*Kirkus Reviews*, February 15, 1999, review of *The Shadow of Albion*, p. 258; May 1, 2002, review of *Beast Master's Ark*, p. 626; March 1, 2005, review of *Three Hands for Scorpio*, p. 267.

*Library Journal*, August, 1990, William Schoell, review of *The Jekyll Legacy*, p. 138, and Jackie Cassada, review of *Black Trillium*, p. 147; June 15, 1993, Jackie Cassada, review of *Golden Trillium*, p. 104; November 15, 1993, Jackie Cassada, review of *Brother to Shadows*, p. 103; September 15, 1996, Susan Hamburger, review of *The Warding of Witch World*, p. 101; November 1, 2000, Michael Rogers, review of *Time Traders*, p. 143; February 15, 2001, Jackie Cassada, review of *Time Traders II*, p. 205; April 15, 2002, Michael Rogers, review of *The Gates to Witch World*, p. 130; October 15, 2002, Jackie Cassada, reviews of *Elvenborn*, p. 97, and *A Crown Disowned*, p. 98; April 15, 2005, Jackie Cassada, review of *Three Hands for Scorpio*, p. 79.

*Life*, July, 1984, Harald Sund and Nellie Blagden, "Otherworldly Women," profile of Andre Norton, p. 112.

*Publishers Weekly*, June 1, 1990, Sybil Steinberg, review of *Tales of the Witch World 3*, p. 50; February 8, 1991, Sybil Steinberg, review of *Storms of Victory*, p. 52; May 17, 1993, review of *Golden Trillium*, p. 70; October 11, 1993, review of *Brother to Shadows*, p. 73; October 18, 1993, review of *Empire of the Eagle*, p. 67; November 29, 1993, review of *On Wings of Magic*, p. 58; May 23, 1994, review of *The Hands of Lyr*, p. 82; September 16, 1996, review of *The Warding of Witch World*, p. 75; January 27, 1997, review of *Derelict for Trade*, p. 82; September 29, 1997, review of *A Mind for Trade*, p. 71; October 25, 1999, review of *Echoes in Time*, p. 56; January 22, 2001, review of *Time Traders II*, p. 307; May 21, 2001, review of *Knight or Knave*, p. 86; July 9, 2001, review of *Star Soldiers*, p. 52; December 2, 2002, review of *Atlantis Endgame*, p. 38; December 1, 2003, review of *The Solar Queen*, p. 45; March 21, 2005, review of *Three Hands for Scorpio*, p. 40; April 25, 2005, review of *Beast Master's Planet*, p. 44.

*School Library Journal*, June, 1996, Steven Engelfried, review of *The Monster's Legacy*, p. 154.

*Times Literary Supplement*, September 28, 1973, "Sorcery for Initiates," p. 1114.


*ONLINE*


*Andre Norton Home Page*, http://www.andre-norton.org (December 10, 2005).

## ■ Obituaries

*PERIODICALS*

*Guardian* (London, England), March 29, 2005.
*Independent* (London, England), March 21, 2005, John Clute, "Andre Norton: Prolific Novelist Who Created Worlds of Wonder and Escape."

*New York Times*, March 18, 2005, Christopher Lehmann-Haupt, "Andre Norton Dies at 93; A Master of Science Fiction," p. B8.

*ONLINE*

*Science Fiction and Fantasy Writers of America Web site*, http://sfwa.org/ (March 17, 2005).*

(Photograph courtesy of Joe Corrigan/Getty Images.)

# ■ Personal

Born 1964 in Brooklyn, NY; daughter of Wallace (a child psychologist) and Ruby (an educator) Nottage; married Tony Gerber (a filmmaker); children: Ruby. *Education:* Brown University, B.A., 1986; Yale School of Drama, M.F.A., 1989.

# ■ Addresses

*Home*—Brooklyn, NY. *Agent*—Olivier Sultan and Corinne Hayoun, Creative Artists Agency, 162 5th Ave., 6th Fl., New York, NY 10010; (film and television) Frank Wuliger, The Gersh Agency, 232 N. Canon Dr., Beverly Hills, CA 90210. *E-mail*—info@lynnnottage.net.

# ■ Career

Playwright. Amnesty International, National Press Officer, 1989-93; visiting lecture in playwriting, Yale School of Drama, 2000—; Voices at the River playwriting residency, Arkansas Repertory Theatre,

# Lynn Nottage

2007; also lecturer, visiting professor, and workshop participant at various institutions. Member of Tony Award nominating committee, 2006.

# ■ Member

PEN, Dramatists Guild, Playwrights Horizons, New Dramatists, New York Foundation for the Arts.

# ■ Awards, Honors

Fellowships from Manhattan Theatre Club and New Dramatists; Whitebird playwriting contest winner; Heideman Award for Ten-Minute Play, Actors Theatre of Louisville, 1993, for *Poof!;* New York Foundation for the Arts fellowships, 1994 and 2004; National Endowment for the Arts/TCG grant for theatre residency at Freedom Theatre, Philadelphia, PA, 1999-2000; TCG residency grant, National Endowment for the Arts, for *A Walk through Time;* AT&T OnStage Award, and Rockefeller grant, both for *Las Meninas;* New York Drama Critics' Circle Award for Best Play, 2004, PEN/Laura Pels Award for Drama, 2004, Outer Critic Circle Award for Best Play, John Gassner Award for Best Playwright, American Theatre Critics' Steinberg New Play Award, Francesca Primus Award, AT&T OnStage Award, Audelco Best Playwright award, and four L.A. Ovation Awards, all for *Intimate Apparel;*

Woodie Award, St. Louis Black Repertory Company, 2005; August Wilson Playwriting Award, National Black Theatre Festival, 2005; Guggenheim Foundation fellowship, 2005; *Village Voice* Obie Award for playwriting, 2005, for *Fabulation; or, the Re-education of Undine;* Lucille Lortel Foundation fellowship, 2007; MacArthur Genius Award, MacArthur Foundation, 2007; Susan Smith Blackburn Prize finalist, 2009; Outer Critic Circle Award for Best Play, New York Drama Critics' Circle Award for Best Play, *Village Voice* Obie Award for Best New American Play, 2009, Lucille Lortel Award for Best Play, 2009, Drama Desk Award for Best Play, 2009, and Pulitzer Prize for drama, 2009, all for *Ruined.*

## ■ Writings

*STAGE PLAYS*

*Poof!* (also see below; first produced in Louisville, KY, at Humana Festival of New American Plays, 1993), Playscripts, Inc. (New York, NY), 2006.

*Por'knockers* (also see below), first produced in New York, NY, at Vineyard Theater, 1995.

*Crumbs from the Table of Joy* (first produced in New York, NY, at Second Stage Theatre, 1995), Dramatists Play Service (New York, NY), 1998.

*Mud, River, Stone* (also see below; first produced in New York, NY, at Playwrights Horizons, 1997), Dramatists Play Service (New York, NY), 1998.

*A Walk through Time,* first produced in Philadelphia, PA, at Freedom Theatre, 2001.

*Las Meninas* (also see below; first produced in San Jose, CA, at San Jose Repertory Theatre, 2002), published in *American Theatre,* 2001.

*Becoming American* (first produced in Louisville, KY, at Actors Theatre of Louisville, 2002), Playscripts, Inc. (New York, NY), 2003.

(With others) *Snapshot* (first produced in Louisville, KY, at Actors Theatre of Louisville, 2002), Playscripts, Inc. (New York, NY), 2003.

*Intimate Apparel* (first produced in Baltimore, MD, at Centerstage, 2003), Dramatists Play Service (New York, NY), 2005.

*Crumbs from the Table of Joy and Other Plays* (contains *Crumbs from the Table of Joy, Mud, River, Stone, Poof, Por'knockers,* and *Las Meninas*), Theatre Communications Group (New York, NY), 2004.

(With others) *The Antigone Project* (includes Nottage's *A Stone's Throw;* first produced in New York, NY, at Woman's Project, 2004), No Passport Press (CA), 2009.

*Fabulation; or, The Re-education of Undine* (also see below; first produced by Playwrights Horizons, 2004), Dramatists Play Service (New York, NY), 2005.

(With others) *Point of Revue* (first produced in Minneapolis, MN, at Mixed Blood Theatre Company, 2006), Playscripts, Inc. (New York, NY), 2006.

*Intimate Apparel [and] Fabulation; or The Re-education of Undine,* Theatre Communications Group (New York, NY), 2006.

*Give Again?* (first produced in London, England, at Tricycle Theatre, 2006), published in *How Long Is Never?: Darfur—A Response,* Josef Weinberger (London, England), 2007.

*Ruined* (first produced in Chicago, IL, at Goodman Theatre, 2008), Theatre Communications Group (New York, NY), 2009.

*By The Way, Meet Vera Stark,* first produced in Costa Mesa, CA, at South Coast Repertory, 2008.

(With others) *The River Crosses Rivers: Short Plays by Women Playwrights of Color,* produced in New York, NY, at Ensemble Studio Theatre, 2009.

Also author of monologues *Banana Beer Bath* and *A . . . My Name Is Still Alice/Ida Mae Cole Takes a Stance.* Contributor to anthologies, including *Life's a Stitch: The Best of Contemporary Women's Humor,* Random House, 2002, and *The Best Women's Stage Monologues 2005,* edited by D.L. Lepidus, Smith & Kraus, 2005.

*OTHER*

(Co-author) *Side Streets* (screenplay), Merchant-Ivory, 1999.

Also author of radio play *Maria Rodriguez and the Hare Krishnas,* and of screenplay *The Dew Breakers.* Coauthor of screenplay *Side Streets.*

## ■ Adaptations

*Poof!* was adapted as a short film, 2003.

## ■ Sidelights

Lynn Nottage, the recipient of the 2009 Pulitzer Prize for drama, is a playwright whose work is intended to lend a voice to the experiences of women, particularly African-American women. Nottage's plays are noted for their depth of research and their capacity for bringing characters alive in a specific time and place. "Though at heart a withering satirist," observed *American Theatre* contributor Randy Gener, "Nottage always goes beyond the external to get to the heart and soul of a place or an era, and she always shows a depth of understanding and respect for her characters—usually restless searchers, forgotten people and alienated folks who are trying to fit in or find a connection or are on a quest for identity." "What I'm interested in as a writer is the people who are marginalized, or the people who don't tend to have their stories told on a larger scale," the playwright told Toronto *Globe and Mail* interviewer Simon Houpt.

Nottage grew up in Brooklyn's Boerum Hill neighborhood. As a child, she began writing plays in her journal, inspired by the tales spun by her relatives. "I think for me the journey begins downstairs at the kitchen table of my house," she recalled in an interview posted on the *Kentucky Educational Television* Web site. "Down there was a gathering place for so many women. To come home from school, and my grandmother would be sitting at the table, and my mother would be sitting at the table. The woman from across the street would be sitting at the table. And they all had stories to tell. They were nurses, teachers; they were activists; they were artists. And I think that is where I got all of my inspiration as a writer."

Nottage attended one of New York City's specialty schools, the High School of Music and Art, then went on to Brown University and the Yale School of Drama, where she earned an M.F.A. in 1989. After graduation, she worked as the national press officer for Amnesty International, the human rights group. Though she found the job frustrating in its mission to bring attention to some of the world's most troubling conflicts, the experience kindled what would be a long-lasting interest in the continent of Africa. "You couldn't get anyone to pay attention," she recalled to Gener. "Reporters were like, 'Where's Burundi?' Many people gave lip service. That's devastating when you're shouting and you're seeing these images from the field of bloated bodies floating down the rivers. I had a lot of anger and frustration—feelings of helplessness and hopelessness."

### Creates Powerful Stage Dramas

During those years, Nottage's playwriting impulse was only dormant, not dead. Sitting down to work on an entry for a short-play competition, she produced the work *Poof!* in one sitting. The drama, which addresses the issue of domestic abuse,

Nottage's *Crumbs from the Table of Joy and Other Plays* contains five of the dramatist's early, acclaimed works. (Theatre Communications Group, 2004. Reproduced by permission.)

premiered in 1993 at the Humana Festival of New American Plays in Louisville, Kentucky, winning the company's Heideman Award and drawing the attention of critics nationwide.

Winning a New York Foundation for the Arts fellowship in 1994, Nottage set to work on several full-length plays. One year later, an Off-Broadway venue, the Second Stage Theater, staged her first full-length play, *Crumbs from the Table of Joy*. Set during the 1950s, the work centers on a displaced African-American family that experiences cultural shock when the father marries a German woman who may have survived a Nazi concentration camp. "As a coming-of-age tale in which a girl discovers that adults are fallible and life an endlessly surprising source of both pain and poetry, *Crumbs* suggests an African-American variation on *A Tree Grows in Brooklyn*," wrote Ben Brantley in the *New York Times*.

In *Por'knockers,* a 1995 work, the playwright deals with the theme of African-American activism. Nottage juxtaposes the solitary life of a Guyanese miner (the "por'knocker" of the title) with the tense situation taking place in a New York apartment serving as a safe house for a five homegrown terrorists. "Nottage uses the image of the striving yet patient por'knocker—alone, hunched over, knee-deep in mud—to convey a theme that cannot be stated by the contentious group, even as they grasp for concise, eloquent phrases that will sum up who they are," Michael Barnwell commented in an *American Theatre* review.

Nottage's play *Mud, River, Stone* was inspired by an article the author read about demobilized soldiers in Mozambique who took hostages because they were never paid for their services. Nottage used the incident as the impetus for her drama concerning an African-American husband and wife who travel to Africa but they find themselves taken hostage by a former soldier turned bellhop. Symbolically, Nottage sought to explore her own relationship to the continent of her ancestry. The work received decidedly mixed reviews. *Back Stage* contributor David Sheward wrote that the play starts out as "clever comedy," but declines into "conventional melodrama." *Variety* reviewer Robert L. Daniels also felt that the play loses focus, but he offered praise for the early scenes, in which "the characters are clearly defined, the landscape picturesque, the dialogue laced with humor."

In the late 1990s Nottage put her writing on hold to devote time to her family. Married to filmmaker Tony Gerber, Nottage moved back to Brooklyn to care for her ailing mother. Her daughter Ruby was born just two months after her mother, also named Ruby, passed away. From 1999 to 2000 Nottage worked at the Freedom Theatre in Philadelphia with the help of a National Endowment for the Arts grant, and produced a children's musical titled *A Walk through Time.* In 2001, she traveled to Africa for the first time, visiting Senegal and Gambia.

## A Return to Form

Nottage was also involved in research for her next plays, and the fruits of her labors showed in *Las Meninas,* which premiered in 2002. It depicts a romance, mostly erased from the historical record, between Marie-Thérèse, wife of King Louis XIV of France, and an African dwarf who had been brought to the French Court. "I felt like I was rescuing these characters from history, uncovering the truth about the relationship between" the queen and her attendant, Nottage explained in an interview with Lenora Inez Brown for *American Theatre.* "This relationship challenges the traditional roles of race and gender in the French court—and yet warrants only one sentence in most history books?!"

Nottage's next play, the award-winning *Intimate Apparel,* debuted in 2003. Based on the life of Nottage's great-grandmother, *Intimate Apparel* centers on Esther Mills, a plain, hard-working seamstress who creates deluxe lingerie for her clients. Although the garments she sews are imaginative and erotic, in her personal life Esther is repressed and has few close relationships. With the help of her clients, however, she begins a correspondence with George, a man working on the Panama Canal, and he eventually comes to New York. Seduced by George's

An adaptation of *Mother Courage and Her Children,* Nottage's *Ruined* stunned audiences and critics alike when it premiered in 2008. (Theatre Communications Group, 2009. Photographs copyright © 2009 by Tony Gerber. Reproduced by permission.)

**Nottage holds the 2009 Lucille Lortel Award, one of several honors she received for *Ruined*.** (Photograph courtesy of Amy Sussman/Getty Images.)

romantic phrases, the illiterate Esther allows herself to be talked into marriage and, then, to handing over her life's savings. "In its account of Esther's reckless leap of faith, the play manages to capture something that is rarely dramatized: the exhilarating newness of freedom," asserted *New Yorker*'s John Lahr in his assessment of its merit. "Esther, unlike her parents and centuries of their ancestors, holds her emotional destiny in her own hands; she is free to make a choice, even a bad one." The play's popularity with audiences and critics alike, Gener asserted, "has to do with its satisfying density: the rare skill by which it builds tension and pathos to a conclusion that is both quiet and emotionally shattering."

Nottage returned in 2004 with *Fabulation; or, The Re-education of Undine* which was written at the same time as *Intimate Apparel* and billed as a modern-day companion piece. The play chronicles the fall from grace of the self-named Undine Barnes Calles, a sharp, successful public relations professional who must return to the Brooklyn housing projects she fled years earlier after she discovers that her South American husband has left her penniless. "For *Fabulation,* I tried to imagine Esther 100 years later, after she's enjoyed the benefits of the women's rights and civil rights movements and become a fully empowered African-American woman, like Condoleezza Rice—and that was Undine," Nottage explained to Gener. "Esther's journey is about becoming empowered, whereas Undine feels completely empowered, so I imagined the opposite journey for her."

Critics offered praise for Nottage's brash comedy. According to Frank Scheck in the *Hollywood Reporter, Fabulation* "serves as an entertaining, moralistic fable for our times." *Daily Variety* contributor Charles Isherwood noted that "as Undine embarks on Nottage's clever inversion of a fish-out-of-water scenario—a reverse-angle photo of a girl from the 'hood making humbling faux pas among her social betters—the play settles on a gently satiric tone that allows us to catch glimpses of the complicated human beings shackled by circumstance to their cliched roles in American culture."

### Pens Her Masterpiece

In 2005 Nottage made a second trip to Africa, visiting Kenya and Uganda to conduct research about the after-effects of war on women and children. She spent time in a female-only village called Umoja, in Kenya, set up for victims of wartime sexual assault who had been turned out by their families and communities. It became a refuge for women fleeing a myriad of domestic violence, and the interviews Nottage conducted became the foundation for her Pulitzer-Prize winning drama *Ruined*. The work also owes a literary debt to the 1939 Bertolt Brecht classic, *Mother Courage and Her Children,* whose title character is a woman who profits from war.

*Ruined* debuted at Chicago's Goodman Theater in 2008. Set during a time of civil war in the Democratic Republic of the Congo, the action takes place in a bare-bones shanty that serves as a brothel for soldiers and miners from the nearby gold mines. Its cast of characters includes Mama Nadi, the brothel-keeper, and the young refugee women who work for her; one of them is Sophie, who suffered irreparable damage in a bayonet assault but works as a bookkeeper and singer. "It is a measure of Nottage's considerable empathetic strength and moral subtlety that she brings nuance and contrast to this harsh world, and that her characters, crucially for themselves but also for the audience, do not simply scrap and scheme but find room to sing, laugh, even hope," noted Rob Weinert-Kendt in *America*. David Rooney, writing in *Variety*, described *Ruined* as a "muscular drama with real, richly textured characters, driven by powerful narrative momentum, pulsating music and heartfelt compassion. It's not structurally perfect, but it's riveting." According to *New York Times* critic Brantley, Nottage "hooks her audience with promises of a conventionally structured, purposefully plotted play, stocked with sympathetic characters and informative topical detail. She delivers on those promises. Yet a raw and genuine agony pulses within and finally bursts through this sturdy framework, giving *Ruined* an impact that lingers beyond its well-shaped, sentimental ending."

In her plays, Nottage has consistently explored new settings and techniques. "In her plays, as in her life, Lynn Nottage is an intrepid traveler," Gener maintained. "With a keenly perceptive eye and an unerring ear for dialogue, as well as a healthy ap-

If you enjoy the works of Lynn Nottage, you may also want to check out the following plays:

Bertolt Brecht, *Mother Courage and Her Children*, 1949.
Suzan-Lori Parks, *In the Blood*, 1999.
Osonye Tess Onwueme, *What Mama Said*, 2003.

preciation for the unusual, the absurd and the hilariously ironic, she will go anywhere and try just about anything to make the theatrical experience full and rewarding." According to Hilton Als, writing in the *New Yorker*, the playwright "has a large, propulsive talent. She works in the tradition of Eugene O'Neill and Theodore Dreiser. Like them, she wants to tell big stories about America." Nottage describes

**A jubilant Nottage celebrates after learning she has received the 2009 Pulitzer Prize for drama.** (Photograph courtesy of Lucas Jackson/Reuters/Corbis.)

herself in somewhat less-glowing terms, however; asked by *New York Times* contributor Jason Zinoman to summarize her career, Nottage simply stated, "I'm a contemporary playwright in a postmodern world."

## ■ Biographical and Critical Sources

*PERIODICALS*

*America,* July 20, 2009, Rob Weinert-Kendt, "A War on Women: Lynn Nottage's Pulitzer Prize-winning *Ruined,*" p. 35.

*American Theatre,* November, 1995, Michael Barnwell, review of *Por'knockers,* p. 10; July, 2001, Lenora Inez Brown, "Dismantling the Box," p. 50; May-June, 2005, Lynn Nottage, "Out of East Africa: The Show Must Go On for Uganda Orphans and Batwa Pygmies, In the Wake of Crossborder Violence, Civil Wars, Disease and Devastation," p. 26; October, 2005, Randy Gener, "Conjurer of Worlds: From Richly Imagined Epochs to Unsparing Satires, Lynn Nottage's Roving Imagination Channels History's Discards into Drama," p. 22; March, 2009, Randy Gener, "Mama Nadi and Her Women," review of *Ruined,* p. 21.

*Back Stage,* June 30, 1995, William Stevenson, review of *Crumbs from the Table of Joy,* p. 36; December 8, 1995, David A. Rosenberg, review of *Por'knockers,* p. 40; December 19, 1997, David Sheward, review of *Mud, River, Stone,* p. 33; December 1, 2000, Mark S.P. Turvin, review of *Crumbs from the Table of Joy,* p. 7; July 2, 2004, David Sheward, review of *Fabulation; or, the Re-education of Undine,* p. 40; February 12, 2009, David Sheward, review of *Ruined,* p. 10.

*Back Stage West,* February 15, 2001, Charlene Baldridge, review of *Crumbs from the Table of Joy,* p. 14.

*Daily Variety,* April 12, 2004, Charles Isherwood, review of *Intimate Apparel,* p. 12; May 26, 2004, Robert Hofler, "Taper Dons New *Apparel,*" p. 5; June 15, 2004, Charles Isherwood, review of *Fabulation; or the Re-education of Undine,* p. 4; February 11, 2009, David Rooney, review of *Ruined,* p. 2; April 21, 2009, Gordon Cox, "*Ruined* Reaps Pulitzer," p. 1; September 24, 2009, David Mermelstein, "Lynn Nottage: Exploring Characters on the Margins," p. 22.

*Economist,* May 23, 2009, "Political Charge: Congo War Play in New York," review of *Ruined,* p. 83.

*Entertainment Weekly,* September 3, 2004, Chris Willman, review of *Intimate Apparel,* p. 83; December 25, 2009, Thom Geier, review of *Ruined,* p. 113.

*Globe and Mail* (Toronto, Ontario, Canada), January 19, 2008, Simon Houpt, "Bringing Light to Life's Grey Areas," p. R3.

*Hollywood Reporter,* July 6, 2004, Frank Scheck, review of *Fabulation; or, The Re-education of Undine,* p. 18; August 6, 2004, Jay Reiner, review of *Intimate Apparel,* p. 24.

*National Catholic Reporter,* April 30, 2004, Retta Blaney, review of *Intimate Apparel,* p. 15.

*New York,* February 23, 2009, Scott Brown, "Misery Times Two: Uncle Vanya's Jumpy, Star-Studded Russian Melancholy, and Lynn Nottage's Grimly Lyric *Ruined,*" p. 136.

*New Yorker,* April 19, 2004, John Lahr, "Unnatural History," review of *Intimate Apparel,* p. 196; March 2, 2009, Hilton Als, "Life during Wartime," review of *Ruined,* p. 72.

*New York Times,* June 22, 1995, Ben Brantley, "Though a Melodrama, Life Is Not a Movie," review of *Crumbs from the Table of Joy;* June 13, 2004, Jason Zinoman, "Lynn Nottage Enters Her Flippant Period," p. AR6; June 14, 2004, Ben Brantley, "A Mighty Diva's Humbling Fall to Rough Roots in the Projects," review of *Fabulation; or, the Re-education of Undine,* p. E1; January 25, 2009, Celia Mcgee, "Approaching Brecht, by Way of Africa," p. 4; February 11, 2009, Ben Brantley, "War's Terrors, Through a Brothel Window," review of *Ruined,* p. C1; March 22, 2009, Charles Isherwood, "Bearing Witness to the Chaos of War," review of *Ruined,* p. 9.

*Star Tribune* (Minneapolis, MN), October 16, 2005, Rohan Preston, "Playwright Lynn Nottage Finds the Historical in the Personal: *Intimate Apparel* Was Lynn Nottage's Search for Her Family History," p. 4F.

*Variety,* December 22, 1997, Robert L. Daniels, review of *Mud, River, Stone,* p. 72; April 1, 2002, Dennis Harvey, review of *Las Meninas,* p. 42; June 21, 2004, review of *Fabulation; or, The Re-education of Undine,* p. 45; February 16, 2009, David Rooney, "Beauty from Brutality," review of *Ruined,* p. 23.

*ONLINE*

*Brooklyn Rail,* http://www.thebrooklynrail.org/ (June, 2004), Sonya Sobieski, "Down the Rabbit Hole with Lynn Nottage."

*Kentucky Educational Television Web site,* http://www.ket.org/ (September 2, 2005), "A Talk with Playwright Lynn Nottage."

*Lynn Nottage Home Page,* http://www.lynnnottage.net (April 1, 2010).

*MacArthur Foundation Web site,* http://www.macfound.org/ (April 1, 2010), "Lynn Nottage."

*Steppenwolf Backstage Online,* http://www.steppenwolf.org/ (September 2, 2005), Alyson Roux, "Lynn Nottage at Steppenwolf," review of *Intimate Apparel,* and Curt Columbus, "The Intimate Conversation."*

# Robert Rauschenberg

(Photograph courtesy of Bob Berg/Getty Images.)

## ■ Personal

Born Milton Ernest Rauschenberg, October 22, 1925, in Port Arthur, TX; died of heart failure, May 12, 2008, in Captiva Island, FL; son of Ernest (a utilities company employee) and Dora Rauschenberg; married Sue Weil, 1950 (divorced, 1952); companion of Darryl Pottorf; children: Christopher. *Education:* Attended University of Texas; studied at Kansas City Art Institute and School of Design, Missouri, 1946-47; Académie Julian, Paris, France, 1947; studied art under Josef Albers, and photography under Hazel Larson, Black Mountain College, North Carolina, 1948-49; Art Students' League, New York, 1949-52.

## ■ Career

Artist. Independent painter, graphic artist, and photographer, 1950-2008, and stage designer, 1955-2008. Mounted first "Happening," with John Cage and others, Black Mountain, NC, 1952; artistic advisor and resident designer for Merce Cunningham Dance Company, New York, NY, 1954-64; cofounder, with Billy Kluver, Experiments in Art and Technology (E.A.T.), 1966; Change Inc., New York, president of the board, 1970; Untitled Press (graphics studio),

Captiva Island, FL, founder, 1971; Trisha Brown Dance Company, New York, president, 1978; director of Rauschenberg Overseas Cultural Exchange (ROCI), 1985-90. Instructor, Black Mountain College, 1952. *Exhibitions:* Work appears in permanent collections at Museum of Modern Art, New York, NY; Guggenheim Museum, New York, NY; Whitney Museum, New York, NY; Museum Ludwig, Cologne, Germany; Stedelijk Museum, Amsterdam, Netherlands; Los Angeles County Museum of Art, Los Angeles, CA; Art Gallery of Ontario, Toronto, Ontario, Canada; National Gallery of Canada, Ottawa, Ontario, Canada; Kunsthaus Zürich, Zürich, Switzerland; and Kaiser Wilhelm Museum, Krefeld, Germany. First solo exhibit at Parsons Gallery, New York, NY, 1951; has exhibited subsequent work in numerous shows worldwide and at museums in the United States, Europe, the Soviet Union, and Japan. *Military service:* Served as a neuropsychiatry technician, United States Naval Reserve, California Naval Hospital, 1942-45.

## ■ Member

American Academy of Arts and Sciences, Royal Academy of Fine Arts (foreign member).

## ■ Awards, Honors

Painting Prize, Art Institute of Chicago, 1960; Ohara Prize, National Museum of Modern Art, 1962; first prize, *International Exhibition of Graphic Art*, 1963;

first prize, XXXII Biennale de Venezia, 1964; William A. Clark Gold Medal, Corcoran Biennial Exhibition of Contemporary American Painters, 1965; Art Institute of Chicago Award, 1966; Logan Award, Art Institute of Chicago, 1976; Mayor's Award of Honor in Arts and Culture, New York, NY, 1977; Creative Arts Medal, Brandeis University, 1978; Chicago Arts Award, 1978; Grand Prize of Honour, *International Exhibition of Graphic Art*, 1979; Special Award, *Biennale of Graphic Arts,* 1979; Gold Medal for Graphics, 1979; named Officier of Ordre des Arts et Lettres, Ministry of Culture and Communication (France), 1981; Skowhegan School Painting and Sculpture Medal, 1982; Grammy Award, 1984, for best album design; Jerusalem Prize for Arts and Letters, Friends of Bezalel Academy, 1984; Band of Honor, Order of Andres Bello (Venezuela), 1985; Golden Plate Award, American Academy of Achievement, 1986; International Center of Photography Art Award, 1987; Algur H. Meadows Award of Excellence in the Arts, 1989; Federal Design Achievement Award, 1992; National Medal of Arts Award, 1993; Second Hiroshima Art Prize, Hiroshima Museum of Contemporary Art, 1993; "Leonardo Da Vinci" World Award of Arts, World Cultural Council, 1995; Lifetime Achievement Award in Contemporary Sculpture, International Sculpture Center, 1996; elected Honorary Royal Academician, Royal Academy of Arts, 2000. D.H.L.: Grinnell College, Iowa, 1967; D.F.A.: University of South Florida, Tampa, 1976; New York University, 1984. Fellow, Rhode Island School of Design, Providence, 1981.

## ■ Writings

(Illustrator) *Robert Rauschenberg's XXXIV Drawings for Dante's Inferno, 1959-1960,* commentary by Dore Ashton, Abrams (New York, NY), 1964.

*Photos In + Out City Limits: Boston,* ULAE (West Islip, NY), 1981.

*Photos In + Out City Limits: New York C.,* ULAE (West Islip, NY), 1982.

## ■ Sidelights

Robert Rauschenberg was one of the most influential figures in twentieth-century American art. During his career, the imaginative and eclectic artist embraced painting, sculpture, collage, lithography, photography, and even dance and performance art. Rauschenberg "defied the traditional idea that an artist stick to one medium or style," Michael Kim-

melman stated in the *New York Times.* "He pushed, prodded and sometimes reconceived all the mediums in which he worked." Once considered the enfant terrible of American modernism, Rauschenberg lived long enough to become a venerable elder statesman in his field, praised by critics, sought after by collectors, and admired for both his work and his interest in world affairs. According to *Time* contributor Robert Hughes, Rauschenberg "is the artist of American democracy, yearningly faithful to its clamor, its contradictions, its hope and its enormous demotic freedom, all of which find shape in his work."

Many critics feel that Rauschenberg's enormous output set the tone for much of the American art of the 1960s and 1970s. "Historically, Rauschenberg got us from Abstract Expressionism to Pop Art—one of the greatest stylistic leaps ever—by introducing those bits of the readymade and the already-seen into the meaty coherence of such abstract 'action painters' as Willem de Kooning," Peter Plagens wrote in *Newsweek.* "With a restless creative energy to rival Picasso's he then crunched, stretched, pounded and exploded the combination of objects and paint into a kind of art full enough and big enough to go way beyond what the critics first called his art—'Neo-Dada'—and to almost get its own 'ism': Rauschenbergism." A reporter in the London *Daily Telegraph* similarly noted, "After Rauschenberg it was accepted that a work of art could be made out of anything and could be shown anywhere, for any duration and any purpose. He was 'the benign uncle' of modern art and it was no surprise that movements ranging from the neo-Dadaists and the Conceptualists to the second wave of Abstract Expressionists sought to claim him as their own." In fact, Rauschenberg did not need to tend his reputation—his successful challenge to the seriousness of abstract expressionism and his prolific mingling of media made him a hero among the younger generation of artists.

### Finding His Own Way

Rauschenberg was born October 22, 1925, in Port Arthur, Texas, an oil refinery town on the Gulf of Mexico. Of mixed German and Cherokee descent, he was christened Milton Ernest Rauschenberg. Neither of Rauschenberg's parents had any particular interest in the fine arts—his father worked as a utilities company employee and his mother cut dress patterns. Raised in the fundamentalist Church of Christ, Rauschenberg, as a teenager, planned to become a preacher until he discovered "it was a sin to dance," he remarked to Michael Ennis in *Texas Monthly.* "And I was quite good at looking through

**Rauschenberg gained fame for his mixed-media works known as "combines," including** *Aen Floga* **(left) and** *Pilgrim*.
(Photograph courtesy of Jacques Demarthon/AFP/Getty Images.)

the Bible and showing how many times they danced in the Bible." As a student Rauschenberg was plagued with nearsightedness and dyslexia, but he did manage to qualify for entry into the University of Texas at Austin after graduating from high school.

Rauschenberg studied pharmacy at the University of Texas, but he was expelled in 1943 after he refused to dissect a frog. Shortly thereafter he was drafted into the U.S. Navy, where he boldly declared that he had no intention of killing anyone. This assertion led to a two-and-a-half-year stint as a neuropsychiatric technician at various naval hospitals in California. "This is where I learned how little difference there is between sanity and madness," Rauschenberg told a contributor in *Time*, "and realized that a combination of both is what everyone needs."

In his brief moments of spare time, Rauschenberg would thumb rides to nearby California towns and visit the local libraries and museums. Wandering into the Huntington Library in San Marino on a

whim, he recognized a number of paintings, including Thomas Gainsborough's *Blue Boy*, from the backs of playing cards. In the words of *Los Angeles Magazine* critic Bernard Cooper, "This revelatory moment (a merging of high culture and low that still resonates through the artist's work) was the first time he realized that art, instead of being a hobby, could be an occupation demanding all his energy and attentiveness."

After his discharge from the Navy, Rauschenberg used the G.I. Bill of Rights to pay his tuition at the Kansas City Art Institute. He studied there through 1946 and 1947, earning spare money by doing store window displays. It was during this period that he changed his first name from Milton to Robert, entirely for professional reasons. In 1948 he set out for Paris, in order to study at the Académie Julian. His tenure there was brief, however, because he did not speak French and therefore could not communicate effectively with his instructors. The *Time* reporter contended that in Paris, the young artist "felt unfocused, self-indulgent and queasy, surrounded by an already academized modern tradition that he could not grasp."

In France Rauschenberg met Susan Weil, another American painter, who would become his wife. Together Rauschenberg and Weil returned to the United States and enrolled at Black Mountain College in North Carolina, where they studied with the pioneer abstractionist Josef Albers. "On the face of it," Michael McNay remarked in the London *Guardian*, "Albers' Bauhaus aesthetics were not ideal for the scruffy and undirected work that Rauschenberg was producing, but he needed and wanted the discipline, and it is possible to see in the delicate discrimination with which he placed the elements

**A museum patron views** *Yellow Moby Glut,* **one of a series of sculptures and paintings on metal by Rauschenberg.**
(Photograph courtesy of AP Images.)

of his collages the influence of Albers' elegant control." During his time at Black Mountain, Rauschenberg also forged close friendships with composer John Cage and dancer Merce Cunningham, ties that would lead to collaborative projects in the 1950s and 1960s.

In 1949 Rauschenberg moved to New York City and continued his studies at the Art Students League. In 1950 he married Weil, with whom he had collaborated on a series of pictures made by running a sun lamp over blueprint paper. Oddly enough, these prints of miscellaneous objects, rendered eerily transparent by the process, became part of a window display at the Bonwit Teller department store. Thereafter Rauschenberg was able to support himself through lean times by doing window displays at the major department stores in Manhattan. With Cage and Cunningham, the young artist became part of a community of dancers, musicians, and painters who were all experimenting with a multimedia approach to art. "I feel that art can be like furniture, static, clumsy," Rauschenberg told Kimmelman. "The whole point of collaboration is to counteract that. For me, art shouldn't be a fixed idea that I have before I start making it. I want it to include all the fragility and doubt that I go through the day with."

### Making His Mark

Rauschenberg's first solo exhibition was held in May of 1951 at the Parsons Gallery. The exhibition featured the predecessors to Rauschenberg's famous all-white, all-black, and all-red canvases, created with the idea that the changing reflections of viewer, lights, and other objects complete the work. Rauschenberg also displayed grass paintings—bundles of soil and seedlings, held together with chicken wire. These early efforts were not received with great enthusiasm, but the underlying philosophy of the works—that a painting's surface could be an impartial collector of images—would become central to Rauschenberg's mature output. Around this same time, Rauschenberg returned to Black Mountain, where he began experimenting with photography. "This became an enduring pursuit— the artist once said he wanted to photograph the world—and he eventually amassed an ever-growing archive of images, which he used for his subsequent silk screens," Barbara Rose stated in *Artforum International.*

Having divorced his wife in 1952, the artist traveled through Italy, Spain, and North Africa, finding inspiration in the collages of German Dadaist Kurt

Schwitters and sculptor-painter Marcel Duchamp. "During this nomadic period, Rauschenberg also made collages on cardboard that prefigured the Combine paintings he would begin upon his return to the United States," Rose explained. "These juxtapositions of divergent and often ephemeral materials evoked brief moments and fugitive experiences. They anticipated the way in which Rauschenberg would eventually cull his subjects and images from his immediate surroundings."

By the mid-1950s Rauschenberg had begun to create innovative works that he called "combines." These collages of cast-off junk, parts of animals and household utensils, and drips of paint were half-painting and half-sculpture, and they created quite a stir among New York's staid art critics. "The Combines are full of jokes, camp replays and caricatures of just about every earnest New York School cliche, as well as startling and unforgettable juxtapositions," commented London *Guardian* reporter Adrian Searle, who added that if the artworks "have any meaning, it is in their profligacy, their inclusiveness, their physical attempt to wrestle with high culture and low—and with no culture at all." Rauschenberg was known to scavenge the streets around his Greenwich Village studio for material; according to Cooper, the artist's "best work suggests that compelling fragments of the world can be found everywhere as long as the artist, and the viewer, are open-minded enough to perceive them. Receptiveness to the world is elevated to a philosophical stance in the combines. They arise from, and enact, a belief in unbounded possibility."

Two works from this period have become particularly famous. *Bed* (1955) features a patchwork quilt and pillow stretched on a frame and spattered with red paint. The suggested violence of the red spatters led Italian critics to ban the work from exhibition at the Festival of Two Worlds. *Monogram* (1959) consists of the head of a stuffed Angora goat, an automobile tire, and a collaged base that incorporates a tennis ball, a shirtsleeve, a rubber heel, and footprints. Critics attached a sexual connotation to *Monogram* because the goat's head protruded from the tire. Whatever their perceived connotations may have been (Rauschenberg never claimed any), the works certainly broke new ground. *New York Times* art critic Grace Glueck noted that the "messy, outlandish tableaux . . . brought the jaded art world to full attention and were later credited with providing a bridge from Abstract Expressionism to Pop." Decades later, the combines still have the power to startle, entertain, and move audiences; in the London *Guardian*, Robert Hughes described the works as "the emblem of [Rauschenberg's] inventiveness. They embody a lavish, anarchic com-

The scope of the artist's vision can be seen in the 1992 metal sculpture *Nile Throne Glut* (front) as well as the 1961 combine *Trophy III (for Jean Tinguely).* (Photograph courtesy of Georgios Kefalas/EPA/Corbis.)

mitment to making everything up as you go along—not 'anarchic' in the sense of totally disordered, but in the sense of not being governed by pre-existing rules."

Between 1955 and 1962 Rauschenberg cultivated a close friendship with Jasper Johns, the other leading artist of the 1950s avant-garde. Rauschenberg and Johns worked together on window displays for department stores, but their most important work was done in the studio, where they critiqued and inspired one another. According to Calvin Tomkins in the *New Yorker*, "The exchange of ideas between Rauschenberg and Johns in those years has been likened to the interaction between Picasso and Braque from 1908 to 1912, when they were jointly inventing Cubism." In an interview with Tomkins, Johns recalled, "We were very close and considerate of one another, and for a number of years we were each other's main audience. I was allowed to question what he did, and he could question what I did."

As his "combines" began to attract attention, Rauschenberg continued to experiment, using everything from lighter fluid to cardboard to newspaper headlines in streams of juxtaposed, fragmentary images. Rauschenberg was also one of the first American artists to turn to the silk screen image. "The silk-screen paintings that Rauschenberg made between 1962 and '65 had a brilliantly heightened documentary flavor," the *Time* contributor remarked. "The canvas trapped images, accumulating them. One was reminded of the shuttle and flicker of a TV set as the dial is clicked: rocket eagle, Kennedy, dancer, oranges, box all registered with the peacock-hued, aniline-sharp intensity of electronic color. The subject was glut."

### A Multi-Talented Artist

The once-vilified experimenter found himself, by 1964, at the pinnacle of success in the international art world. Rauschenberg won the prestigious first prize at the Venice Biennale in l964 and the gold medal at the Corcoran Biennial Exhibition of Contemporary American Painters in 1965. In the words of Kimmelman, "Rauschenberg had, almost despite himself, become an institution." Some wide-eyed critics even dared to compare the painter to Picasso, while the old-school dissenters blamed him for the crass and facile quality of Pop art. Rauschenberg responded to all this attention by returning to collaborative work. He served as an adviser and dancer with Merce Cunningham's company and he started a nonprofit foundation named E.A.T. (Experiments in Art and Technology) that produced multimedia happenings in America and Japan. "Something inherently theatrical about Robert Rauschenberg's talent—always evident in his radical feeling for color, light, composition and new ingredients and juxtapositions—prompted him to his boldest and freshest conceptions when he worked onstage," Alastair Macaulay observed in the *New York Times*.

In the 1970s Rauschenberg returned to the studio, this time involving himself primarily with lithographs and prints. The best known of these works are the "Stoned Moon" series (1970) and the delicate "Hoarfrost" series (1974), done on descending layers of silk, chiffon, taffeta, and cheesecloth. These works, Robert Hughes asserted in *Time*, demonstrate Rauschenberg's "exquisite sense of nuance. It comes out in his complex prints; his Zen-simple paper objects, *Pages and Fuses*, from the '70s; and in the shimmering veils of printed translucent fabric of the Hoarfrost series, image floating over image, as in *Emerald* (Hoarfrost), 1975, with its diver's body vanishing into the deep blue-green." Rauschenberg also escalated his creative use of photography as the decade wore on; in 1979 some six hundred slides he had taken were projected as a backdrop for *Glacial Decoy,* a dance created by choreographer Trisha Brown.

His fame assured, Rauschenberg visited a number of foreign countries through the 1970s and 1980s, including China, India, and Japan. Each country he visited offered him new inspirations and a wealth of local artifacts from which he could create art. These travels culminated in the creation of a foundation, the Rauschenberg Overseas Cultural Interchange (ROCI). Under the aegis of ROCI, Rauschenberg has traveled to more than a dozen countries—including the Soviet Union and other Iron Curtain nations—in order to develop an "international artistic communication." By 1989, some critics estimate, more than two million people had seen themselves and their global neighbors through the idiosyncratic prism of Rauschenberg's art. Initially, Rauschenberg had hoped for corporate sponsorship of ROCI, but with few exceptions he wound up paying for the project himself. "It is hard to imagine a project more quixotic and less feasible than ROCI," Helen Dudar remarked in the *Smithsonian.* Still, financial difficulties didn't bring the project to an

end; Rauschenberg simply wanted to pursue other interests. "Peace and communication and understanding has always been my lifestyle," the artist told Dudar. "I thought I'd made the point."

During the 1970s Rauschenberg began splitting his time between New York City and the Gulf Coast island of Captiva. He eventually acquired more than thirty-five acres of land in Florida, and in 1993 he designed and constructed a 17,000-square-foot, two-story studio. With a team of assistants, Rauschenberg created enormous projects such as *The 1/4 Mile or 2 Furlong Piece,* a "sprawling self-retrospective 'spread' of mixed-medium paintings and sculptures," observed Charles Stuckey in *Art in America.* Despite suffering a stroke in 2002 that paralyzed his right side, Rauschenberg continued to produce art for several more years, directing the staff from his wheelchair. "I usually work in a direction until I know how to do it, then I stop," he told Kimmelman. "At the time that I am bored or understand—I use those words interchangeably— another appetite has formed. A lot of people try to think up ideas. I'm not one. I'd rather accept the irresistible possibilities of what I can't ignore."

**Rauschenberg (left) enjoyed a long-lasting relationship with Merce Cunningham, serving as a designer and artistic advisor for Cunningham's dance company.** (Photograph courtesy of Andrea Merola/EPA/Corbis.)

If you enjoy the works of Robert Rauschenberg, you may also want to check out the following:

The art of French surrealist Marcel Duchamp (1887-1968), American painter Cy Twombly (1928-), and American painter and printmaker Jasper Johns (1930-).

Rauschenberg died of heart failure on May 12, 2008, in Captiva Island. Friends, colleagues, and critics all marked the occasion of his passing. "Rauschenberg confronted every major aesthetic issue facing modern art at a time of crisis and exhaustion," Rose stated. "Rauschenberg was an empirical experimenter who rejected calculation for the far riskier process of trial and error, in which success is predicated not on the repetition of formulas but on prior failures." According to Maria Puente in *USA Today*, the artist will "be remembered for his inventive, eccentric collages of paint and old junk—tires, Coke bottles, shoes, clothing fragments, light bulbs, ladders, newspapers, postcards and other flotsam of city life. They redefined what could be considered high art and introduced conceptual and pop art to a mid-century world then preoccupied with abstract expressionism." Rauschenberg, noted Glenn O'Brien in *Interview*, "not only created work that stands as epic testament to his time, but he was always an activist and an instigator, throwing himself wholeheartedly into the struggle that is history."

## ■ Biographical and Critical Sources

### BOOKS

Bois, Yve-Alain, *Robert Rauschenberg: Cardboards and Related Pieces*, Menil Collection (Houston, TX), 2008.

*Contemporary Artists*, 5th edition, St. James Press (Detroit, MI), 2001.

*Contemporary Photographers*, 3rd edition, St. James Press (Detroit, MI), 1996.

Cowart, Jack, editor, *Rauschenberg Overseas Culture Interchange*, National Gallery of Art (Washington, DC), 1991.

Davidson, Susan, *Robert Rauschenberg: Gluts*, Guggenheim Museum (New York, NY), 2009.

*Encyclopedia of Lesbian, Gay, Bisexual and Transgender History in America*, Scribner's (New York, NY), 2004.

Feinstein, Roni, *Robert Rauschenberg: The Silkscreen Paintings, 1962-64*, Bulfinch Press (Boston, MA), 1990.

Forge, Andrew, *Robert Rauschenberg*, Abrams (New York, NY), 1972.

Hopps, Walter, *Robert Rauschenberg: The Early 1950s*, Houston Fine Arts Press (Houston, TX), 1991.

Hopps, Walter, and Susan Davidson, *Robert Rauschenberg: A Retrospective*, Guggenheim Museum Publications (New York, NY), 1997.

Hunter, Sam, *Robert Rauschenberg*, Rizzoli (New York, NY), 1999.

Hunter, Sam, *Robert Rauschenberg: Works, Writing, Interviews*, Polígrafa (Barcelona, Spain), 2007.

Ikegami, Hiroko, *The Great Migrator: Robert Rauschenberg and the Global Rise of American Art*, MIT Press (Cambridge, MA), 2010.

*International Dictionary of Art and Artists*, St. James Press (Detroit, MI), 1990.

*International Dictionary of Modern Dance*, St. James Press (Detroit, MI), 1998.

Joseph, Branden W., editor, *Robert Rauschenberg*, MIT Press (Cambridge, MA), 2002.

Joseph, Branden W., *Random Order: Robert Rauschenberg and the Neo-Avant-Garde*, MIT Press (Cambridge, MA), 2003.

Kachur, Lewis, *Robert Rauschenberg: Transfer Drawings of the 1960s*, Jonathan O'Hara Gallery (New York, NY), 2007.

Kotz, Mary Lynn, *Rauschenberg: Art and Life*, Abrams (New York, NY), 1990.

Lanchner, Carolyn, *Robert Rauschenberg*, Museum of Modern Art (New York, NY), 2010.

Mattison, Robert S., *Robert Rauschenberg: Photographs*, Pantheon Books (New York, NY), 1981.

Mattison, Robert S., *Robert Rauschenberg: Breaking Boundaries*, Yale University Press (New Haven, CT), 2003.

Rose, Barbara, *Robert Rauschenberg*, Vintage Books (New York, NY), 1987.

Schimmel, Paul, editor, *Robert Rauschenberg: Combines*, Steidl/The Museum of Contemporary Art (Los Angeles, CA), 2005.

*Scribner Encyclopedia of American Lives Thematic Series: The 1960s*, Scribner's (New York, NY), 2003.

Solomon, Alan, *Robert Rauschenberg*, Jewish Museum (New York, NY), 1963.

Steinberg, Leo, *Encounters with Rauschenberg: (A Lavishly Illustrated Lecture)*, University of Chicago Press (Chicago, IL), 2000.

Tomkins, Calvin, *Off the Wall: Robert Rauschenberg and the Art World of Our Time,* Picador (New York, NY), 1980.

*PERIODICALS*

*Art Digest,* September, 1953, Dore Ashton, "Robert Rauschenberg," pp. 20, 25.

*Artforum International,* September, 1997, Thomas Crow, "This Is Now: Becoming Robert Rauschenberg," p. 95; September, 2008, "Material Witness: Robert Rauschenberg," p. 424, Barbara Rose, "Seeing Rauschenberg Seeing," p. 432, Branden W. Joseph, "Media Player," p. 438, and James Rosenquist, "With Bob Rauschenberg," p. 441.

*Art in America,* September, 2008, Charles Stuckey, "Let Us Now Praise Robert Rauschenberg," p. 38.

*ARTnews,* February, 1977, John Gruen, "Robert Rauschenberg: An Audience of One," p. 44; March, 1990, Ruth Bass, "Robert Rauschenberg," p. 174.

*Gay & Lesbian Review Worldwide,* September-October, 2008, Jonathan D. Katz, "The Outness of Rauschenberg's Art," p. 10.

*Guardian* (London, England), September 7, 2000, Michael Kimmelman, "The Secret of My Excess," p. 12; January 26, 2006, Robert Hughes, "Spirit of the Age: Ignored by the Establishment and Derided by Critics, Robert Rauschenberg May Just Be the Most Important American Artist of the Last Century," p. 18; November 28, 2006, Adrian Searle, "Stuff Happens: His Work Is Packed with Jokes, Ideas—and Farmyard Animals," p. 23.

*Interview,* December, 1990, Paul Taylor, "Robert Rauschenberg: I Can't Even Afford My Works Anymore," p. 142; August, 2008, Glenn O'Brien, "Robert Rauschenberg: He Was an Astounding Innovator Who Changed the Course of Art," p. 130.

*Los Angeles Magazine,* August, 2006, Bernard Cooper, "Object Lessons: MOCA Revisits Robert Rauschenberg's Breakthrough," p. 150.

*Newsweek,* January 7, 1991, Peter Plagens, "Back to the Future: Rauschenberg's Golden Oldies at the Whitney Inspire His New Work in Florida," p. 50.

*New Yorker,* May 23, 2005, Calvin Tomkins, "Everything in Sight," p. 69.

*New York Times,* February 16, 1990, Roberta Smith, "An 18-Year Journey Through Rauschenberg's Development"; December 16, 1990, Grace Glueck, "Rauschenberg at 65, with All Due Immodesty," p. H47; August 27, 2000, Michael Kimmelman, "The Irrepressible Ragman of Art," p. AR1; May 16, 2008, Roberta Smith, "Rauschenberg Got a Lot from the City and Left a Lot Behind," p. E34.

*People,* May 19, 1980, Patricia Burstein, "In His Art and Life, Robert Rauschenberg Is a Man Who Steers His Own Daring Course," p. 99.

*San Francisco Chronicle,* August 20, 1998, Kenneth Baker, "Rauschenberg's Reality: A Talk with the Artist Whose Influence Pervades Culture and Whose Early Works Will Reside at SFMOMA," p. E1; December 31, 2005, Kenneth Baker, "Rauschenberg Is 80—How Is His Work Aging?," p. E1; May 24, 2006, Kenneth Baker, "Scavenged Stuff Yields Provocative Pieces in Rauschenberg Survey," p. E1.

*Smithsonian,* May, 1991, Helen Dudar, "The Artist Who Wants to Embrace the Whole World," p. 54.

*Texas Monthly,* March, 1998, Michael Ennis, "The Return of the Native," p. 104.

*Time,* November 29, 1976, "The Most Living Artist"; October 27, 1997, Robert Hughes, "The Great Permitter: A Vast Retrospective Celebrates the Whitmanesque Profusion of Robert Rauschenberg," p. 108.

*ONLINE*

*PaceWildenstein Web site,* http://www.pacewilden stein.com/ (April 1, 2010), "Robert Rauschenberg."

*Public Broadcasting Service Web site,* http://www.pbs.org/ (October 28, 2006), "American Masters: Robert Rauschenberg."

*OTHER*

*Robert Rauschenberg: Inventive Genius* (documentary), Wellspring & PBS Thirteen WNET, 2004.

## ■ Obituaries

*PERIODICALS*

*Daily Telegraph* (London, England), May 14, 2008, "Robert Rauschenberg: American Artist Whose Paintings and Sculptures Anticipated Both Pop Art and Conceptualism."

*Guardian* (London, England), May 14, 2008, Michael McNay, "Robert Rauschenberg: Pop Art Pioneer Whose Wide-ranging Work Evoked the Spirit of the Old Frontier," p. 33; May 15, 2008, Jonathan Jones, "The Trashcan Laureate: Robert Rauschenberg's Generous, Epic Vision Captured the Chaos of Modern America," p. 23.

*Houston Chronicle,* May 14, 2008, Lisa Gray, "Robert Rauschenberg 1925-2008: Art Expressed a Love of Life," p. 1.

*New York Times,* May 14, 2008, Michael Kimmelman, "Robert Rauschenberg, Who Redefined American Art, Dies at 82," p. A1, and Alastair Macaulay, "Rauschenberg and Dance, Partners for Life," p. E1.

*Time,* May 26, 2008, Richard Lacayo, "The Wild and Crazy Guy," p. 49.

*USA Today,* May 14, 2008, Maria Puente, "Robert Rauschenberg's Art Challenged Assumptions," p. 2D.


*ONLINE*

*Newsweek,* May 13, 2008, Peter Plagens, "He Made Art Pop: Honoring the Pre-eminent American Artist of the 20th Century."*

# Richard Serra

(Photograph courtesy of Scott Wintrow/Getty Images.)

## ■ Personal

Born November 2, 1939, in San Francisco, CA; son of a shipyard worker; married Nancy Graves (an artist), 1964 (divorced); married Clara Weyergraf (an art historian). *Education:* University of California at Berkeley and at Santa Barbara, B.A., 1961; Yale University, B.F.A. and M.F.A., 1964.

## ■ Addresses

*Home*—New York, NY, and Nova Scotia, Canada. *Agent*—Gagosian Gallery, 980 Madison Ave., New York, NY 10075.

## ■ Career

Sculptor. Creates sculptures using rubber, fiberglass, and neon, 1966-67; produces *Hands*, a series of short films, 1968; creates sculptures from lead pieces, 1968-71; creates sculptures from sheets of steel, 1969—. *Exhibitions:* Works have been displayed in private and public collections around the world,

including the Castelli Workshop, New York, NY; Gagosian Gallery, New York, NY; Whitney Museum, New York, NY; Museum of Modern Art, New York, NY; Guggenheim Museum, New York, NY; National Gallery of Canada, Ottawa, Ontario, Canada; Tate Gallery, London, England; and Guggenheim Museum, Bilbao, Spain. Exhibitions include first solo show at Galleria La Salita, Rome, Italy, 1966; first U.S. solo show at Leo Castelli Gallery, New York, NY, 1969; installation of *One Ton Prop (House of Cards),* Museum of Modern Art, New York, NY, 1969; retrospective at Museum of Modern Art, New York, NY, 1986; "Threats of Hell," Musée d'art Contemporain, Bordeaux, France, 1990; "Weight and Measure," Tate Gallery, London, England, 1992; "Torqued Ellipses," Dia Foundation, New York, NY, 1997; "Richard Serra: Sculpture 1985-1998," Museum of Contemporary Art, Los Angeles, CA, 1998; permanent installation of *The Matter of Time,* Guggenheim Museum, Bilbao, Spain, 2005; "Richard Serra Sculpture: Forty Years," Museum of Modern Art, New York, NY, 2007; "Monumenta" series, Grand Palais, Paris, France, 2008; and "Blind Spot/Open Ended," Gagosian Gallery, New York, NY, 2009. Public installations include *Tilted Arc,* Federal Plaza, New York, NY, 1981 (removed 1989); *Call Me Ishmael,* Stanford University, Stanford, California, 1998; *The Hedgehog and the Fox,* Princeton University, 2000; and *Wake,* Seattle, WA, 2006.

## ■ Awards, Honors

Yale Traveling fellowship, 1964; Fulbright scholarship, 1965; Goslar Award for Modern Art, 1981;

Skowhegan Sculpture Academy of Arts and Design, Jerusalem, 1983; Carnegie Prize, Carnegie International, 1985; named chevalier of Ordre des Arts et des Lettres, Ministry of Culture and Communication (France), 1985; Wilhelm Lehmbruck Prize for Sculpture, 1991; Praemium Imperiale, Japan Art Association, 1994; Gold Medal for Sculpture, American Academy of Arts and Letters, 2001; elected member, Order of Merit for Science and Art, German government, 2002; International Art award, Cristóbal Gabarrón Foundation, 2005; Louise T. Blouin Award, 2006; named Commandeur of Ordre des Arts et des Lettres, Ministry of Culture and Communication (France), 2008; Cross of the Order of Merit, Federal Republic of Germany, 2009; Prince of Asturias Award for the Arts (Spain), 2010. D.F.A.: California College of Arts and Crafts.

## ■ Writings

(With Clara Weyergraf) *Richard Serra: Interviews, etc., 1970-1980,* Hudson River Museum (Yonkers, NY), 1980.

*Richard Serra: Writings/Interviews,* University of Chicago Press (Chicago, IL), 1994.

(With Hal Foster and David Sylvester) *Richard Serra: Sculpture 1985-1998,* Steidl (Göttingen, Germany), 1999.

Author of introduction, *The Destruction of Tilted Arc: Documents,* edited by Clara Weyergraf-Serra and Martha Buskirk, MIT Press (Cambridge, MA), 1990. Also contributor to periodicals.

## ■ Sidelights

Richard Serra is considered one of America's most significant living artists. The sculptor has garnered acclaim for his large-scale art projects, including such works as *Torqued Ellipses, The Matter of Time,* and the controversial *Tilted Arc,* which are created from massive plates of rolled steel. Art historian Robert Hughes, writing in the London *Guardian,*

**Like many of his monumental sculptures, Serra's** *Torqued Torus Inversion,* **a pair of curved enclosures, seems to defy gravity.** (Photograph courtesy of Thos Robinson/Getty Images for LVMH.)

called Serra "not only the best sculptor alive, but the only great one at work anywhere in the early 21st century." Hughes further remarked that Serra's "achievement has been to give fabricated steel the power and density, the emotional address to the human body, the sense of empathy and urgency and liberation, that once belonged only to bronze and stone, but now no longer does."

Though some of his pieces have been condemned as unsightly and inaccessible, a number of museums, including the Museum of Modern Art in New York City, have created space specifically to hold Serra's monumental work. Known for his bristling attitude and sharp tongue, Serra has alienated many of his colleagues, while at the same time winning their admiration for his innovation in the field. "Like all great iconoclasts, he has lived long enough to see his supposed artistic provocations gradually accepted as groundbreaking statements," Sean O'Hagan commented in the London *Observer.* "His towering curves and sheets of oxidised steel are now an artistic signature, as instantly recognisable as Giacometti's elongated figures or Rothko's swathes of deep, dark colour."

Serra was born in San Francisco, California, on November 2, 1939, the son of a Spanish-born shipyard worker and a Russian Jewish mother. "To compete with my older brother for my parents' affections, I would draw all the time as a boy," he told Richard Lacayo in *Time.* "After about the third grade, my mother started taking me to museums and introducing me as her son the artist. She also told my older brother he was going to become an attorney. And he became an attorney. The strength of a Jewish mother."

Despite his artistic inclinations, Serra decided to study English at the University of California at Berkeley and later transferred to U.C. Santa Barbara, where he continued to take art courses. During the summers, he worked in a steel mill. "I started doing that when I was fifteen, rolling ball bearings in a little plant where I lied about my age," he told Calvin Tomkins of the *New Yorker.* "It was very useful. It's probably why I do what I do." At the urging of his faculty advisor, Serra applied for Yale's School of Art. His classmates there included future luminaries as Chuck Close, Jennifer Bartlett, Brice Marden, and Nancy Graves, who would become his first wife.

### Becoming a Sculptor

Though Serra came out of Yale with the intention to paint, he wasn't sure how to approach the craft. While exploring France on a travel grant, he was introduced to the works of Constantin Brancusi, whose studio had been recreated at the Musée d'Art Moderne de la Ville de Paris. "It was the first time I looked at sculpture seriously," Serra recalled to Tomkins. "I really responded to the strength and simplicity and abstraction of the work. I just found myself being drawn back to that studio every day." Traveling through Europe on a Fulbright scholarship a year later, Serra had a life-altering experience while viewing the works of seventeenth-century Spanish painter Diego Velázquez. "When I saw *Las Meninas,* I thought there was no possibility of me getting close to that," he stated to Tomkins, adding, "That sort of nailed the coffin on painting for me. When I got back to Florence, I took everything I had and dumped it in the Arno. I thought I'd better start from scratch, so I started screwing around with sticks and stones and wire and cages and live and stuffed animals."

An Italian art dealer gave Serra his first show in Rome, an exhibit that began Serra's reputation as an avant-garde artist. His work in the Rome gallery featured caged animals, both stuffed and alive, one of which was a ninety-seven-pound pig. According to O'Hagan, Serra was "on his way to reinventing himself as an artist whose work would hinge on the idea of 'the viewer being the subject of the piece.'" Returning to New York in 1966, Serra immersed himself in the American art scene, studying minimalism and beginning to work with scrap rubber. Influenced by dancers, filmmakers, and musicians in the burgeoning downtown art scene, Serra's interests in process and performance blossomed. He created a long list of active verbs—"to roll, to crease, to fold, to bend, to twist"—that were to inform his later works. "I was very involved with the physical activity of making," he said to Tomkins. "It struck me that instead of thinking about what a sculpture is going to be and how you're going to do it compositionally, what if you just enacted those verbs in relation to a material, and didn't worry about the result? So I started tearing and cutting and folding lead."

In 1969, an exhibit of the artist's performance-sculpture, including a splashed-lead piece, debuted at Leo Castelli's warehouse gallery. The show gathered international attention for Serra, and he began working on free-standing lead prop pieces. The artist didn't weld his pieces, as in traditional sculpture, Lacayo noted, "he simply leaned them against one another in balancing acts that made gravity itself an element of the work. Not to mention the possibility of catastrophic collapse. One of the best known of those pieces, four squares of lead leaned gingerly against one another to form a cube, had a title that said it all—*One Ton Prop (House of Cards).*"

*The Matter of Time,* **an installation of sculptures at the Guggenheim Museum Bilbao, enables spectators to study the evolution of Serra's sculpted forms.** (Photograph courtesy of Rafa Rivas/AFP/Getty Images.)

## Man of Steel

Initially, Serra was hesitant to work with steel, which later became a signature material. "Steel was such a traditional material I wasn't going near it," he told Tomkins. "Picasso, Gonzalez, Calder had all done great things with steel. But then I thought, Well, I can use steel in the way industry uses it—for weight, load bearing, stasis, friction, counterbalance. I knew something about steel, so why not?" He created *Strike* in 1971, a twenty-four-foot-long by eight-feet-high street corner piece, the set-up for which he had to hire industrial riggers. "That's when I left the whole studio idea behind," Serra recalled. "It was a real sea change for me." In 1973, he received a contract to create a large outdoor sculpture in St. Louis, Missouri, for which he built *Quadrilateral,* a triangular shaped structure containing eight sheets of ten-foot-high steel.

Serra's style has always been provocative, which occasionally launches him into the center of controversy. His *Tilted Arc,* a steel wall 12 feet high and 120 feet long, actually landed Serra in court, defending his work. Originally approved by the federal government in 1980 and funded by the National Endowment for the Arts, the work was installed in 1981. Placed in front of the Jacob K. Javits Federal Building in Manhattan, the sculpture blocked the passage of many federal workers, who felt it was both an eye-sore and an obstruction. Serra appeared at a combative public hearing to explain his vision for the piece, but eventually the piece was slated to be removed. Serra launched a $38 million lawsuit against the government for breach of contract, which he lost, and in 1989 *Tilted Arc* was taken down, cut into pieces, and placed in a warehouse, where it remains. "That stuff hurt," he told O'Hagan. "I was standing up for a principle. Artistic ownership. It's your work; nobody has the right to destroy it."

Despite these troubles, Serra's work continued to be featured in galleries and museums around the world. The Museum of Modern Art in New York hosted a retrospective of his career in 1986. The largest piece in the show, *Two Corner Curve,* "enables the public to consider some of the ideas behind *Tilted Arc,*" *New York Times* critic Michael Brenson stated. Brenson added, "From the convex side that greets us, the sculpture pushes towards us, assaulting us like a crowd in a city street at rush hour. From the concave side, however, the work offers a refuge so absolute that it seems like an abandoned amphitheater or monastery." His 1992 installation in Dusseldorf, Germany, titled *Running Arcs, For John Cage,* consisted of three immense steel structures and drew praise from a London *Times* contributor:

"Tilted at various angles, and activating the entire length of the gallery with their menacing yet invigorating dynamism, the entire work showed Serra at his most swaggering."

In the mid-1990s, inspired by the Baroque architecture of Francesco Borromini's San Carlo alle Quattro Fontane church in Rome, Italy, Serra began experimenting with massive plates of curved steel. Called "Torqued Ellipses," his sculptures took the shape of leaning, twisting ovals that could be entered through a gap in the side; Serra's friend Frank Gehry, the acclaimed architect, suspected they would not stand on their own. Serra proved him wrong, and the works appealed to a wider audience than many of his previous pieces. According to *New York Times* contributor Michael Kimmelman, "The drama of the 'Torqued Ellipses' has a lot to do with the fact that they are made of steel: steel treated like rubber seems an impossibility, and the effect is to convey what Mr. Serra calls a kind of 'gravitational pull.' It's easy to picture concrete being cast in eccentric forms, but steel, twisted unexpectedly, is disorienting."

## Pushing the Boundaries

With the success of the "Torqued Ellipses," Serra continued to find ways to twist steel into new shapes. He experimented with spirals and bull horns, bands of rippling metal that resemble a Mobius strip, sheets marked with scars from high temperature exposure or rust. Noting that Serra had long pushed the boundaries of sculpture, doing new and innovative things, Tomkins wrote of a 2002 exhibit at New York's Gagosian Gallery, "What amazed me and many others was how far Serra . . . had moved beyond the breakout innovations of his most recent show, two years earlier. Once again, it seemed, he was carrying the art of sculpture into new areas, taking great risks and pulling them off, and there was something thrilling and deeply reassuring about that."

In 2005 Serra's permanent installation *The Matter of Time* debuted at the Guggenheim Bilbao, a museum designed by Gehry. The sculptures "come in shapes never dreamed of before—massive, tilting, twisting, wildly complicated enclosures whose colors and textured surfaces are the happenstance condition of raw, unpolished steel," Kimmelman stated. The works also drew praise from *Financial Times* contributor Julius Purcell, who stated that the "long, curved arcs from Serra's earlier career are there, but what really draws the eye are the newer works: spirals and concentric ellipses bellying out, then

**Serra opened the 2008 Monumenta at the Grand Palais in Paris with *Promenade*, a series of five enormous steel plates.**
(Photograph courtesy of Horacio Villalobos/EPA/Corbis.)

leaning back in on themselves, like distorted clock springs allowed to uncoil on the floor." *The Matter of Time* "is one of the great works of the past half-century, the culmination of a remarkable fruition in Mr. Serra's career," Kimmelman concluded. "It rejuvenates and pushes abstraction to a fresh level. And it is deeply humane, not least because it counts on individual perception, individual discovery."

When New York's Museum of Modern Art finished an expansion in 2007, room was created to display Serra's large pieces, and floors in the contemporary galleries were built with the weight of Serra's sculptures in mind. In addition to a retrospective, held twenty years after its first exhibit of Serra's work, the Museum of Modern Art incorporated three new works of Serra's. Others were placed in the museum's sculpture garden. The exhibit was "a landmark, by a titan of sculpture, one of the last great modernists in an age of minor talents, mad money and so much meaningless art," noted Kimmelman. To *New York* contributor Karen Rosen-

berg, the exhibit marked how New Yorkers had finally come to terms with Serra's art after the 1985 hearings against the *Tilted Arc*. She wrote, "With this retrospective, the disconnect between the Serra loathed by the public and the Serra lauded by the art world may, finally, be history."

Serra also earned plaudits for his contributions to Monumenta 2008, a show held in the Grand Palais in Paris. Serra's *Promenade*, a course of five rectangular steel slabs, each standing fifty-six feet high and weighing some seventy-three tons, was commissioned by the French Ministry of Culture. The five elements "are precisely placed and angled, leaning 20 inches in or away from their axis, creating shifting lines of sight," explained *New York Times* critic Steven Erlanger. "As the sun moves over the course of the day, casting different latticed shadows from the building, the plates appear at times to bend toward or away from the viewer."

Serra's massive sculptural pieces seek to involve the audience, and their perceptions, in order to complete

If you enjoy the works of Richard Serra, you may also want to check out the following:

The land art of Robert Smithson (1938-1970), the sculptures of American artist Nancy Holt (1858-), and the public artworks of American sculptor Maya Lin (1959-).

the work. "Serra has said that the subject of his sculpture is the viewer's experience in walking through or around it—that what he is doing is not creating static objects but shaping space," wrote Tomkins. "It's about apprehension, how you apprehend the space and the piece," the sculptor told Erlanger. "It's part of the experience of walking around the space in which the art appears—you implicate yourself in the space, and the experience is in you, not in the frame or on the wall." Serra "has been redefining sculpture for four decades," remarked *Financial Times* reporter Jane Ure-Smith. "In the 1960s his choice of industrial materials—rubber, lead, steel—was unconventional but not unique. What set him apart was a belief that time and space were among his raw materials. He talks of the 'substance of space' as if you could reach out and grab it. And in a sense, with the large-scale steel pieces for which he is best known today, you can."

## ■ Biographical and Critical Sources

### BOOKS

*Contemporary Artists,* 5th edition, St. James Press (Detroit, MI), 2001.

Foster, Hal, *Richard Serra: Torqued Spirals, Toruses and Spheres,* Steidl (Göttingen, Germany), 2002.

Foster, Hal, and Gordon Hughes, editors, *Richard Serra: The Matter of Time,* MIT Press (Cambridge, MA), 2000.

Janssen, Hans, editor, *Richard Serra: Drawings Zeichnungen 1969-1990,* Benteli (Bern, Switzerland), 1990.

Kimmelman, Michael, *Portraits: Talking with Artists at the Met, the Modern, the Louvre, and Elsewhere,* Random House (New York, NY), 1999.

Krauss, Rosalind E., *Richard Serra: Sculpture,* Museum of Modern Art (New York, NY), 1986.

McShine, Kynaston, and Lynne Cooke, editors, *Richard Serra Sculpture: Forty Years,* Museum of Modern Art (New York, NY), 2007.

Sussler, Betsy, Suzan Sherman, and Rondale Shavers, editors, *Speak Art!: The Best of Bomb Magazine's Interviews with Artists,* G+B Arts International, 1997.

Taylor, Mark, Lynne Cooke, and Michael Govan, *Richard Serra: Torqued Ellipses,* Dia Center for the Arts (New York, NY), 1997.

Tomkins, Calvin, *Lives of the Artists,* Macmillan (New York, NY), 2008.

### PERIODICALS

*Art and Artists,* March, 1974, John Anthony Thwaites, "Working Out: The Work of Richard Serra."

*Artforum,* September, 1969, Robert Pincus, "Slow Information"; February, 1970, P. Leider, "Richard Serra: Castelli Warehouse"; May, 1972, Rosalind Krauss, "Richard Serra: Sculpture Redrawn."

*Art in America,* February, 2000, Aruna D'Souza and Tom McDonough, "Sculpture in the Space of Architecture"; November, 2005, David Ebony, "Infinite Passages: Serra in Bilbao," p. 138; December, 2007, Carter Ratcliff, "The Fictive Spaces of Richard Serra," p. 116.

*Art Journal,* winter, 1989, Harriet Senie, "Richard Serra's Tilted Arc: Art and Non-art Issues."

*Christian Science Monitor,* September 15, 2006, "Redefining Sculpture Is Richard Serra's Goal," p. 15.

*Financial Times,* June 13, 2005, Julius Purcell, "Several Hundred Tons of Exquisite Poise," p. 15; June 2, 2007, Jane Ure-Smith, "A Journey through Steel and Space," p. 16; October 25, 2008, Edwin Heathcote, "Sculptor with a Heart Of Steel," p. 13.

*Guardian* (London, England), June 22, 2005, Robert Hughes, "Man of Steel: Richard Serra's New Installation at the Bilbao Guggenheim Is Courageous, Sublime—and Even Puts Frank Gehry's Architecture in the Shade."

*New York,* May 28, 2007, Karen Rosenberg, "Richard's Arc: How Serra Went from Being a Steely Pariah to New York's Favorite Sculptor," p. 73.

*New Yorker,* February 7, 2000, Peter Schjeldahl, "Serra Smiles: The New Friendliness of America's Most Fearsome Sculptor," p. 88; August 5, 2002, Calvin Tomkins, "Man of Steel"; June 11, 2007, Peter Schjeldahl, "Industrial Strength," p. 146.

*New York Times,* February 28, 1986, John Russell, "Startling Sculpture from Richard Serra"; March 16, 1986, Michael Brenson, "Richard Serra's Radical Message Is Rooted in Tradition"; September 22, 1989, Michael Kimmelman, "Richard Serra in Shows Of Drawing and Sculpture"; April 2, 1993, Roberta Smith, "Richard Serra's Temporal Monument"; June 14, 1993, John Rockwell, "An Artist a Lot More at Home Away From Home"; November 10, 1996, David Colman, "An Installation That's Worthy Of the Pharaohs"; August 29, 1999, Michael Kimmelman, "A Spectacular Meeting Of Sculpture and Space"; November 23, 2003, Andrew Blum, "A Serra Sculpture Emerges From Its Tomb," p. AR45; June 7, 2005, Michael Kimmelman, "Abstract Art's New World, Forged for All," p. E1; June 1, 2007, Michael Kimmelman, "Man of Steel," p. E25; May 7, 2008, Steven Erlanger, "Serra's Monumental Vision, Vertical Edition," p. E1.

*New York Times Magazine,* October 8, 1989, Deborah Solomon, "Our Most Notorious Sculptor," p. 38.

*People,* April 1, 1985, Peter Carlson, "A Rusty Eyesore or a Work of Art? Sculptor Richard Serra Defends His Controversial *Tilted Arc,*" p. 138.

*Philadelphia Inquirer,* June 17, 2007, Edward J. Sozanski, "Big Steel: The Evocative Sculpture of Richard Serra."

*Observer* (London, England), October 5, 2008, Sean O'Hagan, "Richard Serra: He Emerged out of a Radical Art Scene in the 1960s and Went On to Become One of America's Most Controversial Artists—Provoking Some New Yorkers to Threaten Him with Death," p. 6.

*Sculpture,* January-February, 1999, Jan Garden Castro, "Richard Serra: Man of Steel"; October, 2002, Jonathan Peyser, "Declaring, Defining, Dividing Space: A Conversation with Richard Serra."

*Time,* June 3, 1985, Robert Hughes, "The Trials of *Tilted Arc:* An Unpopular Work Dramatizes the Plight of Public Sculpture," p. 78; October 19, 1998, Robert Hughes, "Steel-drivin' Man: Richard Serra's Massive New Sculptures, as Big as Houses, Create a Wholly Original Spatial Drama"; June 4, 2007, Richard Lacayo, "Size Does Matter," p. 65.

*Times* (London, England), October 9, 1992, "Close Encounter with a Heavyweight: Sculptor Richard Serra," p. 3; July 14, 2007, Morgan Falconer, "Sculptor Shows His Metal," p. 28.

ONLINE

*Museum of Modern Art Web site,* http://www.moma.org/ (April 1, 2007), "Richard Serra: Sculpture: Forty Years."

*Public Broadcasting Service Web site,* http://www.pbs.org/ (April 1, 2010), "Richard Serra."

OTHER

*Richard Serra: Thinking on Your Feet* (documentary), Westdeutscher Rundfunk/ZDF, 2008.*

# Kate Wilhelm

(Reproduced by permission of Richard Wilhelm.)

## ■ Personal

Born June 8, 1928, in Toledo, OH; daughter of Jesse Thomas and Ann Meredith; married Joseph B. Wilhelm, May 24, 1947 (divorced, 1962); married Damon Knight (a writer and editor), February 23, 1963 (died April 15, 2002); children: (first marriage) Douglas, Richard; (second marriage) Jonathan. *Education:* Attended high school in Louisville, KY; Michigan State University, Ph.D., 1996. *Hobbies and other interests:* Gardening.

## ■ Addresses

*Home*—Eugene, OR.

## ■ Career

Writer. Employed as a model, telephone operator, sales clerk, switchboard operator, and insurance company underwriter; full-time writer, 1956—. Co-director, Milford Science Fiction Writers Conference, 1963-76; lecturer at Clarion Fantasy Workshop, Michigan State University, 1968-96.

## ■ Member

Authors League of America, PEN, Science Fiction Writers of America, Authors Guild, National Writers Union, Mystery Writers of America.

## ■ Awards, Honors

Nebula Award nominee for best novel, Science Fiction Writers of America (SFWA), 1965, for *The Clone;* Nebula Award nominee for best short story, SFWA, 1967, for "Baby, You Were Great"; Nebula Award, SFWA, 1968, for best short story, "The Planners"; Nebula Award nominee for best short story, SFWA, 1970, for "A Cold Night Dark With Snow"; Nebula Award nominee for best novella, SFWA, 1970, for *April Fool's Day Forever;* Nebula Award nominee for best novella, SFWA, 1971, for *The Plastic Abyss;* Nebula Award nominee for best novella, SFWA, 1971, for *The Infinity Box;* Nebula Award nominee for best novelette, SFWA, 1971, for *The Encounter;* Nebula Award nominee for best novel, 1971, for *Margaret and I;* Nebula Award nominee for best novelette, SFWA, 1972, for *The Funeral;* Hugo Award nominee for best novelette, 1975, for *A Brother to Dragons, a Companion of Owls;* Nebula Award nominee for best novel, SFWA, 1976, Hugo Award, World Science Fiction Convention, Jupiter Award, and second place for the John W. Campbell Memorial Award, all 1977, all for *Where Late the Sweet Birds Sang;* Nebula Award nominee for best novel, SFWA, 1979, and American Book Award nomination, 1980, both for *Juniper Time*; Nebula Award nominee for best novella, SFWA, 1981, for *The Winter Beach*; Hugo Award nominee for best novella, 1982, for *With Thimbles, with Forks and Hope*; Nebula Award nominee for best novella, SFWA, 1985, and World Fantasy Award nominee for best novella, 1986, both for *The Gorgon Field*; Hugo Award nominee for best short story, 1988, for "Forever Yours, Anna"; Nebula Award for best novelette, SFWA, 1988, for *The Girl Who Fell into the Sky*; Nebula Award for best short story, SFWA, 1989, for "Forever Yours, Anna"; Nebula Award nominee for best novella, SFWA, 1993, for *Naming the Flowers*; Nebula Award nominee for best short story, SFWA, and Hugo Award nominee for best short story nominee, 1995, both for "I Know What You're Thinking"; Hugo Award for best related book, 2006, for *Storyteller*; Solstice Award, SFWA, 2009, for outstanding contribution to the speculative fiction field.

## ■ Writings

*SCIENCE FICTION*

*The Mile-long Spaceship* (short stories), Berkley Publishing (New York, NY), 1963, published as *Andover and the Android*, Dobson (London, England), 1966.

(With Theodore L. Thomas) *The Clone*, Berkley Publishing (New York, NY), 1965.

*The Nevermore Affair*, Doubleday (New York, NY), 1966.

*The Killer Thing*, Doubleday (New York, NY), 1967, published as *The Killing Thing*, Jenkins (London, England), 1967.

*The Downstairs Room and Other Speculative Fiction* (short stories), Doubleday (New York, NY), 1968.

*Let the Fire Fall*, Doubleday (New York, NY), 1969.

(With Theodore L. Thomas) *The Year of the Cloud*, Doubleday (New York, NY), 1970.

*Abyss: Two Novellas*, Doubleday (New York, NY), 1971.

(Editor) *Nebula Award Stories Number 9*, Gollancz (London, England), 1974, Harper (New York, NY), 1975.

*Where Late the Sweet Birds Sang*, Harper (New York, NY), 1976.

*The Infinity Box: A Collection of Speculative Fiction* (short stories), Harper (New York, NY), 1976.

(Editor) *Clarion SF*, Berkley Publishing (New York, NY), 1976.

*Somerset Dreams and Other Fictions*, Harper (New York, NY), 1978.

*Axoltl* (multimedia science fantasy), first produced in Eugene, OR, 1979.

*Juniper Time*, Harper (New York, NY), 1979.

(With husband, Damon Knight) *Better than One* (short stories), New England Science Fiction Association (Boston, MA), 1980.

*Listen, Listen* (short stories), Houghton Mifflin (Boston, MA), 1981.

*Welcome, Chaos*, Houghton Mifflin (New York, NY), 1983.

*Huysman's Pets*, Bluejay Books (New York, NY), 1986.

*Crazy Time*, St. Martin's Press (New York, NY), 1988.

*Children of the Wind* (novellas), St. Martin's Press (New York, NY), 1989.

*State of Grace* (short stories), Pulphouse (Eugene, OR), 1991.

*And the Angels Sing* (stories), St. Martin's Press (New York, NY), 1992.

*"BARBARA HOLLOWAY" MYSTERY SERIES*

*Death Qualified: A Mystery of Chaos*, St. Martin's Press (New York, NY), 1991.

*The Best Defense*, St. Martin's Press (New York, NY), 1994.

*Malice Prepense*, St. Martin's Press (New York, NY), 1996, published as *For the Defense*, Fawcett (New York, NY), 1997.

*Defense for the Devil*, St. Martin's Press (New York, NY), 1999.

*No Defense*, St. Martin's Press (New York, NY), 2000.

*Desperate Measures*, St. Martin's Press (New York, NY), 2001.

*Clear and Convincing Proof*, MIRA Books (Don Mills, Ontario, Canada), 2003.

*The Unbidden Truth*, MIRA Books (Don Mills, Ontario, Canada), 2004.

*Sleight of Hand*, MIRA Books (Don Mills, Ontario, Canada), 2006.

*A Wrongful Death*, MIRA Books (Don Mills, Ontario, Canada), 2007.

*Cold Case*, MIRA Books (Don Mills, Ontario, Canada), 2008.

*"CONSTANCE AND CHARLIE" MYSTERY SERIES*

*The Hamlet Trap*, St. Martin's Press (New York, NY), 1987.

*The Dark Door*, St. Martin's Press (New York, NY), 1988.

*Smart House*, St. Martin's Press (New York, NY), 1989.

*Sweet, Sweet Poison*, St. Martin's Press (New York, NY), 1990.

*Seven Kinds of Death*, St. Martin's Press (New York, NY), 1992.

*A Flush of Shadows: Five Short Novels Featuring Constance Leidl and Charlie Meiklejohn*, St. Martin's Press (New York, NY), 1995.

*The Casebook of Constance and Charlie*, Volume 1 (contains *The Hamlet Trap, Smart House,* and *Seven Kinds of Death*), St. Martin's Press (New York, NY), 1999, Volume 2 (contains *Sweet, Sweet Poison, The Dark Door,* and *An Imperfect Gift*), St. Martin's Press (New York, NY), 1999.

*NOVELS*

*More Bitter than Death*, Simon & Schuster (New York, NY), 1962.

*Margaret and I*, Little, Brown (Boston, MA), 1971.

*City of Cain*, Little, Brown (Boston, MA), 1973.

*Fault Lines*, Harper (New York, NY), 1976.

*The Clewiston Test*, Farrar, Straus (New York, NY), 1976.

*A Sense of Shadow*, Houghton Mifflin (Boston, MA), 1981.

*Oh, Susannah!*, Houghton Mifflin (Boston, MA), 1982.

*Cambio Bay*, St. Martin's Press (New York, NY), 1990.

*Justice for Some*, St. Martin's Press (New York, NY), 1993.

*The Good Children*, St. Martin's Press (New York, NY), 1998.

*The Deepest Water*, St. Martin's Press (New York, NY), 2000.

*Skeletons*, St. Martin's Press (New York, NY), 2002.

*The Price of Silence*, MIRA Books (Don Mills, Ontario, Canada), 2005.

*OTHER*

*The Hindenberg Effect* (radio play), first broadcast by KSOR (Ashland, OR), 1985.

(With son, Richard Wilhelm) *The Hills Are Dancing* (nonfiction), Corroboree (Minneapolis, MN), 1986.

*Storyteller: Writing Lessons and More from Twenty-seven Years of the Clarion Writers' Workshop*, Small Beer Press (Northampton, MA), 2005.

Contributor to anthologies, including *Quark No. 3*, 1971, *Again, Dangerous Visions*, 1972, *Bad Moon Rising*, 1973, *A Shocking Thing*, 1974, and *Epoch*, 1975; contributor to "Orbit" anthology series, 1966-78. Contributor to periodicals, including *Omni, Fantastic, Future, Magazine of Fantasy and Science Fiction, Amazing, Redbook, Cosmopolitan,* and *Strange Fantasy*.

## ■ Adaptations

Several of Wilhelm's novels have been adapted as audiobooks.

## ■ Sidelights

A versatile author, praised for the psychological focus in her fiction, Kate Wilhelm has been called a "serene and powerful talent" by Michael Bishop in the *Magazine of Fantasy and Science Fiction*. Wilhelm feels strongly about the political and social forces shaping the modern world and examines them in her novels, writing about such issues as women's roles in society and the threat of environmental collapse. According to *Magazine of Fantasy and Science Fiction* contributor Gordon Van Gelder, Wilhelm "writes about the things that are important to her; be the subject the over-medication of the mentally ill, a woman's right to choose, or something as 'simple' as the matter of love, she brings wisdom and passion to bear in depicting it."

Wilhelm's short stories and novels have frequently drawn praise for their finely drawn characters and well-crafted narratives, and critics note that she is equally adept at creating thought-provoking works of speculative fiction, perceptive family sagas, and complex mysteries. According to Anne Hudson Jones in the *Dictionary of Literary Biography*, the "body of Wilhelm's fiction shows a steady progression in technical control and thematic complexity," and in *Twentieth-Century Science Fiction Writers* Pamela Sargent remarked that Wilhelm "skillfully uses genre elements—suspenseful plots, scientific or technological notions, and slick prose—to produce fiction as satisfying and as well-rounded as any being written today."

### Stirring the Imagination

Wilhelm was born the fourth of six children in Toledo, Ohio, in 1928. Her verbal acuity was affected by a speech impediment. "For the first five years of my life no one could understand a thing I said," Wilhelm commented in an essay in the *Contemporary Authors Autobiography Series (CAAS)*. Though she spoke quite a bit, her mother and father were the only ones who could interpret her noises. "Very early I stopped trying to communicate, thinking, I suppose, there was little point to it," she noted in *CAAS*. "To a certain extent I became an invisible child, and this continued for most of my life before

I left home. When I got very good grades in school, no one noticed. When I stayed home from school for no particular reason, no one noticed. As a teenager I was never severely questioned about the hours I kept, the many activities I was engaged in. I don't think anyone noticed."

Wilhelm's private world provided her with a rich inner life, however. As a child, Wilhelm's mother read to her a great deal, and she soon began to read on her own without being taught. She related in *CAAS* that "I cannot remember a time when I could not read. Every week my mother went to the library with a shopping bag and brought home the world." Later, Wilhelm was delighted that she was able to get an adult library card. "I read everything in the

branch library," Wilhelm related. "For several years I think I was intoxicated with words. I judged nothing and read everything with equally rapt attention. Mysteries, travel books, westerns, classics, best-sellers. I loved them all."

Although Wilhelm grew up during the Great Depression, her family had been well-off. Her father, a millwright, had found work in factories during the worst years. However, as Wilhelm became a teenager, her father's health declined. Lung infections he had suffered during World War I resulted in long-term damage that did not surface until many years later. He tried to keep his jobs, moving the family to Kentucky, Kansas, and back to Kentucky, but eventually his health declined to the point that he couldn't work anymore. Wilhelm's world was turned around. The many moves split the family apart. Wilhelm had to take on more of the family duties, like cooking dinner. Wilhelm's mother took a job, which helped stabilize the family finances. "Childhood crashed in many ways that year," Wilhelm commented to *CAAS*. "Our family was totally disrupted, totally different." Her older siblings were working and dating, so they were seldom around, and Wilhelm was often called upon to babysit her younger siblings. She used her vivid imagination to keep them amused. "I told them the stories of books I had read, of movies I had seen, and when those ran out, I began to make up stories," she related in *CAAS*. "I reinvented the se-rial, every day leaving our hero in an impossible situation, to be continued the following day. I held my audience."

Wilhelm did well in her classes in high school, especially English, math, and science. "All through high school, teachers encouraged me to write. I was the editor of the school paper, and sometimes wrote the entire issue," she told *CAAS*. Wilhelm showed a proclivity towards science and math, but unfortunately, there were few acceptable career paths for a woman with her talents in those times. "When I told the dean I wanted to be a chemist, she discouraged me. She said I would end up teaching chemistry, and I knew very well I did not want to be a teacher. I believed her although I did not believe any of the teachers who told me to work at becoming a writer," Wilhelm reminisced in *CAAS*. Wilhelm earned a scholarship to a local university and went to investigate the school, but the lack of classes that were interesting to her kept her from pursuing that path.

## Experiments in Fiction

Wilhelm married shortly after high school and worked at several different kinds of jobs, including a telephone operator and a salesclerk, before she

**Wilhelm introduces psychologist Constance Liedl and her husband, private detective Charlie Meiklejohn, in *The Hamlet Trap*, a mystery.** (St. Martin's Press, 1987. Copyright © 1987 by Kate Wilhelm. All rights reserved. Reproduced with permission of Palgrave Macmillan.)

In *The Dark Door,* **Meiklejohn joins forces with an arsonist to combat a renegade alien space probe.** (St. Martin's Press, 1987. Copyright © 1987 by Kate Wilhelm. All rights reserved. Reproduced with permission of Palgrave Macmillan.)

decided to become a full-time writer. "When I began to write at the age of twenty-eight, it was like going home, as if all my life I had been lost and speechless, and was only then finding my way back home, finding I could talk," she remarked in *CAAS*. Wilhelm's first short story, "The Pint-Size Genie," was published in *Fantastic* magazine in 1956, and her first novel, a mystery titled *More Bitter than Death,* appeared six years later. Her first work of science fiction, *The Mile-long Spaceship,* appeared in 1963, and was followed by such titles as *The Clone,* which received a Nebula Award nomination in 1965. "With history to show, it's easy to say now that [Wilhelm]s work didn't blossom until the mid-1960s, when the New Wave opened up the sf field to more experimentation," Van Gelder observed, adding that Wil-

helm's "novels in this period moved away from the more conventional sf elements and began exploring new psychological territory—books like *Margaret and I . . .* and *Fault Lines* went wherever the story took them, regardless of genre conventions."

Wilhelm's Hugo and Jupiter Award-winning novel, *Where Late the Sweet Birds Sang,* explores cloning and its consequences for humanity. After surviving a nuclear disaster on earth, the Sumner family can only perpetuate their line by producing clones who would eventually breed naturally after the danger of radioactive mutation had passed. But the clones, born with telepathic powers, believe they are superior to their human "parents" and plot to transform the earth into a clone utopia. Human individuality eventually triumphs, however; the clones are too dependent on each other to take chances necessary for survival, and in the end, a human escapes the colony to form a new society.

*New York Times Book Review* reviewer Gerald Jonas praised Wilhelm for her technique in *Where Late the Sweet Birds Sang.* While noting that "at times, her prose strains for 'poetic effects,'" the critic maintained that, for the most part, her writing is powerful and effective. "Her cautionary message comes through loud and clear: giving up our humanity to save our skins is a bad bargain no matter how you look at it," Jonas concluded. Jones similarly suggested in the *Dictionary of Literary Biography* that the novel "offers a poignant reminder that human strengths and weaknesses are inextricably bound together. It also serves as a timely warning that altering human reproduction may alter the species itself."

Wilhelm combines the threat of environmental disaster with the possibility of alien contact in *Juniper Time.* During a prolonged drought in the United States, an alien message is discovered in space that many believe contains information to end the drought. Jean Brighton, a young linguist, is the only one capable of decoding it, but instead of relying on the cryptic sign, Jean turns to members of an American Indian tribe who show her how to survive by managing the environment carefully. Jonas believed that Wilhelm creates a parallel between the plot of *Juniper Time* and similar events in history in which contact between cultures totally ignorant of each other has caused the decimation of one of them. "As Montezuma and the Incas learned," Jonas observed, "gods in machines can kill as well as succor. If this fine novel has a moral, it is a cautionary one, not often found in science fiction: Choose your myths with care; the culture you save may be your own."

The style of *Juniper Time* is both muted and evocative, noted Bishop, who contended that *Juniper Time*

"A probing revelation of human character, a pulsing mystery, and a lucid model of chaos theory."
—Katherine Dunn, author of Geek Love

Death Qualified

A MYSTERY OF CHAOS

Kate Wilhelm

In *Death Qualified*, which concerns the murder of a fugitive scientist, Wilhelm blends elements of science fiction and suspense. (St. Martin's Press, 1991. Copyright © 1991 by Kate Wilhelm. All rights reserved. Reproduced with permission of Palgrave Macmillan.)

is written by "completely overstepping the most tenacious and annoying bugaboos of [the science fiction] genre." Sargent likewise observed that Wilhelm's approach brings a unique perspective to her fiction: "Wilhelm's technique, in most of her work, is to introduce a character or set of characters in a commonplace setting, then to reveal the unusual or uncommon elements through the thoughts and actions of the people in it. Her characters are some of the most fully realized people to be found in science fiction." Consequently, the critic continued, "Wilhelm's work gains much of its strength by showing us life as it is lived, as so many works of science fiction do not."

Although Wilhelm has enjoyed tremendous success with her science fiction, she often departs from the genre, such as in her "Constance and Charlie" mysteries, including *The Hamlet Trap* and *The Dark*

*Door,* and in novels such as *The Clewiston Test.* This 1976 work relates a brilliant scientist's growing alienation from her husband. Anne Clewiston Symons has isolated a blood serum that stifles all pain but also causes personality disorders in test chimpanzees, which become violent and then withdrawn. After Anne is injured in a car accident, her husband, Clark—a scientist of lesser ability—takes over her research. Tensions in their relationship mount as Anne withdraws emotionally, and Clark suspects she is taking the serum. In the *New York Times Book Review,* Jerome Charyn pointed out that Wilhelm's craftsmanship in this piece of mainstream fiction is as solid as that of her science-fiction works. "Written in a style that never calls attention to itself," Charyn stated, "*The Clewiston Test* is a horror story that avoids the usual trappings of its genre. Kate Wilhelm isn't interested in futuristic nightmares."

Wilhelm's collection, *Children of the Wind,* also reflects her "earthbound" approach, David E. Jones noted in the Chicago *Tribune Books,* for the five novellas within are "studies of human personalities and relationships." "Lush and intimate, but equally uncompromising," *Children of the Wind* presents nature as "an order that may be frightening to humans, but often has a magical impact," Karen Joy Fowler commented in the *Washington Post Book World.* The collection, which includes the Nebula Award-winning piece, "The Girl Who Fell into the Sky," is "uniformly excellent," Fowler stated. Praising the title story in particular, Orson Scott Card concluded in the *Los Angeles Times Book Review* that Wilhelm's novellas "fully justify her stature as one of the *grandes dames* of the field."

*And the Angels Sing,* a collection published in 1992, consists of twelve previously published short stories, including the Nebula winner "Forever Yours, Anna," and the first appearance of "The Day of the Sharks." Summarizing the common theme of the collection, Rod Clemmons wrote in *School Library Journal* that each story features "an ordinary person caught between unique perceptions and the paradigms of society at large." Wilhelm's examination of "the bizarre, the terrifying, and the beguiling," as Bette Ammon put it in *Voice of Youth Advocates,* centers on the resulting isolation and frustration that each individual experiences when faced with the irrational or unexplained in society. Roland Green praised Wilhelm's "effortlessly graceful prose" in a *Booklist* review of the collection.

## Pens Highly Regarded Mysteries

Wilhelm has also found success with her "Barbara Holloway" mystery series. In *Death Qualified: A Mystery of Chaos,* a fusion of science fiction and mystery thriller, Wilhelm effectively combines courtroom drama with speculation about contemporary chaos theory. As *New York Times Book Review* commentator Jonas observed, the novel is not necessarily concerned with ideas, but "the impact of ideas." Set in Oregon, the plot involves the murder of a fugitive computer scientist who has escaped captive sedation at a research facility, and the false implication of his wife. The woman is defended by Barbara Holloway, a "death qualified" lawyer licensed to represent those accused of capital crimes. Well received, the novel was described by a *Los Angeles Times Book Review* critic as "sensitive, thought-provoking" and "an unqualified success." Though slightly critical of the novel's mystery component, Charles Nicol in a *Washington Post Book World* review acknowledged Wilhelm's "talents for character development" and "acutely observed relationships among an isolated group."

*The Best Defense* places heroine Barbara Holloway in another high profile case, this time involving a woman accused of killing her daughter and setting fire to a shelter where she sought refuge. A *Kirkus Reviews* writer noted the "rousing" trial scenes, in which Wilhelm describes Holloway's struggle to protect her client against right-wing fundamentalists and anti-feminist politics in the Pacific Northwest. According to Mimi Wesson in the *Women's Review of Books*, through the character of Barbara Holloway, Wilhelm "shows us the remarkable possibilities of the feminist courtroom thriller." A *Publishers Weekly* reviewer declared that, with *The Best Defense*, "Wilhelm claims a leading place in the ranks of trial suspense writers."

In *Malice Prepense*, a third novel in the "Barbara Holloway" series, Wilhelm unites the female protagonist with her father to defend Teddy, a man with intellectual disabilities, who is accused of three murders. When Teddy proves to be harmless, the investigation shifts to his father after it is discovered that a murdered congressman was involved in a long-time affair with Teddy's mother. The complex plot also links the murders to newfound gold deposits and a large land development plan. Praising Wilhelm's storytelling, a *Publishers Weekly* reviewer cited the effectiveness of her "clean, clear prose about real people in sometimes loopy legal situations." A *Washington Post Book World* commentator applauded Wilhelm's "gift" for creating tension, especially in "the verbal sparring of the courtroom."

Wilhelm added further entries to the Barbara Holloway series with *Defense for the Devil* and *No Defense*. In *Defense for the Devil*, Holloway must investigate the murder of a violent wife-beater who is somehow

involved in a ring of computer code thieves. *Library Journal* correspondent Susan Clifford called Wilhelm "a masterful storyteller" and added that *Defense for the Devil* has "just the right blend of solid plot, compelling mystery, and great courtroom drama." A *Publishers Weekly* reviewer likewise recommended the novel for its compelling presentation of courtroom procedure and its "sophisticated look at the complex psychology of a jury." *No Defense* finds Holloway and her father tackling a demanding case in which a young wife stands accused of murdering her older, terminally ill husband. The wife's alibi is thwarted when her teenaged son contradicts her, but Holloway, undaunted, uncovers "a labyrinth of legal intricacies and tiny shreds of evidence," to quote Susan Clifford Braun in *Library Journal*. In *Booklist*, George Needham praised *No Defense* for its "outstanding characterization, . . . keen ear for

***Children of the Wind*, a collection of short fiction, includes the Nebula Award-winning novella "The Girl Who Fell into the Sky."** (St. Martin's, 1989. Copyright © 1989 by Kate Wilhelm. All rights reserved. Reproduced with permission of Palgrave Macmillan.)

dialogue, and expert plot construction." Needham concluded: "This well-written novel skillfully captures small-town life in a rural western community with all its benefits and drawbacks." A *Publishers Weekly* contributor concluded that "those who prefer both style and substance in their courtroom dramas will find [*No Defense*] a satisfying read."

In *Desperate Measures,* Holloway defends a young man with hideous physical deformities against a charge of murder. "The consequences of hate, inflexibility, vanity, and a cruel dictatorship within a family are compellingly demonstrated," Carol DeAngelo remarked in *School Library Journal.* When a famous neurosurgeon is found shot to death, his abused wife becomes the primary suspect in *Clear and Convincing Proof,* another mystery featuring Holloway. According to *Booklist* contributor Barbara Bibel, Wilhelm "presents a psychologically complex story with enough action to keep the pages turning." In *The Unbidden Truth,* a talented pianist suffering from childhood amnesia is accused of murdering a bar manager. Bibel applauded the "complex plot that will keep readers interested and make them think about ethical issues." Holloway takes the case of a former pickpocket turned Las Vegas entertainer in *Sleight of Hand,* an "intricately plotted mystery with an ethical dilemma at its core," Bibel stated. In *A Wrongful Death,* Holloway's trip to a remote cabin takes a sinister turn when she tries to assist an injured mother who then mysteriously disappears. The novel, asserted a *Publishers Weekly* reviewer, "proves compelling action can take place outside a courtroom."

With *The Good Children,* Wilhelm fuses Gothic elements with a psychological portrait of a family in dire circumstances. Having moved from place to place for years, the McNair family is finally ready to settle down in Oregon, where the father has found a promising engineering job. Soon after they settle in, however, the father dies—and then the grieving mother also dies in a freak accident. The four siblings decide to pretend their mother is still alive in order to keep their family unit together, but the ruse exacts a huge psychological toll. "Brilliantly plotted, lyrically written, alluring and magical, mesmerizing, terrifying, and heartbreakingly funny, Wilhelm's story is a wrenching masterpiece," Emily Melton wrote in her *Booklist* review of the work.

In *The Deepest Water,* another of Wilhelm's suspenseful tales, the daughter of a prominent, womanizing novelist investigates his murder. Knowing that her father often based his characters on his friends and neighbors, Abby Conners searches her father's manuscripts for clues to the killer's identity and

In *The Unbidden Truth,* one of the "Barbara Holloway" mystery novels, a gifted pianist stands accused of murder. (Mira Books, 2004. Reproduced by permission.)

discovers a number of secrets about her father's past. A critic in *Publishers Weekly* praised the work, calling Abby "a plucky heroine whose steely patience serves her well even amid grief and bewilderment." Set in small-town Oregon, *The Price of Silence* concerns a young journalist who investigates a decades-old mystery involving a series of disappearances. In the work, Bibel noted, Wilhelm "creates a genuinely eerie atmosphere that pulls readers in and keeps them turning the pages."

Widely praised for her adept characterizations and detailed plots, Wilhelm has remained a very readable writer. Sargent concluded that "her stories are easily accessible, but they are not escapist entertainments which one can read and then put aside; the issues she raises are present in our lives." In 2009 Wilhelm was the recipient of the Solstice Award for

If you enjoy the works of Kate Wilhelm, you may also want to check out the following books:

Orson Scott Card, *Speaker for the Dead*, 1986.
Nancy Kress, *Beggars in Spain*, 1993.
Laura Lippman's "Tess Monaghan" mystery series, including *No Good Deeds*, 2006.

her contributions to the genre of speculative fiction. According to Van Gelder, the author "manages to spin out yarns year after year that amuse, enlighten, entertain, and entrance."

## ■ Biographical and Critical Sources

### BOOKS

*Contemporary Authors Autobiography Series*, Volume 8, Gale (Detroit, MI), 1989.

*Contemporary Literary Criticism*, Volume 7, Gale (Detroit, MI), 1977.

*Dictionary of Literary Biography*, Volume 8: *Twentieth-Century American Science-Fiction Writers*, Gale (Detroit, MI), 1981.

Platt, Charles, *Dream Makers: The Uncommon People Who Write Science Fiction*, Volume 1, Berkley Publishing (New York, NY), 1980.

*Twentieth-Century Science-Fiction Writers*, St. James Press (Detroit, MI), 1986.

Wilhelm, Kate, *Storyteller: Writing Lessons and More from Twenty-seven Years of the Clarion Writers' Workshop*, Small Beer Press (Northampton, MA), 2005.

### PERIODICALS

*Booklist*, July 1, 1971, review of *Abyss: Two Novellas*, p. 897; April 15, 1974, review of *City Of Cain*, p. 908; September 1, 1975, review of *The Infinity Box: A Collection of Speculative Fiction*, p. 29; February 1, 1976, review of *Where Late The Sweet Birds Sang*, p. 756; April 1, 1976, review of *The Clewiston Test*, p. 1092; March 15, 1977, review of *Fault Lines*, p. 1070; April 1, 1978, review of *Somerset Dreams and Other Fictions*, p. 1241; March 1, 1981, review of *A Sense Of Shadow*, p. 870; July, 1983, review of *Welcome, Chaos*, p. 1366; January 1, 1986, review of *Huysman's Pets*, p. 643; October 1, 1987, review of *The Hamlet Trap*, p. 221; March 1, 1988, review of *Crazy Time*, p. 1096; October 1, 1988, review of *The Dark Door*, p. 220; February 15, 1989, review of *Smart House*, p. 976; September 15, 1989, review of *Children of the Wind*, p. 147; February 15, 1990, review of *Cambio Bay*, p. 1122; July, 1990, review of *Sweet, Sweet Poison*, p. 2076; May 1, 1991, review of *Death Qualified: A Mystery of Chaos*, p. 1675; February 15, 1992, Roland Green, review of *And the Angels Sing*, p. 1092; June 1 and 15, 1994, Emily Melton, review of *The Best Defense*, p. 1780; February 1, 1998, Emily Melton, review of *The Good Children*, p. 901; December 15, 1999, George Needham, review of *No Defense*, p. 761; May 1, 2001, Mary Frances Wilkens, review of *Desperate Measures*, p. 1643; August, 2003, Barbara Bibel, review of *Clear and Convincing Proof*, p. 1962; September 15, 2004, Barbara Bibel, review of *The Unbidden Truth*, p. 214; October 1, 2005, Barbara Bibel, review of *The Price of Silence*, p. 40; September 1, 2006, Barbara Bibel, review of *Sleight of Hand*, p. 61; September 1, 2007, Sue O'Brien, review of *A Wrongful Death*, p. 60.

*Christian Science Monitor*, July 18, 1979, Chris Lamb, review of *Juniper Time*, p. 18; May 3, 1988, review of *Crazy Time*, p. 20.

*Kirkus Reviews*, November 15, 1975, review of *Where Late The Sweet Birds Sang*, p. 1308; December 1, 1975, review of *The Clewiston Test*, p. 1350; May 1, 1979, review of *Juniper Time*, p. 543; August 15, 1987, review of *The Hamlet Trap*, p. 1199; September 1, 1988, review of *The Dark Door*, p. 1284; July 15, 1990, review of *Sweet, Sweet Poison*, p. 970; January 15, 1992, review of *And the Angels Sing*, p. 76; April 15, 1994, review of *The Best Defense*, p. 510; May 15, 1995, review of *A Flush of Shadows: Five Short Novels Featuring Constance Leidl and Charlie Meiklejohn*, p. 674; June 15, 1996, review of *Malice Prepense*, p. 855; February 1, 1998, review of *The Good Children*, p. 149; January 15, 1999, review of *Defense for the Devil*, p. 100; December 1, 1999, review of *No Defense*, p. 1840; August 1, 2000, review of *The Deepest Water*, p. 1070; May 15, 2001, review of *Desperate Measures*, p. 712; June 15, 2002, review of *Skeletons*, p. 845.

*Library Journal*, May 1, 1975, review of *The Infinity Box*, p. 885; November 15, 1975, review of *Where Late The Sweet Birds Sang*, p. 2176; June 15, 1991, Kathy Armendt Sorci, review of *Death Qualified*, p. 108; February 15, 1992, Jackie Cassada, review of *And the Angels Sing*, p. 200; May 1, 1994, Elsa Pendleton, review of *The Best Defense*, p. 140; June 15, 1996, Susan Clifford, review of *Malice Prepense*, p. 94; February 1, 1998, Susan Clifford, review of *The Good Children*, p. 114; January, 1999, Susan Clifford, review of *Defense for the Devil*, p. 161;

January, 2000, Susan Clifford Braun, review of *No Defense*, p. 164; September 1, 2000, Susan Clifford Braun, review of *The Deepest Water*, p. 254.

*Los Angeles Times*, November 15, 1983, Gregory Benford, review of *Welcome, Chaos*, p. 14; December 3, 1989, review of *Children of the Wind*, p. 13; June 30, 1991, review of *Death Qualified*, p. 6.

*Los Angeles Times Book Review*, December 3, 1989, Orson Scott Card, review of *Children of the Wind*; June 30, 1991, Sherry Gershon Gottlieb, review of *Death Qualified*, p. 6.

*Magazine of Fantasy and Science Fiction*, April, 1968, review of *The Killer Thing*, p. 40; January, 1969, review of *The Downstairs Room and Other Speculative Fiction*, p. 40; September, 1969, review of *Let The Fire Fall*, p. 21; November, 1971, review of *Abyss: Two Novellas*, p. 18; November, 1976, review of *The Clewiston Test*, p. 66; April, 1979, review of *Somerset Dreams and Other Fictions*, p. 33; January, 1980, Michael Bishop, review of *Juniper Time*, p. 37; July, 1985, review of *Welcome, Chaos*, p. 12; February, 1989, Orson Scott Card, review of *Crazy Time*, p. 30; May, 1990, Orson Scott Card, review of *Children of the Wind*, p. 53; February, 1992, Orson Scott Card, review of *Death Qualified*, p. 35; June, 1992, Orson Scott Card, review of *And the Angels Sing*, p. 21; December, 1994, Robert K.J. Killheffer, review of *The Best Defense*, p. 17; September, 2001, Gordon Van Gelder, "Kate Wilhelm: An Appreciation," p. 66.

*Newsweek*, November 29, 1971, review of *Margaret And I*, p. 104; February 9, 1976, review of *The Clewiston Test*, p. 79.

*New York Times*, May 13, 1976, Christopher Lehmann-Haupt, review of *The Clewiston Test*.

*New York Times Book Review*, November 20, 1966, review of *The Nevermore Affair*, p. 82; March 10, 1974, review of *City of Cain*, p. 10; January 18, 1976, Gerald Jonas, review of *Where Late The Sweet Birds Sang*, p. 21; February 22, 1976, Jerome Charyn, review of *The Clewiston Test*; May 8, 1977, review of *The Infinity Box*, p. 51; July 2, 1978, review of *City of Cain*, p. 19; August 26, 1979, Gerald Jonas, review of *Juniper Time*, p. 14; June 3, 1984, review of *Welcome, Chaos*, p. 50; March 9, 1986, Gerald Jonas, review of *Huysman's Pets*, p. 23; September 1, 1991, Gerald Jonas, review of *Death Qualified*, p. 13; February 9, 1992, Gerald Jonas, review of *And the Angels Sing*, p. 20.

*Publishers Weekly*, April 14, 1975, review of *The Infinity Box*, p. 49; November 24, 1975, review of *Where Late The Sweet Birds Sang*, p. 48; April 23, 1979, review of *Juniper Time*, p. 72; March 20, 1981, Barbara A. Bannon, review of *A Sense of Shadow*, p. 58; October 16, 1981, Barbara A. Bannon, review of *Listen, Listen*, p. 63; May 21, 1982, Barbara A. Bannon, review of *Oh, Susannah!*, p. 66; July 29, 1983, review of *Welcome, Chaos*, p. 65; January 3, 1986, review of *Huysman's Pets*, p. 44; August 5, 1988, Sybil Steinberg, review of *The Dark Door*, p. 74; December 16, 1988, Sybil Steinberg, review of *Smart House*, p. 71; September 22, 1989, Sybil Steinberg, review of *Children of the Wind*, p. 42; May 16, 1994, review of *The Best Defense*, p. 53; May 27, 1996, review of *Malice Prepense*, p. 66; January 5, 1998, review of *The Good Children*, p. 56; November 30, 1998, review of *Defense for the Devil*, p. 50; November 29, 1999, review of *No Defense*, p. 52; September 4, 2000, review of *The Deepest Water*, p. 83; June 25, 2001, review of *Desperate Measures*, p. 50; June 24, 2002, review of *Skeletons*, p. 35; August 18, 2003, review of *Clear and Convincing Proof*, p. 59; July 17, 2006, review of *Sleight of Hand*, p. 135; July 9, 2007, review of *A Wrongful Death*, p. 33; June 2, 2008, review of *Cold Case*, p. 29.

*School Library Journal*, April, 1976, review of *Where Late The Sweet Birds Sang*, p. 96; October, 1979, review of *Juniper Time*, p. 164; August, 1981, Ellen Sisco, review of *A Sense of Shadow*, p. 82; May, 1984, Debora Bugbee, review of *Welcome, Chaos*, p. 108; August, 1986, Mary T. Gerrity, review of *Huysman's Pets*, p. 113; July, 1992, Rod Clemmons, review of *And the Angels Sing*, p. 98; November, 1994, Judy Sokoll, review of *The Best Defense*, p. 143; September, 1998, Frances Reiher, review of *The Good Children*, p. 231; October, 2001, Carol DeAngelo, review of *Desperate Measures*, p. 196.

*Tribune Books* (Chicago, IL), December 17, 1989, David E. Jones, review of *Children of the Wind*, p. 7.

*Voice of Youth Advocates*, April, 1992, Bette Ammon, review of *And the Angels Sing*, p. 49.

*Washington Post Book World*, February 6, 1977, review of *Where Late the Sweet Birds Sang*, p. 10; October 29, 1989, Karen Joy Fowler, review of *Children in the Wind*; July 7, 1991, Charles Nicol, review of *Death Qualified*; July 21, 1996, review of *Malice Prepense*.

*Women's Review of Books*, January, 1995, Mimi Wesson, review of *The Best Defense*, p. 22.

ONLINE

*Kate Wilhelm Home Page*, http://www.katewilhelm.com (April 1, 2010).*

# Robert Charles Wilson

## ■ Personal

Born December 15, 1953, in Whittier, CA; became Canadian citizen; married; wife's name Sharry; children: Paul, Devon.

## ■ Addresses

*Home*—Concord, Ontario, Canada. *E-mail*—mcwilson@robertcharleswilson.com.

## ■ Career

Writer.

## ■ Awards, Honors

Philip K. Dick Award nominee, Philadelphia Science Fiction Society, 1986, for *A Hidden Place;* Philip K. Dick Award, Philadelphia Science Fiction Society, 1994, for *Mysterium;* Prix Aurora Award, Canadian Science Fiction and Fantasy Association, 1996, for novelette "The Perseids," 1999, for *Darwinia,* 2002, for *The Chronoliths,* and 2004, for *Blind Lake;* Nebula Award nominee, Science Fiction Writers of America,

1997, for "The Perseids"; Hugo Award nominee, World Science Fiction Society, 1999, for *Darwinia,* 2002, for *The Chronoliths,* and 2004, for *Blind Lake;* John W. Campbell Memorial Award, 2002, for *The Chronoliths;* Hugo Award, 2006, for *Spin;* Theodore Sturgeon Memorial Award for short fiction, 2007, for "The Cartesian Theater."

## ■ Writings

*NOVELS*

*A Hidden Place,* Bantam (New York, NY), 1986.
*Memory Wire,* Bantam (New York, NY), 1988.
*Gypsies,* Doubleday (Garden City, NY), 1989.
*The Divide,* Doubleday (Garden City, NY), 1990.
*A Bridge of Years,* Doubleday (Garden City, NY), 1991.
*The Harvest,* Bantam (New York, NY), 1992.
*Mysterium,* Bantam (New York, NY), 1994.
*Darwinia,* Tor Books (New York, NY), 1998.
*Bios,* Tor Books (New York, NY), 1999.
*The Chronoliths,* Tor Books (New York, NY), 2001.
*Blind Lake,* Tor Books (New York, NY), 2003.
(With Marc Scott Zicree) *Magic Time: Ghostlands,* EOS (New York, NY), 2004.
*Spin,* Tor Books (New York, NY), 2005.
*Axis,* Tor (New York, NY), 2007.
*Julian Comstock: A Story of 22nd-Century America,* Tor (New York, NY), 2009.

OTHER

*The Perseids and Other Stories,* Tor Books (New York, NY), 2000.

*Julian: A Christmas Story* (novella), PS Publishing (Hornsea, England), 2007.

Coeditor, with Edo van Belkom, *Tesseracts Ten,* 2006. Contributor to periodicals, including *Analog Science Fiction and Fact, Asimov's Science Fiction* and *Magazine of Fantasy and Science Fiction.* Contributor to anthologies, including *Star Colonies,* 1996, *The UFO Files,* 1997, *Eternal Lovecraft: The Persistence of H.P. Lovecraft in Popular Culture,* 1998, *The Year's Best Science Fiction Sixteenth Annual Collection,* 1999, and *The New Space Opera: All New Stories of Science Fiction Adventure,* edited by Gardner Dozois and Jonathan Strahan, Eos/HarperCollins (New York, NY), 2009.

## ■ Adaptations

*Spin* was optioned for a feature film by Olympus Pictures and Bits & Pieces Picture Company.

## ■ Sidelights

Canadian author Robert Charles Wilson is "probably the finest science-fiction author now writing," according to famed writer Stephen King, as quoted by *Globe and Mail* contributor James Adams. The author of more than a dozen novels, Wilson has won most of the major science fiction writing awards, including the Philip K. Dick Award, the Theodore Sturgeon Memorial Award, and the Hugo Award. "Known for the way they merge technological fantasy with the psychological and metaphysical," as Thomas March wrote in the *Dictionary of Literary Biography,* "Wilson's novels embody both the hopes and fears that constitute humanity's relationship with scientific possibility." Further praise for the speculative work of this transplanted American came from *Commonweal* reviewer Kurt Luchs, who commented, "There is no writer quite like Robert Charles Wilson, who has done more than anyone else to tease out the imaginative implications of modern cosmological ideas."

Through a series of novels he began in the mid-1980s, including *A Hidden Place, Darwinia,* and *Spin,* Wilson has earned high praise from both readers and critics. In *Twentieth-Century Science-Fiction Writers,* Henry Leperlier stated that the author's "treatment of contemporary themes such as alienation and the loss of identity puts him in the same league with many science fiction and mainstream writers who have managed to resist the passage of time."

### The Making of a Sci Fi Legend

Wilson was born in California in 1953, but he has lived in Canada since he was a nine year old. From a young age, he was drawn to the works of Ray Bradbury, Isaac Asimov, and Robert Heinlein. "All I can say is that for as long as I can remember, from my childhood, I've had a fascination with the strange, the exotic—SF, fantasy, horror," he remarked in a *Challenging Destiny* interview with James Schellenberg and David M. Switzer. "It seemed to come to me so naturally, to be so much a part of my personality, that I can't stand objectively outside it and ask, why do these things attract me? The urge to write was part of my life since the word go—I love to read and I love to write. As soon as I learned to read and write it's what I did."

Wilson grew up in Toronto and also lived for a time in the Western province of British Columbia before returning to Ontario. His first short stories were published in *Analog Science Fiction and Fact* in 1974, but it was not until 1986 that his debut novel appeared. "I broke into the field with short stories, but they were always harder for me than novels," he recalled in his *Challenging Destiny* interview. "I had always read more novels than short stories." Wilson added that his attempts at science fiction tales helped him develop an appreciation for the genre's history: "We existed for decades as a field of short story writers—the people who wrote for the pulp magazines. The novel as a viable SF category didn't really exist until the 50s except as serializations in magazines. I find it hard to be concise enough to write a short story. My short stories tend toward the novelette or the novella."

Wilson gained critical recognition with his first novel, the love story *A Hidden Place,* which is set in a small prairie town. Wilson's consideration of human emotion in the novel brought him comparisons, according to Leperlier, with novelist Theodore Sturgeon. The two human protagonists, Travis Fisher and his girlfriend Nancy Wilcox, come under the influence of a woman from the realm of Faery, Anna Blaise, whose quest is to reunite with her male half, a hobo named Bone who does not remember his true origin. Tom Easton, in *Analog Science Fiction and Fact,* noted that the novel is about misfits, as did Leperlier, who called the characters "estranged persons." According to Easton, the novel contains "salutary vicarious lessons for its readers." In a review of Wilson's second novel, *Memory Wire,* Easton reflected on *A Hidden Place* as "fine and moving and instructive." He liked *Memory Wire* even more, finding it "more plausible" than its predecessor and containing "marvelous science fictional devisings" in its study of a man cybernetically altered to be a perfectly objective "Recording Angel." In *Quill & Quire*, reviewer Kim G. Kofmel found *Memory Wire* "compelling" as an adventure tale, a love story, a "well-drawn" vision of the future, and "an examination of the function of memory, of the freedoms and constraints contained in both remembering and forgetting."

### Blending Genres

Wilson's third novel, *Gypsies*, comprises "a blend of science fiction, mystery, and thriller," according to *Publishers Weekly* critic Sybil Steinberg—a combina-

**Wilson received the Hugo Award for *Spin*, an apocalyptic coming-of-age tale.** (Tor Books, 2006. Reproduced by permission.)

tion she found "spellbinding." The "gypsies" of the title are actually adult siblings, abused in childhood, who possess the power to move among invented worlds. The protagonist, Karen, has settled for a normal married life in Toronto, but divorce and the return of a mysterious "Grey Man" from her past prompt her, and her similarly gifted teenage son, to seek refuge with her sister Laura, who lives in a West Coast utopia of her own invention. More than one critic commented that the novel straddles genres; Sharon Oard Warner, in the *New York Times Book Review*, found the book's turn toward fantasy and away from realism somewhat awkward. Leperlier, while praising the realistic psychology of the work, regretted that its fantastic aspects relied on magic rather than adhering to the conventions of science fiction.

In *The Divide*, Wilson produced what Gerald Jonas, in the *New York Times Book Review*, called "a literate thriller, a superbly crafted novel of character and a thoughtful exploration of what it might feel like to be a superman." The superman in question is John Shaw, who has been created by a government experiment that closes down, leaving Shaw estranged—as so many of Wilson's characters are—from everyday society. Shaw develops a second personality in order to deal with the world around him; a love triangle arises, as each of his personalities is involved with a different woman. Reviewer and science fiction writer Jonas expressed wonder at Wilson's ability to "satisfy the demands of plausibility while contriving a 'happy ending'" for *The Divide*. Pippa Wysong, in *Quill & Quire*, however, found the book's ending "predictable."

Jonas, though continuing to voice admiration for Wilson's gifts, was nevertheless somewhat disappointed by the author's next work, *A Bridge of Years*, in which a young man in the Pacific Northwest, recovering from alcoholism and divorce, discovers a time-travel mechanism that takes him to Greenwich Village in 1962. Writing for the *New York Times Book Review*, Jonas regretted, in particular, a plot turn in which the custodian of the device, a time-traveling cyborg soldier from the future, tries to get it back; the reviewer maintained that the two major plot strands, while separately interesting, interfered with one another. A critic writing in the *Los Angeles Times Book Review* found the novel too intricately plotted but wrote that the protagonist, Tom Winter, is "particularly well drawn" and that Wilson's prose is "lovingly crafted." A Chicago *Tribune Books* commentator found the novel "an entertaining mix of human foible and heroic action, held together by vivid imagination."

Discussing the use of time paradoxes in several of his narratives, Wilson remarked to *io9.com* interviewer Annalee Newitz, "I like to say that science fiction de-privileges the present. Past, present, future—those aren't fixed categories; they're points of view." The author further noted, "The quaintness of the past and the marvelousness of the future are entirely in the eye of the beholder. Messing around with time in fiction is one way we remind ourselves of that truth. Science fiction does it more consciously and consistently than any other genre, and that's one of the things I love about it."

## Award-Winning Novels of Alienation and Philosophy

The Harvest combines an up-to-date science fiction premise with a "cozy" Northwest setting, according to R. John Hayes in Quill & Quire. In the novel an extraterrestrial starship, whose inhabitants are masters of nanotechnology and virtual reality, appears above the earth, offering a high-tech immortality on another world for all humans who choose it. The earth is soon depopulated, except for one-hundredth of one percent of the human species, who have refused the offer for various individual reasons. The novel follows a selected sample of those people and in the process presents a view of human motivation and its emotional complexity. As with The Divide, critics were themselves divided over the book, especially over its ending. In the New York Times Book Review, Jonas called The Harvest "an intelligently conceived, fully realized novel," and singled out the ambiguities of the ending for special praise: "Because he eschews pat answers, Mr. Wilson manages to derive great suspense from the questions that the survivors pose to themselves and to one another." Easton, in Analog Science Fiction and Fact, commented that he "enjoyed The Harvest a great deal," yet found it less satisfying than A Bridge of Years and other works by Wilson, precisely because of the ending's ambiguity.

Wilson's seventh novel, Mysterium, is set in the small town of Two Rivers in the Upper Peninsula of Michigan—a town that, in this fictional treatment, has been transported into an alternate reality, a North America governed by a French-English confederacy whose religion is Gnostic Christian. Searching for the how and why of their startling situation, the townspeople discover that they are to be the subjects of this society's first experiment in exploding an atomic bomb. Their task, from that point on, is to find a way out of their predicament, and they do so with the help of a Nobel-winning physicist, Alan Stern, who never appears in the book but guides its spirit throughout. A Publishers Weekly reviewer wrote of Mysterium: "Wilson . . . blends science, religion, philosophy and alternate history into an intelligent, compelling work of fic-

tion." Other critics were united in praise of Wilson's literary skill, especially his characterizations. Jonas wrote in the New York Times Book Review that "Mr. Wilson is adept at drawing fully rounded characters in a few paragraphs. Everyone in the large cast is seen from the inside." In Quill & Quire, fantasy novelist Michelle Sagara sounded a similar note: "There are no cardboard people in Wilson's hands; even glimpsed for only a page, his people become real. He is that rarest of writers—one who writes both truthfully and with great affection for his characters." Jonas added that the book's ending was "as poignant as it is unexpected." Mysterium won the prestigious Philip K. Dick Award for 1994 and put Wilson solidly in the science fiction canon.

In Darwinia Wilson considers an alternate world in which all of Europe disappears mysteriously in 1912, leaving behind Darwinia, a virgin continent filled with strange animals and plants. While America undergoes a religious revival in response to the enigmatic catastrophe, an expedition is mounted into the heart of Darwinia to discover its secrets. John Mort, in his review of the novel for Booklist, called it "eerie, paranoid, and menacing." Complaining that the novel's point is "dizzyingly abstract," a reviewer for Publishers Weekly nevertheless praised the book's style as "rich, lucid and literate." "If you read only one SF book this year," wrote Denise Dumars in Library Journal, "this wonderfully evocative epic should be it." A Hugo finalist, Darwinia won the Aurora Award, further advancing Wilson's career.

In The Perseids and Other Stories, a collection, all of the stories are centered on Finders, a used bookstore frequented by the characters. "Wilson's slow-building, many-layered yarns shape characters out of the raw materials of loneliness and intellectual isolation," wrote a critic for Publishers Weekly. "Readers in search of thoughtful, resonant writing will enjoy this collection of urban fantasies." A Kirkus Reviews contributor found the stories to be "beautifully observed, skillfully worked out," and believed they "flow subtly, almost imperceptibly, from the prosaic to the preternatural." A further award-winning title was The Chronoliths, which won the John W. Campbell Memorial Award in 2002.

In the 2003 publication Blind Lake, scientist Marguerite Hauser uses new technology to study an alien life form on a distant planet, while trying to raise her young daughter and deal with the fallout from her recent divorce. Marguerite's life at the research facility is further complicated when reporter Chris Carmody comes to Blind Lake looking for a story that will revitalize his floundering career. For reasons unknown, the facility is quarantined shortly after Chris's arrival, leaving Blind Lake's large population of workers and their families completely isolated from the outside world. Marguerite and Chris grow closer as they search for answers to the mysterious lockdown, enraging Marguerite's ex-husband, Ray, who is also trapped in Blind Lake. Jackie Cassada, in an article for *Library Journal*, found *Blind Lake* to be "a taut SF suspense tale."

## A Trilogy and a Change of Direction

In *Spin*, Wilson posits a terrifying "what if" hypothesis when all of the stars in the sky suddenly burn out one night in front of the eyes of young Tyler Dupree and twins Diane and James Lawton. As the friends grow up and apart, the truth becomes clear. The planet is caught in what comes to be known as "the spin," which causes time on Earth to move much slower than the rest of the universe. In the time it takes for one day to pass on Earth, one-hundred million years have passed in outer space. By Tyler's fortieth birthday, the sun will have burned out, leaving the planet barren and the human race extinct. Racing against time, Tyler desperately searches for a way to save his friends and humankind. In an article for the *Magazine of Fantasy and Science Fiction*, writer Michelle Sagara called *Spin* "Wilson's finest work to date." Indeed, the novel won that year's coveted Hugo Award.

*Spin*'s sequel, *Axis*, brings the action to Equatoria, a planet apparently designed for humanity by the Hypotheticals, mysterious machine intelligences that have developed a life-extension technology that is illegal on Earth. Lise Adams arrives on Equatoria to search for her missing father, a scientist determined to crack the Hypotheticals' secrets. Lise hires Turk Findley, a pilot with a criminal past, to help her find her father. As strange mechanical ash falls from space and covers the surface of the planet, Lise discovers that her ex-husband, a Department of Genomic Security employee, is spying on her; at the same time, a top-secret experiment has created Isaac, a child who has been rendered capable of communicating between humans and the Hypotheticals.

A writer for *Kirkus Reviews* considered the novel "equally engrossing and exasperating" because of the many elements it leaves unexplained. *Booklist* reviewer Regina Schroeder, however, lauded *Axis* as an "absolutely, abundantly marvelous" book that "conjures humanity after an event so strange it's almost unimaginable." Expressing similar admiration for *Axis*, *Locus* contributor Gary K. Wolfe

concluded: "Rather than take the expected route of dazzling us with more and bigger billion-year perspectives and alien machines like we saw in *Spin*, Wilson has chosen depth over expansion, and the result is arguably what a middle novel in a trilogy should be, adding weight and density to the narrative instead of merely offering a place-holding intermezzo for the fireworks to come." The sequence of books is intended to conclude with *Vortex*.

However, before venturing on with that novel, Wilson produced a work that is a curious blend of history, steampunk, and dystopia, *Julian Comstock: A Story of 22nd-Century America*. In an interview with a contributor for *Locus*, Wilson mentioned that *Julian Comstock* is his attempt at writing a "post-apocalypse novel that (a) wasn't about survival and (b) was a kind of dystopia that wasn't just an Evil Empire run by the worst human beings—a dystopia more like European monarchies or aristocratic institutions, where there are cracks in the wall; an oppressive set of governmental bodies, but at the same time a lively popular culture. In other words, I wanted something with contradictions built into it. I was tired of dystopias that were triumphant Evil and oppressed Good. Real life isn't like that."

The result is a novel that posits the United States a century into the future after its total collapse in the twenty-first century, a result of ecological disaster, energy pressures, and contagion. The sixty states (including Canada) that constitute the union have been governed by President Deklan Comstock for thirty years. With an administration based in New York City, President Comstock rules with an iron hand. Although it is the twenty-second century, Americans work with nineteenth-century technology, and the nation is no longer a world power. A newfound piety and strong religion possess the country; the years of ruin in the previous centuries are now seen as profligate times. History is seen through a glass darkly; there is little opposition to the new system. A small chink in the armor of Comstock's reign becomes observable, however. A popular hero arises, a certain Captain Commongold who has defeated the Dutch in Labrador, saving the nation and capturing the popular imagination. However, this warrior is no believer in the current orthodoxy and thus President Comstock fears him and wants to destroy him. Then it is learned that this shadowy figure is none other that the president's own nephew, Julian Comstock, and the stage is set for an ultimate showdown between the two men.

*Julian Comstock* won critical applause from many quarters. Writing for *Booklist*, Roland Green termed it "a superior addition to the growing and popular

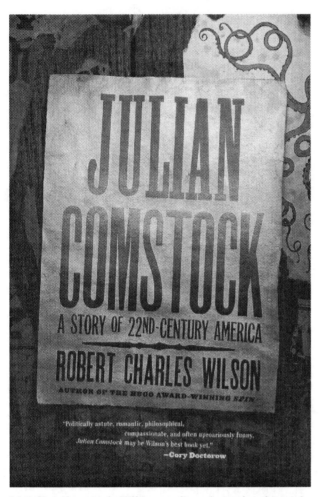

In *Julian Comstock*, **Wilson posits a dystopian future in which a tyrannical president rules over an American nation returned to nineteenth-century technology following a collapse of the social order.** (Tor Books, 2009. Reproduced by permission.)

with engaging and sympathetic, if conflicted, characters, and unlike anything else [Wilson has] done to date." And Cory Doctorow, reviewing the same work on the *Boing Boing* Web site, commented, "Politically astute, romantic, philosophical, compassionate and often uproariously funny, *Julian Comstock* may be Wilson's best book yet."

---

If you enjoy the works of Robert Charles Wilson, you may also want to check out the following books:

Greg Bear, *Darwin's Children*, 2003.
Charles Stross, *Singularity Sky*, 2003.
Joe Haldeman, *The Accidental Time Machine*, 2007.

---

Discussing the virtues of science fiction in his *Challenging Destiny* interview, Wilson stated, "SF is for satisfying your curiosity, for stimulating your imagination. That can be a trivial thing to do, but it can be an important thing too." He continued, "I don't like giving it a literary purpose because it becomes prescriptive. If I decide what SF is good for, it implies SF that doesn't perform this task—whatever we decide this task is at any given moment—is essentially trivial and bad. Whether that task is literary or pragmatic I think it's the wrong genre to be putting these cages around. I think our purpose is to sit outside the other genres and to make up our own purposes, and to be both trivial and profound."

category of postapocalyptic fiction." A *Publishers Weekly* contributor also commended this novel, finding it a "thoughtful tale [that] combines complex characters, rousing military adventure and a beautifully realized, unnerving future." Likewise, *Library Journal* reviewer Jackie Cassada dubbed the novel an "important book" and a "postmodern parable of a nation caught up in extremes." For *School Library Journal* contributor Sandy Schmitz, *Julian Comstock* is a "meaty adventure," while for a *Kirkus Reviews* writer it is an "expertly handled prognostication with more than a touch of somber magnificence." Critiquing the novel on the *Sci Fi Wire* Web site, Paul Di Filippo was also impressed with this work, calling it "poignant, entrancing, [and] thought-provoking." *Locus* magazine reviewer Wolfe pronounced the novel "beautifully written, populated

## ■ Biographical and Critical Sources

*BOOKS*

*Dictionary of Literary Biography,* Volume 251, *Canadian Fantasy and Science Fiction Writers,* Gale (Detroit, MI), 2001.
*Twentieth-Century Science-Fiction Writers,* 3rd edition, St. James Press (Detroit, MI), 1991.

*PERIODICALS*

*Analog Science Fiction and Fact,* September, 1987, Tom Easton, review of *A Hidden Place,* p. 181; July, 1988, Tom Easton, review of *Memory Wire,* p. 178; May,

1993, Tom Easton, review of *The Harvest*, p. 131; November, 1998, Tom Easton, review of *Darwinia*, p. 133; February, 2000, Tom Easton, review of *Bios*, p. 132; December, 2001, review of *The Chronoliths*, p. 134.

*Booklist*, December 15, 1992, review of *The Harvest*, p. 718; April 1, 1994, review of *Mysterium*, p. 1426; August, 1997, review of *A Bridge of Years*, p. 1892; May 15, 1998, John Mort, review of *Darwinia*, p. 1608; August, 2000, Roland Green, review of *The Perseids and Other Stories*, p. 2126; July 1, 2001, Bryan Baldus, review of *The Chronoliths*, p. 1993; August, 2003, Roland Green, review of *Blind Lake*, p. 1969; December 15, 2004, Paula Luedtke, review of *Magic Time: Ghostlands*, p. 716; March 15, 2005, Regina Schroeder, review of *Spin*, p. 1276; September 1, 2007, Regina Schroeder, review of *Axis*, p. 65; May 15, 2009, Roland Green, review of *Julian Comstock: A Story of 22nd-Century America*, p. 28.

*Bookmarks*, January-February, 2008, review of *Axis*, p. 40.

*Books in Canada*, March, 1993, review of *The Harvest*, p. 35.

*Chronicle*, April, 1993, review of *The Harvest*, p. 29; February, 1994, review of *The Harvest*, p. 28; June, 1995, review of *Mysterium*, p. 36; December, 1998, review of *Darwinia*, p. 49; December, 1999, review of *Bios*, p. 41; August, 2001, review of *The Chronoliths*, p. 34; July, 2003, review of *Blind Lake*, p. 34; June, 2005, Don D'Ammassa, review of *Spin*, p. 31.

*Commonweal*, June 19, 2009, Kurt Luchs, reviews of *Spin* and *Axis*, p. 27.

*Globe and Mail* (Toronto, Ontario, Canada), November 22, 2003, review of *Blind Lake*, p. D22; June 30, 2007, James Adams, "Canada's Best-Kept Secrets in the Arts."

*Guardian Weekly*, May 14, 1995, review of *Mysterium*, p. 29.

*Kirkus Reviews*, May 1, 1998, review of *Darwinia*, p. 621; June 15, 2000, review of *The Perseids and Other Stories*, p. 841; November 1, 2004, review of *Magic Time*, p. 1032; January 15, 2005, review of *Spin*, p. 90; August 1, 2007, review of *Axis*; May 15, 2009, review of *Julian Comstock*.

*Kliatt*, July, 1994, review of *Mysterium*, p. 20; March, 2001, review of *Bios*, p. 27; January, 2002, Ginger Armstrong, review of *The Perseids and Other Stories*, p. 21.

*Library Journal*, November 15, 1992, Jackie Cassada, review of *The Harvest*, p. 104; March 15, 1994, Jackie Cassada, review of *Mysterium*, p. 104; August, 1999, Denise Dumars, review of *Darwinia*, p. 176; July, 2003, Jackie Cassada, review of *Blind Lake*, p. 132; November, 15, 2004, Jack Cassada,

review of *Magic Time*, p. 55; September 15, 2007, Jackie Cassada, review of *Axis*, p. 54; June 15, 2009, Jackie Cassada, review of *Julian Comstock*, p. 68.

*Locus*, November, 1992, review of *The Harvest*, p. 17; February, 1993, review of *The Harvest*, p. 57; June, 1993, review of *The Harvest*, p. 56; April, 1994, review of *Mysterium*, p. 17; June, 1994, review of *The Harvest*, p. 60; December, 1999, review of *Bios*, p. 21; September, 2000, review of *The Perseids and Other Stories*, p. 21; November, 2000, review of *The Perseids and Other Stories*, p. 15; September, 2007, Gary K. Wolfe, review of *Axis*; May, 2009, Gary K. Wolfe, review of *Julian Comstock*; June, 2009, "Robert Charles Wilson: The Cosmic and the Intimate," p. 6.

*Los Angeles Times Book Review*, July 29, 1990, review of *The Divide*, p. 6; January 5, 1992, review of *A Bridge of Years*, p. 4.

*Magazine of Fantasy and Science Fiction*, April, 1993, review of *The Harvest*, p. 30; March, 1999, Robert K.J. Killheffer, review of *Darwinia*, p. 35; June, 2000, Michelle West, review of *Bios*, p. 41; October-November, 2005, Michelle Sagara, review of *Spin*, p. 54.

*New York Times Book Review*, May 28, 1989, Sharon Oard Warner, review of *Gypsies*, p. 18; February 11, 1990, Gerald Jonas, review of *The Divide*, p. 29; October 27, 1991, Gerald Jonas, review of *A Bridge of Years*, p. 30; December 27, 1992, Gerald Jonas, review of *The Harvest*, p. 22; July 10, 1994, Gerald Jonas, review of *Mysterium*, p. 30; July 12, 1998, Gerald Jonas, review of *Darwinia*, p. 26; December 3, 2000, review of *The Perseids and Other Stories*, p. 88; September 2, 2001, Gerald Jonas, review of *The Chronoliths*, p. 14; July 7, 2002, Scott Veale, review of *The Chronoliths*, p. 20; December 7, 2003, review of *Blind Lake*, p. 86.

*Prairie Fire*, summer, 1994, review of *Mysterium*, p. 239.

*Publishers Weekly*, November 18, 1988, Sybil Steinberg, review of *Gypsies*, p. 71; November 9, 1992, review of *The Harvest*, p. 80; March 7, 1994, review of *Mysterium*, p. 67; May 11, 1998, review of *Darwinia*, p. 55; July 31, 2000, review of *The Perseids and Other Stories*, p. 76; June 16, 2003, review of *Blind Lake*, p. 55; November 29, 2004, review of *Magic Time*, p. 27; January 31, 2005, review of *Spin*, p. 53; August 6, 2007, review of *Axis*, p. 173; April 27, 2009, review of *Julian Comstock*, p. 116.

*Quill & Quire*, April, 1988, Kim G. Kofmel, review of *Memory Wire*, p. 23; April, 1990, Pippa Wysong, review of *The Divide*, p. 25; March, 1993, R. John Hayes, review of *The Harvest*, p. 49; March, 1994, Michelle Sagara, review of *Mysterium*, p. 70; July, 1998, Colin Leslie, review of *Darwinia*, p. 33.

*School Library Journal*, July, 2009, Sandy Schmitz, review of *Julian Comstock*, p. 109.

*Science Fiction Chronicle*, April, 1993, review of *The Harvest*, p. 29; June, 1995, review of *Mysterium*, p. 36; December, 1998, review of *Darwinia*, p. 49; December, 1999, review of *Bios*, p. 41.

*Tribune Books* (Chicago, IL), October 27, 1991, review of *A Bridge of Years*, p. 6.

*Voice of Youth Advocates*, June, 1993, review of *The Harvest*, p. 106; October, 1994, review of *Mysterium*, p. 228; October, 1998, review of *Darwinia*, p. 291; April, 1999, review of *Darwinia*, p. 16; June, 2000, review of *Bios*, p. 107; April, 2002, review of *The Chronoliths*, p. 16.

*Wilson Library Bulletin*, September, 1989, Gene La-Faille, review of *Gypsies*, p. 117.

ONLINE

*Boing Boing*, http://boingboing.net/(June 24, 2009), Cory Doctorow, review of *Julian Comstock*.

*Challenging Destiny Online*, http://www.challenging destiny.com/ (July 21, 1999), James Schellenberg and David M. Switzer, "Interview with Robert Charles Wilson."

*Curled Up with a Good Book*, http://www.curledup. com/ (July 3, 2008), Midge Bork, interview with Wilson.

*io9.com*, http://io9.com/(May 29, 2009), Annalee Newitz, "Robert Charles Wilson Talks about Movies and Limits to the Singularity," and review of *Julian Comstock*.

*Locus Online*, http://www.locusmag.com/ (March 8, 2006), "Robert Charles Wilson: Alternating Worlds."

*Robert Charles Wilson Home Page*, http://www.robert charleswilson.com (February 2, 2010).

*Sci Fi Wire*, http://scifiwire.com/ (June 17, 2009), Paul Di Filippo, review of *Julian Comstock*.*

# Author/Artist Index

The following index gives the number of the volume in
which an author/artist's biographical sketch appears: